THE DESCENT OF MADNESS

Drawing on evidence from across the behavioural and natural sciences, this book advances a radical new hypothesis: that madness exists as a costly consequence of the evolution of a sophisticated social brain in *Homo sapiens*.

Having explained the rationale for an evolutionary approach to psychosis, the author makes a case for psychotic illness in our living ape relatives, as well as in human ancestors. He then reviews existing evolutionary theories of psychosis, before introducing his own thesis: that the same genes causing madness are responsible for the evolution of our highly social brain.

Jonathan Burns' novel Darwinian analysis of the importance of psychosis for human survival provides some meaning for this form of suffering. It also spurs us on to a renewed commitment to changing our societies in a way that allows the mentally ill the opportunity of living.

The Descent of Madness will be of interest to those in the fields of psychiatry, psychology, sociology and anthropology, and is also accessible to the general reader.

Jonathan Burns is chief specialist psychiatrist at the Nelson Mandela School of Medicine. His main areas of research include psychotic illnesses, human brain evolution and evolutionary origins of psychosis.

D1428410

THE DESCENT OF MADNESS

Evolutionary Origins of Psychosis and the
Social Brain

Jonathan Burns

Routledge
Taylor & Francis Group

LONDON AND NEW YORK

First published 2007
by Routledge
27 Church Road, Hove, East Sussex BN3 2FA

Simultaneously published in the USA and Canada
by Routledge
270 Madison Ave, New York, NY 10016

*Routledge is an imprint of the Taylor & Francis Group, an
informa business*

© 2007 Jonathan Burns

Typeset in Sabon by
RefineCatch Limited, Bungay, Suffolk
Printed and bound in Great Britain by
TJ International Ltd, Padstow, Cornwall
Paperback cover design by Sandra Heath

This publication has been produced with paper manufactured to strict
environmental standards and with pulp derived from sustainable
forests.

British Library Cataloguing in Publication Data
A catalogue record for this book is available from the British Library

Library of Congress Cataloging in Publication Data
Burns, Jonathan, 1968–
    The descent of madness : evolutionary origins of psychosis and the
social brain / Jonathan Burns.
        p.   ;   cm.
    Includes bibliographical references.
    ISBN-13: 978–1–58391–742–8 (hardback)
    ISBN-10: 1–58391–742–X (hardback)
    ISBN-13: 978–1–58391–743–5 (pbk.)
    ISBN-10: 1–58391–743–8 (pbk.)
    1. Psychoses—Etiology.   2. Mental illness—Diagnosis.
3. Evolution.   I. Title.
    [DNLM: 1. Psychotic Disorders—etiology.   2. Evolution.
3. Hominidae—psychology.   4. Psychotic Disorders—genetics.
5. Social Behavior. WM 200 B967d 2006]
    RC512.B87 2006
    616.89—dc

                                                        2006016382

        ISBN13: 978–1–58391–742–8 (hbk)
        ISBN13: 978–1–58391–743–5 (pbk)

For Eliza whose love, companionship, wisdom and patience keep me sane and enrich my every day.

CONTENTS

ACKNOWLEDGEMENTS

In the several years it has taken me to formulate and clarify my thinking and to write this book, there are many individuals to whom I am greatly indebted. As a psychiatric registrar in Cape Town, I was first introduced to the evolutionary approach to mental disorders by Dave Kibel my consultant – he loaned me his copy of *Evolutionary Psychiatry* by Anthony Stevens and John Price – and for planting this seed of interest I am truly grateful. I first met John Price in London a few years later at a Human Behaviour and Evolution Society meeting and I thank him for our conversations and correspondence on that occasion and in the years since. It was John who encouraged me to write a paper on brain evolution and psychosis that marked the beginnings of this book project. Tim Crow has had a profound influence on me over the last 5 or 6 years and I owe him special appreciation. For our conversations, email exchanges and good-natured disagreement on certain issues, I offer him my thanks and humbly acknowledge his genius. To Martin Brüne, I am grateful for friendship and great discussions – also for his helpful comments at different stages of the writing process. Richard Byrne, James Rilling, Sarah Hrdy and Jane Goodall all contributed (either verbally or in writing) their thoughts and insights on human brain evolution and abnormal ape behaviour – I thank them sincerely. And Louis Sass read and offered important suggestions on Chapter 5 for which I am grateful.

Many of the ideas discussed in this book were developed during the open review process of my paper 'An evolutionary theory of schizophrenia – cortical connectivity, metarepresentation and the social brain' published in *Behavioral and Brain Sciences (BBS)* in December 2004. I thank the following individuals who contributed to this open review process (and whose responses are printed in the same volume): Conrado Bosman, Enzo Brunetti and Francisco Aboitiz; André Aleman and René Kahn; Martin Brüne; Tim Crow; Paul Gilbert; Valerie Hardcastle; Ralph Hoffman, Michelle Hampson, Maxine Varanko and Thomas McGlashan; Matthew Keller; Randolph Nesse; Jaak Panksepp and Joseph Moskal; Vadim Rotenberg; Roger Sullivan and John Allen; Rolf Verleger and Rebekka Lencer; and

Glenn Weisfeld. I would also like to acknowledge the wise counsel and welcome encouragement offered by the late Professor Jeffrey Gray, past editor of *BBS*, during the review process of my paper. His personal warmth and intellectual acuity are sorely missed.

While a research fellow in the Department of Psychiatry in Edinburgh during 2001 and 2002, I was fortunate enough to work alongside a number of individuals who are considered leaders in the field of schizophrenia research. Eve Johnstone, David Cunningham-Owens and Steve Lawrie all contributed either directly or indirectly to my thinking and the preparation of this book. To them I extend my gratitude and, in particular, I thank Eve for tolerating my forays away from her project in pursuit of evolutionary ideas. It was in her department that I came to appreciate the significance of the social brain and its disturbance in psychotic illness. I also thank David Semple for the many hours of stimulating discussion out in the rain and for his friendship – many of the ideas I have elaborated in this book were percolated in this intellectual coffee-pot!

I am grateful to my editor Joanne Forshaw and the team at Routledge for their support throughout the preparation of this book. Thank you for guiding me expertly through the process and for your patience with my delays in delivering the manuscript. I am grateful to Sebastian Faulks and Hutchinson Publishers for permission to quote material from *Human Traces*. The extracts are reprinted in Chapter 10 by permission of The Random House Group Ltd.

My mother, Sarah Burns, created two of the illustrations: Figures 6.1 (the primate family tree) and 6.2 (the nut-cracking chimpanzee). I thank her for these wonderful contributions and I am profoundly grateful to both my parents for the multitude of ways in which they have positively influenced my life. As well as providing me with a powerful model of how to live an honest, humane and socially responsible life, they have also instilled a love and respect for the natural world and a curiosity about the workings of the human mind. In my three sons, Noah, Aidan and Luke, I experience true delight every day – they are a boisterous and spirited trio, my three musketeers – my only regret in writing this book is the time it has stolen from being with them. And finally I thank my wife, Eliza, who is the brainy, beautiful and gutsy woman of my life. For her integrity, courage and commitment to real relationship and real community I salute her. For being an awesome mother to our sons I thank her. And for loving me and making me a better man I offer my eternal gratitude. She is the perfect psychiatrist's psychiatrist!

1

INTRODUCTION

THE MEANING OF MADNESS

The meaning of madness is one of the greatest enigmas of the human condition. From before the written word there is evidence that those in our midst of unsound mind and aberrant behaviour have perplexed and unsettled us. Whether we examine archaeological clues, the themes of oral traditions and folklore or the literature of both New World and Old World societies we are struck by the fact that madness has always been a fascination and a challenge for society. Themes of mental suffering and disrupted reasoning pervade our literary and artistic heritage and continue, even into this liberal enlightened age, to evoke strong passions.

Why is it that madness holds such a fascination to human societies the world over? What is it about the 'imbalance' of those afflicted that spurs us on to write about, paint, dramatize and immortalize in our legends caricatures of suffering people? There are several contributory aspects of human nature that fuel this preoccupation.

We are curious animals. We are also discontent. There is a sort of grumbling dissatisfaction with the present, with what we have in hand and with what we have already discovered. Nothing, however great or beautiful, is ever quite enough. I believe this underlies some of the unhappiness that many experience in their lives; indeed, it leads some into the avenues of psychiatric care. But in the same breath I would argue that it is our discontent and our eternal desire for more that drives our creativity and the quest for knowledge. So if the workings of our minds, both in health and ill-health, retain some secrets then we will not rest until all is laid bare.

The other reason we are obsessed with mental aberration is perhaps less laudable and might indeed be a cause for lament. We are selfish and self-serving and ultimately intent on our own successful navigation through the complexities of life. Much of this book is based on a Darwinian view of humans' place on this planet and so this statement resonates well with the themes to be discussed. Survival depends on knowledge and self-belief and a sense of being securely planted upon the ground beneath one's feet. To enter into the fray of daily living I have to believe that I am sane, that my experience is a true reflection of reality. When the competition begins, I will seek out any weakness or disadvantage in my fellow competitors and exploit it to my fullest advantage. If there are odd, eccentric, flamboyant or clearly deranged competitors out there in the world, then I am very interested in them. They will challenge my own sense of being sane, of being 'normal', and I will be very quick to assert the fact that it is I who am normal, not them. As Porter (2002) puts it, 'Setting the sick apart sustains the fantasy that we are whole'. We might couch our interest in madness in a cloak of intellectual and scientific curiosity, but sadly I think this self-preserving instinct underlies much of our motivation in this domain. This too is the essence of stigma – the creation of spoiled identity – an unwelcome bedfellow of the mentally afflicted throughout history and a subject that must be confronted in any discourse on mental illness. The history of society and the ways in which the mentally ill have been perceived and managed by the state tells a sorry tale of the use and abuse of power and domination.

I am using the lay term 'madness' quite freely and before continuing it is appropriate that I define clearly what I am referring to. The *Concise Oxford Dictionary* (*COD*) defines 'madness' as 'a disordered mind; not sane; extremely foolish' (Allen 1990). The first definition is vague but reasonably accurate; the second is quite meaningless; and the third is frankly pejorative. Theoretically, even the COD could be accused of adding to the stigma! (Although to be fair, dictionaries do have a mandate to provide common usage definitions, which illustrates the fact that the word 'madness' is commonly used in a stigmatizing manner.) In terms of this book, 'madness' refers to serious psychotic mental illness where the core symptoms include delusional and divergent thinking, hallucinations and disturbances of mood. Modern psychiatry, like the rest of medicine, operates in terms of diagnoses and has for most of the last 100 years adopted a categorical approach to mental disorders. The pros and cons of categorical thinking regarding psychotic illness is addressed in later chapters, but for now the term 'madness' includes schizophrenia, psychotic depression and psychotic mania. While the latter 'mood disorders' are important in some of the discussion that follows, the main focus of my argument is on schizophrenia.

THE SEARCH FOR MEANING

We are a species obsessed with our mental condition and the mental life and health of our nations. The twentieth century has been called the century of the mind; the 1990s the decade of the brain. It is an age where medical science has supremacy and there are high expectations for answers to some of our most enduring questions. And yet, despite remarkable progress in coming to grips with the molecular biology and therapeutics of vast expanses of human disease and suffering, we are still confounded by the unpredictable and elusive flights of fancy that characterize some of us. Biology, psychology, sociology, anthropology – all have been the domains of a frantic search for this Holy Grail of science. And in each there have been discoveries, new insights and intellectual breakthroughs. But still a clear, well-integrated understanding of the origins, the pathological mechanisms and the most effective ways of preventing and treating madness continue to evade us. Despite all the attention, money, time and creative effort given to the understanding of this perplexing disorder, we are still struggling to integrate the accumulated evidence into a coherent story. Methodologically watertight studies continue to throw up contradictory findings and authoritative journals are filled with conflicting arguments and hypotheses.

I would argue that this failure to reach a consensus is a reflection of a fundamental omission in the whole biomedical enquiry. And that is because we lack an explanatory paradigm in our explorations into madness. There is no attempt to establish the 'meaning' of such an illness in the human species. My use of 'meaning' in this context is as follows: why does such an illness exist and why does it persist despite its clearly maladaptive nature? Putting it crudely, why do some people go mad and what does the existence of human madness imply for our understanding of human nature? These are clichéd and well-worn existential dilemmas that have concerned people throughout history, but I would argue that the apparent 'dead-end' we seem to have encountered in clinical research relates to this absence of a unifying existential framework. There is no basic hypothesis underlying the hundreds of studies of the illness – a hypothesis that integrates all the data into a single conceptual framework.

DARWINISM AND THE MIND

I have said that our scientific endeavours have reaped some rewards in terms of understanding mental disorder, but that a clear and integrated theory of madness is yet to be achieved. I would propose that this failure to construct a unified hypothesis stems from a failure to base our search for the meaning of madness within a strong evolutionary framework. This is extraordinary given the impact of the Darwinian revolution, permeating and shaping almost every avenue of scientific research during the last 100 years. There is hardly a subject in biology that is not situated, in one way or another, within an evolutionary framework. Not so for psychiatry – that is, not during the last 50 years. One might speculate on the reasons for this. It may be a case of 'once bitten, twice shy', for in the decades immediately following the publication of *The Origin of Species* (Darwin 1859) there was a brief flirtation between evolution and psychiatry. Darwin's cousin,

3

Francis Galton, a respected statistician, coined the term 'eugenics' for the application of the principle of natural selection to social stratification. His book *Hereditary Genius* (Galton 1869) outlined his ideas about superior genes and provided grist to the mill of the social scientists who were setting about building 'scientific' justifications for such nefarious political policies as *apartheid* and *Aryan supremacy*. It is said that Josef Goebbels, the Nazi mastermind of racial division and the extermination of Jews, was much taken with eugenic principles.

So, tarred with the brush of the racist and oppressive ideologies it had inspired, eugenics was quite rightly consigned to the rubbish heap of history. Evolutionary thinking was acceptable in terms of natural science as long as it steered well clear of the human species. In the void left behind, behaviourist and sociological models of the mind flourished. The Lockian concept of the mind as a 'tabula rasa' – a blank slate – found favour and human variation at all levels was explained by learned behaviour and social and cultural determinism.

Edward O. Wilson, a biologist at Harvard University, revived the application of Darwinism to the study of human behaviour with the publication of his 1975 classic *Sociobiology* (Wilson 1975). He argued that evolutionary theory can illuminate the social behaviour of not only termites and baboons but also of humans. Immediately branded as genetic determinists, Wilson and his fellow 'sociobiologists' had nevertheless retrieved the study of human behaviour from narrow behaviourist theory and set Darwinian principles centre stage. With the advantage of hindsight some contemporary 'evolutionary psychologists' may distance themselves from sociobiology on the grounds that it too often ignored the mind's role in mediating the links between genes and behaviour, but they will also acknowledge their debt to the discipline for re-establishing evolutionary priority.

EVOLUTIONARY PSYCHIATRY

Despite the assertions of some cynics within the mental health establishment that adopting an evolutionary perspective in attempting to understand psychiatric disorders amounts to telling 'just-so stories', I would argue that this is one of the only ways forward for psychiatry. Conventional methods of research undoubtedly have and will continue to shed light on the causes and mechanisms of mental illness. As a psychiatrist I stand firmly within a biopsychosocial framework and am actively involved in biological research and clinical practice. I have no quarrel with a medical approach to researching and managing serious mental disorders. I do have a problem though with the rigid and blinkered thinking that leads some psychiatrists to reject an evolutionary perspective on the grounds that it is difficult to test. Yes, evolutionary hypotheses are difficult to prove and yes, true science must

4

stand up to empirical testing, but I would argue that the creativity in science lies in developing ingenious methods of testing that which superficially appears unamenable to empirical investigation.

That said, I now want to acknowledge the pioneering contributions of the relatively small number of psychiatrists and psychologists who, over the last 30 years, have offered an evolutionary viewpoint in the search for the meanings of madness. To name some evolutionary psychiatrists and psychologists is possibly unfair on those not mentioned, but it is important for the reader to have some idea of the kind of evolutionary perspective I am talking about. Some of the early contributors were Michael Chance, Russell Gardner, John Price, Leon Sloman and Paul Gilbert who introduced evolutionary principles such as 'rank-hierarchy' and 'dominance-submission' to the understanding of mood disorders. The 'social rank hypothesis of depression' is widely recognized as an important contribution in this field (Price et al. 1994). Paul MacLean's work on 'the triune brain' is similarly acknowledged, conceptualizing the brain in terms of a hierarchy of evolved systems that can be correlated with increasingly sophisticated adaptive behaviours (MacLean 1973). John Price, together with the Jungian psycho-therapist, Anthony Stevens, published *Evolutionary Psychiatry*, a textbook on the subject, in 1996 (Stevens & Price 1996) as well as *Prophets, Cults and Madness* on the origins of schizophrenia in 2000 (Stevens & Price 2000). Randolph Nesse and George Williams have both written on the adaptive features of many medical symptoms, in particular depression and anxiety (Nesse & Williams 1995), while Isaac Marks' book *Fears and Phobias* remains a classic reference on anxiety disorders (Marks 1969). Building on the Nobel Prize winning work of Konrad Lorenz and Niko Tinbergen (Tinbergen 1951), Iraneus Eibl-Eibefeldt (Eibl-Eibefeldt 1971) has exten-sively fostered human ethology by making across-cultural comparisons, while Michael T. McGuire of UCLA co-edited *Ethological Psychiatry* in 1977 (McGuire & Fairbanks 1977) and *Darwinian Psychiatry* in 1998 (McGuire & Troisi 1998).

In the field of developmental psychology John Bowlby's work on attach-ment and separation has had an enormous impact on the theory and practice of psychotherapy (Bowlby 1969, 1973). Paul Gilbert, Kent Bailey, John Pearce, Kalman Glantz, Anthony Stevens, Daniel Kriegman, Alfonso Troisi and Mark Erickson have all adopted an evolutionary perspective in their writings on and practice of psychotherapy (Gilbert & Bailey 2000; Glantz & Pearce 1989). David Bjorkland recently co-published *The Origins of Human Nature*, applying evolutionary principles to developmental psy-chology (Bjorklund & Pellegrini 2002) while Glenn Weisfeld has written *Evolutionary Principles of Human Adolescence* (Weisfelt 1999). Others adopting an evolutionary stance include Jaak Panksepp who compiled his research on emotional systems in *Affective Neuroscience* (Panksepp 1998) as well as Ivor Jones, David Buss (Buss 1991), Leda Cosmides and John Tooby

(Cosmides & Tooby 1992) who have written extensively on personality. Jim Brody and Peter Jensen (Jensen et al. 1997) have written on attention deficit hyperactive disorder (ADHD), Linda Mealey on sociopathy (Mealey 1995), Martin Daly and Margo Wilson on homicide, Denis de Catanzaro on suicide and John Archer and Sarah Blaffer Hrdy (Hrdy 1999) on sexual roles and violence. Leslie Brothers (Brothers 1990, 1997), Jesse Bering (Bering 2002, 2003) and Martin Brüne (Brüne 2001, Brüne et al. 2003) have helped popularize the concept of the 'social brain' in evolution, a concept that is central to this book. Likewise, the work of Simon Baron-Cohen on autism (Baron-Cohen 1995; Baron-Cohen et al. 2000) and Tim Crow (Crow 1995a, 1995b, 1997) on schizophrenia is discussed in some detail in later chapters of this book.

THE CASE FOR AN EVOLUTIONARY THEORY OF SCHIZOPHRENIA

I am arguing that there is a need to integrate recent biological findings from psychosis research into an evolutionary framework based on current insights into the evolution of the human brain. One might ask why the evolutionary paradigm is relevant to our study and understanding of a disorder such as schizophrenia. Since Emil Kraepelin first described *dementia praecox* more than 100 years ago (Kraepelin 1896) this condition has been considered by most people (both professional and lay) as an illness, a disorder of the brain. Individuals with schizophrenia are considered patients and, in both Kraepelin's era and our own era, their problems have been and are regarded as occupying the medical terrain. What relevance has Darwin's great idea for this, a clinical enigma?

In short, the rationale for using evolutionary theory as an explanatory paradigm for the schizophrenic spectrum of disorders comes from attempts to reconcile several seemingly contradictory epidemiological observations. First, from the International Pilot Study of Schizophrenia conducted in nine countries (World Health Organization 1973), it appears that globally, schizophrenia has an incidence of approximately 1 per cent and there is remarkable consistency cross-culturally in the core symptoms of the disorder. One of the 'first-rank' findings of this study was that the evidence points to a significant genetic component in the transmission of schizophrenia (Jablensky 1988). Other evidence suggests that this is a polygenetic disorder (Kendler et al. 2000). The constant global incidence rate of a disorder that is seemingly very similar regardless of continent or culture implies that it may have emerged at a time when modern humans themselves were evolving and spreading across the planet.

Second, it is widely accepted that schizophrenia is associated with lower fecundity (Larson & Nyman 1973) and increased early mortality (Brown

1997). According to strict Darwinian principles of natural selection, a phenotype that is reproductively relatively unsuccessful and where individuals die before they have raised their kin to maturity should be 'weaned' out of the gene pool. But this is not the case with schizophrenia. Despite a selective disadvantage, the phenotype persists with a similar rate of incidence across the human race. This suggests that there may be some trait associated with the disorder that confers an evolutionary advantage.

The final intriguing feature of this condition that has fascinated many who are familiar with it is that there is evidence that some highly gifted and creative individuals either manifest schizotypal traits themselves or have a first-degree relative with schizophrenia (Karlsson 2001; Post 1994). This has led a number of authors to suggest that perhaps schizophrenia (which is apparently maladaptive in evolutionary terms) is compensated for by genetically related individuals who display special traits that might be considered highly adaptive. These somewhat puzzling features of schizophrenia suggest to me (and indeed have persuaded others) that an evolutionary approach is called for. I return to a fuller discussion of this rationale in subsequent chapters of this book.

PSYCHOSIS AND BRAIN EVOLUTION

This chapter began with a reflection on our preoccupation with the meaning of madness. I have raised some issues as to why this subject may have captured our imagination throughout history and why stigma has often characterized attitudes to the mentally ill. I have argued that a theory of madness requires the inclusion of an evolutionary perspective in order to be truly integrated. I have briefly reviewed some of the history of evolutionary thinking in psychiatry and the reader may have noticed that by and large psychotic illnesses do not feature much in this new paradigm. Yes, there are some individuals like Tim Crow who have pushed back the frontiers of our understanding of psychosis and held high the banner of evolutionary theory in psychiatry, but they are few. With increasing evidence amassing from biological research of these serious disorders, it is timely that new ideas are generated that attempt to integrate these findings with evidence from other disciplines in evolutionary biology. This is the central purpose of this book.

I believe that if we take a few steps back from the rock face of psychiatric research and allow new insights from fields as diverse as primatology, paleoanthropology and developmental psychology to inform our thinking, then we can begin to formulate a scientifically satisfying theory of madness. It is my belief that such a theory has to be based within an accepted model of human brain evolution. The brain is the organ of the mind. We must lay to rest the Cartesian notion of a mind–body split. Psychological phenomena, whether healthy or pathological, are based in the physiology of the brain, and so an evolutionary approach to psychopathology must take account of evolutionary changes in the brain. Some evolutionary theories of psycho-pathology have been criticized for being overly speculative and insufficiently grounded in empirical evidence. Sometimes great ideas, full of creative inspiration and truly thought-provoking in their originality, flounder and are discredited as fiction because they lack evidence. In this age of evidence-based research, academic journals and the scientific community as a whole are unlikely to give credence to hypotheses that tell a good story but offer little in the way of supporting data. Hence the dismissive label of 'just-so story' that too often attaches itself to the work of evolutionary psychologists and psychiatrists. Hence, the virtual absence (with a few exceptions) of evolutionary papers in major psychiatric journals. We may quite rightly complain that mainstream psychiatry is narrow and blinkered and lacks imagination, but a little self-examination is called for too. If evolutionary ideas are to penetrate the wall of cynicism that surrounds establishment psychiatry, and if they are to win new 'converts', then these ideas must be supported by good data and convincing evidence.

A METHODOLOGY BORROWED FROM ARCHAEOLOGY

The question of what constitutes truth has preoccupied philosophers for centuries. Epistemology is the enquiry into the nature of truth, and recent postmodern concepts regarding the sociocultural and political construc-tion of truth are helpful when it comes to considering what constitutes 'convincing evidence'. Modern medicine has embraced the 'evidence-based medicine' (EBM) paradigm wholeheartedly (EBM is now a core aspect of medical training) and this has become the 'truth' that guides clinical prac-tice, research and health planning and policy. In psychiatry we chemically alter our patients' brains without even understanding the disordered brain function we are attempting to treat. Confident in our power because our practice is evidence-based we regularly force patients to take our drugs. EBM is the gold standard, the infallible truth, the measure of competent practice and respected research. And yet there are as many studies showing enlarged ventricles in schizophrenia as there are showing normal sized ventricles. Drug trials laud one psychotropic agent over another depending on which pharmaceutical company is funding the trial. Patients are quoted the latest research findings supporting a given treatment and yet they return home dissatisfied because the doctor has failed to understand the real meaning of their suffering. The limits of that vast galaxy, the brain, seem increasingly unreachable as scientists are confronted by a myriad of bizarre planets and hidden worlds. And that modern idol, science, is failing to deliver on its promise to explain the great mysteries of human nature. The point I am

8

making is that any scientific truth is marked by the subjective biases of those human beings who are at the core of constructing that truth. Truth is constructed not discovered because the hypothesis is a human choice and the evidence to support it is selective because, consciously or unconsciously, we include what is compatible with a specific human agenda.

It is not a coincidence that research group A finds support in its data set for hypothesis A, while (across the Atlantic) research group B finds supportive data for hypothesis B. Scientific 'truths' need to be examined, critiqued, and deconstructed so as to reveal the human context within which that truth was created. I am not suggesting that scientists consciously set out to deceive others (and themselves) in their pursuit of knowledge. Rather, I am questioning the authority given to the modern notion of what constitutes 'sound evidence'. I am arguing that, as with any human endeavour, the construction of sound evidence and scientific truth, is subject to individual bias and is coloured with the social, cultural and political identity of those involved in its conception. That is not to say that this method of enquiry is invalid and the knowledge discredited. Indeed, like other academic books, this book contains my biases and my subjectivity – in attempting to convince the reader that my thesis is true, I cannot help but select supportive data and quietly ignore contradictory evidence. It may not be my conscious intention to handle the available data in an uneven fashion, but I have no doubt that this will happen because I have an agenda – a hypothesis to prove. Thus, I am proposing that we adopt a wider and less rigid view of what constitutes 'sound evidence'. If we remain constrained by EBM and other idealized methods of enquiry in science, then we will continue to fail in our pursuit of knowledge. No truer is this, I believe, than in the quest to understand the meaning of madness.

Aleman and Kahn (2004) quote Lewontin (1998), underlining their scepticism regarding the possibility of a scientific theory of human cognitive evolution. I would agree with these authors that it is probably impossible to achieve such a theory if one relies solely upon a narrow empirical method derived from reductionist physics. The construction of a sound evidence base for evolutionary hypotheses is not always easy. How does one generate data about the behaviour and mental state of our ancestors? Relationship dynamics, emotional states and cognitive processes do not readily fossilize like bones – to be examined and analysed and presented as data. This is a problem that several authors have addressed and I will refer to some relevant and helpful conclusions. David Lewis-Williams, a South African 'cognitive archaeologist' and expert on the rock art of the San, has recently published an intriguing book entitled *The Mind in the Cave* (Lewis-Williams 2002), in which he interprets the Palaeolithic art of western Europe in terms of emerging consciousness in early humans. His task is similar to mine in that he is faced with the same constraints when it comes to presenting evidence for his hypothesis. He explains that there are too many gaps in the archaeological record to establish a clear line of argument and this prevents the scientifically reified formal, sequential testing of hypotheses. His solution to this problem is to draw upon the work of Alison Wylie, a philosopher of science (Wylie 1989).

Wylie has described a methodology that incorporates important scientific principles of hypothesis testing and is well suited to the challenge of theorizing about archaeological matters. This method she terms 'cabling'. Unlike some arguments that form a logical 'chain' of sequential links, the cabling method entails the intertwining of numerous strands of evidence. She explains that very often archaeologists construct an argument by drawing in a number of different strands of evidence from varied scientific sources. For example, the utility of an excavated structure might be elucidated by drawing upon ecological, ethnographic and anthropological facts that have a bearing on the site. Lewis-Williams makes use of this method in his enquiry, drawing upon evidence from extant hunter–gatherer traditions, from psychology and from neuroscience in his construction of a hypothesis. He argues that the cabling method is sound in that it is both *sustaining* (a strand may compensate for a gap in another strand) and *constraining* (it 'restricts wild hypotheses that may take a researcher far from the archaeological record') (Lewis-Williams 2002).

In constructing an evolutionary theory of schizophrenia, I am faced with the following problem. Clearly, a study of schizophrenia entails an examination of the workings of the mind. An evolutionary theory of schizophrenia therefore entails an examination of, or attempt at understanding, the archaic mind. As I have stated, the mind itself obviously leaves no fossils to examine. I am therefore forced to draw in strands of evidence from multiple associated scientific sources that have some bearing on schizophrenia and the mind in prehistory. Like Lewis-Williams, I will put my faith in Wylie's 'cabling' method in the construction of a reasonable hypothesis. The strands I will use come from diverse and seemingly unrelated fields of research, but I hope and trust that together, they will form a sturdy and convincing cable of evidence. My hope too is that this approach will prove reliable, and will encourage others who seek answers to similar questions about the origins of the mind and psychopathology to adopt a similar method.

I am very wary of implying that my specific endeavour here will bring us any nearer to the truth about madness and why it exists at all in our species. In fact, I make no claim at all. The conclusions I reach may well be another 'just-so story' and I admit quite openly that much of what follows is speculative and difficult to validate. But I think there is a place for speculation and wonder and the asking of questions and this is my motivation for addressing the enigma of psychosis with an evolutionary eye.

AN OVERVIEW OF THIS BOOK

In this book I have undertaken to integrate current evidence regarding the biology and psychology of schizophrenia into an evolutionary framework that focuses primarily on what we know about brain evolution. As I have stated, there are some authors who have adopted an evolutionary perspective on mental disorders. But very often their hypotheses rely on an adaptationist view of psychopathology. Behavioural and psychological traits are viewed as adaptations that conferred evolutionary advantages on individuals during the 'ancestral environment' (the Palaeolithic). Psychopathologies, they argue, represent a mismatch between traits that were beneficial to our ancestors and the 'grossly abnormal' modern technological age. My problem with this approach (and it seems that many in the mental health field share this concern) is that these hypotheses lack real scientific evidence. They tell a good story, yes, but too often they romanticize the past and underestimate the capacity of the brain to 'cope' in the present. I believe that such speculations without sound evidence merely weaken the case for setting schizophrenia research within an evolutionary paradigm.

Is there a way forward then? I believe there is, if we draw upon current research on the brain and how it evolved in the human line. This is my primary objective. And in doing so, I hope to demonstrate that the evolutionary approach is not just relevant to psychiatry, but also edifying in our existential search for meaning.

In short, I argue that under the selective pressure of social group living, the primate brain first enlarged and then reorganized during the period 16–2 million years ago (mya). Complex neural circuits linking the prefrontal cortex to the temporal and parietal cortices evolved as a substrate for complex social cognition. Interconnected with the deeper and more ancient limbic system, this circuitry has been called 'the social brain' and constituted a basis for adaptive social behaviour in human ancestors. I cite paleoanthropological, anthropological and comparative primate data that suggests that hominids evolved complex cortical interconnectivity (in particular frontotemporal and frontoparietal circuits) in order to regulate social cognition and the intellectual demands of group living. I also suggest that the ontogenetic mechanism underlying this cerebral adaptation was an evolutionary process known as sequential hypermorphosis[1] and that it rendered the hominid brain vulnerable to genetic and environmental insults. I then argue that further changes in genes regulating the timing of neurodevelopment occurred prior to the migration of *Homo sapiens* out of Africa 150–100,000 years ago giving rise to the schizotypal spectrum. While some individuals within this spectrum may have exhibited unusual creativity and iconoclasm, this phenotype was not necessarily adaptive in reproductive terms. However, because the disorder shared a common genetic basis with the evolving circuitry of the social brain, it persisted. Thus, schizophrenia emerged as a costly trade-off in the evolution of complex social cognition. I believe that this approach represents a sound 'evidence-based' evolutionary theory of schizophrenia.

In searching for the evolutionary origins of schizophrenia, it is necessary to look back into history and even further back into pre-history in order to consider the question of whether our earliest ancestors had the cognitive 'capacity' for psychosis. Several authors have questioned the validity of attempting to reconstruct human cognitive evolution (Aleman and Kahn 2004; Lewontin 1998). Richard Byrne, an evolutionary psychologist and primatologist at St Andrews University in Scotland, has defended this exercise, outlining a methodology for inferring the history of primate cognition (Byrne 2000). Byrne stresses the importance of establishing a reliable pattern of descent and he argues that cladistic analysis is a tool that does just that: it provides us with a family tree relating both modern humans and extant primates to each other and to our common ancestors.

Furthermore, there is strong data from comparative psychology, molecular biology and physical anthropology confirming the close evolutionary relationship between simian and ape species and modern *Homo sapiens*. So, since mental phenomena do not fossilize, this question is best addressed by examining the literature on our nearest extant relatives – the great apes. In Chapter 2, I draw upon psychological research conducted on apes both in the field and in captive populations and address the question of 'madness in the family': Is there convincing evidence for 'psychotic-like' behaviour in apes? Clearly, the absence of language ability in apes makes this a complex task, forcing one to rely solely upon behaviour and its aberrations. I argue that while there is some evidence for a model of 'primitive psychotic illness' in apes, this does not approximate the complexity of human madness. This suggests the obvious (and a theme that I develop during following chapters) – that human cognitive ability may lie on a continuum with that of apes (and there may be few human-specific cognitive abilities), but the mental gulf is truly wide.

Historically, and in the present, the role of shamans, substances and 'altered states of consciousness' (ASC), is linked to psychotic phenomena. I consider how the evolutionary history of shamanism, mind-altering substances and altered states can inform our thinking about the origins of schizophrenia. Is early shamanism evidence for the existence of the schizotypal spectrum in prehistory? Can modern analyses of the neurobiology of substance use and altered states inform us in any way about the possible functioning of the brain during evolution? Does Lewis-Williams' interpretation of Palaeolithic rock art in the caves of western Europe as the product of shamanistic hallucinations imply that our ancestors had brains capable of psychotic experience? And if so, could schizophrenia have occurred 20,000 years ago? These (and other) questions are addressed and I argue that there is strong evidence to suggest that the capacity for schizophrenia-like illness originated together with the earliest fully modern mind/brain.

The next step is to consider how far back in recordable human history it is possible to trace psychotic-like illness. Some authors (and indeed some evolutionary thinkers) have suggested that schizophrenia is a recent disorder and represents a modern response to the stresses of the industrial and technological age. I draw on ancient records as well as the historical literature of several traditions (Western, Islamic, African and Asian) in arguing that there is evidence for schizophrenia in early human history. Some background is required to this analysis and hence I briefly review some of the dominant philosophies in history that shaped our evolving concepts of the human mind. This enables us to better identify historical references to disturbances of the mind such as psychosis. It may be that historically the illness was expressed and interpreted in different ways from the present, and in some cases the phenomena may have been accorded a positive and contributory status in early societies, but it is my belief that schizotypal behaviour and schizophrenic illness have ancient origins in almost all cultures.

Chapter 3 provides an overview of existing evolutionary approaches to psychosis. I introduce the popular Darwinian principles of 'natural selection' and 'adaptation' that have dominated the thinking of evolutionary psychologists and psychiatrists in recent years. The 'adaptationist programme' regards observable mental phenomena in terms of their adaptive qualities – traits survive selection if they serve to enhance the 'fitness' of the individuals displaying them. This approach views mental disorder as follows: a behavioural trait evolved because it conferred an advantage on the individual in the 'ancestral environment'; but now, in our vastly different and psychologically stressful world, there is a mismatch between the evolved trait and the modern environment; the result is mental disorder. While appealing and in some cases probably true, I believe this is a problematic model for schizophrenia. In this chapter I critique the adaptationist programme and argue that its validity in constructing an evolutionary theory of schizophrenia depends on rigorous adherence to an appropriate methodology.

Tim Crow popularized the notion of a continuum of psychotic illness and this features prominently in previous efforts to develop an evolutionary theory of schizophrenia. Schizophrenia is not a discrete disorder with clearly demarcated boundaries. Instead, the condition should be regarded as the severe end of a spectrum of divergent thinking and perceptual experience that stretches from normality to disorder. This concept of a spectrum of mental function and dysfunction is critical to one of the central adaptationist arguments considered; that is, maladaptive conditions exist simply because other phenotypes on the genetic spectrum harbour particularly adaptive traits. So, with a disorder such as schizophrenia, genetically related but unaffected individuals who share some of the milder features of the illness (termed 'schizotypy') may possess some kind of evolutionary advantage that enhances fitness and balances the Darwinian scale. The schizotypy spectrum also has significant clinical and biological overlap with the affective disorders (bipolar disorder and psychotic depression) (Bentall 2003). While there is some evidence for independent disorders, they are better conceptualized as opposite ends of a continuum of psychotic illness. These two axes (schizotypy–normality; and schizophrenia–affective psychosis) are important concepts that require elucidation early in this book and are important concepts in the construction of an evolutionary model of schizophrenia.

Several authors (e.g. Allen & Sarich 1988; Farley 1976; Kellett 1973; Stevens & Price 2000) have proposed evolutionary models of schizophrenia and I briefly review these in this chapter. These are in the main theories of 'ultimate causation' and take for granted the model of an adaptive continuum. Ultimate causation refers to the factors that may have contributed to the structure of the human genome over millions of years of selection pressure. Thus, in terms of the psychoses, theories of ultimate causation address the very question posed by this model: what was it about the psychotic genotype that conferred an advantage on 'carriers' and ensured that they did not die out? A number of hypotheses have been put forward and this chapter summarizes them and offers a critique. While some of these proposals are appealing in that they invest the schizotypal personality with a special role in the origins of culture and society, I attempt to convey to the reader some of my scepticism regarding this mechanism. While initially impressed by classic theories of ultimate causation, I have latterly begun to question whether schizotypy is in fact adaptive. The critical question is whether these individuals actually have a reproductive advantage that can balance and account for the persistence of a clearly maladaptive phenotype.

Tim Crow has been at the forefront of evolutionary thinking about schizophrenia in recent years and in the final section of Chapter 3, I review and critique the core principles of his hypothesis. While I agree that the emergence of schizophrenia is closely related to the evolution of complex cortical circuitry in the hominid brain, I differ with Crow in his focus on its links with asymmetry and language. I also question his reliance on sexual selection as the mechanism of evolutionary change in schizophrenia. While not an adaptationist approach, I believe his theory is flawed on several counts, not least because it is not robustly supported by current data from either schizophrenia research or from research on the evolution of the human brain. Another important and increasingly popular evolutionary concept with some psychiatrists (including Crow) warrants debunking before I begin to build my own evolutionary theory of schizophrenia. This is the issue of 'speciation' in *Homo sapiens* – a theory strongly advanced by Crow (2002) and integral to his evolutionary theory of schizophrenia. I briefly introduce the reader to the contrasting principles of 'speciation' versus 'gradualism' and then cite important evidence that I believe supports the latter process in human brain evolution. While the human brain and cognitive ability are certainly 'superior' to that of apes, I believe that it is a matter of degree rather than kind. Language is unique, yes, but represents an elaboration and continuation of cognitive processes underpinning communication in other primates – there is no need to invoke a saltational (or 'sudden-leap') explanation to account for advanced human cognitions.

In Chapter 4, I turn to genetics, in particular evolutionary genetics and consider several genetic mechanisms that could account for the epidemiology of schizophrenia and other psychoses. The central enigma is the persistence of a phenotype that is reproductively maladaptive. I consider a variety of models derived from evolutionary biology that may be helpful in respect of the origins of psychosis and argue that a 'balanced polymorphism' model[2] (favoured by many authors) is inappropriate in this context. Rather, I argue that a model termed 'antagonistic pleiotropy' is highly relevant and potentially applicable to psychosis. In essence, it is possible that a number of 'susceptibility alleles'[3] (SAs) for psychosis have been selected for their pleiotropic contribution to the evolution and development of the human brain. Up to a certain threshold, these alleles have a beneficial effect, regulating both the phylogenetic and ontogenetic development of social brain networks. There is variation between individuals in the number of SAs and the presence of increasing numbers enhances reproductive fitness up to a threshold. The increasing number of SAs corresponds with an increase in the magnitude of the phenotypic trait, which in this case is cortical connectivity and increasingly sophisticated social cognition. Beyond the threshold (or 'cliff-edge') the presence of additional SAs results in a sharp decrease in the fitness effects of the phenotype. Both schizotypal individuals and those with schizophrenia lie beyond the threshold and exhibit reduced fitness, thus there is no need to invoke a balanced polymorphism model in explaining the evolutionary enigma of this disorder. This chapter also considers the role of epigenetic factors in the origins and emergence of psychosis.

Chapter 5 focuses on the subjects of social behaviour, intersubjectiveness and adaptive group living as well as the neural basis for social cognition. I review the literature on the normal development of interpersonal behaviour and social cognition in human and non-human juveniles and focus on the fascinating subject of developmental neural sensitization to social stimuli. How does the growing brain become increasingly attuned to the discernment of social signals? This chapter does not cover the *evolution* of the social brain but rather focuses on the nature and function of social cognition. Aspects of social cognition such as 'theory of mind' (TOM) are introduced and I consider these under the rubric of the 'upper social brain' locating it within higher cortical circuits. I also introduce the notion of a 'lower social brain' based in the primitive limbic system, which is responsible for basic motivational drives (fight/flight, rank, etc) that contribute to

15

social behaviour. Thus, social behaviour and social cognition emanate from both 'top-down' and 'bottom-up' interactions between the 'upper' and 'lower' social brain and the social world around it. In the 'normal' individual, interaction between upper and lower social brain processes and the social world leads to normal social behaviours and cognitions pertaining to social hierarchy, affiliation, in-group/out-group relations, social identity and interpersonal distance. This has relevance to the discussion of socially impairing psychotic symptoms in later chapters.

The theme of Chapter 6 is the evolution of social cognition and the social brain. Drawing on primate and palaeontological data, I argue that the need to discern and manipulate social signals and social behaviour within expanding hominid groups constituted a powerful driving force for the enlargement and reorganization of the brain during evolution. Of particular interest is the question of how social selective pressures increased neural sensitization to socially salient stimuli. Starting with the concept of the metamind, I trace the evolution of complex social cognition and TOM in apes and human ancestors. Evidence suggests that social selective pressures gave rise to an increase in brain size during the period 40–16 mya. Importantly, primitive forms of communication are evident in extant monkeys and baboons. From 16 mya, continuing enlargement of the brain in ape ancestors was accompanied by reorganization within the brain. It is this later proliferation of interconnectivity, in particular intra-hemispheric connectivity, which contributes to what is termed 'the social brain' and provides a substrate for social cognition and a TOM. Complex cortical circuits of the social brain began to emerge and evidence of this comes from the fossil record and also from comparative primate studies of the brain and cognition. I argue that extant apes show both anatomical and psychological evidence for an immature and basic form of language and social cognition.

For example, asymmetry of the language areas of the brain (thought to be unique to humans and to correlate with the unique human capacity for speech) has recently been demonstrated in great apes. Asymmetry and the lateralization of language areas in the dominant hemisphere seem to have earlier origins than was previously thought and this has implications for assessing the validity of Crow's hypothesis that links the evolution of asymmetry to the evolution of psychosis. I contest Tim Crow's argument that language and cerebral asymmetry are unique to *Homo sapiens* and I instead suggest that asymmetry has more ancient origins and is related to evolving cortical connectivity in the common ancestors of apes and humans. Likewise, human-specific speech has a less-developed equivalent in gestural and non-verbal communicative behaviour in apes. Thus, rapidly evolving cortical connectivity is the link between the ape brain/cognition and the more advanced manifestation in humans. There is continuity and thus a 'gradualist' model is better supported than the 'speciation hypothesis'.

For decades psychiatrists have struggled to apply an inadequate and reductionist system of classification to the illnesses of their patients. Time and again they have discovered that the clusters of symptoms and patterns of mental disturbance experienced by the individual seeking help do not fit comfortably into a rigid diagnostic category prescribed by textbooks. The same 'disorder' more often than not appears dissimilar in different patients while the identical symptom (e.g. hearing voices) is experienced by two individuals with completely separate diagnoses. For example, all the symptoms we attribute to schizophrenia manifest also in other psychiatric disorders. No truer is this than for the symptoms of impaired social cognition as Martin Brüne has observed (Brüne 2004a; Brüne et al. 2003). In Chapter 7 the phenomenology of the psychoses is considered in detail and like Brüne (Brüne 2004a) and Bentall (2003) I argue for a symptom- rather than syndrome-based approach. For me, the core symptoms of schizophrenia are those that reflect social deficits and this is the major thrust of this chapter. However, social dysfunction is evident in other disorders also, such as autism, bipolar disorder, psychopathy and dementia and imaging research confirms this has a neural basis. So it is necessary to accommodate these facts in an expanded model of the social brain and psychopathology. As Brüne has suggested it may be that 'virtually all psychiatric disorders fall into the category of "social brain disorders"' (Brüne 2004b).

Drawing upon the work of such authors as Chris Frith, Stephen Mithen, Paul Gilbert, Richard Bentall, Martin Brüne and Jesse Bering, I develop a cognitive model of psychosis (and schizophrenia in particular) in Chapter 8 that lays a foundation for examining the anatomy of psychosis. This model conceives the modern mind as a highly integrated and connected system that 'allows' for complex social cognition and consciousness itself. During our evolutionary history, the previously 'modularized' mind (Fodor 1983; Cosmides and Tooby 1992, etc.) developed increasing interconnections allowing for the integration of previously independent cognitive abilities. This allowed for metarepresentation that is the hallmark of modern human cognition. Schizophrenia can be considered a syndrome in which these interconnections are disordered. The symptoms too can be seen as the result of a failure to integrate information. What we see in schizophrenia, in cognitive terms, are multiple deficits in the integration of information related to social behaviour, metarepresentation and the attribution of intentionality.

This leads to a review of state-of-the-art evidence that supports the so-called dysconnectivity hypothesis of schizophrenia. In short, there is evidence that the disorder is characterized by deficits in the functional integration of information between the prefrontal cortex and temporal and parietal cortices. 'Functional connectivity' refers to the normal healthy integration of cortical regions and circuits, and recent imaging and neuro-psychological research in schizophrenia shows that there is impairment of normal functional connectivity. Thus, the cognitive model elaborated above has a basis in current research evidence. Until very recently, however, the question of whether 'functional dysconnectivity' in schizophrenia translates into 'structural dysconnectivity' has not been addressed. In other words, are there structural correlates for impaired functional connectivity in the disorder? A study designed to examine this question was conducted by me and others in the Department of Psychiatry in Edinburgh (Burns et al. 2003). We used a new structural imaging technique called diffusion tensor imaging or DT-MRI to examine the structural integrity of white matter tracts connecting the prefrontal cortex to the temporal and parietal cortices in schizophrenia. The results confirmed that these circuits are structurally impaired in schizophrenia. I outline this study and argue that schizophrenia represents a disorder of the cortical circuits comprising the social brain. Thus, the condition can justly be considered a disorder of the highly evolved social brain in *Homo sapiens*.

In Chapter 9, I consider the neuropathology of schizophrenia and introduce the widely accepted notion that schizophrenia is a disorder of neurodevelopment. This is relevant to this book in that it establishes the pathological basis for the findings of disordered cortical connectivity. I cite evidence that suggests that very early insults (probably genetic) to the developing brain give rise to an abnormal pattern of cortical connectivity and that this renders the individual vulnerable to later schizophrenia. Developmental and environmental events at puberty combine to precipitate psychosis.

But can evolutionary theory regarding brain evolution inform our understanding of the genesis of the schizophrenic brain? I believe it is relevant to examine and contrast brain development in humans and other primates in order to understand how ontogenetic events have changed over the last million years under various selection pressures. In this chapter I introduce the evolutionary concept of heterochrony and review the contributions of developmental theorists from Bolk (1926) to Bjorklund & Pellegrini (2002) to our understanding of the origins of neurodevelopment and psychopathology. Heterochrony describes the process by which changes have occurred in the timing of neurodevelopment during evolution, so that descendants' brains develop at a different rate from those of their ancestors. I cite evidence supporting the heterochronic mechanism of 'sequential hypermorphosis' as a mechanism responsible for the evolution of the social brain. Sequential hypermorphosis refers to the progressive prolongation of each stage of neurodevelopment in subsequent generations. I argue that schizophrenia represents a phenotype in which there is *further* prolongation of neurodevelopment, relative to normal phenotypes. Thus, the mechanism employed during brain evolution is the same mechanism responsible for aberrant neurodevelopment in schizophrenia. Therefore, in terms of ontogeny also, schizophrenia is a trade-off in the evolution of the social brain in *Homo sapiens*.

18

In Chapter 10, I draw together the evidence I have gathered from various disciplines, and elucidate an integrated theory of the evolutionary origins of psychosis. My premise is that schizophrenia exists in our species as a costly legacy in the evolution of cortical connectivity and social cognition. Between 16 and 2 mya, human ancestors began to evolve complex cerebral interconnectivity and specialized neural circuits in order to regulate social cognition and the intellectual demands of group living. The neurodevelopmental changes responsible for the emergence of this sophisticated social brain in *Homo sapiens* were associated with increasing vulnerability to disorder. Thus, the advantages in terms of becoming socially adept were gained at the cost of this enormous vulnerability of the developing circuits to both genetic and environmental events. Then in the region of 100–150,000 years ago, prior to the migration of *Homo sapiens* out of Africa and across the Palaeolithic landmasses, a genetic event or series of events gave rise to the schizotypal spectrum. Although the exact mechanism is not yet fully understood, I propose that up to a certain threshold, the presence of increasing numbers of schizophrenia susceptibility alleles was critical to the evolution and development of complex connectivity and social cognition. However, beyond this threshold, the resultant phenotype was characterized by a disruption of developing cortical circuits and psychotic illness. Brain research in schizophrenia and in schizotypy has provided some clues as to which stage/s of ontogeny might be culpable and I examine this evidence. As I noted earlier, the idea of a genetic spectrum is important, but only insofar as it explains the extreme variability in clinical presentation and the apparent continuum with eccentric and sometimes gifted personality. The inherently *maladaptive* schizotypal genotype has remained in the human gene pool because susceptibility alleles for the disorder play a role in critical aspects of brain development in our species and cannot be eliminated. 215,398

Finally, in conclusion, I revisit the subject of human–ape differences (specifically addressing the question of whether psychosis could manifest in other primates); revisit the question of altered states of consciousness (in the light of my hypothesis); and consider the implications this hypothesis might have for our beliefs about and attitudes to mental illness. I conclude by suggesting several implications of this hypothesis for our understanding of the human mind, our relationship to other primates and of course our conceptualization of the meaning of madness. In particular, I believe that if this illness is rightly considered a disorder of the social brain that emerged as a legacy in the emergence of the modern human brain/mind, then this fact alone should serve to heighten our sensitivity and compassion towards individuals afflicted with psychosis. It should also cause us to reassess our priorities in terms of management. This model highlights the importance of social deficits in schizophrenia and other psychotic disorders and consequently a large part of our clinical and research effort should be dedicated to understanding and confronting the social, cultural, economic and political obstacles that face our patients. If these vulnerable individuals, who have particular difficulties with comprehending and responding to the social world, are isolated, stigmatized and subjected to societal prejudices, then they have no hope of averting a lifelong struggle with incapacitating mental illness.

2

A HISTORY AND PRE-HISTORY OF MADNESS

MADNESS IN THE FAMILY

In July 1995, in need of a change after a year at a rural mission hospital in the subtropical north-east corner of South Africa, I accompanied a group of British gap-year students to Borneo. I was the 'expedition doctor' and besides one unhappy girl with malaria, my patients were a pretty healthy lot who required little more than the occasional antidiarrhoeal tablet or antifungal ointment. Naturally, I involved myself with the projects at hand – building jetties and renovating staff huts on the banks of the Sekonyer River in the Tanjung Puting Reserve. For five weeks we worked under the supervision of locally employed carpenters, attempting to avoid constant distraction from three other residents of the camp – ex-captive juvenile orang-utans who were slowly being rehabilitated back into the forest by park rangers. This is a profoundly difficult task for the orangs are socialized to human company and have either never been exposed to or have forgotten the skills they require to survive in the rainforest. Although a challenge, the rangers have some success and probably because of their commitment to the apes, they have managed to teach a number of individuals how to find fruit, build treetop nests and avoid predation. However the task of resocializing their charges into orang-utan social life is much harder and often unsuccessful. There have been a handful of triumphs, for example an ex-captive orphan who was successfully adopted by a wild mother who had recently lost her infant. But for the most part the social deficits of the youngsters and the strangeness of the habits of their wild cousins meant there was a bridge too wide to cross. As we sawed planks and hammered in nails our three young ape cousins alternately stood with arms outstretched waiting to be picked up – an appeal almost impossible to resist – or snatched at a hammer or saw before leaping into the branches where they mimicked our sawing and hammering actions. Soap too was a favourite item to snatch before swinging under the jetty out of our reach.

Early one morning I awoke to find my mosquito net and those of my neighbours being systematically dismantled by one orang who had squeezed through the window and was clearly enjoying the prank as well as the resulting distress of the rudely awakened. It was impossible not to react to these young primates as one would normally react to a juvenile human; and with the greatest resolve in the world not to be anthropomorphic, one could not help but experience a range of very human emotional responses. It struck me that these orangs were exhibiting a pattern of behaviour reminiscent of human juvenile delinquents. They were defiant, deceitful, thieving and aggressive and then at other times lovable and seemingly fragile. The stories of their early experience and development bore a striking similarity to the clinical histories of conduct-disordered kids I had encountered in practice: inadequate or absent maternal care, an inconsistent and unpredictable environment and very often abuse at the hands of adults. Young orang-utans remain dependant on their mothers for up to eight years and these individuals had been removed soon after birth to be sold as pets and curiosities to an illegal market predominantly in the Far East.

Observing the unnatural behaviour and personality traits of these orangs in the Tanjung Puting Reserve started me on a process of questioning the meaning of madness and the mental relationship between human and non-human primates. To what extent do these wild cousins of ours share our consciousness, emotions, reasoning and in particular our capacity for mental suffering and disorder? Why does madness exist in *Homo sapiens* and is it unique to our species or is there evidence for a form of madness in other primates? If there is then we can safely assume that our last common ancestors living approximately five million years ago also experienced psychosis in their midst. And if that was the case, does it follow that madness is an inherent aspect of the human condition – a costly legacy of our evolved human nature? Clearly, in order to answer these questions it is necessary to establish whether our nearest living relatives, the apes, show evidence of psychotic behaviour.

A number of authors have documented behaviour in captive chimpanzees that could be construed as psychotic in nature. These animals have been studied in zoos, research and rehabilitation centres and regrettably in pharmaceutical laboratories. Consequently, almost all these chimps have been subject to some form of human interference, whether that be the administration of drugs, the manipulation of the environment and social relationships for research purposes, or simply the presence of regular human contact. Enculturation has taken place and this proves to be a major confounding variable in the interpretation of recorded behaviours. An added problem is the fact that chimps do not have language ability and it is thus almost impossible to determine the presence of so-called positive symptoms of psychosis. In 1980 Professor Tim Crow of Oxford University proposed a classification of psychotic symptoms into positive and negative symptoms (Crow 1980). Positive (or productive) symptoms include hallucinations, delusions and disorganized thoughts and behaviour while negative (or deficit) symptoms include emotional or affective flattening, alogia (reduced volume and content of speech), avolition and apathy, loss of interest and motivation and social withdrawal.[1] Clearly, one cannot reliably determine whether a chimp is hallucinating, deluded or has disorganized thought processes. It is therefore necessary to describe a *psychotic behavioural syndrome* (PBS), largely based on negative symptoms that could be identified in disturbed individuals.

Some researchers have documented a range of abnormal behaviours in both chimps (Hook et al. 2002; Nash et al. 1999; Walsh et al. 1982) and other primates (Capitanio 1986; Erwin & Deni 1979; Goosen 1981). For example, Walsh et al. (1982) provided operational definitions for abnormal behaviours observed in 45 captive chimpanzees. They included behaviours such as coprophagy, faeces-smearing, regurgitation, rocking, repetitive body movements, hair-pulling, self-slap and spitting. Nash et al. (1999) suggested that some abnormal behaviours in chimps may be a result of social learning rather than indicative of reduced psychological well-being. In a separate study, Hook et al. (2002) demonstrated variance in the expression of abnormal behaviour across eight chimp groups suggesting that social learning processes are involved in the propagation of these behaviours. However, they also concede that in some cases social transmission is unlikely and the behaviours derive from inherent psychopathology. Table 2.1 lists a number of abnormal behaviours that together might constitute a PBS in chimps and possibly other apes. Evidence for such a syndrome in specific individuals would support the argument that our closest extant primate relatives do have the potential for psychotic disorder. It would also suggest that extinct hominids encountered psychosis in their midst.

If a PBS is to be identified in chimps and other apes, one would anticipate that disturbed individuals would display some of the behaviours listed in Table 2.1. As with human psychosis, one would not require all the behaviours to be present, neither would one expect different individuals to manifest exactly the same cluster of 'symptoms'; like humans, there is likely to be variability in the expression of psychosis between affected individuals. Furthermore, the demonstration of a PBS in captive apes would only suggest that apes have the potential for *induced* psychotic experience, since there are many confounding aetiological factors associated with the captive environment, for example: abnormal physical conditions; contrived social groupings; abnormal diet; human contact and enculturation; trauma associated with capture, separation from a natural group and introduction to artificial conditions; and finally exposure to drugs, surgery and other experimental procedures (in the case of experimental animals). In order to assert that a *spontaneous* PBS (equivalent to the functional human psychoses) occurs in apes, a cluster of symptoms would need to be documented in wild individuals exposed to a minimum of human interference. Since human functional psychosis is often precipitated by various stressors in constitutionally

Table 2.1 Proposed 'ape equivalents' of the human psychotic syndrome

Psychotic syndrome in humans	Psychotic behavioural syndrome in apes
Disorganized appearance and behaviour	Disorganized appearance and behaviour, e.g. aggression; bizarre behaviour, e.g. eating objects
Auditory and visual hallucinations	Hallucinatory behaviour, e.g. attending to abnormal stimuli
Paranoid delusions	Hypervigilance; suspicious, paranoid behaviour
Grandiose delusions	Increased dominance behaviour; increase in rank; hypersexual behaviour; increased risk-taking behaviour
Affective restriction or blunting	Loss of facial expression and reduced non-verbal communication
Impaired social cognition	Poor facial affect recognition; inappropriate social interactions
Social withdrawal, apathy, avolition	Social withdrawal; apathy; loss of interest in play and other activities; loss of rank
Ambivalence	Ambivalent responses to other individuals
Mannerisms, stereotypies, catatonia, posturing	Mannerisms; catatonia; posturing; and stereotyped ritualistic behaviours, e.g. rocking, scratching, hair-pulling, regurgitation, etc.

vulnerable people, the existence of *naturally* occurring precipitants in cases of PBS in wild apes would not invalidate the claim that these were examples of spontaneous psychotic illness.

As stated earlier in this chapter, behaviours suggestive of psychosis have been described in captive chimps and a range of other primates such as macaques and baboons. For example, experimental induction of psychotic behaviour has been achieved with surgical lesioning (Aggleton 1992; Bachevalier et al. 1999; Dicks et al. 1969; Málkova et al. 1997), administration of amphetamines (Castner & Goldman-Rakic 1999; Nielsen et al. 1983; Peffer-Smith et al. 1983; Ridley et al. 1982) and cocaine (Post et al. 1976), rearing in isolation (Dienske & Griffin 1978; Harlow & Harlow 1962; McKinney 1974; Turner et al. 1969) and manipulation of the social environment (Harlow & Novak 1973; Lutz et al. 2003; Sackett 1969; Suomi 1997). Lesion experiments responsible for the induction of psychotic symptoms typically involve surgical ablation of limbic temporal lobe structures such as the amygdala, hippocampus and uncus. This is an interesting detail since brain-scanning research in schizophrenia has consistently demonstrated both structural and functional abnormalities in these same limbic structures suggesting that the lesioning experiments are an appropriate model of human psychosis. Pharmacological precipitants of psychosis in both human and non-human primates boost the neurotransmitter dopamine in diffuse brain regions, thus modelling the well-recognized hyperdopaminergic states in schizophrenia and other functional psychoses.

Finally, experiments that involve manipulation of developmental and environmental conditions provide a crude representation of the complex and diverse psychosocial factors that often precede the onset of psychotic illness. In terms of the abnormal behaviours defined as constituting a PBS in apes and monkeys, the most commonly identified behaviours in these experiments are the following: stereotypies such as rocking, scratching, hair-pulling, regurgitation and licking; coprophagy; hyperactivity and hypervigilance; aggression; restriction of facial expression; hallucinatory behaviour; and social withdrawal. For example, Ellison describes the hallucinatory effects of implanted amphetamine pellets in the brains of monkeys: 'The animals behaved as though seeing imaginary enemies and then fleeing, or experiencing bugs under the skin, or pouncing on objects that could not be detected by human observers' (Ellison 1979). And in an early experiment that thankfully would not be permitted now, Davenport and Menzel (1963) compared stereotyped behaviours of sixteen chimpanzees raised from birth in restrictive environments with three wild-born chimpanzees brought to the Yerkes Laboratories as infants. The captive-born individuals were kept individually in cages for nearly three years and exhibited stereotypies such as rocking, repetitive head movements and posturing while their wild-born cousins, housed together in an enriched environment, showed almost negligible abnormal movements. This and similar deprivation studies confirm that disturbed behaviours reminiscent of human psychosis can be induced in a range of higher primates through manipulation of developmental and environmental conditions. Thus, in captive non-human primates, there is strong evidence to support the notion of an induced PBS. I would propose that this strongly supports the existence of an evolutionarily naïve form of human psychosis in non-human primates. Of course, the concern remains that this syndrome may be an artificial phenomenon directly attributable to human contact and intervention. In order to feel confident that *spontaneous* examples of PBS occur, equivalent to the human functional psychoses, it is necessary to look to the literature from field studies of primates in the wild.

Louis Leakey, the elder statesman of East African palaeoanthropology, who founded a dynasty of fossil hunters that included his wife Mary, his son Richard and his daughter-in-law Meave, initiated and mentored a programme of field research on the great apes of Africa and Southeast Asia. Under his guidance and with his support, three young women, Jane Goodall, Dian Fossey and Biruté Galdikas, established the first long-term field studies of the chimpanzee, gorilla and orang-utan during the 1960s. Until these studies very little was known of the behaviour of these close human relatives within their natural habitat and over the following decades a huge volume of data steadily accumulated from field sites in Tanzania,

Rwanda and Borneo. Some individuals have argued that the behaviours documented at these and other study sites[2] cannot be completely objective records of natural ape behaviour since many of the observations have been assisted by provisioning methods and habituation of the wild apes to regular human contact. Nevertheless, they remain the best we can hope to obtain. While few cases of grossly disturbed behaviour have been documented in wild ape studies, there are some records of individual animals manifesting behaviour reminiscent of psychosis. Jane Goodall (personal communication) attributes the relative paucity of documented accounts of abnormal behaviour to the difficult conditions of the field where small numbers of individuals are observed for brief periods and in differing social settings. Nevertheless, in her many years of close involvement with the chimpanzees of Gombe in western Tanzania, Goodall has encountered certain chimps that forced her to entertain the possibility of mentally illness in her subjects. For example, she describes the deterioration in behaviour of Merlin, a young male, who lost his mother while still suckling her at the age of three:

> As Merlin entered his sixth year his behaviour was becoming rapidly more abnormal. Sometimes he hung upside down, like a bat, holding onto a branch by his feet and remaining suspended, almost motionless, for several minutes at a time. Often he sat, hunched up with his arms around his knees, rocking from side to side with wide open eyes that seemed to stare into the far distance. And he spent much time grooming himself during which he pulled out hair after hair, chewed at their roots, and dropped them.
>
> (Goodall 1971)

This young chimpanzee was clearly exhibiting stereotyped behaviour including rocking, hair-pulling and posturing. He also dropped considerably in rank, was inadequate and disinterested in play behaviour with peers and displayed a range of socially inappropriate behaviours that included both sudden aggression and excessive submissiveness. For example, in response to the pant-hoots of a dominant male Humphrey who was commencing an arrival display, Merlin failed to move away as his companions did, but instead . . .

> . . . began moving fast towards Humphrey, pant-grunting in submission. Humphrey, who had already started to display, ran straight at Merlin, seized him by one arm and dragged him for several yards along the ground. As the big male charged away Merlin, screaming, rushed to embrace Miff. He had behaved like a small infant who does not yet appreciate the signals of impending aggression in his elders.
>
> (Goodall 1971)

This, and countless other bizarre social encounters, demonstrated that Merlin was unable to read, interpret and respond appropriately to the social signals of other chimps in his group. Time and again he was assaulted by displaying males because he ran towards them instead of getting out of the way, and with peers of a similar age he displayed unpredictable aggression that lead to his inevitable social isolation. His tool-using abilities were also inappropriate and he was particularly inept at termite fishing, using twigs that were too short and yanking them roughly out of the burrow so that he rarely caught any termites. These deficits in social behaviour and intuition suggest that Merlin suffered significant problems with social cognition and normal mind-reading. Furthermore, his behaviour and its social consequences provide a clear illustration of the survival advantages associated with healthy social cognition – Merlin's social disabilities put him in regular physical danger and at risk of starvation and isolated him within his own family group. Perhaps due to his reduced state, he succumbed to polio before he reached adolescence.

The naturalistic studies at Gombe have been criticized on the basis that human contact and food provisioning created an unnatural stress on the chimpanzees and influenced behaviours otherwise assumed to be species traits. Margaret Power, for example, suggests that human proximity altered the social ecology and social organization of the Gombe and Mahale chimps (Power 1991). She argues against the well-documented and substantiated view of chimp society as hierarchical, territorial and aggressive and instead promotes a more peaceful and optimistic view. Horacio Fábrega, in his book, *Origins of Psychopathology*, discusses Power's position and points out that many recent studies in the Tai and Kibale forests have confirmed the traditional view and thus weaken 'Power's controversial generalizations' (Fábrega 2002). In addition, he highlights the somewhat refuted group selectionist approach adopted by Power and argues that her conclusions are misguided. For the purposes of this discussion I would agree with Fábrega that in most cases documented behaviours at Gombe and other sites were likely to represent 'natural' or 'spontaneous' traits rather than the product of human interference. Merlin suffered a major developmental insult in losing his mother while still young and his appearance, behaviour and presumably mental state deteriorated into a syndrome that I would argue was most likely psychotic. Of interest is the fact that Merlin's case seemed to be exceptional. Goodall describes other orphans at Gombe (e.g. Flint) and while some may have manifested signs suggestive of a bereavement or even depressive illness, none displayed aberrations reminiscent of Merlin. This suggests a variation in chimpanzee vulnerability to stress similar to the notion of variable resilience[3] in human infants. It also suggests variability in the specific manifestation of psychopathology – a concept I address in detail in later chapters.

What does this mean for our understanding of the origins of psychosis in the human line of descent? The last common ancestor of modern *Homo sapiens* and *Pan troglodytes* (the common chimpanzee) is estimated from molecular studies to have lived in Africa between five and six million years ago. One can assume that this last common ancestor had the capacity to experience psychotic illness similar to the psychotic behavioural syndrome observed in chimpanzees. The manifestation of this illness in the last common ancestor and in subsequent hominid races evolving over the last five million years would have varied according to two major factors. Fábrega commits several chapters in his detailed book (Fábrega 2002) to the discussion of the factors that influenced the expression of psychopathology in hominids but essentially they group into two themes: the social ecology and the cognitive status of the specific hominid in question. In modern psychiatry we are well accustomed to the concept of a biopsychosocial approach to the causation and expression of mental illness. A broad interpretation of this model includes environmental and cultural factors and so intuitively we can assume that biological, psychological, social, environmental and cultural factors all interfaced during human pre-history to determine the specific manner in which psychosis expressed itself in hominid ancestors. For example, William Calvin presents a dramatic case for the role of global climactic change in shaping and driving hominid brain evolution (Calvin 2002) and it is no great leap of the imagination to surmise that the freezing arctic conditions of the Ice Age would have presented different stresses to evolving hominids from those resulting from life in a tropical rainforest. Similarly, David Horrobin in *The Madness of Adam and Eve* (Horrobin 2001) argues that periods of relative deficiency in essential fatty acids during hominid brain evolution increased our ancestors' vulnerability to schizophrenia-like psychosis.

These theories and others are examined in some detail in later chapters of this book, but for now it is important to recognize that psychotic illness, if it existed in pre-human communities, would have differed significantly from modern psychosis in terms of its expression. One can imagine that the earliest hominids such as *Australopithecus afarensis*, close to the last common ancestor, displayed a syndrome similar to the PBS I have described in extant chimps. As social dynamics became more complex and language began to emerge, it is likely that psychotic illness increasingly resembled the syndrome we recognize in modern psychiatry. But are there any other indicators along the road of human evolution that can inform our understanding of the origins of madness? In the next section I consider a period which spanned perhaps 100,000 years, beginning with the very first fully modern *Homo sapiens*. Archaeological evidence from this period suggests that these early humans regularly experienced psychotic-like phenomena in the context of shamanic ritual practices and psychoactive substance use.

SHAMANS, SUBSTANCES AND ALTERED STATES

The Ndedema Gorge lies in the foothills of the Drakensberg, a volcanic range separating the lowlands of KwaZulu-Natal from the highlands of the mountain kingdom of Lesotho. As a child I was taken hiking in the Ndedema almost every year so that the yellowwood forests, the high backdrop of Cathedral Peak and the numerous caves became a familiar and unforgettable part of my childhood. On summer trips, some days were spent boulder-hopping up the Ndedema River and swimming in its countless deep clear rock pools. On other days we climbed up from Poachers' Cave, our nightspot, onto the plateau to cross into an adjacent valley. After a water and apple break at Leopard Cave we headed for our landmark – a notch in the ridge at the head of the valley – before descending a steep slope to our destination. It wasn't marked on the map, but Eland Cave was a well-kept secret and it was our good fortune that my brother had been shown the cave by a conservationist friend. Today, I understand this awesome site is a popular tourist attraction for top-paying guests at a luxury lodge built less than a mile away. But 25 years ago one arrived alone at what felt like a remote and undisturbed wonder of the ancient world. No more than a shallow overhang of sandstone and basalt, the white face of the cave stretched at least 20 to 30 metres and formed a natural gallery for literally thousands of rock paintings. Great panels and friezes of yellows, browns, white and black showed images of human stick figures, the animals that populated their world and bizarre characters, half-human and half-mystical. This is the rock art of the San, the indigenous hunter–gatherers of Southern Africa who found refuge from northern invaders in these secluded valleys for several thousand years. In the latter half of the nineteenth and the early decades of the twentieth century they were systematically hunted and driven out of the mountains, fleeing west to their final refuge in the Namib and Kalahari Deserts. Today, their descendants are few and mostly poor, their society fragmented and plagued with alcoholism – a bitter legacy of the 'dop system'[4] which kept them harnessed as trackers for the South African apartheid army of occupation.

For many years the rock art was misunderstood as simple representations of the people and animals that made up the day-to-day existence of the San. The most common animal depicted was the eland, a large antelope that once flourished in these grassy foothills and provided the hunters with their major source of meat. And so it seemed obvious that the art reflected this relationship of dependence, with numerous images of this yellowish-brown cow-like creature with a pale head and neck. Obvious too because a simple narrative interpretation of the art fitted well with the popular (and politically motivated) view of the San as primitive simple 'savages' whose less than human status justified their extermination.

Then, thankfully for our rehabilitated view of the San and our awakened appreciation of their complex cosmology and cultural heritage, a new and informed interpretation of their art emerged during the latter decades of the twentieth century. Foremost among the scientists who pioneered this new understanding was David Lewis-Williams, Professor Emeritus in the Rock Art Research Institute at the University of the Witwatersrand in Johannesburg. In 1988 Lewis-Williams and his colleague Thomas Dowson drew considerable critical fire when they suggested that altered states of consciousness (ASC) played a role in the production of both European Upper Palaeolithic cave art and the rock art of the San (Lewis-Williams & Dowson 1988). This 'neuropsychological model' relates certain recurring motifs in the paintings to visual phenomena known to occur in ASCs. For example, during trance-like states induced by sensory deprivation, rhythmical drumming and dancing or ingestion of psychotropic substances, the individual may experience a number of predictable visual phenomena and hallucinations. Lewis-Williams (2002) describes three stages of trance '. . . each of which is characterized by particular kinds of imagery and experiences'. During Stage One, the lightest stage, various 'entoptic phenomena' are experienced consisting of geometric lines, dots, grids, zigzags and 'fortification structures'. These originate from 'hard-wired' stimuli in the brain, specifically in the connections between the retina and visual cortex and are found universally irrespective of cultural context. Thus, they are an inherent characteristic of the human mind in an altered state of consciousness. In Stage Two of the trance, the individual attempts 'to make sense of entoptic phenomena by elaborating them into iconic forms, that is, into objects that are familiar to them from their daily life' (Lewis-Williams 2002). The deep Stage Three of the ASC is associated with a transition through a 'swirling vortex' into a state of complex hallucination in any of the five senses, often superimposed on residual entoptic phenomena from the earlier stages. The imagery of this deep state is experienced as entirely real and is based upon emotionally salient memories, experiences and beliefs that are individually and culturally specific. Lewis-Williams quotes Erika Bourguignon[5] in making the point that while 'the capacity to experience altered states of consciousness is a psychobiological capacity of the species, and thus universal, its utilization, institutionalization, and patterning are, indeed, features of cultures, and thus variable' (Bourguignon 1973).

Lewis-Wiliams and Dowson argued that the European Upper Palaeolithic parietal art and the later art of the San (dated from the earliest in Apollo 11 cave in Namibia at 27,000 years ago to the most recent in the Drakensberg at the end of the nineteenth century) was not 'art for art's sake' as popularly believed, but was in fact the product of ASCs induced during shamanistic rituals (Dowson 1988; Lewis-Williams 1981; Lewis-Williams 1997; Lewis-Williams & Dowson 1999). In support of this hypothesis – and there has been no shortage of scepticism[6] – they tested their model against both the rock art of the San and that of the Numic people of the Coso Range on the western edge of the Great Basin, which occupies a large part of the American Southwest. Working in association with Lewis-Williams and Dowson, David Whitley conducted an in-depth analysis of the Numic ethnographic record and concluded that the rock art of these hunter–gatherers (dating from 500 to 4000 years ago) was largely shamanistic in nature (Whitley 1994, 1998, 2000). Both the San and Numic art contained motifs similar to the phenomena experienced in each stage of an ASC. Encouraged by these results, Lewis-Williams and Dowson applied their neuropsychological model to the Upper Palaeolithic cave art of western Europe and concluded that this too was produced in association with shamanistic ASCs. In addition to the famous caves of Lascaux in the Dordogne, Chauvet in the Ardèche and Altamira in Cantabrian Spain, thousands of subterranean caverns contain evidence of prehistoric art. At least 300 of these date to the Ice Age and the oldest radiocarbon-dated drawing is of a rhino in Grotte Chauvet approximately 32,400 years old (Clottes 1996).

Lewis-Williams, Dowson and other advocates of the neuropsychological model drew further support for their radical position (that complex art emerged almost simultaneously with the emergence of fully modern *Homo sapiens*) from laboratory and ethnographic studies of ASCs and the cognitive and emotional effects of psychoactive substances. The history of psychedelic research, from Albert Hofmann and LSD in the 1940s to twenty-first century functional brain imaging, is a book unto itself,[7] but for our purposes it is suffice to say that entoptic phenomena, elaborated iconic images and complex multisensory hallucinations are well-established products of drug-induced ASCs. For example, Klüwer (1966) classified four constants among the visual phenomena accompanying hallucinogenic states: (1) gratings, latticework, fretwork, filigree, honeycomb, chessboard; (2) cobweb figures; (3) tunnels, funnels, alleys, cones, vessels; (4) spirals. These phenomena are seen with eyes open or closed and appear variable in size, colour and brightness and are also associated with migrainous headaches and trance states. Later researchers elaborated these 'entoptic phenomena' (adding grids, zigzags, dots, circles and catenary curves) and identified the iconic forms and complex hallucinations common to deeper stages of trance (see discussion in Pearson 2002: 104). The fact that these phenomena are common to trance states, whether induced by substances or by other methods (such as rhythmical drumming, etc.) suggest that modern humans the world over have the capacity to experience a predictable and uniform pattern of ASC. If this is the case then it is implicit that our brains have a common structural and physiological basis for ASCs and that this capacity has evolved in conjunction with the emergence of modern *Homo sapiens*.

Brain research confirms the role of particular neuroanatomical structures and the presence of specific neurophysiological changes in altered states of consciousness. For example, Fritzsche (2002) argues that a breakdown in general sensorimotor information-processing may trigger ASCs. A number of authors have identified an increase in electroencephalogram (EEG) alpha and theta wave production during meditation (Jevning et al. 1982; Schuman 1980) and rhythmic drumming (Jelik 1982; Maxfield 1994) and Mandell (1980, 1985) attributes ecstatic transcendental states to slow-wave hyper-synchronous activity in deep temporal lobe structures (hippocampal-septal area). According to Mandell this has the effect of increasing inter-hemispheric coherence and integration. Interestingly, Ayahuasca, a hallucinogenic beverage brewed in the Amazon basin, has been shown to induce 'inter-hemispheric fusion' (Frecska et al. 2003). In a review of the neurophysiology of ASCs, Wright (1995) highlights the importance of temporal lobe disinhi-bition and 'kindling' in the generation of hypersynchronous slow-waves. Her model also explains the central role of serotonin in ASCs: various fac-tors such as hallucinogenic substances, sensory isolation and meditation decrease serotonin release resulting in a loss of serotonergic inhibition in the temporal lobe (Wright 1989). Changes in frontal lobe activity are also recognized in ASCs with a predominance of alpha waves and transient hypofrontality (Dietrich 2003).[8]

The metabolic effects of hallucinogens (such as mescaline, psilocybin and ketamine) have been demonstrated using functional imaging and include increased metabolism in the prefrontal cortex (especially the right side) and temporal cortex (Hermle et al. 1992; Gouzoulis-Mayfrank et al. 1999; Vollenweider et al. 1997a; Vollenweider et al. 1997b). Hallucinogens are known to act as partial agonists at serotonin $5HT_{2A}$ receptors (Aghajanian & Marek 1999; Nichols 2004), which are found in high densities in pre-frontal and temporal cortices, and it is thought that long-term activation of these receptors may alter gene expression at these sites (Nichols et al. 2003). Acute psychedelic stimulation of serotonin receptors gives rise to a cascade of other neurotransmitter shifts including the release of dopamine and glutamate (Aghajanian & Marek 2000; Vollenweider et al. 1999) – both implicated in the pathophysiology of schizophrenia.[9]

It is clear then that the human brain demonstrates a common pattern of activity in ASC, whether induced by substances or other techniques. The historical and contemporary use of psychoactive plants and shamanic rit-uals to induce ASCs is well documented (Dobkin de Rios & Winkelman 1989; Eliade 1989; Metzner 1998; Schultes 1998; Vetulani 2001) suggest-ing that our brains evolved the hardwiring necessary for altered states long ago. But how long ago? Winkelman (1989) used a large cross-cultural study to show a correlation between hunter–gatherer societies and the presence of shamanism. This fact, along with other ethnographic evidence, seems to indicate that shamanism has been a worldwide phenomenon since the earliest hunter–gatherer societies of the Palaeolithic era (Ripinsky-Naxon 1993). The earliest evidence of medicinal use of plants comes from Shanidar Cave in the Zagros Mountains of northern Iraq where nine Neanderthal skeletons dated between 50,000 and 80,000 years old were excavated from what appears to have been a burial site (Trinkaus 1983). Large quantities of pollen from eight different spring flowers were recovered from the 'flower burial' of Shanidar IV, a large male, and Leroi-Gourhan has shown that seven of these are known to have medicinal properties (Leroi-Gourhan 1975).

In his book *Shamanism and the Ancient Mind*, James Pearson asks, '. . . if they [the flowers] were placed with the remains because of their healing properties, as many surmise, is it such a giant leap to infer the beginnings of some type of shamanistic activity?' (Pearson 2002: 66). Since at least one of the Shanidar fossils (Shanidar I) survived to advanced age with what is probably a congenital withered arm and Eric Trinkaus has argued that this is proof of care-giving behaviour (Trinkaus 1983), it seems very likely that Pearson's conjecture is correct. The earliest depictions of hallucinogenic plants in rock art date to the late Stone Age: approximately 12–15,000 years ago. For example, in the Tassili-n-Ajjer plateau of southern Algeria shamans are portrayed clutching handfuls of mushrooms. Some figures have mushrooms sprouting from their bodies and are surrounded by geometric motifs reminiscent of entoptic phenomena. McKenna argues that these were depictions of the hallucinogenic psilocybin-containing *Stropharia cubensis* mushroom, endemic to the tropics wherever cattle grazed and left their manure as a fungal culture (McKenna 1992). There are many other examples of prehistoric use of psychedelics including the discovery in the Cuatro Cienagas Basin, Mexico of peyote remains and mescal beans together with human artifacts dated to 8000 years ago (Adovasio & Fry 1976) and evidence for the use of fly agaric, the mushroom *Amanita muscaria*, on the Siberian plateau as early as 10,000 years ago (Wasson & Wasson 1957).

If it is accepted that psychoactive plants featured prominently in the lives of early humans and that shamanistic rituals, similar to those of contemporary cultures such as the southern African San and the Indians of the Columbian Orinoco, facilitated their exposure to ASCs, then we have something of a window into the cognitive potential of Palaeolithic *Homo sapiens*. Clearly, they were capable of experiencing hallucinations, mood alterations, divergent thoughts and dissociative phenomena such as depersonalization and derealization. Their brains too must have already evolved the necessary structural and functional characteristics that would permit altered states to occur. Thus one can hypothesize that serotonergic and dopaminergic systems as well as prefrontal and deep temporal structures were present at this early stage. Lewis-Williams (2002) argues that the geometric and iconic images present in rock art arose fully formed from the evolved neurocircuitry of the brain. Since we know that the occipital and parietal association cortices of the brain play a major role in regulating our perception and interpretation of visuospatial information, it seems likely that these cortical regions (and their connections) were also highly evolved in early *Homo sapiens*.

In a later chapter I review the evolution of these important cortical structures in higher primates and hominids and what will emerge is the importance of the neural connections that link them together. This web of neural pathways allowed our ancestors to begin to integrate different information arising in previously modularized regions of the brain. Winkelman believes that ASCs contribute to 'psychointegration', that is, 'the integration of information across different functional systems of the brain' as well as the development of 'a greater degree of flexibility and conscious control of biological and mental systems' (Winkelman 2000: 129–130). He maintains that altered states are adaptive experiences since they contribute to 'an enhanced understanding of the nature of human consciousness, knowledge and awareness, and the ability to selectively and deliberately access a greater range of aspects of consciousness as needed'. The inherent quality of our capacity for ASCs is emphasized by Pearson (2002) who quotes Weil (1972): '(the) desire to alter consciousness periodically is an innate normal drive analogous to hunger or the sex drive'. And Sullivan and Hagen (2002) support their argument that psychotropic substance-seeking has ancient origins and possibly represents a human adaptation by drawing upon the biological evidence for a 'co-evolutionary relationship' between humans and psychotropic plants. They state that:

> ...this 'deep-time' relationship is self-evident both in the extant chemical-ecological adaptations that have evolved in mammals to metabolize psychotropic plant substances and in the structure of plant defensive chemicals that have evolved to mimic the structure, and interfere with the function, of mammalian neurotransmitters.

Finally, Terence McKenna, in his provocative and somewhat controversial book, *Food of the Gods: A Radical History of Plants, Drugs and Human Evolution*, attributes the reorganization of the brain's information-processing capacity to the influence of psychoactive chemical compounds in the diet of early humans (McKenna 1992). He argues that constant exposure to naturally occurring psychotropics constituted a positive selection pressure during the Palaeolithic. 'Alkaloids in plants, specifically the hallucinogenic compounds', he states, '. . . could be the chemical factors in the protohuman diet that catalyzed the emergence of human self-reflection' (McKenna 1992: 24). A bold hypothesis indeed; one whose merits will be debated in some depth later in this book.

Of central importance to our investigation of the origins of psychosis in humans is the question of the relationship between psychosis and altered states of consciousness. Are they similar phenomena and if so does the fact that our ancestors regularly experienced ASCs imply that they also had

34

experiences of psychosis? Certainly there is a significant overlap in the phenomenology of ASCs and psychosis – hallucinations, divergent thought processes, dissociation and mood alterations characterize both conditions. Bizarre and unusual beliefs too are common features of psychotic disorders and we know that while experiencing altered states the individual may believe that he or she is invested with special powers, is transformed into another being or is transported to a world that an observer may regard as pure delusion. At the level of the neuron there are similarities too between the two states. As we have seen from the discussion above, ASCs are characterized by alterations in neurotransmitter levels, specific electrophysiological changes on EEG and activation of specific cortical regions such as the prefrontal, medial temporal and parietal cortices. Research findings from schizophrenia, bipolar disorder and the major functional psychoses, demonstrate similar abnormalities of dopamine, serotonin and glutamate, provide evidence of EEG disturbance and implicate the same cortical regions in the genesis of psychotic symptoms. And certain hallucinogens (e.g. psilocybin, lysergic acid diethylamide (LSD) and phencyclidine (PCP)) have on some occasions the capacity to generate ASCs and on other occasions the effect of inducing psychosis.

Are we then to conclude that altered states are in fact a form of psychosis or vice versa? Are we to assume that the shamans of prehistory and the present are in fact culturally sanctioned sufferers of psychotic mental illnesses? Was the first art a mere product of 'acceptable' derangement? There are authors who have argued in the affirmative (Devereaux 1956; La Barre 1970; Silverman 1967), who maintain that shamans were and are the 'mad' of 'primitive' societies who have found a place and a role and a function, in contrast to those of 'developed' society who have been excluded and overlooked as mere 'lunatics' who play no useful role or purpose. For example Polimeni and Reiss (2002) state, 'A resemblance between schizophrenia and shamanism seems to be more easily observed in less technologically advanced societies' and they go on to suggest that, 'In hunting and gathering societies, individuals with schizophrenia-like symptoms may have been instrumental in initiating and maintaining spiritual ceremonies'. In other words, shamans were and are in fact schizophrenics! To my mind this conclusion is naïve and smacks of paternalism. It is naïve because it ignores a fundamental difference between the shaman and the psychotic, between altered states of consciousness and psychosis, that is, social and functional status. For Eugene Bleuler, the originator of the term 'schizophrenia', and for many others including myself, the defining feature of schizophrenia is the loss of social and functional competence.

By contrast, shamans are invariably respected, highly functional members of their communities who '. . . not only control their hallucinatory experiences but are able to distinguish clearly between external reality and their visions' (Stephen & Suryani 2000). Furthermore, Noll (1983) has identified other distinguishing characteristics of shamanism such as the positive nature of visions and voices and the enriching experience of submission to greater powers rather than disintegration of the sense of self. The confusion of the two states goes further with suggestions that psychosis may actually constitute a form of trance or ASC (Castillo 2003) or delirium (Charlton 2000). However, it is clear that they differ epidemiologically, phenomenologically, prognostically and in terms of social function. What then is the relevance of shamanism and ASCs during prehistory for our understanding of the origins of psychosis?

During the summer of 2003 I visited two painted caves and saw for myself the black bison of the Salon Noir in Niaux (in the French Pyrenees) and the child handprints on the walls of Castillo (in Cantabrian Spain). It was an awesome experience and the familiarities between these Palaeolithic creations and the San art of 10,000 years later were striking. Was this the work of shamans, the master artisans of altered states of consciousness? Lewis-Williams and Dowson's hypothesis is controversial without doubt, but for me it rang true as I descended far into these dank and silent caves to behold this extraordinary rock art. And it bore no resemblance to the normally disorganized bizarre character of psychotic art. So the evidence for 'archaic techniques of ecstasy' (Eliade 1989), whether it comes from shamanic rock art or from the fact that we share a long evolutionary relationship with hallucinogenic plants, is not evidence for psychosis in prehistory. But it is evidence for the emergence of complex brain reorganization and the cognitive potential for psychotic-like experience in early *Homo sapiens*. Clearly these ancestors of 100–30,000 years ago had the capacity to hallucinate, harbour bizarre and supernatural beliefs and experience extremes of emotion. Is it too much of a stretch of the imagination to conclude that the first modern humans knew the meaning of psychosis within their social groupings and were forced to respond to the mental distress of some individuals in their midst? This is a scenario we consider further in a later chapter. In the concluding part of this chapter, however, we move forward to the period that is recorded in the evolution of humankind and examine the evidence for historical descriptions and understanding of madness.

FROM NEBUCHADNEZZAR TO NIETZSCHE

31 . . . a voice came from heaven, 'This is what is decreed for you, King Nebuchadnezzar: Your royal authority has been taken from you. You will be driven away from people and will live with the wild animals; you will eat grass like cattle.

33 Immediately what had been said about Nebuchadnezzar was fulfilled. He was driven away from people and ate grass like cattle.

His body was drenched with the dew of heaven until his hair grew like the feathers of an eagle and his nails like the claws of a bird.

34 At the end of that time, I, Nebuchadnezzar, raised my eyes towards heaven, and my sanity was restored.
(From Daniel 4, Holy Bible NIV. Reprinted with permission.)

The author of the Book of Daniel provides a vivid account of the punishment meted out on the King of Babylon for his pride and vanity and failure to acknowledge God's supremacy. He is afflicted with madness and for seven years crawls in the fields with the beasts until his repentance sees the restoration of his sanity. The discovery in a cave of four scraps of parchment, the Dead Sea Scrolls, provides a remarkable confirmation of this Old Testament legend. Inscribed in Aramaic during the second half of the first century BC, the *Prayer of Nabonidus* tells of a Babylonian king who falls ill, is isolated for seven years and becomes convinced of the truth of the monotheistic creed.[10] The story of Nebuchadnezzar, whether fact or fiction, reveals an important truth about the perception of 'madness' during the millennia before Christ: madness came from the gods (or God) and was a spiritual punishment for sin and disobedience. This theme is echoed in the Homeric epics, the Hindu *Vedas*, the Egyptian *Book of Hearts* and the Chinese text *The Yellow Emperor's Classic of Internal Medicine* (*c.* 1000 BC).

There are authors who have argued that schizophrenia did not exist until the early 1800s, and then '. . . once [schizophrenia] was adequately described clinically in 1809 . . . the disease seems to have become visible all over the Western world and to have increased rapidly for a hundred years' (Gottesman 1991). Gottesman (1991) has summarized a number of theories accounting for what he views as the complete absence and then sudden appearance of schizophrenia in human history. The first is that the tendency to develop the disorder always existed, but that it was only with the increased stress of the industrial and urbanized age that it emerged as an incapacitating illness. Another theory posits that with the introduction of asylums in western Europe, large numbers of mentally ill people were for the first time concentrated together and could be observed and differentiated diagnostically. A third and more radical theory (which Gottesman seems to support) suggests that schizophrenia as a disease did not actually exist earlier in history and that the sudden increase in numbers of patients was due to an infectious agent such as a virus.

None of these explanations satisfies the issue for me for the following reason: 200 years ago, the clinicians who described the 'schizophrenic syndrome' were operating within a specific cultural framework that regarded psychosis as a pathology, an illness to be cured medically. Their interpretation of psychotic phenomena as 'illness' was as much a social and cultural

37

construction as the ancients' view that madness came from the gods. In every age and context human perception and interpretation of phenomena is coloured and influenced by the social, cultural and political norms of that context. We define the schizophrenic syndrome and understand it as a medical disorder because we live in an age of reason where science is venerated as a pure and objective discourse. Science continues to have authority – it is a yardstick that will protect us from fanciful myths and irrational charlatans. Not surprisingly, postmodernism constitutes a threat and is frequently decried as a meaningless philosophy. The postmodern movement, as represented by thinkers such as Michel Foucault, Jacques Derrida, Jean-Francois Lyotard and Richard Rorty, is characterized by relativism. Thus, as Muir Gray (1999) puts it '. . . there are no such things as objective facts and . . . reality has a plurality of meanings and is contingent'. He goes on to say 'Postmodernism also challenges the objectivity that science has claimed is its defining characteristic . . .'.

Pat Bracken and Phil Thomas, both consultant psychiatrists working in Bradford's multicultural communities, have articulated the need for a postmodern approach to psychiatry that they term 'postpsychiatry' (Bracken & Thomas 2001). They argue that human experiences of distress require an appreciation of individual context in order to be fully engaged with and understood. They explain: 'Contexts, that is to say social, political and cultural realities, should be central to our understanding of madness'. In their approach, Bracken and Thomas draw upon the inspiration of such philosophers as Wittgenstein and Heidegger who emphasized the importance of meaning and interpretation in knowledge. They entreat us not to abandon the empirical approach to psychiatry but rather to be aware of the social, cultural and political dynamics that surround and influence our modern construction of distress. Undeniably, the supreme advantage and confidence that characterizes the medical concept of mental disorder as biologically determined has a lot to do with the extraordinary success of the Enlightenment project in western Europe, which led to an almost religious faith in the power of science to answer our deepest questions about existence. But this faith has waned in many erstwhile believers as the limitations and failures of science to deliver answers have become increasingly apparent. Hence, the emergence of the postmodern condition.

Deconstructing madness therefore entails being aware of the lenses through which we experience the world and construct our truths about it. It also means being open to other lenses through which people in other times and places experience the world and construct their truths about it. As Krippner and Winkler (1995: 163) explain, the key to understanding the 'lenses' of other people living in a different context is language. They state: 'People in each culture construct experience in terms of the categories provided by their own linguistic system, coming to terms with a "reality" that has been filtered through their language. Each culture has a specialized terminology regarding those aspects of consciousness important for its functioning and survival.'

So, if we are to look for evidence of schizophrenia or psychosis in other cultures and at other times during human history then we cannot expect to find descriptions of the syndrome with which we are familiar. Gottesman (1991) and other authors who maintain that schizophrenia is a modern disease are correct only insofar as the schizophrenic syndrome is a modern construction of the scientific age. But they are wrong in their conclusion that a schizophrenia-like condition could not have existed prior to the 19th century. The key to finding evidence for its prior existence is to take the advice of Krippner and Winkler, and that is to look at language. And by 'language' I mean the socially, culturally and politically constructed world-view and means of expression of each culture and in each historical context. One needs to learn the 'language' of a people in order to understand the manner in which they would have constructed their experience of madness. Nebuchadnezzar crawled in the fields with the beasts, growing his hair and nails long and languishing for seven years in isolation and exile from his community. The author of Daniel lived in a context where deranged behaviour signified punishment from God. Thus, any recorded examples of psychosis are likely to be represented in terms of divine punishment and wrath. We see this repeated in the Old Testament:

> 15 But it shall come to pass, if thou wilt not hearken unto the voice of the LORD thy God, to observe to do all his commandments and his statutes which I command thee this day; that all these curses shall come upon thee, and overtake thee:
>
> 28 The LORD shall smite thee with madness, and blindness, and astonishment of heart:
>
> (Deuteronomy 28: King James Bible)

We also see it in Ancient Greece in Homer's accounts of his heroes, buffeted like 'puppets, in the grip of terrible forces beyond their control – gods, demons and the Furies – which punish, avenge and destroy; and their fates are decided largely by decree from above' (Porter 2002). As Porter explains, these heroes were not yet aware of 'the inner life, with its agonizing dilemmas of conscience and choice'. But with the emergence of Athens' Golden Age during the fourth and fifth centuries BC, the 'protagonists are the *conscious* subjects of reflection, responsibility and guilt' (Porter 2002). In Sophocles' *Ajax* we hear of his madness and violence, followed by guilt, remorse and self-blame when sanity returns:

> In the dead of night when the evening lamps were no longer aflame,
> he seized a two-edged sword and wanted to leave on an aimless

foray. Then I admonished him and said, 'What are you doing, Ajax? Why do you set out unsummoned on this expedition, neither called by messenger, nor warned by trumpet? In fact the whole army is sleeping now.' But he answered me curtly with that trite jingle: 'Woman, silence graces woman.' And I, taking his meaning, desisted, but he rushed out alone. What happened out there, I cannot tell. But he came in with his captives hobbled together – bulls, herding dogs, and his fleecy quarry. Some he beheaded; of some he cut the twisted throat or broke the spine; others he abused in their bonds as though they were men, though falling only upon cattle. At last he darted out through the door, and dragged up words to speak to some shadow – now against the Atreidae, now about Odysseus – with many a mocking boast of all the abuse that in vengeance he had fully repaid them during his raid. After that he rushed back again into the house, and somehow by slow, painful steps he regained his reason. And as he scanned the room full of his disastrous madness, he struck his head and howled; he fell down, a wreck amid the wrecked corpses of the slaughtered sheep, and there he sat with clenched nails tightly clutching his hair.

(Sophocles: *Ajax* from v. 285)

The Greek philosophers of the fourth and fifth centuries BC deposed the gods and grounded human experience in the physical reality of the body and its natural properties. Aristotle defined 'man' as a rational animal with reason as the shield against turmoil and chaos. Mental life, both healthy and deranged, was located in the brain as Hippocrates (1931) states: '. . . only from the brain spring our pleasures, our feelings of happiness, laughter and jokes, our pain, our sorrows and tears. . . . This same organ makes us mad or confused, inspires us with fear and anxiety . . .' Furthermore, both physical and mental illness represented imbalance of the humours.[11] For example, people with excess bile in the brain (*phrenitis*) were 'noisy, evildoers and restless, always doing something inopportune' (Hippocrates 1931).

The Roman writer Celsus (first century AD) described three forms of madness, the most disabling being a chronic illness usually resistant to treatment (Celsus 1935). Patients remained physically robust but could remain mentally ill their entire lives. Evans and colleagues suggest that Celsus' reference to patients who were 'duped not by their mind but by phantoms' (Celsus 1935) may describe the 'hallucinated and or the deluded' (Evans et al., 2003). They also suggest that the phrase, 'become foolish in spirit . . . fatuous or foolishly amused' may be a description of mania or disorganized schizophrenia. The first clinical description of 'schizophrenic types' is generally accepted as that of Aretaeus during the 1st century AD (Palha & Esteves 1997).

Aretaeus is considered a pioneer of the unitary model of psychosis, stating that the many forms of mental disorder all belonged to the same order (thus pre-empting contemporary advocates of the unitary model by 2000 years). In their review of classic literature and historical records, Evans et al. (2003) identify several other accounts that may suggest psychosis. These include Herodotus' (c. 484–430 BC) accounts of the madness of King Cleomenes of Sparta and also King Cambyses of Persia; Plutarch's (c. 50–120 AD) reports of a deluded and hallucinated stranger who sat on Alexander the Great's throne in Babylon – and was executed because the king regarded this an ill omen foreshadowing his own death; and finally Plutarch's descriptions of two famous generals, Dion and Brutus, who saw 'phantoms' or 'apparitions'.

With the rise of Christendom following Constantine's declaration of the faith, the human being became a battlefield whereon the Holy Ghost and the devil battled for possession of the soul. According to Porter (2002), 'the marks of such "psychomachy" might include despair, anguish and other symptoms of disturbance of mind'. The first asylums were created in a humanitarian spirit, influenced by Arab philosophers such as Rhazes, Avicenna and Averroës (living between 850 and 1200 AD) and soon asylums sprang up at Gheel, Belgium (thirteenth century), at St Mary of Bethlem, London in 1243 and in Granada, Spain in 1365. In his account of this period, Gottesman (1991) points out the paradox, 'that while the medieval period regressed to antiscientific explanations of mental illness, yet treated the ill humanely, the Renaissance's intellectual enlightenment brought history's darkest hour in mental health treatment'. A Papal Bull authorizing the genocide, largely inspired the witch-hunts that saw the extermination of more than 50,000 people across western Europe between 1460 and 1680. In 1484, two Dominican monks, Heinrich Kraemer and Johann Sprenger, prompted Pope Innocent VIII to issue the Bull, thus opening the way to the Inquisition and its grotesque excesses. As if they had not done enough, Kraemer and Sprenger produced *Malleus Maleficarum* ('The Witches Hammer') in 1486 – a handbook for finding witches and devising their punishments.

In order for us to appreciate the causes of this radical shift in attitude towards the mentally ill, it is first necessary to comprehend the social, cultural and political changes that influenced the common (hu)man's construction of madness. Porter (2002) explains how the naturalistic philosophy and medicine of the Classic era continued to influence medieval thinkers in both the Islamic and Christian world. For Porter, the arrival of the Renaissance 'brought no Copernican revolution in psychiatry . . . it was rather the culmination, and the conclusion, of the Classical tradition' (Porter 2002). And as for the witch-hunts, Gottesman (1991) cites a number of contributory social and political factors giving rise to this heinous public response to madness. These include: 'power struggles between

Protestants and Catholics, economic greed, the disempowerment of women, the expression of repressed sexuality in Christian doctrine, and the cruel scapegoating tendencies of our species when placed under stress'.

The philosophers of the Enlightenment, Descartes, Hobbes, Locke and others revived the rationalist and materialist focus of the Classic era. They also made the mind a subject of central importance. Descartes committed his life to the pursuit of logic and reason, arguing that nothing besides his own consciousness was free of doubt – 'I think therefore I exist'. The mind he equated with the soul as an immaterial phenomenon responsible for consciousness, morality and immortality and suggested that it was located in the pineal gland of the brain. Descartes' separation of mind (which is ethereal) from body (which is tangible) had a major influence on philosophy, science and medicine throughout the Enlightenment and modern era and has become known as 'Cartesian dualism'. The implications of Cartesian dualism for the social construction of madness were significant. No more could demons and devils be invoked in the causation of madness, for now the mind was grounded in substance, albeit elusive. In addition, the rise of technology and mechanistic industry during this period (17th–19th centuries) impacted on concepts of body and mind. The mind was a machine, thus healthy reason reflected a well-oiled functioning machine, while insanity reflected a loss of reason and consequent malfunction of the machine. This reductionist approach was to dominate thinking for the next 300 years as psychiatry emerged as a formal response to madness. Its influences are apparent in all the major theoretical schools within psychology and psychiatry, including the Behaviourist and Psychoanalytic Movements and indeed the 'golden age' of biological psychiatry.

Sadly, the advances in science that characterized the Enlightenment era did not translate into a more compassionate view of the mentally ill. In fact, the veneration of reason carried with it an almost moralistic contempt for 'unreason'. Individuals who were intellectually disabled or mentally ill were regarded as 'degenerates' and were locked away in asylums where they could not contaminate sane society. By the end of the eighteenth century, conditions in the asylums had reached rock bottom with overcrowding, poor hygiene and routine 'treatments' designed to punish and correct the disturbed 'indulgences' of inmates. It took a social and political cataclysm in Europe to bring an end to this shameful era of exclusion and debasement of the mad. The age of asylums and shackles, condemned by Foucault as 'the great confinement' (Foucault 2001) and portrayed by Hogarth in his series depicting 'Rake's Progress' through Bedlam, came to an end when, in the spirit of the French Revolution, Philippe Pinel struck off the chains from his charges. In 1793, only four years after the storming of the Bastille and inspired by the ideals of liberty, equality and fraternity, Pinel introduced radical reforms at the Bicêtre and Salpêtrière Hospitals in Paris. Shortly afterwards reforms spread to England where William Tuke, a Quaker, founded the York Retreat in 1796. Liberation and compassion for the mad, therefore, followed directly from a dramatic transformation in the way people viewed themselves as autonomous beings and as worthy members of society.

In concluding this chapter, it is worth considering the following statement: psychosis has its origins with the emergence of the first *Homo sapiens* 100–150,000 years ago. Forms of psychotic-like behaviour are evident in our nearest extant primate relatives and were likely manifest in hominids such as *Australopithecus, Homo habilis* and *Homo erectus*. However, it was only with the evolution of a mature social mind based in the interconnected circuits of a fully integrated social brain that the first modern humans manifested a capacity for true psychotic illness. Insights from the archaeology and anthropology of Palaeolithic cave art, psychotropic substance use and shamanic practices of altered states of consciousness, teach us that these early humans were well acquainted with quasi-psychotic phenomena and were likely familiar with full-blown psychosis too. Finally, the absence of written descriptions of the schizophrenic syndrome prior to the end of the 19th century cannot be interpreted as the absence of functional psychosis prior to that period. Rather, if one appreciates the cultural, political and religious belief systems of each historical epoch, from Old Testament Palestine to the current age, then one discovers a multiplicity of accounts of functional psychotic illness in the written records and literature of that age. The key to discovering these accounts is to acknowledge the process by which knowledge is constructed in the language and socio-cultural idiom of the times. As Bracken and Thomas (2001) state, 'Contexts, that is to say social, political and cultural realities, should be central to our understanding of madness'.

Thus, it is apparent that madness is as old as humankind itself. The origin of our species was the origin of complex interpersonal relationship and the ability to truly mindread. However, with this evolutionary advantage came another phenomenon – psychosis – a trait, it turns out, that rendered the afflicted individual disadvantaged in the Darwinian contest for survival. In the next chapter we turn our attention to evolutionary biology and consider the attempts of several authors to explain the evolutionary paradox that is psychosis. The survival of human madness is paradoxical because here we have a situation where a trait persists, universally and at a constant prevalence, despite the obvious evolutionary disadvantage conferred on the sufferer.

3

EVOLUTIONARY PRINCIPLES OF THE ORIGINS OF PSYCHOSIS

THE ADAPTATIONIST PROGRAMME

Certain events stand out from my memories of childhood. One such memory is an experience my classmates and I had at about 15 or 16 years old. Our English teacher, who we addressed as Ken and for whom we had the utmost respect, took our class of 20 or so boys camping in the Umgeni Valley, a protected wilderness area. As with any group of adolescents we were a mix of studious and not so studious pupils and we certainly had our complement of jokers who played the fool, disrupted lessons and generally stressed out the teachers. The first 24 hours of the camping trip progressed as expected – mud fights in the river, illicit cigarettes secretly puffed behind trees and not much sleep for anyone. On the second morning Ken led us to a sunny spot upriver and invited us to make ourselves comfortable and then he began to tell us a story – the story of Hamlet. In his usual fashion this 'lesson' was more a conversation and interactive discussion than a lecture. And the striking feature of this experience (and of others over the subsequent few days) was the extraordinary change in both the attitude and behaviour of the group. The normally disruptive and disinterested boys were captivated and became vocal participants in the discussions. Suddenly individuals written off as poor achievers had extraordinary things to say and the treachery of Claudius, the madness of Ophelia and the anguished soul-searching of the Prince became themes that surfaced again and again over the following days. Perhaps even more importantly the group witnessed another dimension to these stereotyped 'bad boys' for they seemed to shed their macho skins revealing a depth and sensitivity previously hidden. In a sense this 'bush-school' interlude probably taught the group more about life and literature and human experience than an entire year in the classroom.

In my current clinical practice near Durban, a swelling metropolis on the east coast of South Africa, I run a clinic one day a week at a district hospital that serves a relatively deprived local community. Every week I see two or three children who have been referred by their schoolteachers for Ritalin.

44

The complaints are a familiar list of so-called attentional and hyperactivity behavioural problems and the usual demand is for me to confirm the diagnosis as attention deficit hyperactivity disorder (ADHD) and start the troublesome child on stimulant medication. This will 'solve the problem' and enable the child to progress in his or her schooling. The pressure on parents is massive: 'Put your child on Ritalin or we are no longer prepared to teach him/her'. In most cases there are a host of socioeconomic, familial and developmental reasons for the child's misbehaviour – poverty, parental conflict, substance abuse, physical abuse in the home and exposure to trauma are just some of the environmental scourges impacting on the child's life. Inevitably and regrettably I end up writing the script since the resources required to remedy the true causes of the 'ADHD' do not exist. And for a struggling parent, having a child passing school on Ritalin is vastly prefer-able to a child failing and sitting at home on no treatment. The fact is that these kids are exhibiting behaviour that they learn outside the classroom and to a certain extent they need to survive.

This may sound strange and not very scientific but I am certainly not the first person to suggest that some of the behavioural traits of ADHD may represent adaptations that evolved in our hunter–gatherer past. Peter Jensen at NIMH for example has argued 'that evolutionary perspectives can explain the presence of ADHD traits in *some* children' (Jensen et al. 1997). He and his colleagues propose that in the ancestral environment the core 'symptoms' of ADHD – hyperactivity, inattention and impulsivity – may have represented advantageous traits that aided survival, namely, 'high motor activity', 'hypervigilance and high-scan ability' and 'impulsive, imme-diate response'. These traits characterize the 'response-ready individual' who is well adapted to the unsafe, resource-scarce, ancestral environment, where response time is critical. These authors maintain that the modern classroom environment favours 'problem-solving' traits such as low motor activity, non-impulsivity and focused attention. Clearly this phenotype rep-resents the opposite end of a spectrum extending to the response-ready individual and they conclude that children diagnosed with ADHD and their parents should be 'encouraged to seek situations and potential success areas where "response-ready" traits are more adaptive' (Jensen et al. 1997).

Perhaps this evolutionary reframing of a 'clinical disorder' sheds some light on the transformation in behaviour I witnessed in some of my school-mates during our outdoor learning experience in the Umgeni Valley 20 years ago. I would argue that it also helps provide a better understanding of the problems experienced by 'response-ready' kids forced to participate in a 'problem-solving' classroom environment. As a psychiatrist I may still have to dish out the Ritalin but at least this evolutionary perspective adds a deeper level of meaning to the child's experience and hopefully the child, parent and doctor leave the consultation with a little more wisdom and compassion.

This approach to ADHD is an example of what has become known as the 'adaptationist programme', a research strategy that extends to most of the biological and social sciences. The term originates from a landmark paper by Stephen Jay Gould and Richard Lewontin in which these two giants of modern evolutionary theory question the wholesale use of 'adaptationist' thinking in evolutionary studies (Gould & Lewontin 1979). According to Gould and Lewontin, adherents to the adaptationist programme seek to discover an adaptive purpose for every biological trait, leaving no room for chance or evolutionary constraint in the survival of some features of the phenotype. Just like the spandrels[1] of St. Mark's Cathedral in Venice, they argue, some features of the organism may represent epiphenomena or by-products of the evolutionary process that serve no adaptive function themselves. They attribute this overuse of the concept of adaptation not to Darwin but to among others Alfred Russel Wallace, the co-discoverer of the principle of natural selection. The adaptationist programme, they state, is rooted in a belief in: '. . . the near omnipotence of natural selection in forging organic design and fashioning the best among possible worlds. This programme regards natural selection as so powerful and the constraints upon it so few that direct production of adaptation through its operation becomes the primary cause of nearly all organic form, function and behaviour' (Gould & Lewontin 1979).

Ernst Mayr, another doyen of modern evolutionary theory, mounted a qualified defence of the adaptationist programme, arguing that 'the adaptationist question, "What is the function of a given structure or organ?" has been for centuries the basis for every advance in physiology' (Mayr 1983). Mayr argues that our current understanding of the purpose and function of such organs as the thymus, spleen, pituitary and pineal glands is a result of adaptationist questions being asked in biological research. He maintains that the criticisms levelled by Gould and Lewontin are justified when restricted to reductionist atomistic use of the adaptationist programme; for example reducing an organism to its most basic traits and then searching for 'the ad hoc adaptation of each smallest component'.

The elaboration of an appropriate methodology to establish adaptive significance is, according to Mayr and others (Daly & Wilson 1994; Durrant & Haig 2001; Nesse 1999), essential for any credible evolutionary programme. Evolutionary psychologists, Martin Daly and Margo Wilson, concede that some evolutionary psychologists erroneously misconstrue adaptationist theorizing as a claim that fitness itself is what organisms strive for. It is as if the attainment of perfect evolutionary fitness is the direct objective or motivator of adaptation by natural selection. This notion has a historical context in that it hearkens to the pre-Darwinian notion of creative design. The impact of Darwin, says Sober (1984), relates chiefly to his replacement of a purposeful creator by a blind process. A divine creator has a purpose or goal 'in mind' when designing an object or organism and progress is an essential aspect of the designing process because there is progression towards the ultimate goal. This concept is teleological in nature because it deals with the purposes, goals or ends of a process or action.

The term 'teleology' comes from the Greek word *telos* meaning 'final purpose' and teleological explanations attempt to explain X by saying that X exists or occurs for the sake of Y. According to Sober (1984), 'science progresses by replacing teleological concepts with ones that are untainted by goals, plans and purposes'. Bernado Dubrovsky (2002) of McGill University, Montreal, maintains that Darwin legitimized the notion of 'chance' in evolution by invoking natural selection as the mechanism acting upon a random assortment of variable traits in any given instant. As Mayr (1983) states, 'the important role of chance at the first step, the production of variability, is universally acknowledged . . . What is usually forgotten is the important role chance plays even during the process of selection'. In his critique of the use of adaptationist thinking in evolutionary psychology, Dubrovsky (2002) argues that this is the error commonly committed by these theorists. Influenced more by evolutionists such as Herbert Spencer (1862) than by Darwin himself, evolutionary psychologists such as Cosmides and Tooby (1992) overlook the 'strictly a posteriori nature of an adaptation' (Mayr 1983) and view natural selection teleologically rather than as a chance process.[2] For example Cosmides and Tooby (1992) state: '. . . the field of evolutionary biology summarizes our knowledge of the engineering principles that govern the design of organisms, which can be thought of as machines built by the evolutionary process . . . Modern evolutionary biology constitutes, in effect, an "organism design theory."'

If we are to heed Mayr (1983) and others therefore and focus on establishing a valid methodology in pursuing adaptationist lines of enquiry within psychology and psychiatry, we need to be cautious and not invest natural selection with teleological potential. The algorithmic nature of cognitive processes so popular with evolutionary psychologists (e.g. Cosmides & Tooby 1992; McGuire & Troisi 1998; Nesse & Williams 1995; Stevens & Price 1996) is, according to Dubrovsky (2002), erroneous since this view implies that mental events 'are produced by executing a programmatic list of logically connected instructions that, once started, go ahead regardless of circumstances so that it is sure to attain the preset goal'. Thus, algorithms are innate hardwired programs comparable to computer programs and, in Dubrovsky's view, imply evolutionary design. It seems therefore that much of the criticism levelled at evolutionary psychology as a discipline may be at least partly justified, since they are largely based on a teleological view of natural selection and adaptation.

If then there is a place for adaptationism within cognitive science and psychiatry, how do we go about developing a methodology that is robust and not guilty of the errors so despised by Gould and Lewontin (1979)? Several authors have proposed criteria to establish adaptive significance of traits, whether they be physical or mental. For example Mayr (1983) draws on the work of Traub (1980) (on adaptive modification in fleas) and explains: '. . . the methodology consists in establishing a tentative correlation between a trait and a feature of the environment, and then to analyze in a comparative study, other organisms exposed to the same feature of the environment and see whether they have acquired the same specialization' (Mayr 1983).

Clearly, Mayr (and Traub) are drawing on the evolutionary principle of 'convergence' whereby two or more unrelated organisms arrive at the same trait because of their exposure to similar environmental conditions. Daly and Wilson (1994) add support for this across-species comparative method. They explain that in evolutionary terms, appropriate research needs to take account of species similarities and differences in relation to 'species-characteristic ecologies and the adaptive problems they entail'. According to Durrant and Haig (2001), one of the developments in evolutionary biology following Gould and Lewontin's (1979) landmark critique of the adaptationist programme was an appreciation of the importance of phylogenetic analyses and the comparative method. Mayr (1983) continues by stating that if this comparative approach leads to falsification of the hypothesis, then experimental tests become the next step. These tests, says Mayr, need to be holistic in nature, addressing 'the possible adaptive significance of a larger portion of the phenotype' rather than focusing on individual select traits. He states:

> Aristotelian 'why' questions are quite legitimate in the study of adaptations, provided one has a realistic conception of natural selection and understands that the individual-as-a-whole is a complex genetic and developmental system and that it will lead to ludicrous answers if one smashes this system and analyses the pieces of the wreckage one by one.
>
> (Mayr 1983)

Mayr supports Gould and Lewontin's (1979) appeal for a pluralistic approach to evolution but argues that their 'alternatives to immediate adaptation' are all ultimately based on natural selection. Gould and Lewontin cited Darwin himself in their paper,[3] making a case for non-selective mechanisms such as exaptation and cultural adaptation. But Mayr's contention is that natural selection is a satisfactory explanation for change as long as it is properly conceived. A pluralistic view requires us to take account of numerous factors – most unavailable in Darwin's era – including the developmental physiology, genetics, demography and ecology of an organism. These factors act as constraints on evolution so that an adaptation is 'the best of the available variants of a trait' rather than 'the perfect adaptation'. And finally, the pluralistic approach ensures that one does not forget the fact that natural selection acts on complete genotypes rather than individual traits. Mayr believes that Dobzhansky expresses the appropriate view of the adaptationist programme:

> It cannot be stressed too often that natural selection does not operate with separate 'traits.' Selection favours genotypes ... The reproductive success of a genotype is determined by the totality of the traits and qualities which it produces in a given environment.
>
> (Dobzhansky 1956)

This appeal for a pluralistic approach to adaptationism seems to support the methodology I outlined in Chapter 1. Incorporating multiple dimensions such as developmental, genetic and ecological features of the organism amounts to a 'cabling' method of evolutionary enquiry. It is my hope that such an approach will validate my attempt to develop an empirically sound evolutionary theory of psychosis. Natural selection is undoubtedly the major mechanism giving rise to change on our planet and it is highly likely that it has played a significant role in the evolution of the brain in our species. This fact implies that adaptationism is a concept that cannot be ignored, but must instead be grappled with in excavating the origins of mental disorder. The adaptationist example (of ADHD) that I provided at the beginning of this chapter has a ring of truth about it – in terms of clinical realities it makes a lot of sense – but I have elected not to submit this particular hypothesis to the criteria advocated by Mayr and others (for robust adaptationist research). Instead I will return to the focus of this book, psychosis, and try to hold in mind the principles I have outlined above as I first critique existing evolutionary theories of psychosis and then go about building my own.

A CONTINUUM OF PSYCHOSIS

In Chapter 1, I presented the rationale for an evolutionary discourse on psychosis. The epidemiology of the disorder calls for a Darwinian analysis since we have observed the paradoxical survival of a highly genetic condition despite the apparent maladaptive nature of the phenotype. In response, several authors have examined the phenotype itself – schizophrenia or bipolar disorder or the atypical functional psychoses – asking the question as to whether there is some hidden physiological evolutionary advantage in being psychotic (Carter & Watts 1971; Huxley et al. 1964). For example, perhaps if you have schizophrenia you have some kind of immunity against certain infections?[4] Or perhaps psychotic individuals in early hunter–gatherer communities fulfilled a role as charismatic leaders (e.g. Stevens & Price 2000)? More popular though has been a slightly different strategy that

49

has emerged as a result of certain clinical observations regarding the phenomenology of psychotic disorders. These observations have bothered psychiatry as long as it has been a recognized discipline. The fact is that our classification system is problematic and does not adequately account for the varieties of psychosis that we encounter in clinical work. This issue has some history to it that is worth a brief digression.

The medical literature of the nineteenth century was largely characterized by a myriad of clinical descriptions and classifications of psychotic illness. Kahlbaum described *katatonie* in 1868 and French psychiatrists characterized manic-depressive insanity. The concept of *paranoia* was developed at this time also by Kahlbaum. Importantly, the classification of psychoses was variable and lacked a unifying and simplifying formulation. Emil Kraepelin, a German psychiatrist in the Heidelberg Clinic, revolutionized the conceptualization of psychosis, with the publication of the fifth edition of his textbook in 1896 (Kraepelin 1896). He divided the functional psychoses into two distinctive groups, and in doing so set the course for psychiatry for the next 100 years. He based the division upon the long-term course: *manic-depressive insanity* following a fluctuating pattern with full recovery; and *dementia praecox* (schizophrenia) following a steadily deteriorating course to a chronic disabled state. This basic dichotomy provided a workable platform for research and the development of a clinical approach to the two 'disorders'. However, Kraepelin's classification was troubled by the obvious presence of individuals who manifested classic symptoms of schizophrenia, but whose course improved and had a favourable long-term prognosis. In fact, Kraepelin (1913) himself later conceded that a complete recovery occurred in 12.5 per cent of cases.

This controversy, initiated by his division of the psychoses into two basic groups, has continued to occupy psychiatry throughout the last 100 years. The recognition that there are patients who defy classification into one or other group and rather seem to straddle the divide has generated numerous nosological efforts. Kasanin (1933) coined the term 'schizo-affective disorder' and this has survived into DSM-IV, while other categories such as schizo-depression and schizophreniform disorder have been suggested (Kendler et al. 1998; Langfeldt 1939).

This categorical approach in dealing with the complex and variable manifestations of psychosis has drawn strong criticism, both prior to and since Kraepelin. The opposing 'unitary model' of psychosis dates back to Griesinger in 1845 – he described a single mental condition with his term *die einheitpsychose* (Griesenger 1845). Later Menninger resuscitated this unitary concept, reasoning that one cannot divide psychosis into discrete disorders (Menninger et al. 1958). Recent work has demonstrated that the psychoses cannot be reliably separated in terms of symptoms (Kendell & Brockington 1980; Kendell & Gourlay 1970), genetics (Kendler et al. 1998) or epidemiology. Crow (1997, 1998) has proposed that psychotic illnesses should be viewed as lying on a *continuum of variation* and that we need to think dimensionally instead of categorically. In his recent book *Madness Explained: Psychosis and Human Nature* Richard Bentall of the University of Manchester has outlined in detail the evidence for a dimensional approach to the functional psychoses (Bentall 2003). Bentall and others have also argued the case for a spectrum of variation stretching from 'sanity to madness' (Bentall 2003) – or from 'normality' to 'trait' to 'disorder'.

As early as the turn of the 19th/20th century, Eugen Bleuler, the Swiss psychiatrist who coined the term 'schizophrenia', argued that the differences between sanity and madness are but a matter of degree. Ernst Kretschmer, a professor from Tübingen, Germany, maintained that psychoses represented variations in normal personality. However, it was only within the last 40 years that this proposed spectrum of variation was examined experimentally. Bentall attributes this new interest to a speech presented by Paul Meehl to the American Psychological Association in 1962 (Meehl 1962). According to Bentall (2003), Meehl proposed that individuals inherit a *vulnerability* to psychosis rather than the disorder itself and he termed this predisposition 'schizotaxia'. This led to the concept of 'schizotypy' whereby an individual harbours a vulnerability to psychosis and manifests some traits such as eccentricity and magical thinking, but does not manifest frank psychosis. The adoption studies of Seymour Kety and his colleagues in Denmark provided empirical evidence for a genetic relationship between schizotypy and schizophrenia – a notion they called 'schizophrenia spectrum disorder' (Kety et al. 1975). Further validation for the concept of a genetically mediated schizotypal spectrum followed, with key contributions from researchers such as Gordon Claridge in Oxford (Claridge & Beech 1995), the Chapmans in Wisconsin (Chapman et al. 1994) and Bentall himself (Bentall et al. 1989). Recent evidence from neuroimaging and neuropsychology studies suggests that schizotypal individuals have milder but similar deficits to patients with schizophrenia (Buchsbaum et al. 1997a, 1997b; Cadenhead et al. 1999; Dickey et al. 2002). That these deficits are also found in relatives of patients with schizophrenia suggests a genetic cause (Byrne et al. 1999; Lawrie et al. 2001) and supports the idea of a genetic continuum.

Having outlined the well-supported concept of a continuum of variation (from mood disorder to schizophrenia), as well as the equally wellsubstantiated notion of a schizotypal spectrum (from normality to frank psychosis), I can now return to the evolutionary endeavours within psychiatry and psychology that have sought to explain the survival of a maladaptive psychotic phenotype. In essence, the existence of a spectrum in the expression of the genotype has provided a suitable model for those authors wishing to consider just where the adaptive value might reside. So, instead of vainly attempting to conjure up some aspect of this disabling disorder that might be considered 'adaptive', it seems legitimate to focus on individuals in the schizotypal spectrum and seek to identify adaptive traits in this population that may compensate for the former group's lack of fitness. Thus, a popular assumption among evolutionary psychiatrists is that unaffected individuals in the schizotypal spectrum may be at some kind of reproductive advantage, thus compensating for the apparent disadvantage of the psychotic phenotype. In genetic terms this effectively describes a 'heterozygous advantage' or 'balanced polymorphism' model.[5]

THEORIES OF ULTIMATE CAUSATION

Within evolutionary theory a distinction is made between *proximate* and *ultimate* causes. According to Dewsbury (1999) this distinction dates back to William James' 1890 *Principles of Psychology* where James clearly distinguished between the function and the immediate causation of behaviours (James 1890). Biologists such as Julian Huxley (1916) and J.R. Baker (1938) made use of this distinction but it was Ernst Mayr (1961) who developed and popularized the two concepts. Evolutionary thinkers in the behavioural sciences, especially in psychology and psychiatry, make liberal use of this distinction in their adaptationist approaches to mental and behavioural phenomena. In this context the ultimate cause of a trait refers to the evolutionary history of that trait and the selective pressures that, over millennia, gave rise to that trait. Proximate causes on the other hand refer to the systems active in the individual's lifetime that give rise to the trait. For example, McGuire and Troisi (1998), both evolutionary psychiatrists, describe the implications of this distinction for evolutionary approaches to behaviour:

> Short-term changes in behaviour are mediated by nervous system structures that have physiological, psychological, and anatomical properties. Proximate mechanisms – or proximate causes, another term often used – is the term applied to systems that are responsible for short-term behavioural changes. Ultimate causation explains why proximate mechanisms have been selected. Proximate mechanisms explain the workings of mechanisms within specific time frames. Ultimate and proximate causes are not alternative explanations of behaviour. Rather, they are complementary. Behaviour has both ultimate and proximate contributions.
>
> (McGuire & Troisi 1998)

McGuire and Troisi maintain that research in psychiatry has focused on proximate causation such as alterations of receptor function with pharmacological agents or behavioural desensitization. They argue that our understanding of psychiatric disorders will expand significantly if we begin to examine the ultimate mechanisms that underlie our cognitive and behavioural traits. They cite a number of examples of 'ultimately caused traits': parent–offspring bonding; male and female possessiveness and jealousy; cooperative and reciprocal behaviour among nonkin; parent–offspring conflict; sibling rivalry; preferential investment in kin; menopause; and deception and self-deception. All humans, they state, are predisposed to engage in these behaviours – they are hardwired as 'algorithms' – and these predispositions 'act as constraints that limit the scope of proximate functions and their development' (Dubrovsky 2002).

Having introduced the concepts of 'adaptationism', 'continuum of psychosis' and 'ultimate causation', it is now possible to review the efforts of previous authors over the last 30 years to develop an evolutionary theory of psychosis. These are theories of ultimate causation and, in the main, rely on balanced polymorphism or heterozygous advantage models. Julian Huxley, grandson of 'Darwin's bulldog' Thomas Henry Huxley, collaborated with Ernst Mayr and others in a 1964 *Nature* paper, 'Schizophrenia as a genetic morphism', drawing attention to the central evolutionary paradox of schizophrenia, namely, that schizophrenia is apparently genetic but is associated with a fecundity disadvantage (Huxley et al. 1964). Their conclusion – that this disadvantage is balanced by an advantage to the affected individual in terms of better resistance to wound shock or stress – has derived little empirical support.

Kuttner et al. (1967) were quick to point out the problems with Huxley et al.'s hypothesis. Instead, these authors suggested that the compensatory advantage must lie in the realm of psychological functions such as intelligence, social behaviour and language – they opted for 'the sphere of social behaviour' – and they proposed that the advantages lay in kin rather than in the individuals themselves. Kellett (1973) addressed the functional psychoses, both schizophrenic and affective types and, like Kuttner et al. (1967), opted for the social domain as the site of advantage. Notably, in his model, Kellett makes use of the spectrum concept, specifically the notion of variation from normality to psychosis. He states: 'These psychoses ... reduce fertility and would have been bred out of the population if they did not represent an advantage to the species, at least in the "heterozygote" form' (Kellett 1973). Thus, heterozygote individuals in the affective psychosis spectrum occupied an advantage in hierarchical societies where agonistic encounters prevailed; whereas heterozygote 'schizoids' occupied an advantage in territorially dominated societies, where survival depended on disengagement from group loyalties and commitment to the family unit.

The work of John S. Allen and Roger J. Sullivan in Micronesia probably best exemplifies a balanced polymorphism model of schizophrenia (Allen & Sarich 1988; Sullivan & Allen 1999, 2004), arguing that the disorder represents one extreme of a 'sociality versus asociality scale'. Non-psychotic carriers of the gene(s) had an advantage in the ancestral environment by virtue of their ability to balance their own interests against the demands of group living. In some cases, this advantage might emerge in their greater creative potential. They also maintained that schizophrenia is a 'disease of civilization' and that the greater tolerance manifest in more modern societies may account for the survival of schizophrenia genes in the population.

This brings us to a sentiment that has characterized Western culture as far back as Aristotle; namely that there is some relationship between exceptional ability and mental illness. The association of creative genius with madness reached its zenith during the Romantic period in Europe and provided a foil to the philosophies of Kant and Descartes who were preaching the omnipotence of reason. Byron, Blake, Rousseau, Shelley – these were the figures that epitomized in the public mind the archetypal union of madness and genius. 'Great wits are sure to madness near allied; And thin partitions do their bounds divide' wrote Dryden, while a seventeenth century etching by Melancolicus proclaims 'the price of wisdom is melancholy'. In the modern era a number of authors[6] have researched this phenomenon, seeking empirical support for the notion of 'creative advantage'. For example, Karlsson investigated epidemiological records in Iceland and demonstrated an increased incidence of psychotic illnesses including schizophrenia in a cohort of particularly gifted artists, philosophers and politicians (Karlsson 1970, 1984). And Kay Redfield Jamison[7] has examined historical and biographical material, pointing out the high incidence of mood disorders in creative individuals such as Schumann, Shelley, Byron and Van Gogh (Jamison 1993, 1995b).

In a fascinating study conducted recently at Cambridge University, Baron-Cohen et al. (2001) have demonstrated higher than expected scores for Asperger syndrome/high-functioning autism among postgraduate scientists and mathematicians. This is of relevance since there is a genetic (and often clinical) overlap between autistic spectrum disorders and the functional psychoses. A contemporary example of the 'genius-madness' phenomenon is the Nobel Laureate, John Nash, whose remarkable story is the subject of the book and recent movie *A Beautiful Mind*. Another that springs to mind is James Joyce whose daughter had schizophrenia (and was unsuccessfully treated by Carl Jung) – an attempted reading of *Ullyses* must raise some questions as to Joyce's own mental state. Interestingly the style employed by Joyce in *Ulysses*, often termed 'stream of consciousness', is phenomenologically almost identical to 'formal thought disorder', which is a hallmark of psychotic thinking and language.

While evolutionary advantages such as creativity have been attributed to non-psychotic carriers within the psychotic spectrum, most authors supporting this claim have focused on advantages to individual and kin. However, in recent years there has been a resurgence of support for the concept of *group selection* in biology. Elliott Sober and David Sloan Wilson, contemporary advocates of group selection, explain that 'natural selection sometimes acts on *groups*, just as it acts at other times on *individuals*. An altruist may have fewer offspring than a nonaltruist within its own group, but groups of altruists will have more offspring than groups of nonaltruists' (Sober & Wilson 1998, their italics). Although Darwin did not deal extensively with the notion of group selection, he did use this principle in *The Descent of Man* to explain the evolution of human morality: 'It must not be forgotten that although a high standard of morality gives but a slight or no advantage to each individual man and his children over the other men of the same tribe, yet that an increase in the number of well-endowed men and advancement in the standard of morality will certainly give an immense advantage to one tribe over another . . . and this would be natural selection' (Darwin 1871: 166).

For 50 years or more after Darwin's death in 1882, group selection, as a mechanism of natural selection, attracted numerous supporters, such as Dobzhansky (1937), Fisher (1930) and Wynne-Edwards (1962). However, the emergence of the 'modern synthesis' in evolutionary biology coincided with vociferous attacks on group selection theory.[8] Advocates of the 'selfish gene' theory such as Richard Dawkins (1976) decried the notion that natural selection could act on anything other than the gene. Group selection was equated with Lamarckism as a redundant and almost heretical evolutionary dead-end. The so-called 'Darwin Wars' that dominated the 1970s, 1980s and 1990s revolved around a number of issues in evolutionary biology; one of the most controversial of these was (and still is) the question of the level/s of selection. Lined up on the side of the selfish gene were George Williams, William Hamilton, Robert Trivers, John Maynard Smith and of course Richard Dawkins. Harvard biologists Stephen Jay Gould and Niles Eldredge, together with geneticist Richard Lewontin, challenged these theorists, accusing them of being reductionist and 'ultra-Darwinist'. Gould and his supporters wanted to create a more open and pluralist approach within evolutionary biology and they argued for multiple levels of selection including group selection.

The revival of group selectionist theory during the 1990s opened the way for psychologists and psychiatrists to invoke this mechanism in their evolutionary analyses of mental disorders and the psychoses in particular (e.g. Polimeni & Reiss 2002; Price & Stevens 1996, 2000). Stevens and Price have argued in their two books, *Evolutionary Psychiatry* (1996) and *Prophets, Cults and Madness* (2000), for a 'group-splitting hypothesis' of schizophrenia. In the ancestral environment, they suggest, a group would reach a critical size at which it began to outgrow its resources. At this point a schizotypal individual, having undergone a 'mazeway resynthesis' and spurred on by his or her iconoclastic ideas and possible 'voices of the gods' (Jaynes 1976), would offer a vision of a new and better 'promised land' to those who would follow.

The power of the schizotype was such that followers would enter his or her delusional world (or at least go along with it) and the group would split. The converted and their leader would either remain (and enter into a genocidal conflict for resources with the 'outgroup') or set off on a migration, dispersing human ancestors across the planet. Thus, the particular personality and behaviour of the schizotype proved adaptive for the group, according to these authors. They cite a number of clearly schizotypal but also paranoid and psychopathic cult leaders such as David Koresh, Jim Jones and Adolf Hitler as examples of this phenomenon in recent times,[9] and interestingly note that both Koresh and Jones fathered many children – suggesting increased fitness as a result of their schizotypal personalities. The eventual failure of these modern 'gurus' may reflect greater social intolerance and censure relative to the ancestral environment. Emmanuelle Peters has studied members of a number of religious cults in Britain and discovered a high level of near-psychotic delusional beliefs (Peters et al. 1999). This suggests that schizotypal traits flourish in cults or that schizotypes flock to them and, according to Stevens and Price, it may also support the notion that in the ancestral environment, where cults may have had a greater impact on society, these traits could have played a significant role in the splitting and dispersal of groups.

While group selection theory seems to have emerged as a credible model for the evolution of altruistic behaviour, this particular group-splitting model is to my mind problematic as an explanation for the origins and survival of the human functional psychoses. Jane Goodall observed and described what might be termed 'group-splitting' in wild chimpanzees (Goodall 1990); and while I do argue for a degree of cognitive continuity between great apes and humans, the schizotypal group-splitter, as conceived by Stevens and Price, would surely have been a human-specific phenotype. If group-splitting in both humans and great apes was related to the presence of psychotic influences within these groups, one would have to argue that Goodall's chimpanzees were responding to a charismatic 'chimp-guru' in their midst.

My other more serious concern with the validity of this group selectionist model (and in fact with most of the theories of ultimate causation discussed in this section) relates to a glaring error in the logic of these authors. They have invoked natural selection as the mechanism responsible for the persistence of psychosis in our species and yet they have ignored a fundamental Darwinian principle, namely, that creative and political advantage does not necessarily equate with *reproductive advantage*. These authors have drawn links between schizotypy and genius, and between divergent thinking and creativity, as if these associations automatically imply that these individuals have a selective advantage. And herein lies the error. The evidence is not convincing that schizotypal individuals have a reproductive advantage. In fact, the studies of relative fertility in schizotypal disorder are contradictory and most fail to demonstrate an advantage (Avila et al. 2001; Haukka et al.

56

2003; Kendler et al. 1998). An exception is a study by Avila et al. (2001) that demonstrates an increased number of children in first-degree relatives of people with schizophrenia. However, the recent study by Haukka et al. (2003), which concludes that there is no fertility advantage in siblings of people with schizophrenia, is large enough and has sufficient power to confirm this position. In fact, I would argue that the statistical strength of this study almost rules out the balanced polymorphism model as a mechanism explaining the survival of schizophrenia in modern *Homo sapiens*.

If simple balanced polymorphism models dealing with individual, kin or group advantage are not supported by epidemiological research, then is there another mechanism that might account for the persistence of the functional psychoses? Polimeni and Reiss (2003), in their review of evolutionary approaches to schizophrenia, distinguish between theories advocating 'schizophrenia as an evolutionary advantage' and those advocating 'schizophrenia as a disadvantageous by-product of human brain evolution'. Among the latter category of theories they cite an important contribution by Farley (1976), who emphasized the fact that many social skills and responses, which are of adaptive value, are under a significant degree of genetic control. Multiple genes contribute to these innate functions and there is considerable variation between individuals. He maintains that this variation in 'adaptiveness' means that 'individuals at the extremes of the distribution tend[ing] to be maladjusted, chronically overaroused, and vulnerable to psychotic breakdown'. Of significance is the fact that Farley is not invoking the idea of specific pathological 'psychosis genes' in the origins of psychosis, but is rather suggesting that *normal* adaptive genes confer vulnerability on the individual – albeit specific combinations of normal genes at the extremes of a (poly)genetic spectrum. This model has much in common with my conceptualization of the evolutionary genetics of psychosis, as will become evident in Chapter 4. However, before progressing to the subject of evolutionary genetics, I must first introduce one of the most persuasive recent theories of the origins of psychosis. For nearly two decades Professor Tim Crow of the University of Oxford has grappled with the issue of the origins of the functional psychoses and particularly schizophrenia. His theory has evolved into its current form in which he links the emergence of schizophrenia to a genetic 'speciation event' in early *Homo sapiens* that gave rise to cerebral asymmetry and language.

SPECIATION, LANGUAGE AND PSYCHOSIS IN MODERN *HOMO SAPIENS*

Crow's theory rests on a number of important assumptions and it is important for the reader to be aware of these so that his ideas can be examined critically. First, he is aligning himself with those thinkers who argue that our species arose suddenly and decisively, thus marking a distinct separation from our hominid ancestors. The transition was a 'leap' from one form to another; rather than a gradual metamorphosis through multiple intervening forms. Second, Crow suggests that this speciation event occurred approximately 100–150,000 years ago, prior to the migration of *Homo sapiens* out of Africa. This 'out of Africa' (Stringer & Andrews 1988) theory of human origins has drawn much support among palaeontologists and molecular biologists alike and is opposed by an alternate hypothesis, that of 'multiregional continuity'.[10] Third, Crow argues that the speciation event involved a certain 'protocadherin' gene that is homologous on the X and Y chromosomes and he invokes the evolutionary mechanism termed 'sexual selection' as responsible for its selection and propagation in early humans (Crow 2002). Fourth, he believes this genetic event involving protocadherin initiated the beginnings of lateralization in the human brain and the specialization of the language area on the left side.

Thus, the speciation event was also responsible for language in our species. Importantly, this assumes that both cerebral asymmetry and language are unique phenomena in modern *Homo sapiens*. Finally, and perhaps of most relevance to the central subject of this book, Crow is convinced that these evolutionary changes in the brain provided the neural and cognitive substrate necessary for the emergence of psychosis. I have the greatest respect for this 'giant' of modern psychiatric thought and so it is with reservation that I take issue with most of these arguments. In subsequent chapters, I discuss critically each aspect of his theory, but for now it is important to address the concept of 'speciation' in the emergence of modern *Homo sapiens*.

In making his case for speciation, Crow is continuing a long tradition of sometimes heated debate over the exact nature of our descent. Darwinists, faithful to the principle of gradualist change by natural selection, have, for more than a 100 years, come up against sceptics (from Alfred Russel Wallace – the co-discoverer of the theory – to Stephen Jay Gould) who cite the discontinuities in the fossil and archaeological record, as well as the emergence of complex symbolic art and human-specific language, as evidence for 'saltational' or sudden change (Gould 1982; Schwartz 1999; Wallace 1858).

I do not find it necessary to invoke a saltational explanation for the emergence of psychosis in humans. Crow's theory depends on two assumptions for which I believe there is insufficient evidence thus far. First, other species do not have a capacity for psychosis – in Chapter 2, I outlined the evidence for a primitive form of psychotic behavioural syndrome in non-human primates. Second, he relies upon discontinuity in evolution to explain the emergence of language. While speech itself is unique to humans, there is increasing evidence (Deacon 1998; Pinker 1994) supporting a gradualist model of language development within a number of higher mammalian species, for example anthropoid primates and cetaceans (whales and dolphins). In *The Descent of Man*, Darwin (1871) committed himself to a gradualist theory of language evolution, and a 100 years later this idea retains wide support: 'Nor, as we have seen, does the faculty of articulate speech in itself offer any insuperable objection to the belief that man has been developed from some lower form . . . The lower animals differ from man solely in his almost infinitely larger power of associating together the most diversified sounds and ideas; and this obviously depends on the high development of his mental powers'.

Thus, articulate speech emerges from a gradual process of evolving communication in higher mammals and, as Darwin predicted, the unique properties of human thought and language relate to increasing cognitive complexity and specialization of phylogenetically old neural networks for communication, rather than a speciation event. In the following chapters I argue that the social brain, as represented by prefrontal cortical connectivity, became highly developed within the human line, providing a substrate for consciousness and articulate speech, but that this reflected a continuation of a phylogenetically ancient process, as evidenced by 'immature' forms of social cognition and communication in some extant primates (Baron-Cohen 1999; Byrne 2001) and cetaceans (Marino 2002).

In conclusion, therefore, I maintain that while adaptationist models of human behavioural evolution may enlighten our understanding of both normal and pathological phenomena in our species, they will remain no more than 'just-so stories' without a robust methodology. The concept of a psychotic continuum is strongly supported by good research but its existence may only serve to explain variants gifted with extraordinary cognitive and social abilities. Whether this continuum is sufficient to account for the survival of psychosis is questionable and theories that rely on balanced polymorphism models and group selection must be critically scrutinized. Like Farley (1976), I propose another explanation for the evolutionary origins of psychosis; that is, madness represents a costly and disadvantageous by-product of human brain evolution. Crow has asked whether 'schizophrenia (is) the price that *Homo sapiens* pays for language?' (Crow 1997). I don't think so. Instead, in the pages that follow, I argue that psychosis is the price paid by our species for our unique and complex social mind.

4

EVOLUTIONARY GENETICS OF PSYCHOSIS

A struggle for existence inevitably follows from the high rate at which all organic beings tend to increase. Every being, which during its natural lifetime produces several eggs or seeds, must suffer destruction during some period of its life, and during some season or occasional year, otherwise, on the principle of geometric increase, its numbers would quickly become so inordinately great that no country could support the product. Hence, as more individuals are produced than can possibly survive, there must in every case be a struggle for existence, either one individual with another of the same species, or with the individuals of distinct species, or with the physical conditions of life. It is the doctrine of Malthus applied with manifold force to the whole animal and vegetable kingdoms; for in this case there can be no artificial increase of food, and no prudential restraint from marriage. Although some species may be now increasing, more or less rapidly, in numbers, all cannot do so, for the world would not hold them.

(Darwin 1859)

On 3 October 1838, Charles Darwin happened 'to read for amusement Malthus on population'. As Huxley and Kettlewell (1965) comment: 'we must be eternally grateful that Darwin had such a peculiar notion of amusement!' For it was during this relaxing diversion that the stunning idea of natural selection suddenly appeared chimera-like in the great man's mind. This was Darwin's Eureka moment, his personal epiphany. The Reverend Thomas Malthus, a clergyman turned academic economist, had published anonymously his major work *Essay on the Principle of Population* in 1798 and his ideas proved hugely influential on the social and economic policies of the Whig government during the early nineteenth century. Malthusian philosophy gave rise to the social constructs of free enterprise, the emergence of the middle classes and the erosion of the nobility. This was a turbulent time in British politics with the Tories bemoaning their loss of the old order and the working classes rioting against policies that punished and excluded the poor and disadvantaged masses. Against this backdrop entered Darwin, desperate to find the solution to the problem of how some individuals survive in the fierce scrum of life. The answer of course was simple and so obvious that once it had dawned on him, Darwin was amazed he had not thought of it before: Those individuals best suited or adapted to an ecological niche will displace others from the ongoing battle for resources.

On the day he read Malthus, Darwin wrote in his *Notebook on Transmutation of Species*: '. . . there is a force like a hundred thousand wedges trying to force every kind of adapted structure into the gaps in the economy of nature, or rather forming gaps by thrusting out weaker ones' (Darwin 1960). One of Darwin's grand insights in his theory of natural selection was his recognition that competition for resources occurs predominantly between members of the *same* species, rather than between members of *different* species. This is because the former compete for the same resources and ecological niches and only the fittest get to pass on their genes. Obviously the fierceness of competition increases as the population size of a group increases; up to a certain threshold, there are enough resources for all members to coexist and reproduce. But beyond a threshold, where numbers of individuals begin to outweigh fixed resources, natural selection begins to weed out the weak and the population size falls.

In thinking about alternative mechanisms (other than balanced polymorphism) that may account for the survival of maladaptive psychosis genes, Darwin's great idea provides a useful metaphor or model. In order to explain clearly what I mean by this statement, it is first necessary for me to review the current thinking on the genetics of psychotic disorders. It is also important that I outline several possible explanations that have been proposed for the survival of psychosis in our species. These I will critique and dismiss in favour of a model that merges two concepts, termed 'antagonistic pleiotropy' and 'cliff-edge fitness'.

The functional psychoses are known to be largely genetic in nature. For example, the risk of schizophrenia increases from 1 per cent in the general population to 10 per cent in first-degree relatives and 50 per cent in monozygotic (identical) twins. This fact, as well as the great molecular research successes with numerous Mendelian diseases, sparked a multitude of genetic studies on schizophrenia and the affective psychoses over the last two decades. Kato et al. (2002) reviewed the research on schizophrenia (which has included linkage analyses, gene association studies and several other more complex strategies) and came to the conclusion that 'not a single gene causing or predisposing to schizophrenia has been identified thus far'. They discuss the possible reasons for this spectacular failure. First, the mode of inheritance of the disease is unclear – few cases follow a quasi-Mendelian pattern and most cases are sporadic. Second, the disease may well result from the interaction of numerous susceptibility genes of minor effect.

These epistatic[1] interactions include gene-to-gene and gene-to-environment interactions and this obviously makes the mode of inheritance incredibly complex. And finally, there is a major phenotypic variation in the clinical presentation of schizophrenia, which, together with the inadequacies of the DSM system of classification, means that molecular research on the disorder is not necessarily standardized.

In their discussion of possible future strategies in researching the genetics of schizophrenia, Kato et al. (2002) clearly favour a focus on 'the epigenetic regulation of gene expressions'. They conclude: 'The epigenetic research program may provide a new framework for the integration of genetic and environmental interactions in schizophrenia . . .' (Kato et al. 2002). Thus, in developing an evolutionary model for the survival of the functional psychoses, it would seem imperative that such a model addresses both the issue of epigenetic interaction of multiple genes and the issue of the regulation of gene expression.

If we consider the various possibilities other than a balanced polymorphism model for the evolution of psychosis, we find there is a range of theoretical standpoints. Some authors, like Hardcastle (2004) and Weisfeld (2004) take the view that schizophrenia is a benign trait not subject to natural selection because, they argue, reproduction occurred at an earlier age than the onset of the disorder in the ancestral environment. Weisfeld's image of the Paleaolithic environment with abundant food, nurturing families and limited stress on vulnerable individuals is, to my mind, somewhat romantic. This harkens to a past era where anthropologists idealized the 'noble savage' and is in contradiction to most evidence that supports a harsher and more stressful ancestral lifestyle (Bogin 1999). A more severe world where drought, disease and threat of predation was the norm would have pushed the reproductive age into or beyond the usual age of onset of schizophrenia, thus rendering the disorder subject to natural selection.

One evolutionary mechanism whereby genes not subject to natural selection may survive is the 'neutral theory of random genetic drift'. In this scenario the genes for schizophrenia would represent random mutations or 'neutral genes'. In 1968, Kimura put forward a revolutionary thesis that shook the biological community; he suggested that most mutations responsible for molecular variability in populations are neutral (rather than advantageous) and became fixed as a result of random genetic drift (Kimura 1968). Given the fact that human ancestors experienced several significant 'bottlenecks' during evolution, with dramatic reductions in population size, it is theoretically possible that the mutations responsible for the schizotypal spectrum were 'neutral' and were fixed in the human genome by this mechanism. However, as we shall see, there are much stronger and more relevant explanations.

It is also remotely possible that care-giving behaviour by a family or group may have allowed individuals with less adaptive schizotypal traits to

62

survive. There is some evidence that Neanderthals and early *Homo sapiens* cared for those with disabilities. For example, burial sites have been discovered where individuals have lived to a fair age with deformities, where they could not have survived without care (Stringer & Gamble 1993; Trinkaus & Shipman 1993). Furthermore, observations of caring behaviour by chimpanzees towards sick or disabled group members (Aureli & de Waal 2000; Goodall 1990) suggest that care-giving behaviour has ancient origins.

A more likely viewpoint comes from Panksepp and Moskal (2004) who suggest that schizophrenia 'is not actively maintained in the genome' and that certain genes make one vulnerable to 'epigenetic and environmental factors that promote schizophrenic phenotypes'. This is close to the model that I present later in this chapter for I certainly agree that the genetic basis of schizophrenia should best be conceptualized as conferring a vulnerability to disorder rather than a disorder itself. Twin studies have shown that genes contribute no more than 50 per cent to aetiology, leaving a major role for developmental and environmental factors. However, these authors give too much weight to non-genetic factors, instead depending on cultural transmission as a means of survival of the psychotic phenotype. They state: 'Our fascination with human quirks may have created cultural spandrels for the survival and propagation of individuals who survived less well without such cultural supports' (Panksepp & Moskal 2004).

But the complexity of madness lies partly in the fact that it is perpetuated by neither genetics nor sociocultural factors alone but by an interaction of both. This is largely why psychosis manifests as a protean, multidimensional and heterogeneous phenomenon rather than a clearly defined and uniform disease. And this is also why the epigenetic approach gives us a useful tool for beginning to unravel the tangled relationship that exists between the genes that create vulnerability and the environmental factors that contribute to expression of disorder. The fact that environment plays a role is not sufficient reason to exclude an evolutionary scenario since one would still expect genes that confer a 50 per cent risk of vulnerability to an 'unfit phenotype' to be subject to negative selection and thus removed from the human genome. The enigma remains and a putative mechanism for the survival of these genes is still required. In my view, to attribute both past and present survival of schizophrenic phenotypes to 'cultural spandrels' is to avoid this central challenge.

But if we return to Darwin's great insight during the autumn of 1838, there is a clue that I believe guides us to a workable solution to our problem. At the end of the previous chapter I suggested that psychosis might represent a costly by-product of human brain evolution. At the genetic and epigenetic level, how might this have come about? Let us consider the following: If schizotypal genes are associated in some way with genes that code for some faculty essential to the human condition, then the disorder may persist by virtue of this association. In other words, maladaptive traits survive into the next generation because they are associated, at a genetic level, with traits that are highly adaptive and which confer a reproductive advantage on the individual. I will argue that these 'adaptive genes' are genes (or alleles) that are involved in regulating the evolution and development of the social brain in humans.

There are several mechanisms that could be considered to explain this 'association' between maladaptive and adaptive genes. The first is that the loci for schizotypal genes may be close on the chromosome/s to the loci for the adaptive genes and that they are 'dragged' in selection. Sober (1993) makes the distinction between 'selection for' a trait and 'selection of' a trait and this distinction may be useful in clarifying this mechanism. 'Selection for' a trait describes the process of discriminating between phenotypes, but this process is not entirely 'clean' and linked traits that do not necessarily increase fitness may be 'dragged' along in the inheritance process (i.e. 'selection of' a trait). Thus, while there may be 'selection for' the social brain, there may in conjunction be 'selection of' schizophrenia. In his commentary on my 2004 *Behavioural and Brain Sciences (BBS)* target article (Burns 2004), Keller (2004) explains why this is an unlikely mechanism: '... if susceptibility alleles "hitchhiked" alongside adaptive alleles due to physical proximity on the chromosome, the susceptibility alleles would be at fixation in the population along with the adaptive alleles, which offers no explanation for genetic differences predisposing to schizophrenia'.

A second possibility is that schizotypal genes are defective alleles of the adaptive genes, but the problem with this scenario is that one would expect defective alleles to have been selected against during evolution. However, Keller offers an explanation as to how this form of *mutation-selection balance* might explain the survival of schizophrenia susceptibility alleles:

> In mutation-selection models, maladaptive alleles are maintained at an equilibrium that results from their introduction via mutation and their eventual removal (usually many generations later) via selection ... The key insight, championed by Houle, is that 'downstream traits,' those that are affected by many biological processes, have very high trait-level mutation rates because downstream traits subsume a large number of loci (Houle, Morikawa, and Lynch, 1996). To the degree that many loci are involved in schizophrenia, mutation-selection balance may provide an explanation for a substantial portion of susceptibility alleles.
>
> (Keller 2004)

A third possibility is that genes (subsequently responsible for schizophrenia) were already embedded in the genome before the social brain evolved in all its complexity in modern humans. In this scenario, the emergence of novel neural architecture may have served to 'activate' the schizotypal genes. In other words, the genes responsible for schizophrenia existed prior to modern *Homo sapiens* (perhaps with neutral or even adaptive functions). With the emergence of a novel brain environment, characterized by a host of novel gene functions, the previously benign schizotypal genes changed (either through mutation or altered expression or gene interaction) and became the malignant genes responsible for schizophrenia.

For want of a better term, I will call these models (in which maladaptive genes are associated with adaptive genes) the 'pleiotropic model' of selection; but we have still not clarified exactly the nature of this association, since the three possibilities above fall short of a comprehensive and workable model.

We have established that the genetic basis of psychosis is almost certainly 'polygenic'; that is, multiple genes contribute to the trait. Presumably, different numbers or combinations of these genes, interacting with environmental factors, give rise to a range of differing phenotypes – hence the presence of a spectrum in the clinical expression of psychosis. Now instead of hypothesizing different genes (or alleles) for psychosis that are somehow associated with adaptive genes, let us consider the following alternative: Perhaps there is only one kind of gene? Perhaps the *same* genes that give rise to psychosis are also responsible for some critical and adaptive human trait? In this scenario one could hypothesize that certain numbers or combinations of these genes are adaptive, but that an excess number results in a maladaptive trait. So, for example, smaller numbers of these genes might code for the normal development of the social brain, but additional genes cause a disruption of normal development, which results in psychosis. One can imagine there being a threshold, above which there is a reduction in fitness. The Malthusian concept of increasing numbers of individuals reaching a threshold, above which fitness falls, thus provides a metaphor for this kind of genetic model. But there is no need to reinvent the wheel since these concepts of increasing fitness, a threshold and then a drop in fitness, are contained within existing evolutionary genetic models termed 'cliff-edged fitness' and 'antagonistic pleiotropy'.

In their commentaries of my 2004 *BBS* target article (Burns 2004), Nesse (2004) and Keller (2004) suggested the application of 'cliff-edged fitness' and 'antagonistic pleiotropy' models respectively in my construction of an evolutionary genetic model of schizophrenia. Hoffman et al. (2004) provided another useful perspective derived from their work on computer-simulated models of psychosis. In my author's response, I attempted to integrate these ideas into a workable model and this is what follows below. However, these concepts first require some explanation. The British ecologist David Lack addressed the question 'Why don't birds lay more eggs?' in his 1954 book *The Natural Regulation of Animal Numbers* (Lack 1954). The assumption usually made is that a fit individual will have as many offspring as possible, thus ensuring maximum surviving progeny. However, studying starlings and their breeding patterns, Lack demonstrated that these birds have the greatest number of surviving offspring if they lay no more than five or six eggs (Futuyma 1998: 572). The parents are unable to feed larger broods adequately, so that increasing clutch size above a threshold results in decreased overall survival. Lack proposed that a parent's fitness is maximized by laying an *optimal* clutch size (rather than maximal clutch size); that is, a size that yields the greatest number of surviving offspring. Lack's work on clutch or litter size was advanced by Mountford (1968).

More recently, Nesse and Williams (1995) have invoked cliff-edged fitness functions in a number of other situations. For example, they explain how humans have higher levels of uric acid than other primates and this probably helps protect against oxidative tissue damage. However, it also causes gout in a small number of unfortunate individuals, whose levels rise above a threshold. Another example provided by Nesse (2004) is the case of the racehorse. He states: 'Breeding has resulted in longer and thinner leg bones that increase running speed but are vulnerable to catastrophic failure, as is tragically obvious to race fans who see a champion put down after breaking a leg'. In each case a trait is maintained because of its adaptive character, but if it is expressed above a critical threshold, fitness falls dramatically and the result is often damaging to the individual. One can see, however, how the maladaptive genotype survives natural selection.

The concept of 'antagonistic pleiotropy' was introduced by Rose (1982) and has become a 'central part of life history theory, evolution of senescence and other topics in evolutionary ecology' (Hedrick 1999). Evolutionists such as Charlesworth (1987, 1994) have developed the concept, specifically in regard to the evolution of senescence. Antagonistic pleiotropy is a form of *balancing selection* where 'two or more alternative alleles are maintained at relatively high frequencies at equilibrium because their marginal fitness effects are equal to each other' (Keller 2004). According to Keller (2004), balancing selection may be invoked as a potential mechanism accounting for the survival of schizophrenia. He explains:

> Applied to schizophrenia, this would imply that susceptibility alleles have the same fitness, on average, as non-susceptibility alleles, which seems unlikely given that schizophrenia shows reduced fitness in modern populations (Markow and Gottesman 1994). Such evidence does not necessarily preclude balancing selection as an explanation for schizophrenia however. For one, modern fitness effects can differ from ancestral ones. Secondly, a small number of susceptibility alleles may be beneficial (perhaps improving creativity, as mentioned in Burns' article) while too many may be maladaptive. Models have shown that this latter possibility, which is a form of antagonistic pleiotropy, is unlikely to account for much genetic variation (Hedrick 1999; Prout 1999). Nevertheless,

balancing selection cannot be ruled out in general as an explanation
for the existence of some proportion of susceptibility alleles.

(Keller 2004)

Finally, Ralph Hoffman and colleagues at Yale University have conducted
a number of experiments using computer 'pruning' models to simulate
the production of psychotic symptoms and their findings are instructive
(Hoffman et al. 2004). These experiments are based on well-supported evidence regarding the neurodevelopmental and neuropathological processes
operant in schizophrenia. In Chapter 9, I address this subject in detail in
developing an integrated theory of the evolutionary ontogeny of psychosis.
But for now a brief summary of the major mechanisms will suffice in order
to provide a context in which we can appreciate Hoffman et al.'s findings.

There is good evidence that schizophrenia is a disorder of neurodevelopment; that is, it is caused by a disruption of normal brain development. In
normal development there is a cascade of events spanning foetal, childhood
and adolescent life, in which neurons are generated, migrate to their final
destinations in the cortex, connect up through synaptic branches and then,
in later adolescence, are 'pruned' of faulty connections leaving a refined
neural network. In schizophrenia there appears to be a disruption of this
process, so that neurons locate to the wrong cortical layers, synapse incor-
rectly and are pruned excessively. The result macroscopically is a subtle loss
of brain volume, particularly in the prefrontal and temporal cortices. At
the microscopic level, however, there are numerous abnormalities of arborization (neuronal branching), synaptic connections and neuronal growth
factors (that facilitate normal synaptogenesis). Recent research suggests
that there are specific abnormalities of the white matter tracts that connect
prefrontal and temporoparietal cortices (Burns et al. 2003). These findings
support the hypothesis that schizophrenia is a disorder of functional and
structural connectivity linking different regions of the cortex to each other
and to deeper subcortical structures of the brain (Frith et al. 1995; McGuire
& Frith 1996).

Ralph Hoffman's group have attempted to replicate these disturbances
in normal brain development using computer-generated models whereby
connected circuits are pruned of the weakest links. The quality and power
of information-processing by these 'neural networks' is quantified as the
programme 'eliminate(s) connections based on "Darwinian principles"'
(Hoffman et al. 2004). Hoffman et al.'s findings are intriguing and converge with the concepts of antagonistic pleiotropy and cliff-edge fitness
that I have elaborated above. For they found that 'Darwinian pruning
of networks to levels just below the "psychotogenic threshold" actually
enhanced network performance in detecting linguistic meaning' (Hoffman
et al. 2004; Hoffman & McGlashan 1997). Further pruning above this
threshold resulted in the emergence of 'attractor states that intrude into

information-processing'; this leads to the production of 'spurious outputs', which they argue simulate hallucinated voices. Thus, there is progressive enhancement in performance up to a threshold, beyond which further pruning results in a steep decline in function and the emergence of pathological phenomena that mimic psychosis. While this data is impressive and seems to support the argument that susceptibility alleles for psychosis may survive natural selection because they are subject to cliff-edged fitness functions, I must also convey my scepticism about using computer technology as an accurate model of brain function. Conrad (1989) was a pioneer in investigating biological information-processing and strongly supported what he termed the 'brain-machine disanalogy'; that is the fact that computer modelling cannot be absolute in replicating complex brain function. Despite rapid sophistication in this field, most of his views have been confirmed in the decade since he published his major thesis (Ziegler 2002). Nevertheless, the work of Hoffman's group is a valuable contribution to the development of an evolutionary genetic model of psychosis.

I have attempted to describe as succinctly as possible the ideas proposed by Keller, Nesse and Hoffman et al. in their 2004 *BBS* commentaries (on my target article – Burns 2004). I hope I have also succeeded in elucidating clearly the overlaps between these models. Keller's interpretation of antagonistic pleiotropy seems to describe a similar model of fitness effects as Nesse's cliff-edged fitness model; and the work of Hoffman's group seems to converge with both these models. So I believe that I am now in a position to draw on each of them in constructing a specific model for the evolutionary genetics of psychosis. And in doing so, I hope to provide a robust alternative to previously suggested models such as balanced polymorphism and group selection. Importantly, I am considering the functional psychoses as a single entity, albeit an entity that encompasses spectra of variation between the schizotypal and affective phenotypes and between the normal and psychotic ends of a continuum. Consider the following:

(1) All humans have at least one susceptibility allele (SA) for psychosis because these alleles have been selected for their pleiotropic contribution to the evolution and development of the social brain.

(2) There is variation between individuals in the number of SAs, and the presence of increasing numbers of SAs enhances reproductive fitness up to a threshold.

(3) An increasing number of SAs corresponds with an increase in the magnitude of the phenotypic trait. In this model the trait is increasing cortical connectivity with associated neural pruning at the histological level and increasingly sophisticated social cognition at the behavioural/psychological level.

(4) At a certain threshold (or cliff-edge), the presence of increasing numbers of SAs results in a sharp decrease in the fitness effects of the phenotype.

These 'post-threshold' phenotypes constitute the borderline – psychotic spectrum (as conceived by Crow 1998). With reference to Hoffman et al., both the borderline and psychotic phenotypes exhibit reduced fitness. Since an increasing number of SAs corresponds to an increase in synaptic connections (both normal and abnormal) and increased peri-adolescent pruning, the borderline–psychotic brain is characterized by reduced final cortical connectivity (which is consistent with recent research findings (Burns et al. 2003).

(5) As suggested by Hoffman et al. (2004), the at-risk carrier (the borderline) exhibits normal or reduced fitness, thus negating the need for a balanced polymorphism model. Additional SAs, environmental factors and epigenetic effects convert some of these at-risk individuals to full-blown psychotic disorder.

This model is depicted in Figure 4.1 and incorporates Nesse's concept of 'cliff-edged' fitness effects as well as Hoffman et al.'s (2004) proposal that both 'at-risk' borderline psychotics and those with psychosis fall beyond the threshold and therefore exhibit reduced fitness. It also acknowledges the role of environmental and epigenetic effects in the conversion of the at-risk phenotype to the disorder phenotype as stressed by Panksepp and Moskal (2004) in their 2004 *BBS* commentary. Finally, the model is consistent with Keller's account of antagonistic pleiotropy.

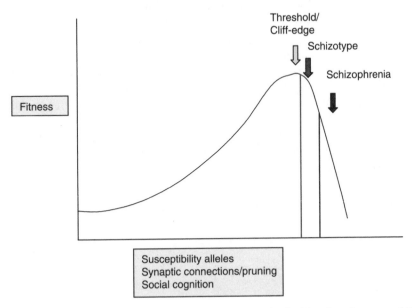

Figure 4.1 Evolutionary genetic model for the 'survival' of schizophrenia susceptibility alleles.

So there we have it: a model that I believe accounts for the survival of psychosis genes (or rather susceptibility alleles for psychosis). The SAs survive natural selection because all humans carry at least one or more SA; these alleles are adaptive in that they play a vital role in the regulation of brain development. Specifically, they are involved in regulating the development of the social brain in modern *Homo sapiens*. However, as is the case with most traits, there is variation between individuals in terms of the numbers of SAs they possess in their genome. This creates a spectrum with some individuals developing better social cognitive skills than others; and in the next chapter I argue that better social skills give these individuals a fitness advantage. But there are some individuals who inherit an excess of SAs, which takes them beyond a threshold and over a cliff-edge; their adaptive fitness plummets as their disrupted neurodevelopmental processes result in faulty social brain circuitry and disabled social cognition and behaviour. Perched on the cliff-edge or maybe just over the edge are a number of individuals whose fitness is either neutral or slightly disadvantaged.

Occasionally, among these borderline cases, there is a unique variant – someone whose brain is connected and pruned in such a way that he or she is gifted with extraordinary ability. These are the eccentric and flamboyant geniuses in our midst, who sometimes hover on the brink of madness, but whose off-beat and iconoclastic way of looking at the world often takes them and the rest of humanity to greater heights of achievement. Finally, there are those outliers upon whom fortune has not smiled. They inherit too many SAs and, in the context of the stresses and strains of life, this genetic bequest interacts with factors from the world around them and the result is frank psychosis. Like the ecosystem that has outgrown itself, where too many individuals vie for fixed resources causing the weakest to die, there is a cost that must be paid. Humans are uniquely social animals and this has proved advantageous in the evolution of our species. But this heirloom has come at a price and that price is borne by a few, not all. They suffer madness in its many guises – they see visions, hear voices, feel persecuted and are rocked by destructive extremes of emotion – but perhaps worst of all, every single one, in one way or another, is socially disabled and maladapted to his or her social world.

5

A SOCIAL BRAIN FOR
A SOCIAL WORLD

A PHILOSOPHY OF INTERPERSONAL
RELATEDNESS

Ubuntu is very difficult to render into a Western language. It speaks of the very essence of being human. When we want to give high praise to someone we say, 'Hey, so-and-so has *ubuntu*.' Then you are generous, you are hospitable, you are friendly and caring and compassionate. You share what you have. It is to say, 'My humanity is caught up, is inextricably bound up, in yours.' We belong in a bundle of life. We say, 'A person is a person through other persons.' It is not 'I think therefore I am.' It says rather: 'I am human because I belong. I participate, I share.' A person with *ubuntu* is open and available to others, affirming of others, does not feel threatened that others are able and good, for he or she has a proper self-assurance that comes from knowing that he or she belongs in a greater whole and is diminished when others are humiliated or diminished, when others are tortured or oppressed, or treated as if they were less than who they are.

(Desmond Tutu 1999)

I grew up in apartheid South Africa and I am now a citizen of post-apartheid South Africa. My experience of the dehumanizing character of apartheid was sheltered by virtue of the privilege I experienced as a white, middle-class, English-speaking person. Fortunately, I had progressive and compassionate parents whose consciences led them into involvements that exposed my brothers and me to some of the heinous realities of our corrupt society. My mother's activities in a women's protest organization, the Black Sash, began early in the 1960s before I was born and thus we had some awareness of and contact with the suffering lives of millions in our country. I clearly recall tagging along to endless political meetings, being introduced to my mother's crazy but wonderful friends and listening to her debriefs with my father over a drink on the veranda after a 'stand'.

One story sticks in my memory: My mother and her companions held a silent protest with placards on a busy street in Durban. The police would only allow one person to stand with a placard, so the others would wait and monitor the protest at a discrete distance. My mother was taking her turn with the placard and was approached by several young men who stopped in front of her and began to verbally abuse her, calling her a 'stupid communist bitch' and spat in her face. The Catholic Archbishop of Durban, Dennis Hurley, who was a man of great integrity and courage and a prominent anti-apartheid activist, was standing with the other 'Sashers' and observed my mother's plight. He quietly stepped forward, took the placard from my mother's hands and faced up to the thugs in his purple robes. Perhaps shamed (or perhaps cowed) by this fearless priest, they skulked away without another word. Like Desmond Tutu and many other moral giants who emerged to confront the dehumanizing spectre of apartheid, Archbishop Hurley took seriously and lived out the conviction that individual human freedom depends on freedom for the rest of humanity. In the words of another hero for justice, Dietrich Bonhoeffer (1971)[1]: 'In truth, freedom is a relationship between two persons. Being free means "being free for the other," because the other has bound me to him. Only in relationship to the other am I free'.

This concept of human freedom, which is in essence the full and unfettered expression of human worth through healthy interpersonal relationship, became a major focus in the work of the great humanist psychologist Erich Fromm. As a Jewish German refugee to America, Fromm applied psychological principles to the pressing social, economic and political issues of the era. His book *The Art of Loving* (2000) has been translated into 50 languages and has sold over 25 million copies, while *Fear of Freedom* is recognized as one of the great psychological studies of the conflicting human drives for individual freedom and community. Fromm was politically active in America and Mexico during the 1950s and 1960s and, in collaboration with Albert Schweitzer, Paul Tillich, Martin Buber and other outspoken humanists, he advocated an alternative to rising western capitalism and Soviet communism, based on the principles of peace and self-realization. Fromm maintained that the human drive for individualism and autonomy, which characterized both the ontological development of the child into adult and also the emergence of society from the bondage of the Middle Ages into the 'freedom' of the Enlightenment and Modern era, could result in two separate outcomes. Healthy 'individuation' led one to full self-realization and expression that becomes manifest in interpersonal relationship and commitment to community. Conversely, in their 'escape from freedom', many individuals retreat into cult-like packs, idealizing oppressive and dehumanizing fascist ideologies led by paranoid fanatics.

This emphasis on social relationship as the key to individual freedom and fulfilment has its root deep in the history of most human societies. In

Southern Africa there is an ancient proverb, *umuntu ngumuntu ngabantu* – a person depends on persons to be a person – from which derives the concept of *ubuntu* (elaborated by Desmond Tutu in the extract above from his book *No Future Without Forgiveness*). In his discussion of the implications of the *ubuntu* philosophy for post-apartheid South Africa, Shutte argues, 'the traditional African conception of community (as expressed in such proverbs as "ubuntu") is crucial to the reconstruction of a just society' (Shutte 1993). While many of us of non-African origin might feel a sense of disillusionment at the apparent decadence and selfishness of capitalist Europe and America, there is some consolation in the fact that the *ubuntu* philosophy has been visible at a number of junctures during the long course of 'western' history. These sometimes brief 'sightings' have usually coincided with a context in which a people find themselves oppressed and striving for freedom.

For example, the preachings of Jesus Christ for love, compassion and forgiveness came into a context of Jewish slavery to the Roman Empire and a zealous groundswell for violent rebellion. Christ's call was not for freedom of the individual through self-liberation and self-aggrandizement, but was rather for freedom of entire societies and all of humanity through interpersonal affirmation and the building of community. Likewise, as described by Mary E. Clark in her extraordinary book *In Search of Human Nature*, the Indian emperor Asoka (who reigned from 272 to 232 BC) was so 'appalled by the slaughter of innocents in the wars he led . . . [and] deeply moved by the teachings of Buddha . . . [that he] instituted among his people a period of peace and justice based on compassion' (Clark 2002). Clark argues that ' "compassion" and "love" for others are universally found in the world's major religions'. She quotes ethicist Paul Gordon Lauren, a student of the history of human rights, and his summation is worth quoting here in full:

> All of the major religions of the world seek in one way or another to speak to the issue of human responsibility for others . . . This concern is approached through various revelations, narratives, poetry, edicts and commandments, and stories and parables dealing with right and wrong, moral responsibility, ethical principles of justice and fairness, compassion, the essential dignity of each person, and the kinship and common humanity of all.
>
> (Lauren 1998)

The function of religion in society is a subject that evokes strong debate within the social and behavioural sciences. There is the strongly supported view that religious belief fulfils some sort of human existential need in life. Psychological and evolutionary theorists argue that there is an inherent drive to believe in some sort of external nurturing force or being, a being that transcends and represents freedom from the frightening boundaries of mortal life. But Clark suggests another function or role for religion, beyond that of providing an answer to our existential insecurities. She explains how rising civilization and the development of hierarchical social structures created in the individual a feeling of anxiety and alienation from 'those three innate human propensities for bonding, autonomy and meaning' (Clark 2002). She states:

> The feelings of rejection, worthlessness, and injustice that people tended to have . . . could be psychologically ameliorated by practicing compassion and love for one's neighbours and forgiveness of oppressors. The natural need to be bonded and the powerful health-promoting effects of belonging were as well served as might be possible by the tenets of all these religions, given the inevitable psychic suffering in hierarchical systems.
>
> (Clark 2002)

So Clark is suggesting that religion served and continues to serve as a 'rescuer' from the psychologically damaging sense of dislocation and social detachment induced by hierarchical societies. The rule of law and the power of social stratification that accompanied the formation of states throughout the last millennium estranged the common man and woman from his or her innate need for social connection and egalitarian community. And power relations do not merely manifest in the hierarchies created between social classes, but are also powerfully tangible in the economic, educational, gender-related and cross-cultural dynamics of society. The rise of industrialization, the steady advances in education and the current wildfire of globalization have served to widen the gap between rich and poor, developed and developing, educated and uneducated, powerful and weak. So perhaps now more than ever we are witnessing the psychological consequences of human isolation and dislocation from what Erich Fromm terms 'a feeling of communion and "belonging"' (Fromm 1942/2003). In *Fear of Freedom*, Fromm recognizes another fundamental human need, besides the physiologically rooted drives to eat, drink, sleep and reproduce. This need, he argues, is rooted in 'the very essence of the human mode and practice of life' – it is 'the need to be related to the world outside oneself, the need to avoid aloneness'. This inherent compulsion is so strong that to fail in achieving relationship and connectedness with the world is to risk 'mental disintegration just as physical starvation leads to death'. Fromm maintains that the feeling of belonging need not imply physical proximity to others but may take the form of a connectedness 'to ideas, values, or at least social patterns'. The absence of this connectedness he terms 'moral aloneness' and he later equates this to insanity.

This emphasis on the social nature of humanity represents a change in focus from the individual-centred psychology of Freud and his followers

74

in the psychoanalytic movement. It also signifies a divergence from the Cartesian model of the mind and the world as separated entities. It is quite likely that the ideas of Rene Descartes and Sigmund Freud have had the greatest impact on our view of ourselves as a conscious species with an inner mental life. Not surprisingly our psychology is focused on this inner life of the individual, and we speak of unconscious drives, dynamics and complexes. Likewise, the phenomenology of our psychiatric, psychological and religious sciences is a phenomenology of the individual, derived from the Cartesian account of human reality. In Christianity, for example, we witness the influence of Cartesian dualism. The supreme project of the Reformation was to disembody spiritual life by putting aside the aesthetic trappings of Catholicism and ridding inner spirituality of its messy earthly connections.

The Archbishop of Canterbury, Rowan Williams, has attributed much of the existential suffering in contemporary Western culture to this disembodiment of faith (Williams 2000). Descartes separated the soul from the body (and the world) and he reasoned that the only thing one can be sure about is the fact that one is thinking; hence his epithet, 'I think therefore I am'. This has been termed the 'Cartesian cogito' and has heavily influenced the major phenomenologists such as Edmund Husserl (1859–1938) and Karl Jaspers (1883–1969). Husserl's phenomenology divided the world of individual consciousness from the 'world outside it'; and Jaspers, who followed his framework, later produced the most influential work of descriptive mental phenomena in twentieth-century psychiatry, *General Psychopathology* (Jaspers 1963). The 'symptoms' we identify in our patients today are inherited from Husserl and Jaspers and are, without exception, framed in terms of an internal individual psyche. Depressed mood states, delusions, hallucinations and 'thought disorder' are all descriptor terms that we apply to the mental state of an individual person – an isolated psyche, viewed as separate and detached from the world around. We do not evaluate a patient's feeling state or motivation or pattern of thought *relative to* or *in conjunction with* phenomena 'outside' his or her individual consciousness. Cartesian dualism is so pervasive in our psychiatric attitudes, language and culture that we are oblivious to the interpersonal, social and existential aspects of our patient's experience. We automatically react to 'clinical signs' that we have detected in his or her mind as though we are enumerating the pathological features of a diseased organ on an operating table. And while this 'clinical' method may give us a sense of security and reassure us that we are real physicians practising a valid medical science, its Cartesian foundation and framework means that it is a method which prevents us from seeing the whole truth about our patient's experience.

In the introductory chapter of this book, I expressed my view that modern psychiatry and neuroscience had failed to bring us close to a true understanding of madness. In Chapter 2, I introduced some of the ideas of 'postpsychiatry', a postmodern approach to mental disorder and its interpretation as pioneered by thinkers such as Philip Thomas and Patrick Bracken. I argued that our way forward to a more fruitful exploration and understanding of madness is to begin to deconstruct our assumptions and our inherited belief systems about the mind. The predominant notion of madness is based upon the Cartesian cogito. We have seen that over a 100 years of efforts to unravel this mysterious human malady from a Cartesian perspective have failed and we must ask ourselves why this is so. I would suggest that a postmodern approach to psychosis requires us to re-evaluate the philosophical basis for our understanding and study of madness. Is the Cartesian 'project' the most appropriate heuristic for our purpose? I would suggest that it is not and the failure of modern psychiatry is the evidence. If *Homo sapiens* is a socially conscious animal, and if psychological and emotional well-being depends on a healthy and appropriate social relationship and connectedness, then surely we should abandon an explanatory system (Cartesianism) that represents humans as isolated and solitary mental beings. Instead, we should look for a new philosophical framework that reflects this interpersonal understanding of mental life.

In this chapter I argue that such a philosophy must abandon Cartesian dualism and must acknowledge the thoroughly social nature of human experience. It must also re-embody the mind within the physiology of the brain. Mental life reflects a dynamic two-way interaction between the social world 'out there' and the neuronal function in the brain of the individual. The human brain is a 'social brain', highly evolved and finely tuned to interact with other brains that populate our social landscape. My thesis is the following: When we reorientate our approach within psychiatry away from the Cartesian legacy and towards a 'social neuroscience' model that investigates and describes the dynamic interaction between individual brain and social world, only then will we begin to understand mental disorder. And, in particular, it is only then that we will begin to unravel the mystery of psychosis.

Before proceeding with this enquiry, however, I think it is worth stating that there is considerable empirical support from the biological sciences for this notion of the human being as a social animal with a socially evolved and socially sensitive brain. In the second half of this chapter and in the next chapter I review this evidence in detail, drawing on state-of-the-art research in the neurosciences, behavioural sciences and animal sciences. I also feel it is important to consider briefly a concept that has emerged within psychiatry and psychology during the last two decades, and which goes some way towards redressing the error of the Cartesian project – the 'biopsychosocial' approach to mental disorders. The biopsychosocial framework, elaborated by George Engel (1980), represents an attempt to acknowledge the role played by not just biology in mental disturbances, but also that played by psychological and social factors. The student is now taught to formulate the patient's problems in terms of biological, psychological and social factors and similarly he or she is taught to consider therapeutic interventions under these three headings. This is certainly a better model than previous reductionist attempts to understand mental disorders as purely biological or psychological or indeed sociocultural phenomena. However, it is a model that continues to view the mind of the individual and the world around it as separate entities. The 'mind' is still understood in Cartesian terms as an internally derived entity, shaped and driven by inherent processes, be they molecular and physiological or 'unconscious' and 'instinctual'. Consider this passage from the introduction to an influential and widely used psychiatric textbook:

> The biopsychosocial model is derived from general systems theory: The biological system deals with the anatomical, structural, and molecular substrates of disease and the effects on patients' biological functioning; the psychological system treats the effects of psychodynamic factors, motivation, and personality on the experience of, and reaction to, illness; and the social system examines cultural, environmental, and familial influences on the expression and experience of illness.
>
> (Kaplan & Sadock 1998)

So each 'system' is separate and has its own specific material to contribute to an individual's experience of illness and distress. Although these systems are seemingly given equal status in terms of their relative contributions, it is implied that the biology of the individual is central and that psychodynamic and social systems merely express or impinge upon the biological origins of disorders. Furthermore, they are viewed as parallel rather than integrated and interactive systems and the role for 'the social system' is limited to mere 'influences on the expression and experience of illness'. The social world of the patient is paid lip-service as an entity that only modulates and colours mental phenomena *that already exist*. These phenomena, be they joy or sorrow or delusional belief, emerge already formed from the depths of the individual's mind; and the 'world outside the mind' merely performs a bit of window-dressing. So the biopsychosocial model perpetuates the Cartesian myth and does not adequately reflect the interpersonal nature of consciousness, nor does it provide an appropriate framework within which we can begin to understand human madness.

In seeking a suitable philosophy that better reflects the social nature of human experience we need not look far. Patrick Bracken, whose contributions to a new 'postpsychiatry' I have already noted, has addressed the clinical constructs of trauma and anxiety in his book *Trauma: culture, meaning and philosophy* (Bracken 2002). His thesis is based on the same criticism of modern psychiatry that I have elaborated above. He too argues that we

77

need to move away from the Cartesian framework in understanding mental life and he draws on the work of the early twentieth-century German philosopher Martin Heidegger in formulating a new approach. In his introductory chapter he states: 'Heidegger's thought is a powerful antidote to the dominance of Cartesianism in the humanities and the human sciences ... His work is the central reference point for existentialism, hermaneutics and postmodern approaches' (Bracken 2002). Bracken explains this change in focus from a Cartesian to a Heideggerian perspective as follows:

> Traditionally, both philosophy and psychology begin theorizing with a mind relating to a world outside it. This is their starting point. The major challenge for both has been to understand how these two realms (mind and world) are connected. However, it is clear that for the most part we live our lives without assuming that we have a mind that relates to an outside world at all. We simply get on with things. Having the thought that there is a mind relating to a world outside is a theoretical move. It is a thought that only becomes possible when we stand back from our practical involvement in life. This practical involvement is primary, more basic. To be human is to be involved, implanted, immersed in the everyday world. Heidegger wants to engage with human experience at this more basic level, at a level before we have moved to a theory involving separation.
>
> In fact, he wants to philosophize in the opposite direction: away from notions of 'mind', 'world' and 'representation' ... It is ourselves who give meaning to the world that we inhabit: we construct our world as we live in it ... We are simply not 'in' a world that is separate from ourselves. Rather, we allow a world to be by our very presence. Heidegger uses the composite term 'being-in-the-world' in an attempt to describe the complexity of our involvement with our worlds.
>
> (Bracken 2002)

Bracken goes on to explain that for Heidegger, the world exists 'a priori', or before, our human representation of it as thought. What is in the mind of the individual is a construct derived from social and cultural information in the world around him or her. He explains:

> A human world only becomes possible to us because we live in that world with other people and in the midst of a culture. The opening up of a world is never an individual act ... I experience the world with words, beliefs, emotions and patterns of thought that come from the social world in which I live. Human reality is both individual and social at the same time ... This position allows

Heidegger effectively to reverse the Cartesian cogito, which confidently asserts the primacy of detached thought: 'cogito ergo sum' (I think, therefore I am). For Heidegger the reverse is the case: 'I am, therefore I think.' Existence, in the sense of lived human existence, involved and embedded in the world, is the necessary precedent and the enabling condition of thought.

(Bracken 2002)

In his description of *ubuntu*, Desmond Tutu makes an almost identical statement: 'It is not "I think therefore I am." It says rather: "I am human because I belong. I participate, I share"' (Tutu 1999). Thus, the notion of *ubuntu*, and Heidegger's philosophy of human reality as a socially derived phenomenon, coincide and speak to Fromm's emphasis on social relationship as the key to individual freedom and fulfilment.

THE INTERPERSONAL NATURE OF EVERYDAY LIFE

So much for philosophy, but is there evidence from everyday experience that we are primarily social beings and that our mental life is socially derived? In order to answer this question, we need to consider all aspects of human experience and behaviour, across the lifespan, during aloneness and in social settings. This enquiry naturally draws upon observations within the anthropological, psychological and sociological sciences and it is a subject that has been addressed with considerable skill by Leslie Brothers in her book *Friday's Footprint: how society shapes the human mind* (Brothers 1997). She discusses the work of developmental psychologists such as Ina Uzgiris, Andrew Meltzoff and Alison Gopnick who have shown how mothers use imitation games to ' "teach" shared experience to their babies' and how 'the infant's basic faith in a shared world of subjectivity emerges from a matrix of physical interactions' (Brothers 1997). Trevarthen and Aitken (2001), who have researched 'the emergence and development of "self-and-other" awareness', refer to 'infant intersubjectivity' Brothers states:

The intersubjective faith is clearly expressed by around age 1, when infants show by their attempts at communication that they believe minds can be interfaced with one another through mutually comprehensible signals. They first use signals, such as pointing and gaze direction, to establish joint topics of attention with their mother at around 9 months of age. By persisting and repeating their signals when messages have not been understood, and by timing their gestures to make themselves understood, infants show they believe

persons can share understandings. Such a belief in shared understandings is a prerequisite for creating deliberate exchanges of
meaning, such as that which occurs later in pretend play. Social
pretend play involves the active co-construction of a detailed intersubjective world . . . All these findings outline how infants come to
believe in a shared world, and how young children then go on to use
shared frameworks for creating and sustaining social activity.

(Brothers 1997)

Brothers goes on to discuss the work of George Herbert Mead (1863–
1931) who, together with other Americans, William James and John Dewey,
was one of the founders of social psychology. Mead studied the development of the infant's sense of 'self' and conceptual meaning. According to
Brothers, he argued that 'meanings . . . arise in social interaction', and that
'self-consciousness arises in the process of social experience. The generalized attitude of others toward oneself becomes linked with the sensations of
one's body, to produce the feelings of personal existence with which we
are familiar' (Brothers 1997). Thus, individual consciousness is derived
from collective meanings and, following the Austrian philosopher Ludwig
Wittgenstein (1889–1951), words and language only have meaning that is
derived from the social context of which they are a part. As Brothers states:
'Language simply embodies the shared beliefs and practices of the community of language users'. Isolated from everyday experience within interpersonal contexts, the meaning of words, symbols and associations is lost
for the individual. We learn these meanings through our experience of and
immersion within the social world. In neuroscientific terms we might concur with the developmental psychologist Lev Vygotsky who maintained that
our cognitive processes – thoughts, beliefs, memories and language – have
their origins in communal behaviour and discourse (Vygotsky 1978). Again,
it is worth quoting Brothers who eloquently explains:

[Vygotsky] held that the transactions in which infants participate
are internalized to create the structure of individual mentation.
Children learn social scripts and conventions by participating in
them; individual cognition subsequently bears the stamp of its
social origins. This would imply, in accordance with Mead, that the
child's concept of itself, like its other concepts, arises from interactions with others, rather than existing a priori . . . only brains in a
social field can generate the kind of consciousness that includes 'I.'

(Brothers 1997)

It is notable that in recent years the field of consciousness studies is
increasingly preoccupied with this social view of the origins of human
consciousness. In his famous *The Phenomenology of Perception*, the French

phenomenologist Maurice Merleau-Ponty described the mind as an 'embodied' phenomenon, constructed by and engaged in the physical world of the body and society (Merleau-Ponty 2002). And Dan Zahavi argues that perceived objects in the environment of the developing child are invariably social objects that derive their meaning from their social connotations (e.g. a chair is defined by virtue of the fact that it is something a person sits on and uses) (Zahavi 2001). Thus, perception itself is embodied in the world around us. As Thomas Fuchs explains:

> Conscious experiences are thus essentially characterized by having a subjective 'feel' to them, a quality of 'what it is like' to have them. This holds true not only for bodily experience itself, but for emotions, moods or even perceptions as well: what is it like to taste an apple, to feel the sand of a beach, or to hear the rhythmic sound of a drum. Infant research has shown that the child's perception is permeated with bodily feelings and dominated by felt similarities of rhythm, intensity or tone. There is a primordial layer of a 'bodily felt sense', a 'sensus communis' that precedes the separation of proprioception, perception and emotion.
>
> (Fuchs 2002)

According to Fuchs (2002), we experience a resonance or similarity between the 'outward expressivity of others and our own bodily expressivity, which in turn is in resonance with our emotional states'. Thus, there is a mirroring within our bodies and our mental processes of the perceived physical and mental states of others. Merleau-Ponty termed this form of empathic perception the 'transfer of the corporeal schema'; and Fuchs points out that infant research supports this claim. For in the newborn baby's ability to imitate facial expressions of others, we witness this interpersonal 'transfer' of feeling states. 'By the mimetic capacity of (infants' bodies), they also transpose the seen gestures and mimics of others into their own feelings' (Fuchs 2002). He concludes, 'There is a sphere of embodied sensibility and mutual resonance that we all share from the beginning with others as embodied subjects'. Later in this chapter I introduce the 'mirror neuron', which constitutes a biological substrate for the transposition of, or mirroring of, psychological phenomena and felt states between individuals. I point out that neuroscience is now providing us with empirical evidence and support for a phenomenology and philosophy of interpersonal experience.

BRIDGING THE CARTESIAN DIVIDE

In acknowledging the primary role of the social world in the development of individual mental life, we must be weary of implying that the 'mind' is a

81

blank slate, or 'tabula rasa', as theorized by the seventeenth-century empiricist, John Locke. We are not suggesting that the mind is wholly created from nothing by the 'world outside'. Indeed, there is plenty of human and animal research that supports the innateness of many properties of the mind and behaviour, from attachment formation[2] to altruistic behaviour.[3] Other 'motivational drives' attributed to innate properties of the genome and brain include: territoriality; dominance-submission behaviour; affiliative bonding; mate selection and sexual reproduction; threat detection; intraspecific aggression; protection of kin; and parenting strategies. The fields of ethology, sociobiology and evolutionary psychology have focused on the evolved biological basis of these and other human and non-human behaviours. Unfortunately, the Cartesian myth has perpetuated itself within these disciplines. In their fervent desire to re-establish the human 'mind' firmly within the biological and evolutionary sciences, scientists within these disciplines have denounced any role for the social world in the origin and manifestation of these behaviours. The 'social world' and environment is acknowledged in terms of the entity 'out there' to which the organism is either preferentially adapted or maladapted.

There is still a separation between organism and environment; the latter serving as a kind of counterpoint to the traits of the former. Over time and the course of many generations, the 'world out there' does help to determine the emergence of adaptive traits through natural selection, but the Cartesian gulf remains, especially when it comes to describing the role played by society in the emerging behavioural and psychological traits of the individual. Thus, in phylogenetic terms (i.e. over evolutionary time), the social world is credited with a role in the ultimate causation of traits; but in ontogenetic terms (i.e. in the development of the individual) the social world is separated off as *the environment within which innate traits are expressed*. For the developing individual the social world is seen as separate from innate evolved traits and the interaction between the two entities is described in terms such as 'cultural influence' or 'cultural expression' or 'social stress'. In the biopsychosocial model of behaviour and mental experience, the social world plays the backseat role of 'precipitating factor' or 'cultural idiom of distress'.

If one begins to talk about an active social world that directly influences and modulates the degree to which innate genetically determined traits are expressed, suppressed or distorted during development, one is viewed with suspicion. And if, God forbid, one suggests that these active influences of the social world on the expression of genetic material in the individual may in fact be transmitted to subsequent individuals in future generations, one is immediately labelled Lamarckian[4] (a serious insult within evolutionary biology!) But, as we shall see, there is in fact emerging experimental evidence that supports a more prominent and persistent role for the social world/ environment in modulating and altering both the course of development in the individual and the expression of traits in descendants of that individual. This evidence is profoundly important because it serves as a bridge across the gulf that traditionally separates 'body' from 'mind' and 'individual mind' from 'social mind'. It allows us to abandon the Cartesian split and finally acknowledge the dynamic interrelatedness of physical, mental and social phenomena. The social world does impact significantly on the way in which inherited material in the brain is expressed in the behaviour and mental life of the individual.[5]

The interplay between physical, mental and social factors is dynamic, reciprocal and ongoing throughout development and this can now be demonstrated in the laboratory. Thus, it is possible to reorientate our understanding and study of the 'mind' away from the generally accepted view of the mind as individual, innately derived and isolated from the 'world out there'; and towards an interpersonal and thoroughly social view of the mind that reflects the philosophies of *ubuntu* and those of western thinkers such as Erich Fromm, Martin Heidegger and Maurice Merleau-Ponty. More importantly, in my opinion, this concept of a 'social mind' makes sense when one looks at the behaviours and mental experiences of people living and interrelating around one. A social view of the mind also makes sense of the perplexing disturbances of experience and behaviour evident in people suffering mental disorders such as psychosis. Finally, it makes sense when one begins to examine the structure and function of the human brain, both in its extant form and in its evolutionary history.

THE DEVELOPMENTAL SYSTEMS APPROACH

Before we consider the absolutely social nature of the human brain, in terms of both its anatomy and physiological function, it is important to elaborate my argument that the social world plays an active role in the neurodevelopment of the individual. This requires us to adopt an ontogenetic view and address the age-old question of 'nature versus nurture' in the emergence of the individual mind. Traditionally, evolutionary thinkers have been accused of 'biological determinism' when they suggest that traits are innate or have evolved. Prominent scientists such as Richard Dawkins have reinforced this view by focusing on the gene as the sole unit of selection (see Dawkins' hugely popular book *The Selfish Gene*). On the other hand, according to evolutionary psychologists, John Tooby and Leda Cosmides, a form of 'cultural determinism' (which they label the standard social science model) has dominated academic study of human behaviour through most of the twentieth century. This latter view denied a role for inherited genetic influences in the development of individual cognition. How then does one resolve the nature versus nurture problem and ascribe a more than backseat role to the social world (or environment) in the development of the seemingly gene-driven mind-brain? The answer seems to lie in the so-called 'developmental systems approach'.

Developmental psychologists, David Bjorklund and Anthony Pellegrini, address this problem of gene–environment interactions in the development of human cognition in their book *The Origins of Human Nature: evolutionary developmental psychology* (Bjorklund & Pellegrini 2002). They draw on the work of another developmental psychologist, Gilbert Gottlieb, in arguing for a 'developmental systems approach' (DSA). In essence this approach revolves around the concept of *epigenesis*, which is defined by Gottlieb as 'the emergence of new structures and functions during the course of development' (Gottlieb 1991a). In Chapter 4, I briefly introduced this concept in my evolutionary genetic model of psychosis, but the current topic requires us to examine epigenesis in greater detail. Epigenesis refers to the dynamic interaction of biological and environmental factors during development so that the resulting organism represents a unique individual despite species-specific or group-specific genes in common. Experimentally, it has been demonstrated that experiential or environmental factors can directly alter the expression of genes during development. According to Bjorklund, Pellegrini and Gottlieb there are a number of levels, both biological and experiential, that interact and modulate each other in a bidirectional manner. Gottlieb (1991b) states: 'Individual development is characterized by an increase of complexity of organization (i.e., the emergence of new structural and functional properties and competencies) at all levels of analysis (molecular, subcellular, cellular, organismic) as a consequence of horizontal and vertical coactions among the organism's parts, including organism-environment coactions'. This means that activity at one level (e.g. genes) influences activity at another level (e.g. protein molecules), which in turn influences activity at the next level (e.g. nerve cells). But, conversely, activity at 'higher' levels influences activity at lower levels also – thus the interactions are bidirectional (see Figure 5.1, adapted from Gottlieb 1992). As Bjorklund and Pellegrini state:

> ... Activity of these and surrounding cells can turn on or off a particular gene, causing commencement or cessation of genetic activity. Also, self-produced activity or stimulation from external sources can alter the development of sets of cells. From this viewpoint, there are no simple genetic or experiential causes of behaviour; all development is the product of epigenesis, with complex interactions occurring among multiple levels.
>
> (Bjorklund & Pellegrini 2002)

Jean-pierre Changeux, the French neurobiologist and author of *Neuronal Man: the biology of mind*, emphasizes the fact that a relatively small number of genes give rise to the incredibly complex system that is the human

Bidirectional Influences

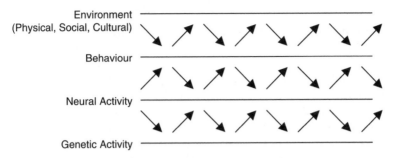

Figure 5.1 A simplified schematic of the developmental systems approach, showing a hierarchy of four mutually interacting components. (Adapted from *Individual Development and Evolution: the genesis of novel behaviour* by G. Gottlieb, Oxford University Press, p. 186. © 1992.)

cerebral cortex (Changeux 1997). He writes of an 'economy' within the developmental system. Just a few genes can spawn a myriad of complex differentiated cells, which in turn generate unimaginable numbers of neural pathways and networks simply because there are horizontal, vertical and temporal bidirectional interactions between gene, protein, cell and environment. Regulatory genes operate to control and vary the expression and timing of maturation of other genes; certain proteins such as *nerve growth factor* equally modulate the interaction of cells and the formation of synapses in the developing cortex; and the amazing phenomenon of the neuronal *growth cone*, discovered by Ramón y Cajal, which 'navigates "visually", steering itself [across the developing cortex] by the cells it meets' (Changeux 1997), are all examples of this bidirectional process. Changeux explains how neuronal impulses are detectable in the developing nervous system of the foetus, which originate from perceived environmental stimuli. These impulses contribute epigenetically to synaptic formation and stabilization. He states:

> Impulses travel through the neuronal network even at very early stages of its formation. They begin spontaneously, but are later evoked by the interaction of the newborn with its environment . . . The evolution of the connective state of each synaptic contact is governed by the overall message of signals received by the cell on which it terminates. In other words, the activity of the postsynaptic cell regulates the stability of the synapse in a retrograde manner.
>
> (Changeux 1997)

Thus, the development of the synapse, which is the site of major postnatal brain growth, depends not on information arising centrally but rather from stimuli derived from the peripheral sensory and perceptual systems. The source of these stimuli is the environment as perceived by the perceptual organs. We therefore have clear evidence for epigenetic regulation of neuro-development by the 'world out there'. Of significance is the fact that nearly 80 per cent of human brain growth occurs after birth – this reflects the growth of axons, dendritic branches and synapses as well as myelin sheaths around the axons – so we are a species readily adapted to maximize on epigenetic control of development. Furthermore, *Homo sapiens* experiences a prolonged juvenile period relative to non-human primates and hominid ancestors; this extends the period during which there is relative plasticity or flexibility in brain structure and cognitive function. Epigenetic processes operate when neural circuits retain plasticity; later on, once neural material is committed to specialized functions, brain and behavioural flexibility is reduced. This has given rise to the notion of 'critical periods' during development, when neural plasticity 'allows' for considerable change. Beyond a critical period, flexibility is lost and the potential for change diminished. A good (but tragic) example of this comes from work done with Romanian orphans rescued from the grossly deprived institutions of the dictator Ceausescu's regime.

O'Connor et al. (2000) demonstrated that orphans rescued and adopted before the age of 6 months had an equivalent mean IQ at six years to their British counterparts. However, those orphans who were older at the time of their adoption had a significantly lower mean IQ at six years than their British counterparts. Reversal of early deprivation was possible if the child was still within the critical period; those unfortunates rescued beyond the critical period had lost developmental plasticity and were disadvantaged in terms of benefiting from the epigenetic effects of an enriched environment.

Bjorklund and Pellegrini (2002) point out the seeming contradiction between the concepts of 'developmental plasticity' and 'genetic innateness'. 'This perspective' [plasticity], they state, 'seems to be at odds with evolutionary psychology's contention for universal, "innate" features' and is difficult to explain when 'almost all members of a species (human or otherwise) develop in species-typical pattern'. How are these two seemingly contradictory positions reconciled? If there is substantial plasticity one would expect greater variation between individuals, even within the same species; not the seemingly 'universal' traits one observes within specific species. These authors explain that 'the answer lies in the fact that humans (or chimpanzees or ducks) inherit not only a species-typical genome but also a species-typical environment'. Thus, common traits emerge in conspecific individuals as a result of both innate genetic factors and a common ecological and social niche.

The 'species-typical environment' of *Homo sapiens* is a predominantly social environment, characterized by interpersonal relationship. Healthy brain and psychological development depends on continued exposure to an adequate social world. Deprived or distorted experiences of the 'world out there' during critical periods of development prevent the normal expression of inherited genetic information. Likewise, exposure to an enriched social environment during early development can often mitigate the detrimental influence of 'bad genes'. These facts have huge implications for our understanding and management of mental and behavioural disorders such as the psychoses and neurotic disorders. We are fundamentally social beings with an evolved brain-mind that develops in response to social stimulation and interface with the world outside. It should then be no surprise that mental disorders are primarily problems of social functioning, social navigation and social understanding. This is a subject that is addressed later in Chapter 7 but for now I return to the social brain and attempt to convince the reader that this 5 kg spongy lump of tissue within our skulls is, in both its structure and function, brilliantly adapted to negotiating and interacting with other spongy lumps of tissue; and that taken together, all these brains form a substrate for that complex and dynamic organism we call society.

THE NEUROPSYCHOLOGY OF SOCIAL COGNITION

Social cognition is a concept that has emerged within the neurosciences over the last 30 years in parallel with the development of the cognitive sciences. It reflects an attempt to locate the basis of human social behaviour within the functioning of the brain and relies heavily on a mechanistic understanding of neural information-processing. Interestingly, the development of social cognition as a science has not come from the arena of academic social psychology but rather from evolutionary approaches to cognitive psychology. Placing human behaviour within an evolutionary context has led to a greater focus on the basic motivations or drives that lie behind the variety of social behaviours that typify our species. For example, it is clear that the individual experiences two contrasting motivations in attempting to negotiate the social world: on the one hand there is an evolved drive to be part of a group (which brings security, companionship, mating opportunities and greater access to resources); while on the other hand there is the drive to be more successful than others within the group (who compete for rank, food and mates). As Humphrey (1976) puts it: 'In a complex society such as those we know exist among higher primates, there are benefits to be gained for each individual member both from preserving the overall structure of the group and at the same time from exploiting and outmanoeuvring others within it'. Thus, the group-living or social individual needs to develop a finely tuned ability to detect, interpret and respond optimally to the motivations of others within that group. This ability has evolved in many social animal species from weavers to whales but it is in primates that it has emerged in its greatest complexity.

Among primates we see a phylogenetic increase in the sophistication of social cognitive ability; in other words, the more recently evolved and therefore genetically closer a primate is to humans the greater its repertoire of navigational skills for managing its social environment. Thus, the common chimpanzee and its rarer cousin the bonobo (or pygmy chimpanzee), which shares approximately 98.5 per cent of the genome with *Homo sapiens*, demonstrates an extraordinary social cognitive ability. But it is in humans that we encounter unmatched proficiency at interpreting and manipulating the social world. This is because our evolutionary history was characterized by millions of years of group living and the evolution of our brains was 'driven' by a continuous need or pressure to adapt to and survive living in human society. Our brain is a social brain, first and foremost adapted to a social lifestyle.

Leslie Brothers, a Californian psychiatrist, described 'the social brain' as the higher cognitive and affective systems in the brain that evolved as a result of increasingly complex social selective pressures (Brothers 1990). These systems underlie our ability to function as highly social animals and provide the substrate for intact social cognition, social behaviour and affective responsiveness. Broks (1997) defines 'social cognition' as information-processing that contributes to 'the perception of the dispositions and intentions of other individuals ... the construction and maintenance of a viable concept of self ... [and] the production and regulation of behaviour in social contexts'. Thus, in order to 'mindread' (Whiten 1991) successfully, an individual requires both an evolved perceptual system in order to detect social signals, as well as an information-processing 'module' that draws on stored emotions and memories in interpreting the mental state of conspecifics. Grady and Keightley (2002) include the following functions within social cognition: face perception; emotional processing (including both perception of emotional information in the environment and regulation of mood); 'theory of mind' (see below); and self-reference and working memory. It is important to recognize these functionally separate aspects of social cognition, for most terms used in relation to it encompass all aspects as an integrated unit. Indeed, I would argue that, when social cognition is described in modular terms, there is the risk that we view the social brain as a single anatomical region, rather than as a distributed network of interconnected systems that include both cortical and subcortical structures.

As is common in the behavioural sciences, a range of terminology has emerged in relation to the concept of social cognition. For example, in relation to apes' capacity to recognize or infer mental states in other individuals, Dick Byrne and Andrew Whiten of the University of St Andrews in Scotland have used the term, 'metarepresentation' (Byrne & Whiten 1991).

As Brüne (2001) puts it, one has 'metarepresentations about the social world' and this in turn indicates the possession of 'social metacognition'. And drawing on the social machinations of Machiavelli's *The Prince*, Frans de Waal of the Yerkes Primate Sanctuary at Emory University introduced the term 'Machiavellian Intelligence' to describe the social and political behaviour of chimpanzees (de Waal 1982). Others have referred to 'mentalizing' (Morton 1980), 'folk psychology' (Wellman 1991) and 'the intentional stance' (Dennett 1987). Finally, within the psychiatric literature at least, 'theory of mind' is the concept most familiar to clinicians and researchers alike. So much for terminology: in this book I restrict myself to the use of the terms, 'theory of mind', 'metarepresentation' and 'social cognition' and, in referring to the neural systems that regulate this faculty, I use the term 'social brain'.

The term 'theory of mind' (TOM) was coined in a landmark *Behavioural and Brain Sciences* paper by Premack and Woodruff in 1978 in relation to chimpanzees' capacity for deception (Premack & Woodruff 1978). In essence, it refers to the assumption one makes during communication that another individual possesses a mind just like one's own. TOM is the ability to attribute mental states to others and thus forms the very basis of social interaction and communication. This is because it is critical to understand the beliefs and intentions of others in social discourse. Having TOM ability enables individuals to engage cognitively in the social arena. Thus, it is a core aspect of social cognition. A number of authors have argued strongly for the existence of TOM or elements of TOM in the great apes (Premack & Woodruff 1978; Russon 1999; van Schaik et al. 1996). However, as noted by Frith (1994), evidence for TOM in apes is questionable and other explanations of recorded deceptive behaviours have not been ruled out (Povinelli & Eddy 1996; Premack 1988). This leads Baron-Cohen (1999) to conclude that only primitive elements of a TOM may exist in apes and that the same could be said of the last common ancestor of apes and humans. This is a topic we discuss again in the next chapter. As for the development of full TOM in normal healthy children, it is generally accepted that this is achieved by four years of age (Perner 1991; Wimmer & Perner 1983). Avis and Harris studied Baka pygmy children in Cameroon and concluded that this is reliable cross-culturally (Avis & Harris 1991). However, Lillard argues that in terms of the actual manifestation of TOM, cultural variations do exist (Lillard 1998).

In terms of testing social cognition in an individual, the assessment of TOM ability as described above is a major component. However, there are particular cognitive faculties that can inform one's appraisal of another's social abilities and these are most easily appreciated by adopting an ethological view. Adolphs (1999) outlines this approach well. He argues that most mammals use olfaction and touch as key sensory channels for social communication – in humans this is perhaps best evidenced in maternal and sexual behaviours. Auditory communication is based on often complex signals that are adapted to a species' particular environment; for example whale songs that can travel great distances underwater or ultrasonic separation cries of small mammals that are inaudible to predators. There is no doubt that there are species or even individual-specific auditory signals in humans that contribute to social cognition. The separation cry of the infant elicits a parental response while tone of voice imparts significant meaning in a social interaction. The sensory modality that has been the subject of most experimental work in social cognition, in both humans and primates, is vision.

Emery (2000) argues that eye gaze plays an important signalling role in conveying emotional and mental states between individuals. In 'higher primates' the following and interpretation of gaze is an essential part of TOM ability and social cognition. So too is the ability to recognize the facial expression and direction of attention in others. In primates these visual signals are a critical part of dominance–submission encounters, affiliative behaviour and threat detection. Baron-Cohen (1999) has described three developmentally earlier modules underlying the achievement of a full TOM, namely the 'intentionality detector' (ID), the 'eye-direction detector' (EDD) and the 'shared attention mechanism' (SAM). All three modules depend on visual stimuli and the EDD specifically functions in response to perceiving eye movements and detecting direction of gaze.

THE ANATOMY OF SOCIAL COGNITION

I now wish to examine the neural basis of social cognition. Drawing on imaging studies conducted in normal individuals, on evidence from autism research and from neurological case studies, and on primate lesion studies, I argue that the anatomy of the social brain is best understood in terms of a network of complex neural interconnections linking the frontal lobes to the temporal and parietal lobes of the brain. These networks are primarily cortical and they principally connect frontal and posterior cortical regions to each other, but there are also vertical links connecting the superficial cortex to deeper and phylogenetically older structures of the brain.[6] A number of authors have critiqued a cognitive view of the social brain on the grounds that it 'ignore(s) too many of the foundational social circuits of the cross-mammalian limbic brain' (Panksepp & Moskal 2004). Gilbert (2004) warns against emphasising 'top-down' processes to the exclusion of 'bottom-up' effects on social cognition, while Weisfeld (2004) argues for a greater integration of the ethological perspective in constructing a model of the social brain. Clearly, the construction of such a model must incorporate both an analysis of basic limbic-driven social emotions and motives, and an appreciation of higher cortical processes, to account for hominid-specific social cognition. Thus, it may be useful to consider the social brain a system of integrated circuits, including both limbic and cortical structures and functionally operating in terms of both 'top-down' and 'bottom-up' processes. Within such a system one could, anatomically, identify both an *upper social brain* and a *lower social brain*, the former being the cortical aspects and the latter the subcortical aspects.

In terms of my model this distinction is artificial since I do not support a modular view but rather an integrated 'fluid' view. However, this may be a useful model since it acknowledges both primitive and newer aspects in the system. Top-down processes include the function of the heteromodal cortex 'elaborat(ing) theories of mind and complex sociocognitive strategies' as suggested by Panksepp and Moskal (2004) and involve attentional, working memory and executive functions. Bottom-up processes originate in the primitive subcortical regions and regulate basic emotions, motives and drives (as discussed by Gilbert 2004 and Weisfeld 2004). This two-tiered social brain is discussed further in later chapters, but for now I turn to a different approach that focuses on specific components of social cognition.

Adolphs (2001) has proposed a simple model that describes the various component processes of social cognition. I believe this is a useful model for the purposes of this discussion of the anatomy of the social brain. Adolphs describes three major stages in social cognition: *social perception*, which is the detection of social stimuli; *central social cognition*, which entails the recognition, evaluation and interpretation of material; and *social behaviour*, which is the effecting of the individual's response. In terms of social perception he identifies the sensory and association cortices (including the fusiform gyrus and the superior temporal sulcus (STS)) as the primary sites involved. The central processes include the amygdala, the orbitofrontal cortex (OFC), the anterior cingulate cortex (ACC) and the right somatosensory cortex. Finally, the areas implicated in social behaviour include the motor cortex, the basal ganglia, the hypothalamus and the brainstem. Importantly, the central processes operate at multiple levels – cognitive, emotional and motivational – and draw upon memory systems for the recognition and evaluation of stimuli and the preparation of the organism's response.

Adolphs' selection of brain structures involved in the central component is very similar to that of Brothers (1990) who proposes that there is a specific brain module[7] that is dedicated to social cognition which is predominantly innate. The structural correlates of this module form a distributed brain system which, according to Brothers, includes the STS, the amygdala and the OFC. Brüne includes the dorsolateral prefrontal cortex (DLPFC) and the ACC in addition to the above areas as candidate areas for social cognition (Brüne 2001). Using the model proposed by Adolphs, I now want to address each of his components of social cognition and ascertain whether the research literature supports the identification of these brain regions as constituting the social brain.

Social perception

Adolphs attributes social perception to the fusiform gyrus and the STS. This is derived from both primate and human studies that have focused on neuronal responses to socially important visual stimuli. In primates a number of studies have identified neurones in the OFC, the amygdala and the STS that respond selectively to facial expression, eye gaze and intended action (Emery 2000; Perrett et al. 1985; Perrett et al. 1992). Other primate studies have identified neurones responsive to eye gaze in the amygdala (Brothers et al. 1990; Brothers & Ring 1993). Human studies have largely corroborated these findings. For example, electrophysiological studies in epileptic patients have found regions of the STS that respond to socially salient visual stimuli (especially facial motion) (Adolphs et al. 2000), while functional imaging studies have identified a 'fusiform face area' on the lateral fusiform gyrus that is 'specialized for face perception' (Haxby et al. 1994; Kanwisher et al. 1997; McCarthy et al. 1997a).

The STS has also been identified, using functional imaging, as implicated in face perception (Puce et al. 1998; Haxby et al. 2001). Haxby et al. (2002) argue that 'face perception is mediated by a distributed neural system in humans that consists of multiple bilateral regions'. They describe a 'core system', consisting of the fusiform gyrus and STS, which mediates the visual analysis of faces. The former, they argue, is responsive to invariant aspects of faces (i.e. identity), while the latter is responsive to changeable aspects (i.e. expression). The 'core system' connects with a number of regions from other neural systems involved in other cognitive functions (e.g. amygdala) forming the so-called 'extended system'. This interaction between core and extended systems allows for the extraction of meaning from faces. Of the amygdala, Haxby et al. (2002) say: 'it plays a central role in processing the social relevance of information gleaned from faces'. Thus, in terms of Adolphs' model of social cognition, the 'extended system' for face-processing forms part of the 'central processes', and I shall discuss this in the next section.

Central processes of social cognition

To recap on Adolphs' description of the 'central processes': a network of structures including the amygdala, the OFC, the ACC and the right somato-sensory cortex mediates the recognition, evaluation and interpretation of socially related stimuli. Clearly, these stimuli are presented to the individual in predominantly the visual and auditory modalities, and the central processing entails integration of these stimuli with emotional, memory and higher cognitive systems. Before addressing the particular role played by the amygdala, OFC and somatosensory cortices (as well as a few other key brain regions in social cognition), I wish to return to the matter of face processing with particular reference to Haxby et al.'s (2002) 'extended system'.

The 'extended system' and face processing

Visual material from the perception of faces is distributed from the core system to a number of regions in the extended system where it is invested with meaning. Specifically, information such as gaze direction and head position is processed within the neural systems for spatial attention and perception in the intraparietal sulcus and the frontal eye fields (Hoffman & Haxby 2000). Phonemic information from speech-related lip movements is processed within the neural system for auditory verbal comprehension in the STG and STS (Calvert et al. 1997; Puce et al. 1998). Perception of identity and retrieval of semantic knowledge about a person recruits neural systems in the anterior temporal lobes (Gorno-Tempini et al. 1998; Nakamura et al. 2000). Finally, the emotional content of expression is processed in the amygdala, insula and other parts of the limbic system (Breiter et al. 1996; Streit et al. 1999).

The amygdala and emotional responses

The amygdala forms an interface between the information-processing activities of the neocortex and the autonomic and endocrine functions of sub-cortical structures such as the hypothalamus and brainstem. Thus, it is well placed to perform its function as the brain's emotion-regulation system, integrating emotional, motivational and cognitive processes (Le Doux 1994). The important array of connections the amygdala has with cortical and subcortical regions is critical to its task. Importantly, though, two connections that are known to play a central role in processing social material are between the lateral nucleus of amygdala and the STS, and between the amygdala and the OFC (Amaral et al. 1992).

Evidence from primate studies (Leonard et al. 1985; Nakamura et al. 1992), from human studies on patients with amygdala lesions (Adolphs et al. 1994; Jacobson 1986; Young et al. 1995; Young et al. 1996), and from autism research (Baron-Cohen et al. 2000) supports the central role played by the amygdala in the recognition and interpretation of facial expressions of emotion. In particular, the amygdala seems to play a role in detecting and responding to threat and danger and mediating the fear response. Amygdala lesions in macaques result in a loss of fear responses to threatening objects (Amaral 2002), while functional imaging in normal subjects has demonstrated amygdala activation when viewing facial expressions of fear[8] (Morris et al. 1996). It appears that this structure is critical for vigilance and recognition or evaluation of potential threat and therefore, in evolutionary terms, the amygdala plays a vital adaptive role for the organism and one can speculate that its origins are extremely ancient.

In addition to fear responses there is a wealth of evidence for the key involvement of the amygdala and its anterior connections in more general affective and social responsiveness (Barbas 2000; Breiter et al. 1990; Davis 1992; Le Doux 1994). For example, work with autism links the well-described abnormalities of this structure to a broad array of emotional and social deficits (Baron-Cohen et al. 2000). As an important structure in the central processes of social cognition, the amygdala facilitates recognition of emotionally salient stimuli. Its role in emotional memory is supported by functional imaging of normal individuals, where emotionally charged information is remembered better than neutral information and this correlates with activation in the amygdala (Cahill et al. 1996; Hamann et al. 1999). In patients with amygdala lesions, this function is also impaired (Adolphs et al. 1997).

Finally, the amygdala and its connections with the OFC have been attributed a major role in establishing and maintaining social bonds. Studies in rodents have shown how oxytocin and vasopressin, two key peptides involved in affiliative behaviour, effect their action by modulating the amygdala and parts of the ventral striatum (Young 2002). Monkeys with lesions placed in the amygdala, the anterior temporal pole or the OFC, show varying degrees of social isolation and marked reductions in affiliative behaviours (Kling & Steklis 1976). Having said this, it is important to note that Amaral (2002) reports relatively normal affiliative behaviour (except for a loss of the fear response) in young monkeys following lesioning of bilateral amygdalae, suggesting that an intact OFC may be more important than intact amygdalae in mediating affiliative behaviour.

The orbitofrontal cortex and social behaviour

The classic case of Phineas Gage sticks in every medical student's mind because it illustrates the central role of the OFC in regulating socially appropriate behaviour. This unfortunate railway construction foreman was blasting rock in the Vermont Mountains in 1848 when an accidental explosion blew his 'tamping iron' through his head, specifically his OFC. He was transformed from a socially responsible and polite man to an irreverent and grossly profane individual, so much so that his friends are recorded to have stated that he was 'no longer Gage'! If Gage's case is deemed unreliable because of the diffuse frontal injury he sustained, then there are a number of case reports of surgically placed lesions in the OFC that might convince one of the selective social impairments resulting from OFC damage (Eslinger & Damasio 1985). In humans, damage to the OFC is notable for a diminished capacity to respond to punishment, stereotyped and sometimes inappropriate social manners, and an apparent lack of concern for other individuals, all in the face of otherwise normal intellectual functioning (Damasio 1994).

In primates, David Perrett of the University of St Andrews and colleagues have identified neurons sensitive to facial expression, not just in the amygdala and STS, but also in the OFC (Perrett et al. 1985; Perrett et al. 1992). The human OFC appears to have cells similarly sensitive to socially and emotionally aversive visual stimuli (Kawasaki et al. 2001).

The OFC (as well as the ventral prefrontal cortex) is implicated in Damasio's 'somatic marker hypothesis', an adaptive mechanism by which we acquire, represent and retrieve the values of our actions (Damasio 1994). These structures generate representations (or 'somatic markers') of emotional or somatic states that correspond to the anticipated future outcome of decisions, thus steering the decision-making process towards those social outcomes that are advantageous for the individual (Adolphs 1999). Studies using a gambling task have shown that subjects with damage to the OFC are unable to represent choice bias in the form of an emotional hunch or 'gut feeling' (Bechara et al. 1997). Thus, impairment of the OFC and its circuits may result in ambivalence and impulsivity rather than carefully considered decision-making in social situations.

As mentioned in the previous section on the amygdala, the OFC is ascribed an important role in affiliative behaviour. Lesions placed in the OFC in monkeys result in dramatic reductions in sociability as well as shifts in social ranking (Butter & Snyder 1972; Kling & Steklis 1976). A dominant alpha male will drop in rank to a submissive, low-ranking and depressive individual if a surgical lesion is placed in his OFC. Furthermore, the density of certain serotonin receptors in the OFC correlates with a monkey's social status and pharmacological manipulation of serotonergic neurotransmission results in changes in its social status and rank (Panksepp 1998; Raleigh et al. 1996). Other neuromodulatory compounds known to have an important role in maternal behaviour, such as oxytocin, oestrogen and prolactin, have high numbers of receptors in the OFC (Leckman & Herman 2002). Affiliative behaviour (the making and maintaining of social bonds) is vital for the individual's survival and sanity. Two components of affiliative behaviour, the ability to empathize and the ability to forgive others, have been studied with functional magnetic resonance imaging (fMRI) in normal individuals. Farrow et al. (2001) used fMRI to demonstrate the role of the OFC and the anterior temporal lobe in the social phenomena of empathy and forgiveness. Finally, the OFC is one of the regions that activates during theory of mind (TOM) tasks. As stated above, TOM ability is a core aspect of social cognition. The role played by the OFC in TOM is discussed later in this chapter, where the anatomical basis of TOM ability is reviewed.

The anterior cingulate cortex and social behaviour

The ACC plays a key role in emotion and social behaviour (Devinsky et al. 1995; Maddock 1999). A unique type of neuron, the 'spindle-cell', is found in the ACC of humans and apes (Nimchinsky et al. 1999) and it is thought that these neurons play a role in complex tasks of motor control and control of cognitive impulsivity (Brüne 2004b). In the next chapter we discuss the significance of spindle-cells in the evolution of the social brain. Damage to the ACC can result in a gross loss of motivation[9] and this region is activated in normal subjects by emotional versions of the Stroop task (Bush et al. 2000), supporting the idea that it helps to monitor errors and response conflicts (Adolphs 2001). An fMRI study by MacDonald et al. (2000) identified the ACC as playing a central role in the monitoring of performance and conflict monitoring (in other words, the evaluating and selecting of choices and reactions to stimuli). Importantly, the ACC, together with other connected regions, mediates attention and working memory and it goes without saying that these are centrally important cognitive processes in social cognition and behaviour.

As with the amygdala and OFC, the ACC has a role in affiliative behaviour. A neuroethological study using fMRI, linked parental and infant separation to the ACC (Lorberbaum et al. 1999). Mothers were scanned while listening to recorded infant cries, and the activity demonstrated in the ACC suggests that this structure plays a role in attachment and bonding, arguably the ontogenetic precursors to human sociability. Finally, the ACC is implicated, along with other structures, in TOM ability.

THE NEURAL BASIS OF THEORY OF MIND

Earlier in this chapter I discussed the concept of TOM as a cognitive module that evolved in humans as a means of representing the mental states of others, and therefore enabling our species to engage in complex social behaviour. I now want to examine the anatomical basis for this cognitive function.

In the last ten years functional imaging in particular has been applied, using a variety of study designs, to examine normal TOM ability. The three earliest studies, using PET and SPECT, imaged normal subjects as they performed TOM tasks (including recognition of mental states and the inferring of intentions to others) and showed activation in the left medial pre-frontal cortex (PFC) (in two studies), the OFC and the left temporal cortex (Baron-Cohen et al. 1994; Fletcher et al. 1995; Goel et al. 1995). Of these anatomical regions, the medial PFC has been most commonly identified in subsequent studies of this nature (Brünet et al. 2000; Calder et al. 2002; Castelli et al. 2000; Gallagher et al. 2000; Gusnard et al. 2001). These studies used PET or fMRI and TOM paradigms that included affective responses, mental state attribution, eye gaze detection and attribution of intentions. Within the medial PFC, the ACC specifically has been identified in a number of studies (Brünet et al. 2000; Vogeley et al. 2001).

The other regions that most commonly activate during TOM imaging studies are in the temporal lobes and include the STS, the STG and the anterior temporal poles (Brünet et al. 2000; Calder et al. 2002; Castelli et al. 2000; Gallagher et al. 2000; Vogeley et al. 2001). Baron-Cohen et al.'s (1994) finding of OFC activation during a TOM test has been replicated by Levine et al. (1999) using a test of self-regulated social behaviour. Other structures that have only occasionally shown activation during similar experiments include the paracingulate sulcus, the posterior cingulate, the temporoparietal junction and the PFC (Fletcher et al. 1995; Gallagher et al. 2000; McCabe et al. 2001). The only experiment that showed PFC activation was an fMRI study using cooperation games in a 'prisoner's dilemma'-type paradigm (McCabe et al. 2001).

Thus, it is obvious that the neural structures and regions that are active during TOM tasks correspond with those implicated in general experiments on social cognition. This rather dense review of the literature seems to support the conclusions of social brain scientists such as Ralph Adolphs, Leslie Brothers and Martin Brüne. The neuroanatomical basis for social cognition, which we might call 'the social brain', is to be found in the distributed neural networks and interconnected regions of the prefrontal, temporal and parietal association cortices.

A SPECIALIZED CELL FOR SOCIAL COMMUNICATION

At a neuronal level, how do we represent the mental states of others? What is happening at the level of cells when we engage in TOM activity? Earlier in this chapter I talked about the bidirectional transfer of information between multiple levels of the nervous system and the social environment. Development of synapses and neural circuits depends on this dynamic process as the social brain is actively 'created'. But if we focus in on a single exchange of social information between two individuals, we must ask what is happening at the level of the neuron that enables such an exchange to occur. How is a person's mental state or intention represented in the brain of an observer? How do we empathize in cellular terms? To answer these questions we need to turn to an area of research that germinated in an Italian laboratory 20 years ago.

The search for a neural substrate for social cognition took a major upturn when Giacomo Rizzolatti and his team in the Department of Neuroscience at Parma University, Italy, identified so-called 'mirror neurons' in the prefrontal cortex of macaque monkeys (di Pellegrino et al. 1992). From the early 1980s he and his colleagues had systematically investigated neuronal function in macaques and in 1992 reported their discovery of these extraordinary cells, which were to revolutionize the neuroscience of interpersonal behaviour. Situated in the cortical area of the macaque known as F5, which lies in the ventral premotor cortex and is homologous with Broca's (speech) area of the human brain, mirror neurons discharge both when the macaque performs a particular goal-directed action, and when it observes another individual performing a similar action. Thus, mirror neurons serve to mirror or simulate observed actions within the motor cortex of the observer. According to Jeannerod (1994), these cells form a motor image of an observed action in the brain; and it is these same cells that will later activate when the observer unconsciously plans and prepares to imitate this action. Thus, mirror neurons are neurons that internally 'represent' an action (Jeannerod 1994; Rizzolatti et al. 1996).

Subsequent research reveals that neuron discharge requires an interaction between the action's agent (monkey) and its object; 'neither the sight of the agent alone nor of the object alone was effective in evoking the neuron's response' (Gallese 2003a). Thus, it is the *intention* of the action rather than the action itself that is represented – mirror neurons register *goal-directed action*. In a later study (Kohler et al. 2002), the presence of 'audiovisual mirror neurons' was demonstrated: constituting about 15 per cent of mirror neurons, these cells were additionally shown to respond to goal-directed sounds only (i.e. in the absence of visual presentation). According to Gallese et al. (2004), these cells 'represent actions independently of whether these actions are performed, heard or seen'.

So far I have discussed the mirror neuron system (MNS) in monkeys. But what of humans: does a similar system underlie action recognition in *Homo sapiens*? In 1995 a study by Fadiga et al. (1995) revealed that a mirror system does in fact exist in humans. Subsequent studies have confirmed this and have demonstrated that the neural basis for action recognition in humans is comprised of a mirror-matching system located in a cortical network consisting of Broca's area, the premotor cortex, the superior temporal sulcus (STS) and the posterior parietal cortex (Buccino et al. 2001; Decety & Grèzes 1999; Grafton et al. 1996; Rizzolatti et al. 1996). A functional MRI study by Buccino et al. (2001) confirmed that (as in the macaque), when one observes goal-directed behaviours executed with the mouth, hand or foot, specific regions of the premotor cortex become active. Thus, during observation of an action, our mirror neurons activate as if we were performing the same action. According to Gallese (2003a), 'This *implicit, automatic,* and *unconscious* process of embodied simulation enables the observer to use his/her own resources to penetrate the world of the other without the need of explicitly *theorizing* about it'. Gallese describes a shared intersubjective space across which the MNS maps a 'multimodal representation of organism-organism relations'. She terms this space 'the shared manifold of intersubjectivity' and argues that it underpins our capacity to share feelings and emotions with others. Thus, it is within the neural circuits of the MNS that human empathy is possible as an embodied phenomenon (Decety & Jackson 2004; Gallese 2003a). Gallese uses the term 'empathy' broadly to describe the cognitive, emotional and bodily identification of one individual with another. So it is not just the capacity to understand another person's anger, joy or sadness.

Empathy also enables us to identify with the quality of a sensation experienced by another, such as tickling, touch or pain. This identification is automatic and embedded in the MNS and does not necessitate any interven-ing cognitive mediation. In another paper, published in *The Philosophical Transactions of the Royal Society of London*, Gallese (2003b) extends her argument regarding empathy to include other components of interpersonal relations, namely imitation and mind reading or TOM. She argues that these different aspects of social cognition 'share, at a basic level, a crucial common feature: they all depend on the constitution of a shared meaningful intersubjective space'. At a functional level this 'shared manifold' relies on a specific mechanism – 'embodied simulation'; and at an anatomical level this simulation occurs within the cells of the MNS.

In the mirror neuron system, therefore, we have an embedded mechanism for actively engaging in and responding to interpersonal stimuli emanating from the social world in which we exist. What is significant in my view is the fact that these socially sensitive and active neurons are to be found in the very same interconnected cortical regions that I have argued comprise the social brain in our species. Furthermore, the presence of a neural system that mediates the bidirectional interaction of the human brain with the social world 'out there' provides us with empirical evidence and support for a philosophy of interpersonal relatedness. The Cartesian legacy is indeed a myth and the insights of Fromm, Heidegger and Merleau-Ponty must now take centre stage as we move forward towards a deeper understanding of the mind and its relationship to the social world.

THE EVOLUTION OF THE
SOCIAL BRAIN

Nevertheless the difference in mind between man and the higher animals, great as it is, certainly is one of degree and not of kind. We have seen that the senses and intuitions, the various emotions and faculties, such as love, memory, attention, curiosity, imitation, reason, etc., of which man boasts, may be found in an incipient, or even sometimes in a well-developed condition, in the lower animals.

(Darwin 1871)

WHY ARE PRIMATES SO BRAINY?

The 1997 Newsmaker of the Year for the Johannesburg Press Club was a 250 kg lowland gorilla named Max. Earlier that year an armed robber who was also wanted for rape escaped from a crime scene by fleeing through the Johannesburg Zoo. In his panic the villain jumped into an enclosure only to be confronted by the adult male gorilla. Max, in defence of his territory and his mate, Lisa, attacked and mauled the man who was then arrested by police and zoo staff. During the fracas the gorilla sustained two gunshot wounds to the jaw and shoulder, the suspect was shot in the groin by the police, and two policemen were bitten by the angry primate as they attempted to remove the man from the enclosure. Max received emergency surgery at a nearby hospital and made a good recovery, only to be hailed a hero in the fight against rampant crime in the city. The national and international press had a field-day, the gorilla was honoured by the Press Club and a company that manufactures security doors and equipment 'adopted' him as their mascot. Political commentators quipped that Max's actions outstripped the crime-fighting efforts of local authorities and law-enforcement agencies. And when Max died of natural causes at the age of 33 years in May 2005, a website was established for the public to record their condolences and express their mass grief. The zoo decided to erect a memorial garden near his enclosure where mourners could queue to leave their handprints in wet concrete. An artist involved in building the garden was quoted as saying, 'After Max died the zoo was inundated with messages from the public who felt the loss and wanted to be involved in saying goodbye to him. We realized the public needed it'.

I have chosen to relate this story because it raises a number of issues that I believe cut to the central theme of this chapter. The behaviour of the gorilla is certainly of interest – charging to attack an intruder into his territory, an intruder who may also have posed a threat to his mate – but in truth there is nothing particularly unusual or special about a male gorilla acting aggressively towards a sudden intruder. What is of more interest, to my mind, is the public reaction to this animal's act of aggression. Clearly, the situational facts of the case significantly coloured the human response and contributed greatly to Max's heroic status. The city of Johannesburg is renowned for violent crime and unfortunately there is the widely held perception that many criminals escape justice for a lack of an efficient and effective crime-prevention service. Thus, the apprehension of a violent criminal is welcome news to a fearful and disillusioned public. In addition, the fact that a wild animal – in particular a wild animal that is recognized as biologically close to our own species – was responsible for the villain's capture, serves to evoke a range of human emotions directly related to our self-consciousness as a species that straddles the divide between beast and immortal. We want to believe that Max the gorilla acted against the man because he was recognized as a criminal fleeing from justice, not simply because he was an unfamiliar intruder entering the ape's territory. We want to endow Max not just with the ability to act intentionally but also with a sense of moral indignation and a desire for justice. Max is eulogized in the press as 'The Second Best Known Living South African In The World' (presumably after Nelson Mandela) because it is somehow gratifying to imagine that he consciously set out to do his bit in 'the fight against crime' when he attacked the unfortunate man. Furthermore, in doing his bit, Max 'took the bullet' as a true patriot – a gorilla patriot – and showed up his human cousins who generally speaking are too corrupt and degenerate to be so self-sacrificing!

Although anthropomorphic in the extreme, the tale of Max deals with the vexing questions of whether non-human animals have the ability to act intentionally; whether they are capable of empathy and altruism; and to what degree their capacity for complex social behaviour approximates that of modern *Homo sapiens*. Anthropomorphism within the behavioural sciences is strongly discouraged as the young Jane Goodall discovered when she first began to report on her Gombe chimps in the scientific literature. She was criticized for giving names to the chimps she studied – they were supposed to be identified with a number – but true to her independent and indomitable spirit, she ignored the objections of the primatological purists. Another respected primate expert is Robert Sapolsky who, fully cognizant of the decorum expected of field scientists, quite brazenly went about naming his baboons after biblical prophets! His wit and self-confidence are a refreshing respite from the dry rigidity of research papers and I cannot resist a short detour from the topic of this chapter so as to include this extract from his book *A Primate's Memoir*:

> I have always liked Old Testament names, but I would hesitate to inflict Obadiah or Ezekial on a child of mine, so I ran wild with the sixty baboons in the troop. Plus, clearly, I was still irritated by the years I spent toting my Time-Life books on evolution to show my Hebrew school teachers, having them blanch at such sacrilege and tell me to put them away; it felt like a pleasing revenge to hand out the names of the patriarchs to a bunch of baboons on the African plains. And, with some sort of perversity that I suspect powers a lot of what primatologists do, I couldn't wait for the inevitable day that I could record in my field notebook that Nebuchanezzar and Naomi were off screwing in the bushes.
>
> (Sapolsky 2002)

The question of social intelligence in apes and other 'higher' mammals such as cetaceans (whales and dolphins) has received considerable attention over the past 50 years or so; and it is of central relevance to my thesis that the modern human brain is a social brain that evolved over millennia in response to the selective pressures of negotiating complex social relationships. The first scientists to suggest that social dynamics might constitute the major driving force in hominid brain evolution were Chance and Mead who, in their 1953 paper 'Social behaviour and primate evolution', stated that:

> ...the ascent of man has been due in part to a competition for social position, giving access to the trigonal sphere of social activity in which success was rewarded by a breeding premium, and that at some time in the past, a group of primates, by virtue of their pre-eminent adaptation to this element and consequent cortical enlargement, became pre-adapted for the full exploitation of the properties of the mammalian cortex.
>
> (Chance & Mead 1953: 48–9)

Chance and Mead's insight was largely overlooked for the next two decades, although a handful of authors such as Alison Jolly (1966) and Hans Kummer (1967) touched on the theme of social intelligence in their analyses of the social behaviour of lemurs and Hamadryas baboons, respectively. According to primatologists Richard Byrne and Andrew Whiten, in their edited volume *Machiavellian Intelligence* (1988), it was Nicholas Humphrey's essay 'The social function of intellect' (1976) that really served to 'fire the imaginations' of those who have subsequently pursued empirical research on social cognition in evolution. In his paper Humphrey asked the question: Why do modern humans have such advanced creative intelligence when most 'important practical problems of living actually demand only relatively low-level intelligence for their solution'? Natural selection does not usually give rise to unnecessary complexity in an organism, which will be wasted because it is excess to that organism's needs.[1] In Humphrey's view, the life of humans and great apes:

> ... may not require much in the way of practical invention, but it does depend critically on the possession of wide factual knowledge of practical technique and the nature of the habitat. Such knowledge can only be acquired in the context of a social community – a community which provides both a medium for the cultural transmission of information and a protective environment in which individual learning can occur. I propose that the chief role of creative intellect is to hold society together.
>
> (Humphrey 1976)

Humphrey thus argues that social cohesion is fundamental to a context in which the transmission and learning of skills and knowledge necessary for survival can occur. And social cohesion within a group depends on the possession of complex social cognitive skills by members of that group. Group dynamics are not static – they are often ambiguous and fluctuate constantly. Thus, in order to survive, group members need to be skilled in the arts of detection, interpretation and calculation of the relative benefits and costs of chosen behaviours. Using the analogy of chess, Humphrey (1976) explains how each individual or 'social gamesman' needs to be 'capable of a special sort of forward planning'. It is not sufficient merely to perceive the current 'state of play'; one needs to anticipate various alternative responses from the other player and plan one's rebuttal accordingly. Furthermore, strategizing one's social involvements requires a great deal of time – time spent familiarizing oneself with others in the group, choosing allies and building up alliances, and planning the next move. Balanced against this within-group gamesmanship is the contrasting need to maintain group cohesion so that the native group is well prepared and unified to deal with inter-group conflicts. Humphrey maintains that the exhaustive work of social inter-relationship leaves little time for basic 'chores' such as foraging and hunting, raising young and securing the environment. He argues that improved technologies such as tool use emerged as a solution to the problem of 'time given up to unproductive social activity'. He states: 'if an animal spends all morning in non-productive socialising, he must be at least twice as efficient a producer in the afternoon'. Hence, the evolutionary advancement of technology in great apes and hominids was a consequence rather than a primary cause of evolving social cognition.

This new focus on social adaptation as the engine driving primate brain evolution and intelligence represented a departure from existing theories. According to Byrne and Whiten (1988), the two major alternative hypotheses are that the brain/intelligence (a) 'evolved in response to an increasing technological sophistication of tools' and (b) 'evolved to deal with the spatial memory problem of finding widely dispersed, ephemeral, but predictable food resources'. Of course, Tim Crow's (1997) hypothesis regarding the origins of language represents a third alternative – namely that the emergence of language constituted the driving force for brain evolution and intelligence in ancestral humans. As we shall see, all three factors undeniably played a role in primate brain evolution and the emergence of intelligence, but the social brain hypothesis has more support and in fact subsumes these other factors within a broad version of the theory.

Until Jane Goodall first reported tool use in chimpanzees to a disbelieving scientific community in 1963, it was assumed that Benjamin Franklin's phrase, 'Man the Tool-maker' encapsulated the essence of human uniqueness. As Richard Byrne (1999) explains, several non-human species are known to *use* tools (such as sea otters and Galapagos woodpecker finches), but only the great apes have been observed to *make* tools to solve problems. As Humphrey (1976) suggested, tool manufacture may have arisen as a means of maximizing productivity so as to accommodate non-productive time spent on social activity. In terms of spatial memory requirements and brain evolution, most species of monkey and ape show remarkable ability to remember the seasonality and location of tropical forest trees that often fruit unpredictably on non-annual cycles (Milton 1981). Undoubtedly, this feat requires enormous cognitive capacity; and this is confirmed by neuroanatomical studies that demonstrate generalized neural networks underpinning visuospatial memory in primates, rather than specialized domains (as exist for the same task in various bird species). This great expansion in memory capacity served another purpose though – the management of social relationships – and it may well be that this latter requirement constituted the major selective pressure driving cognitive and intellectual evolution.

THE EVOLUTION OF SOCIAL COGNITION IN PRIMATES

In the introductory chapter of this book, I referred to the evolutionary method known as 'cladistic analysis' and briefly alluded to evolutionary psychologist Richard Byrne's argument that in this method we have a means of exploring the probable cognitive status of extinct ancestral species. Regarding human ancestors, this method requires us to consider traits shared by closely related extant or living primate species that form a 'clade'.[2] So, for example, the last common ancestor (LCA) of modern

104

humans and chimpanzees is estimated from mitochondrial DNA analyses to have lived approximately five million years ago (mya); the LCA of chimps, gorillas and humans lived approximately eight mya; the LCA of all living great apes (humans, chimps, gorillas and orang-utans) lived approximately sixteen mya; the LCA of monkeys and great apes lived approximately forty mya; and the LCA of all primates (great apes, monkeys and prosimians) lived approximately sixty mya (see Figure 6.1). Thus, comparing traits among living species within a clade allows us to make some predictions about the corresponding traits that manifest in the LCA. So, if we want to speculate about the likely social cognitive abilities of species ancestral to *Homo sapiens*, it follows that we should consider the social repertoire of living relatives, making use of the cladistic method. This exercise enables us to construct a likely evolutionary phylogeny of social cognition in primates.

Most species of primate show evidence of some degree of social skill beyond that of the majority of non-primate species. Obviously, there are exceptions but there is no other order besides primates where social skill is such a pervasive trait across all species within that order (except perhaps for cetaceans – whales, dolphins, etc. – and this is a case of parallel evolution). Alison Jolly has studied prosimian lemurs in Madagascar and concluded that these earliest primate relatives of modern humans (the LCA was approximately 60 mya) recognize and 'differently respond to other individuals as kin, friends, or menaces, and to some extent seem to predict others' behaviour' (Jolly 1966). However, prosimians fall short of complex three- and four-part social interactions. Thus, we can assume that by 60 mya, the first primates had evolved basic social skills allowing them to discriminate between kin and nonkin, friend and foe, and to react adaptively according to this recognition. Experts agree that these simple skills required little more than good learning and memory capability.

By contrast, anthropoidea (monkeys and apes) demonstrate a whole range of complex social behaviours including three- and four-part interactions and the calculation of other's knowledge and desires. Byrne (1999) includes the following social skills within the repertoire of monkeys and apes:

- They use alliances and cooperation extensively, when directly competing for resources (Harcourt 1988).
- They acquire dominance ranks on the basis of support given by others, particularly kin (Chapais 1992).
- They show long-lasting 'friendships' which predict the distribution of mutual help (Cheney et al. 1986; Smuts 1983, 1985).
- They devote considerable time and effort to others, in Old World species principally via social grooming (Dunbar 1988), using this as a way of building up friendships with potentially useful individuals (Seyfarth & Cheney 1984).

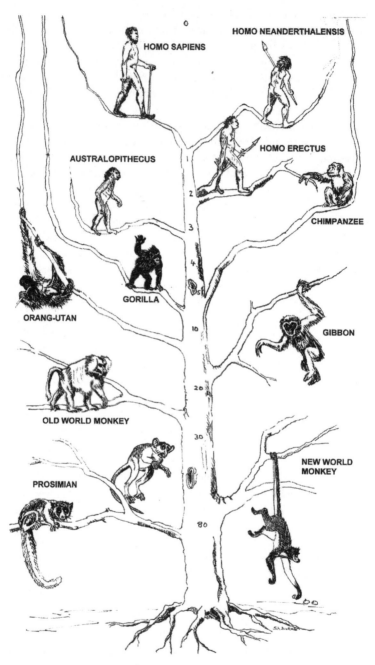

Figure 6.1 The primate family tree. In millions of years before the present. (Original drawing by Sarah Burns.)

- When friendships are perturbed by conflict, some species repair these relationships by targeted reconciliation after conflict (Cords 1997; de Waal & van Roosmalen 1979).
- They show knowledge of the personal characteristics and affiliations of other members of the social group (Cheney & Seyfarth 1990).
- They use techniques of social manipulation, to gain personal ends while minimizing social disruption, including deception (Byrne & Whiten 1985, 1992; Whiten and Byrne 1988).

The LCA of New World monkeys and humans lived approximately 40 mya, while that of Old World monkeys and humans lived approximately 30 mya. This means that complex social skills such as remembering and orchestrating alliances, engaging in reconciliation behaviour and making use of tactical deception had evolved in primate ancestors between 30 and 40 mya. A number of authors have argued that these skills could be explained solely on the basis of learning and adequate working memory capacity (Byrne 1997; Byrne & Whiten 1990, 1992); however others disagree. Byrne and Whiten (1988) suggest that this level of social manipulation might be regarded as 'the first rocket-stage' of Machiavellian intelligence; the second rocket-stage emerged within hominids (apes and humans) several million years later. In his discussion of 'Machiavellian intelligence', Byrne (1999) attributes the first use of the term to Frans de Waal in his 1982 volume *Chimpanzee Politics*. In his book, de Waal compared the political strategizing and manipulative tactics of Niccolo Machiavelli – in his 1532 book *The Prince* – with the social manoeuvring of chimpanzees (de Waal 1982). In advice given to an aspiring prince, Machiavelli (1532/1979) states: '(It) is useful, for example, to appear merciful, trustworthy, humane, blameless, religious – and to be so – yet to be in such measure prepared in mind that if you need to be not so, you can and do change to the contrary'.

Various authors have argued for the existence of a theory of mind (TOM) or elements of TOM in the great apes (Premack & Woodruff 1978; Russon 1999; van Schaik et al. 1996). This claim has proved to be one of the most controversial topics in cognitive ethology with as many authors arguing against TOM in non-human primates as those supporting the claim (for reviews of this debate see Premack 1988; Tomasello & Call 1997). Richard Byrne, who has researched primate social cognition in depth, argues that apes demonstrate the ability to represent 'thoughts' in mind in the absence of a direct stimulus, an ability not found in other primates (Byrne 1999). He terms this 'representational intelligence' and cites complex tool use by chimps (McGrew 1992) and orang-utans (van Schaik & van Hoof 1996), ability to perform false belief tasks (Byrne & Whiten 1991), complex political dynamics (de Waal 1982, 2000), and the ability to attribute causality (Limongelli et al. 1995) as examples of representational intelligence. He estimates that the origin of this further step in the evolution of mind dates from approximately 16–13 mya when orang-utan ancestors (such as Sivap-ithecus) split off from the African apes, and was complete by 5 mya when human ancestors split from those of the chimpanzees. He suggests that the biological basis for this cognitive step was an organizational change in the brain, allowing for increased flexibility. He also suggests that the selective pressure for such change in the apes was the need to evolve complex new strategies for food acquisition in order to compete with monkeys who were better adapted for tree climbing. These new strategies include tool use to extract embedded foods (Parker 1996; Parker & Gibson 1977) and novel ways of manipulating nutritious plant foods; for example, nut cracking (Byrne & Russon 1998) (see Figure 6.2).

Figure 6.2 Common chimpanzee cracking nuts in the Bossou forest, Guinea. (Original drawing by Sarah Burns.)

On the other hand, Baron-Cohen (1999) argues that our LCA with chimps, 5 mya, could only have possessed immature elements of a TOM. His evidence comes from TOM tests in apes that showed only a limited ability to attribute mental states and intentionality to others (Povinelli & Eddy 1996; Premack 1988). He suggests that our common ancestor may have possessed an 'intentionality detector module' and an 'eye detector module', both of which are apparent in chimps. He puts the time frame for the evolution of a full TOM at approximately. 150–40,000 years ago, supported by archaeological records, which show the earliest fictional art and symbolic adornments dating from that period (Henshilwood et al. 2002; Mithen 1996).

Suddendorf agrees, putting the emergence of the 'metamind', which is first evident during a child's fourth year, at approximately 2 million to 100,000 years ago, as evidenced by the complex Acheulian tool culture of *Homo ergaster/Homo erectus* (Suddendorf 1999; Suddendorf & Corballis 1997). Unlike the Oldowan tradition of *Homo habilis* that predated this epoch and was within the scope of modern chimpanzee tool culture, the Acheulian tools required planning, precision and a concept of the future, and implied cultural learning.

Finally, Whiten (1999) argues that hominids evolved a 'deep social mind' as a 'cognitive niche' (Tooby & deVore 1987) in order to compete for food with better-adapted monkeys in the trees and carnivores on the savannah during the Pleistocene period. This cognitive advance, which is probably synonymous with Byrne's TOM and Suddendorf's metamind, resulted from social interdependence and involved the refinement of cooperative behaviour, cultural and social learning and transmission, and mind-reading ability. Thus, most commentators seem to agree that complex mind-reading ability originated in hominoid ancestors between 16 mya and 5 mya, accelerating to a full TOM in the human line between 150,000 and 40,000 years ago (see Table 6.1).

EVOLUTION OF BRAIN SIZE IN PRIMATES – IS BIGGER BETTER?

Having traced the evolution of mind-reading or TOM ability in primates, we now come to the question of what lies behind this emergence of social cognition in terms of brain changes in our ancestors over the last 30 million years. This question has proved to be somewhat controversial, often evoking heated and even acrimonious debate in the pages of journals and books. For many years opinion was divided into two basic camps – those who argued that cognitive and intellectual evolution can be attributed to a steady *increase in the size* of the brain; and those who maintained that superior cognition emerged as a consequence of *increasing complexity* in brain

Table 6.1 Table illustrating the stages in the evolution of brain and cognition NB: IBNS (increasing brain and neocortex size); TOM (theory of mind); FT (fronto-temporal); FP (frontoparietal)

	Species	Anatomical changes	Cognitive changes	Evidence
100 thousand years ago	H. sapiens	IBNS + complex FT and FP connectivity	Full TOM	– Complex social cognition – Culture, religion, etc.
2	H. erectus/ ergaster	IBNS + evolving connectivity	'Metamind'	– Acheulian tool culture – Symbolic art
5	H. habilis Australopithecus	IBNS + evolving connectivity		– Oldowan tool culture
15	Great Apes	IBNS + evolving connectivity	'Representational Intelligence' and early TOM	– Complex tool use – Attribute causality – TOM tasks
30	Old and New World Monkeys	IBNS	Increasing memory and social skills	– Group relations – Finding fruit
40 million years ago				

structure and organization. Within these camps one found some diversity of focus. For example, regarding brain size, some authors focused on regional enlargement (e.g. relative cortex size, relative prefrontal cortex size, etc.) rather than gross brain expansion. In recent years most authors would now agree that both parties are correct: during primate evolution, the massive advances in cognitive ability have related to *both increasing size and complexity of the brain.* Furthermore, size increase and complexity are in some cases interdependent factors; in other words, one factor is sometimes due to the other. As Striedter (2005) explains: 'Since at least some of those organizational changes are causally linked to changes in brain size, an old debate about whether human brains changed mainly in size or in organization (see Holloway, 1974) turns out to have been moot: They have changed in both. Just like the brains of other vertebrates, human brains are special in a multitude of different but causally entangled ways.'

Contrary to popular belief, humans do not have the biggest brains – several species such as elephants and whales have larger brains (elephants up to 5.7 kg and some whales as large as 10 kg). Clearly, the main factor determining increased brain size is an increase in body size. However, Jerison (1973) has shown that within vertebrates the increase in brain size does not strictly parallel the increase in body size, so that smaller animals actually have greater brain:body ratios than larger animals – a phenomenon called 'negative brain allometry'. Furthermore, among mammals, primates and cetaceans have relatively larger brains than other orders. Obviously, body size alone cannot be the sole determining factor of brain size. Roth suggests (2001, Ch. 19: 570): 'Thus, during the evolution of birds and mammals and more specifically of cetaceans and primates, genetic and epigenetic systems controlling brain size have undergone substantial changes in favour of relatively larger brains. These changes resulted in enlargements of brains beyond that associated with body size . . .'

Jerison developed the so-called *encephalization quotient* (EQ) as an attempt to quantify this brain enlargement 'beyond that associated with body size' (Jerison 1973). EQ indicates 'the ratio between the actual relative brain size of a group of animals to the relative brain size as expected on the basis of brain allometry determined by body size alone' (Roth 2001). Putting it simply, the higher the EQ for a species, the greater other factors (besides pure body size) play a role in brain enlargement. Thus, one finds that the EQ for humans is about seven times larger than that of an average mammal and about three times larger than that of the chimpanzee.

Turning now to hominid ancestors, we can use cladistic methods to show that an increase in relative brain size commenced in the common ancestor of Old and New World monkeys and hominoids approximately 35–40 mya. As discussed earlier in this chapter, several authors have argued that this relative increase in brain volume occurred under the selective pressures of increased social complexity as a result of group living (Byrne & Whiten 1988; Chance & Mead 1953). One way to test this hypothesis is to compare EQ measures for different species against measures of social intelligence and it turns out that in fact EQ is not a good measure of social intelligence.

Robin Dunbar of the University of Liverpool developed an alternative measure of brain expansion, the *neocortex ratio* (NR) (Dunbar 1992). NR is the ratio of the size of the neocortex to the size of the remainder of the brain and in non-human primates NR tends to correlate with absolute neocortical size. However, NR and neocortical size are not the same measure of intelligence since NR may decrease for a species if other parts of the brain are relatively enlarged (e.g. the gorilla has the largest neocortices of the non-human primates, but their NR is relatively small due to the disproportionately enlarged cerebellum of the gorilla) (Gibson et al. 2001). In a classic study, Dunbar attempted to compare NR in primates against social intelligence and showed a constant relationship between NR and group size – the latter being a crude measure of social complexity (i.e. the number of relationships the animal has to keep track of) (Dunbar 1992; 2001). On the other hand, NR does not correlate with simple measures of environmental complexity such as the relative size of the home range (Byrne 1999). Interestingly, NR does correlate with rates of tactical deception in non-human primates (Byrne 1996), 'supporting the interpretation that brain enlargement is required for the efficient memory needed to manage complex social interactions' (Byrne 1999). Kudo and Dunbar have suggested that there may be a number of ways in which neocortex size constrains group size. For example:

> (T)he constraint might lie in the number of other group members with whom an individual can maintain a coherent relationship (and this might include being able to monitor relationships between third parties). Alternatively, the extent to which an animal can manage a large number of relationships may be related to the kinds of subtle social strategies that it can bring into play, and this in turn may be constrained by neocortex size . . . A third possibility arises from the fact that coalitions are a peculiarly characteristic feature of primate societies (Harcourt 1992): the constraint may therefore lie with the number of other individuals with whom an animal can maintain a special relationship.
>
> (Kudo & Dunbar 2001)

Thus, NR seems to be a useful measure of social intelligence although there are some limitations on its use in this regard. For example, Byrne has pointed out that apes do not have an increase in NR relative to monkeys, yet apes show increased cognitive abilities (Byrne 2001). He also notes the smaller group size in some apes (e.g. single or mother–child pair in orangutans) and argues against the extrapolation of Dunbar's hypothesis to the hominoid super-family. Furthermore, measures of social intelligence such as tactical deception can be misleading since:

> . . . as delineated by Byrne (1996), deception can entail greater or lesser degrees of understanding of the minds of the deceived on the part of the deceiver. Baboons, who have large neocortical ratios and high rates of deception, nonetheless appear to have lesser degrees of understanding of others minds than do the great apes (Byrne 1996) . . . Hence, neocortical ratio does not predict mental differences between apes and monkeys.
>
> (Gibson et al. 2001)

In addition, as Gibson et al. (2001) point out, increasing NR implies a reduction in the relative contribution of other neural structures, such as the cerebellum, hippocampus and amygdala to total brain volume. And yet we know that these structures contribute greatly to higher cognitive functions such as memory and learning. 'Moreover,' these authors argue, 'the neocortex does not function in isolation, but rather as part of several major neural circuits involving both cortical and subcortical structures'.

Recent developments in neuroimaging techniques have enabled researchers to further enlighten the controversial topic of evolving brain size in primate ancestors. For example, Katrina Semendeferi has analysed data from *in vivo* MRI scans of the primate brain (collected by James K. Rilling and Thomas R. Insel at Yerkes Regional Primate Centre) and has demonstrated that, with increasing brain size, the frontal lobe does not increase relative to total hemispheric size in hominoids (Semendeferi 2001; Semendeferi et al. 1997; Semendeferi et al. 2002). Likewise, the parieto-occipital lobes enlarge consistently relative to total hemispheric size. However, the relative temporal lobe size (relative to whole brain size) is greater in humans than in apes (Rilling & Seligman 2002). Interestingly, the size of the cerebellum is progressively reduced (with significance) as one moves from the phylogenetically older apes to humans (Rilling & Insel 1998; Semendeferi & Damasio 2000).

The observation that the frontal lobes are not relatively larger in humans is not new. Von Bonin first described this in 1948 (Von Bonin 1948, 1950) and later Holloway (1966, 1968, 1975) reiterated this in a number of papers. Holloway has challenged the popular supposition that size alone correlates with cognitive ability. He cites as evidence the case of microcephalics who do obtain some language ability; as well as the extensive variation in brain volume (without variation in cognition) noted in both fossil hominids and modern humans. More recently Aboitiz has proposed that increasing brain size only produces increases in processing capacity if accompanied by significant connectional rearrangements (Aboitiz 1996). Clearly, size is important as a number of authors have argued (Falk 1985; Gibson et al. 2001; Jerison 1973), but in the tradition of Holloway, I would maintain that size increase alone is insufficient to account for the social cognitive advances during human descent.

CORTICAL REORGANIZATION AND CONNECTIVITY IN EVOLUTION

As discussed previously, we know that humans are genetically very close to the African apes (98.5 per cent of the genome is identical (Allen & Sarich 1988)) and especially close to the two species of chimpanzees (Waddell & Penny 1996). Therefore, human cognitive advances are only 5–6 million years old, the date of our last common ancestor, which is very quick by evolutionary standards. Mesulam (2000) argues that increased brain size alone could not accommodate and explain adequately the enormous cognitive advances that occurred during this short period. He argues that it was the evolution of cerebral connectivity that allowed for the huge leaps forward.

Holloway (1966, 1967, 1975, 1995, 1996) is generally cited as the first author to seriously raise the argument that evolutionary changes in cognition reflect reorganization of systems internal to the brain rather than increased brain size as championed by Jerison (1973). Drawing upon both endocast analyses and archaeological evidence of complex cognitive skills in *Australopithecines*, Holloway (1975) suggested that reorganization dates to at least 2.5–3 mya and, in his 1973 James Arthur Lecture, he tied the role of social behaviour into a theory of human brain evolution.

More recently, Hofman (1989) demonstrated, what in my view is a fact of major importance in our understanding of human brain evolution, that in hominoids it is *white matter that increases* substantially (relative to brain size) rather than grey matter; and latterly this has been confirmed using MRI (Rilling & Insel 1999a; Semendeferi et al. 1994). Furthermore, it is specifically *intra-hemispheric connectivity* that increases disproportionate to increasing brain size and neocortical surface area (Rilling & Insel 1999b). Conversely, *inter-hemispheric connectivity*, as expressed by the cross-sectional area of the corpus callosum, decreases with increasing brain size. (This in turn suggests that Crow's (1995b) reliance on the corpus callosum in his cerebral asymmetry hypothesis is flawed – a subject I address later in this chapter.)

This leads me to consider comparative primate data, as well as fossil evidence, regarding the specific frontotemporal (FT) and frontoparietal (FP) interconnected regions I identified in the previous chapter as constituting the social brain in *Homo sapiens*. Extrapolating from the insights of Hofman (1989) and Rilling and Insel (1999b), one might anticipate that these major *intrahemispheric* circuits have been subject to significant evolutionary change in the hominid line. So, if we examine comparative primate as well as fossil data, we could expect to find evidence for major evolutionary change in prefrontal, temporal and parietal interconnected cortical circuits. Is this the case?

I am encouraged in this task by the findings of Rilling and Seligman (2002) regarding temporal lobe evolution in primates. They scanned 11 species of anthropoid primates using MRI and found that the human temporal lobes were larger than expected for brain size, and that the departure from allometry was most pronounced for the white matter of the temporal lobes. This is particularly noteworthy, as it implies selection for deviation from typical rules of brain growth in anthropoids. The authors note that each of the four main functional subdivisions of the primate temporal lobe projects heavily to the PFC, and they suggest that a possible interpretation of their finding of 'the disproportionate size of the human temporal lobe white matter' is that this 'reflects an augmented number of connections linking temporal and prefrontal cortex' (Rilling & Seligman 2002). (They

114

further speculate that this augmentation may relate to the evolution of language.) This statement is supported by a very recent study by Schoenemann et al. (2005) who demonstrated disproportionately larger white matter volume (than grey) in the prefrontal cortex (PFC) of humans compared with non-human primates.

Thus, we may conclude from these two studies that interconnected temporal and prefrontal cortical white matter was indeed subject to major evolutionary expansion during hominoid descent. With the advent of new imaging techniques such as DT-MRI (which is explained in Chapter 8), it is feasible that these connections might be examined in greater detail in hominoids, giving us a clearer understanding of the evolution of FT and FP white matter tracts such as the *uncinate fasciculus*, the *arcuate fasciculus* and the *anterior cingulum*.[3]

Another strategy one can apply in furthering our understanding of the evolution of FT and FP circuits is to examine comparative data on individual regions comprising the prefrontal, temporal and parietal cortices. These regions include the anterior cingulate cortex (ACC), the orbitofrontal cortex (OFC), the amygdala and the parietal association cortex (PAC) – in fact the same regions that I argued in Chapter 5 comprise the social brain in our species.

THE EVOLUTION OF THE SOCIAL BRAIN IN PRIMATES

ACC circuits

The first region of the social brain I wish to consider then is the ACC and its connections. There is recent evidence from a comparative primate study that the ACC evolved a unique type of projection neuron in the hominoid clade (Hof et al. 2001; Nimchinsky et al. 1999). This large spindle-shaped cell that is characterized by immunoreactivity to the calcium-binding protein, calretinin, is unique to hominoids and increases in density as one compares the ACC of the orang-utan with that of the gorilla, with that of the chimpanzee and finally is greatest in humans. The authors note that these specialized neurons are not detected in areas of the ACC involved in somatic motor function. Rather, they are located posteriorly and dorsally and 'might represent a population of specialized neurons that could integrate inputs with emotional overtones and project to highly specific motor centres controlling vocalization, facial expression, or autonomic function' (Nimchinsky et al. 1999). Nimchinsky et al. argue that this indicates that the ACC experienced strong adaptive pressure related to communication during the past 16 million years of primate evolution. They conclude that the ACC plays a significant role in recently evolved cognitive processes including self-awareness, attention, emotional control and communication.

OFC circuits

The second, region of the social brain I wish to consider is the OFC. A comparison of the macroscopic and microscopic morphology of the OFC in great apes supports both the notion that this region is implicated in social cognition and my argument that it has been subject to reorganization in hominoids. Semendeferi compared Brodmann areas 10 and 13 across hominoids and demonstrated that area 13 is significantly smaller in orang-utans than in gorillas and chimpanzees (and humans) (Semendeferi 1994; Semendeferi et al. 2001). Area 13 lies posteriorly and medially in the OFC and is considered to be part of a circuit connecting to the limbic temporal lobe that is relevant to emotion, particularly related to social stimuli. As mentioned previously, ablation of this area in wild monkeys results in significant reductions and losses of behaviours that are considered important for the maintenance of social bonds (Kling & Steklis 1976). Furthermore, in terms of the cytoarchitecture of area 13, Semendeferi has demonstrated a marked decrease in cortical cell density in the orang-utan relative to the African hominoids, especially in infragranular layers V and VI (which have connections with subcortical limbic structures). Thus, it appears that there is decreased representation of the 'limbic' OFC in the orang-utan, a phylogenetically more distant species. She suggests that this region is important for the survival of members of complex social groups and speculates that the relative immaturity of the frontal limbic cortex in orang-utans may relate to the more solitary lifestyle and less complex social organization of this primate compared with its African cousins (Semendeferi 1999; van Schaik & van Hoof 1996). Further speculation might suggest that the OFC has, like the ACC, experienced strong adaptive pressures related to social living during the course of hominoid evolution.

Amygdala circuits

As discussed in Chapter 5, the primate amygdala contains neurons that respond selectively to facial expression and eye gaze, and when surgical lesions are placed in this structure, the animal fails to evaluate new stimuli and puts itself at risk. This is a clear example of a brain structure that has evolved in relation to social demands on the individual. Obviously, the fear response is a very primitive adaptation and comparative studies have confirmed that the amygdala is present in most vertebrate species. However, when the amygdala is divided into its component nuclei, there is evidence of extensive variation in mammals including primates. Barton and Aggleton (2000) have compared amygdaloid nuclei across 43 species of primates and shown that the relative size of the corticobasolateral (CBL) nucleus is significantly greater in primates than in insectivores, and among primates is significantly greater in apes and monkeys than in prosimians. This is complemented by histological evidence for increasing organization of this nucleus during phylogeny (Pitkånen & Kemppainen 2002). Barton and Aggleton (2000) also found that CBL size correlates with neocortex size as well as social group size in monkeys and apes, suggesting that this nucleus and its connections with higher cortical regions were subject to social selective pressures. The CBL has been shown to have far more widespread cortical connections in monkeys than in cats (Young et al. 1994) and has extensive reciprocal connections with the OFC (via the *uncinate fasciculus*) and the STG. Barton and Aggleton conclude that this amygdaloid nucleus has experienced disproportionate enlargement and connectedness in higher primates as part of a recently evolved network regulating social cognition.

PAC circuits

Preuss has pointed out that the frontal, temporal and parietal association cortices account for most of the increased brain area in humans compared with apes (Preuss 2000). In humans the primary visual cortex (V1, BA 17) is displaced posteriorly, being approximately 121 per cent *less* than its allometrically expected size, thus allowing for the greater expansion of the parietal association cortex (PAC) (Holloway 1995). According to Holloway, endocasts from two *Australopithecine* fossils (the Taung specimen and Hadar AL 162–28) reveal an intermediate position of the lunate sulcus, between that of the human and that of the chimpanzee, suggesting that the PAC was significantly enlarged and reorganized as early as three mya (Holloway 1972, 1975, 1983a, 1984, 1985). The lunate sulcus separates the primary visual cortex from the PAC, is notoriously difficult to identify on endocasts, and thus its position in these specimens is a point of controversy in physical anthropology (see Falk 1980, 1985, 1986 for opposing viewpoint). Controversy aside, it is clear that the PAC has enlarged and reorganized significantly during hominid descent. Comparative primate studies support this also. For example, functional imaging suggests that the human intraparietal cortex (IPC) contains visuospatial processing areas that are not present in monkeys (Vanduffel et al. 2002). Regarding the IPC specifically, Gilissen has scanned chimps using MRI and shown that this structure is more symmetrical in chimps than in humans (Gilissen 2001). While there is some right-greater-than-left asymmetry of the IPC in chimps, it does not compare with the marked asymmetry in humans, suggesting that the human right IPC (a notable component of the social brain) has enlarged disproportionately in the human line.

In summary, therefore, there is good evidence that the social brain has evolved markedly in hominids, through a process of brain reorganization and increasing intra-hemispheric white matter connections linking the PFC to the temporal and parietal association cortices. Conversely, inter-hemispheric connectivity has diminished during hominoid phylogeny, posing a serious problem for Crow's asymmetry hypothesis.

CEREBRAL ASYMMETRY AND LANGUAGE

The study of cerebral asymmetry and the evolution of language has old origins, and the literature and controversies are manifold and are certainly beyond the scope of this book. Of relevance to my hypothesis, however, are two issues: first, Crow (2002) has founded his evolutionary hypothesis of schizophrenia upon the premise that both asymmetry and language have recent origins and are associated with a speciation event in modern *Homo sapiens* (see also Chapter 3 for a discussion of speciation); And second, in the study of schizophrenia, abnormalities of both cerebral asymmetry and language are well recognized (Crow 1990; De Lisi 2001; Luchins et al. 1979). In terms of my thesis, I would argue that human cerebral asymmetry has ancient origins within the hominoid lineage and that it represents an aspect of brain reorganization as suggested by Holloway and de la Costelareymondie (1982) and Holloway (1983b). Several authors have argued that leftward brain asymmetries may have evolved as a consequence of reduced interhemispheric connectivity and the increase in more efficient localized networks in each hemisphere (Rilling & Insel 1999b; Hopkins & Rilling 2000). For example, Hopkins and Rilling (2000) report a study they conducted using MRI in 45 primates, including New and Old World monkeys, lesser apes, great apes and humans. They compared measures of asymmetry against measures of the corpus callosum (CC) relative to brain size. Their findings indicated an inverse relationship between asymmetry and relative CC size, so that species showing marked asymmetry had smaller relative CC size. They argue that as brains enlarged during primate evolution and became increasingly organized:

> ... inter-hemispheric connections became longer and slower and it became more efficient to process information in small local networks with shorter axons. Therefore, long-distance axonal projections, including inter-hemispheric connections via the CC, were pruned in larger brains. This had the effect of confining certain functions to a single hemisphere that had previously been bilaterally distributed. In other words, increased laterality of function may have been an emergent property accompanying brain enlargement in primate evolution.
>
> (Hopkins & Rilling 2000)

Le May's work on cortical petalias[4] (Le May 1976; Le May et al. 1982) boosted the study of cerebral asymmetry in primates and linked it to handedness. These (Le May et al. 1982) and other authors (Geshwind & Galaburda 1984) have found petalia asymmetries in pongids similar to the human pattern, while Holloway and de la Costelareymondie argue, on the basis of their examination of 190 hominoid endocasts, that the human petalia pattern is specific to both modern and fossil hominids (e.g. *Homo habilis* and *Homo erectus*) (Holloway & de la Costelareymondie 1982).

However, when it comes to specific structures within the language networks, the evidence for very early origins of lateralization/asymmetry is quite convincing. While the fossil record has yielded only one specimen that shows evidence of a modern human-like Broca's speech area (the KNM-ER 1470 habiline) (Holloway 1976), comparative data in extant primates offers more clarity. For example, in their seminal paper, Gannon et al. (1998a) reported in *Science* their discovery of marked asymmetry in the chimpanzee planum temporale (PT) – a key site in Wernicke's posterior language area. They found that the left PT was significantly larger in 94 per cent (17 of 18) of chimpanzee brains examined post-mortem and they state: 'The evolutionary origin of human language may have been founded on this basal anatomic substrate, which was already lateralized to the left hemisphere in the common ancestor of chimpanzees and humans 8 million years ago' (Gannon et al. 1998a).

A number of further studies, one post-mortem (Gannon et al. 1998b) and three using MRI to image the brains of a variety of sedated primates (Cantalupo et al. 2003; Hopkins et al. 1998; Hopkins et al. 2000), confirm the asymmetry of both the PT and Heschl's gyrus as well as the insular region of the sylvian fissure in the great apes but not in monkeys. Another study by Cantalupo and Hopkins, reported in *Nature*, demonstrates left-right asymmetry of Broca's 'language' area (Brodmann's area 44) in three great ape species, *Pan troglodytes, Pan paniscus* and *Gorilla gorilla* (Cantalupo & Hopkins 2001). It should be noted that at least one histological study (Buxhoeveden 2001) has confirmed that there are some human specific features of PT asymmetry architecture.

Gannon et al. (2001) argue that these findings set the date for the origins of a lateralized 'proto-linguistic' area in great apes and humans, at approximately 16–18 mya, just after the gibbon ancestor diverged from that of the other hominoids. Furthermore, they argue for a polymodal role for the PT in a connectionist model of 'language' perception. In other words, a diffuse network of lateralized neuronal connections corresponding to the left PT and related association areas constitute a region underlying communicative skills in great apes and humans. These authors cite the following findings in support of their argument:

- The complex communicative skills of great apes, including both referential and intentional gesturing and vocalization (Corballis 1992) and their use of sign language (Savage-Rumbaugh 1990; Savage-Rumbaugh et al. 1978; Shapiro 1982; Shapiro & Galdikas 1999).

- Evidence from functional imaging of deaf-from-birth humans that signing activates classic left hemisphere language areas (Neville et al. 1998).
- Auditory hallucinations in psychotic individuals activate language areas without discernible motor or audible components (Suzuki et al. 1993).

Notably, there are strong arguments from 'neural network theory' against Chomsky's idea of a domain-specific, innate 'human language organ' (Chomsky 1972), and in favour of 'broadly distributed, domain-general neural systems' that subserve complex communication in humans and great apes (Bates & Elman 2000). Thus, my conclusions regarding language are that: cerebral asymmetry and 'language areas' began to evolve 16–18 mya as a part of emerging cortical reorganization and are found in all extant great ape species; these areas are diffuse and involve connectivity rather than localized domains; they represent regions involved in complex communication rather than pure language; and finally, that these findings do not support Crow's hypothesis that asymmetry and language evolved suddenly with a speciation event marking a saltational leap to *Homo sapiens*. When one examines the anatomical and fossil evidence concerning the emergence of communication and language in hominoid ancestors, one can only conclude that these sophisticated cognitive abilities have a long and gradual history with their origins represented in the first gestural hand movements of the earliest bipedal apes.

CONCLUSION

In this chapter I have presented evidence supporting my claim that the human brain evolved in response to a social selective pressure to manage and succeed at living in sophisticated social groups. Throughout the course of primate evolution, we have observed the need to store important information regarding other individuals, the need to foster alliances and strategize political behaviours, the absolute imperative of detecting, interpreting and responding to social signals and the adaptive significance of such abilities as tactical deception and reconciliative behaviour. In apes we have seen the emergence of primitive forms of mind-reading or TOM ability, which in turn only matured into its complete form with the advent of modern *Homo sapiens*. The use of cladistic methods as well as the hominid fossil record has enabled us to trace the evolution of the social brain in hominoids.

I believe, and I hope I have convinced the reader, that the most striking feature of recent brain evolution in our ancestors is the rapid expansion of structures and circuits comprising the social brain. Certainly, the brain has enlarged mightily in overall size and also in terms of specific regional size (e.g. the prefrontal cortex). However, as Holloway has insisted for decades, the cognitive superiority of modern humans has more to do with brain reorganization than mere enlargement. The evidence supports my thesis that frontotemporal and frontoparietal cortical regions and circuits were subject to marked increase in size and connectivity during the last 15 million years of hominoid evolution. 'Driven' by escalating pressure to succeed in the increasingly complex social environment they occupied, human ancestors evolved highly connected brains – which today we call the social brain. Darwin himself was astute enough to recognize the significance of what he termed 'the social instinct' in the genesis of modern humanity:

> Under circumstances of extreme peril, as during a fire, when a man endeavours to save a fellow-creature without a moment's hesitation, he can hardly feel pleasure; and still less has he time to reflect on the dissatisfaction which he might subsequently experience if he did not make the attempt. Should he afterwards reflect over his own conduct, he would feel that there lies within him an impulsive power widely different from a search after pleasure or happiness; and this seems to be the deeply planted social instinct ... Such actions as the above appear to be the simple result of the greater strength of the social or maternal instincts rather than that of any other instinct or motive; for they are performed too instantaneously for reflection, or for pleasure or pain to be felt at the time; though, if prevented by any cause, distress or even misery might be felt.
>
> (Darwin 1871)

7

SCHIZOPHRENIA AND THE
SOCIAL BRAIN

In the severer forms of schizophrenia the 'affective dementia' is the most striking symptom. In the sanatoria there are patients sitting around who for decades show no affect no matter what happens to them or to those about them. They are indifferent to maltreatment; left to themselves they lie in wet and frozen beds, do not bother about hunger and thirst. They have to be taken care of in all respects. Toward their own delusions they are often strikingly indifferent . . . Moreover the affective expressions are usually somewhat unnatural, exaggerated or theatrical. Consequently the joy of a schizophrenic does not transport us, and his expressions of pain leave us cold. This becomes especially plain if one has occasion to observe the reaction of little children to such expressions. Just as little do the patients sometimes react to our affects. Thus one speaks of a defect in the emotional rapport, which is an important sign of schizophrenia. One feels emotionally more in touch with an idiot who does not utter a word than with a schizophrenic who can still converse well intellectually but who is inwardly unapproachable.

(Bleuler 1923)

A SYMPTOMS APPROACH TO PSYCHOSIS

Since Eugene Bleuler, the socially disabling symptoms of schizophrenia such as withdrawal, emotional restriction and functional deterioration have aided clinicians in diagnosis, helping to differentiate the disorder from the affective disorders. In recent times this symptom cluster has been referred to as 'deficit symptoms' or 'negative symptoms'. And yet, until quite recently, the focus of research and treatment has been on hallucinations, delusions and disorganized thought and behaviour (so-called 'positive symptoms'). In this chapter I focus on what Bleuler termed the 'affective dementia' of schizophrenia – a 'psychological dementia' I believe he implied in the sense of the gross emotional and interpersonal detachment one experiences in an individual with schizophrenia (rather than an irreversible physiological impairment of the brain).[1] Social deficits or aberrations of social behaviour and functioning are also to be found in other mental disorders and I briefly address this topic. The heart of the chapter consists of a review of the substantial evidence for conceptualizing schizophrenia as a disorder of social brain anatomy and function. However, the story would not be complete without attending once again to the broader matter of the social brain and general psychopathology. Martin Brüne has argued that there is good support for including the entire continuum of functional psychosis within the definition of social brain disorders (see Brüne et al. 2003 for a review); and one might even have to concede that most forms of mental disorder involve impairments or disturbances of social brain functioning.

This is not entirely surprising if we cast our minds back to the discussion in Chapter 3 of the inadequacies of current psychiatric classification systems and the marked overlap of symptoms one witnesses in different disorders. The issue of classification has plagued psychiatry for more than a 100 years, and the present DSM system – which arose primarily as a research tool as well as a handy manual for managed care companies in America – represents a poor compromise rather than a good solution. The diversity of symptoms both within and without the psychoses, and their tendency to manifest across categorical diagnostic boundaries, has led some authors such as Bentall (2003) to advocate the complete abandonment of syndrome-based nomenclature. In *Madness Explained: psychosis and human nature*, Bentall argues for a symptom-oriented approach to mental distress and its treatment. Ever the psychologist, Bentall expresses his discomfort with this term 'because of the medical connotations of the word "symptom"' – he proposes that this new orientation might rather be considered as *post-Kraepelinian psychiatry*! Like others before him (e.g. Tim Crow), Bentall favours a dimensional rather than a categorical approach. He states:

> We should abandon psychiatric diagnoses altogether and instead try to explain and understand the actual experiences of psychotic people. By such experiences and behaviours I mean the kinds of things psychiatrists describe as symptoms, but which might be better labelled complaints, such as hallucinations, delusions and disordered speech . . . An advantage of this approach is that it does not require us to draw a clear dividing line between madness and sanity.
>
> (Bentall 2003)

Although no doubt this approach will have its detractors,[2] there is some support from various quarters within academic psychiatry (see Andreasen & Carpenter 1993 and Berner 1997 for reviews). This approach may well suit a dimensional approach to psychiatric disturbances better than the current categorical system. Likewise, as Bentall points out, focusing on symptoms allows us to accommodate the spectrum that, in reality, extends from madness to sanity (or perhaps better stated: from disorder to 'normality').

If one considers specific symptoms and symptom clusters, one certainly encounters overlap between various disorders as they are currently conceptualized. Kurt Schneider's classic first-rank symptoms of schizophrenia – which have largely been assimilated into DSM-IV – provide a classic example. 'Audible thoughts', 'voices arguing' and 'voices commenting on one's actions' are supposed to be pathognomonic of schizophrenia. However, it is common to find these kinds of voices experienced by patients with manic or depressive psychosis. Similarly, individuals suffering a psychotic illness induced by substances such as cannabis, cocaine or amphetamines, often report such hallucinations. Depersonalization and derealization phenomena are in our modern nomenclature attributed to dissociative disorders. And yet they are common to the early stages of schizophrenia (Spitzer et al. 1997). Joseph Parnas and Peter Handest of the University of Copenhagen quote a schizophrenic patient of theirs describing his sense of disembodiment as follows:

> I am no longer myself (. . .) I feel strange, I am no longer in my body, it is someone else; I sense my body but it is far away, some other place. Here are my legs, my hands, I can also feel my head, but cannot find it again. I hear my voice when I speak, but the voice seems to originate from some other place. Am I here or there? Am I here or behind? One might think that my person is no longer here (. . .) I walk like a machine; it seems to me that it is not me who is walking . . .
>
> (Parnas & Handest 2003)

A PHENOMENOLOGY OF SOCIAL ALIENATION IN SCHIZOPHRENIA

In Chapter 5, I introduced the philosophies of Martin Heidegger and Marcel Merleau-Ponty, which moved away from the Cartesian cogito towards a social and embodied concept of mind. I argued that the construction of a so-called 'philosophy of interpersonal relatedness' is much more in keeping with modern discoveries in neuroscience that point towards a dynamic two-way relationship between the brain and the outside world. The 'mind' of the individual emerges during development from the continuous interplay between innate inherited DNA and the highly social world around. It is therefore truly 'embedded' in the physical matter of the brain, body and social world. As Heidegger described it, the world exists a priori, or before, our human representation of it as thought, and is 'the necessary precedent and the enabling condition of thought' (Bracken 2002).

In Chapters 5 and 6, we saw that our human brain is primarily an organ adapted for social interrelationship – in its anatomical structure and its physiological functioning, the derived brain of modern *Homo sapiens* constitutes an ideal 'location' for the embodied mind. Perception, thought, emotion and memory are embedded and expressed in terms of bodily interaction with the physical and social world that is our environment. It is thus not surprising that disturbances of mental functioning manifest predominantly as disruptions to the normal sense of embodiment in and contact with the social world. And it is in schizophrenia perhaps that we witness the most radical alienation and expression of disembodiment from that social world.

Bleuler wrote of an 'affective dementia' in his patients at the Burghölzli near Zurich. He believed that schizophrenia 'is characterized by a specific kind of alteration of thinking and feeling, and of the relations with the outer world that occur nowhere else' (Bleuler 1923). Underneath the often obvious but also varied symptoms such as hallucinations and delusions, there existed, argued Bleuler, a less obvious inner unity. He characterized this unity in terms of four 'basic symptoms' – which are known to this day as Bleuler's 'A's'.

The *disturbances of association* are perhaps best known and find their modern day place in the DSM as 'disorganized speech'. Normal logicality and train of thought and speech is lost and incoherence results, which in its grossest form is termed 'formal thought disorder'. As Bleuler described it: 'The normal associative connections suffer in strength; any other kinds take their place. Thus links of association following one another in sequence may lack all relation to one another so that thinking becomes disconnected' (Bleuler 1923).

The second basic symptom is *affective disturbances* by which Bleuler meant the constricted, depthless, and often inappropriate expressions of feeling and emotion he observed in his patients. He wrote of the strange coincidence of a general 'character of indifference' with moments of 'over-sensitiveness' – where patients would display a 'temporary reduction of emotivity or contradictions in the interplay of the finer feelings'. Bleuler, a man who spent countless hours every day in the company of his patients, experiencing them directly and writing his observations in a notebook, had a deep appreciation of the quality of his patients' moods and affects. He is very clear in his description of disturbed affect that these aberrations reflected a *qualitative* rather than a *quantitative* change. He states:

> Under no conditions has the affectivity disappeared altogether. By touching on the complexes one can very often provoke, even in apparently very indifferent cases, lively and adequate reactions, and in the dereistic ideas of apparently vegetating patients one finds

fulfilments of active wishes and endeavours or even of fears; the analysis of schizophrenic delusions and logical mistakes shows that thinking is dominated more by the affects than it is in healthy people.

(Bleuler 1923)

Thus, in his description of this basic symptom, Bleuler had a specific meaning in mind that the schizophrenic affect differed (from normal) in terms of its quality as a means of expression and communication of inner states to others in the world around. This is a very important point for the following reason. I believe Bleuler's original meaning regarding affective disturbance in schizophrenia has been lost in contemporary constructs of the phenomenon as a 'negative' or 'deficit' symptom. In DSM language, 'affective disturbance or blunting' implies a *loss of or absence of affect and emotion* (author's emphasis). The very terms 'negative' and 'deficit symptoms' are, according to Sass and Parnas (2001), suggestive of 'the *absence* or *diminishment* of processes or phenomena that would normally be *present*'. Louis Sass, Professor of Psychology at Rutgers University, and Joseph Parnas, Professor of Psychiatry at the University of Copenhagen, have explored this issue in depth (Sass 1994, 2001; Sass & Parnas 2001, 2003) and trace this 'deficiency' concept of negative symptoms back to Hughlings Jackson.[3] Sass and Parnas state: 'negative behaviour signs are typically assumed to indicate a paucity of psychological activity or even a dimming of subjective life, perhaps especially of higher forms of consciousness or mental life' (Sass & Parnas 2001).

But recent research on subjective reports has proved this assumption erroneous. Patients judged by observers to have marked negative symptoms such as impoverished thoughts, avolition and restriction or blunting of affect, in fact, do not report having the subjective experiences of impoverished thoughts, volition and feeling (Selten 1995; Selten et al. 1998). And other research by the same authors reveals that there is no correlation between the level of distress actually experienced by schizophrenics with 'negative symptoms' and their observed severity; whereas, subjective and objective reports of negative symptoms are highly correlated in people with depression (Selten et al. 1998, 2000). Sass and Parnas (2001) draw on earlier work by Cutting and Dunne (1989) in concluding: 'Whereas depressive patients report a quantitative decline in energy, mental intensity, and the ability to think efficiently, schizophrenia patients typically report a qualitative alteration of thought and perception that is far more difficult to describe'.

Bleuler's third basic symptom was *ambivalence*. The patient with schizophrenia often experiences contrasting feelings, thoughts and volitional tendencies in the same moment. 'The schizophrenic defect of the associational paths makes it possible that contrasts that otherwise are mutually exclusive exist side by side in the psyche' (Bleuler 1923). Thus, patients may coincidently feel love and hatred towards someone – 'affective ambivalence'; 'they do what they do not want to do as well as what they want to do (ambivalence of the will)'; and may 'in the same moment . . . think, "I am a human being like you," and "I am not a human being like you"' – 'intellectual ambivalence' (Bleuler 1923: 382).

Finally, Bleuler regarded *autism* as a basic symptom of schizophrenia and used the term 'to describe detachment from outer reality and immersion in inner life' (Stanghellini 2001). Eugene Minkowski (1885–1972), a student of Bleuler's, defined schizophrenic autism as 'loss of vital contact with reality' (Minkowski 1926, 1927) and viewed it, not as a symptom, but as a global phenomenon investing the whole person. In his review of Minkowski's concept of autism, Stanghellini states:

> Autistic activity consists in the reduced capacity to interact with the external world. Autistic thought is characterized by its lack of communicative action. The pragmatic deviance of autistic language is a good example: The autistic person is not interested in communicating her inner world to others; language is not a means of communication which serves mutual understanding, a cooperative process whose aim is interlacing one's own world with that of others. The autistic person's use of language is much like a soliloquy, the monologue of the solitary thinker more focussed on expression – the outward portrayal of immanent contents of consciousness – than on dialogue – the exchange of meanings between speaker and listener. Moreover, each meaning is presented in its manifold profiles or adumbrations and the task of selecting the context-relevant meaning is left to the listener.
>
> (Stanghellini 2001)

In a fascinating (and well-worth reading) paper in the journal *Philosophy, Psychiatry and Psychology*, Sass (2001) reviews the phenomenological contributions to our understanding of schizophrenic autism of three twentieth-century thinkers: Eugene Minkowski, Wolfgang Blankenburg and Kimura Bin. Sass believes that although these individuals differ in their approach to schizophrenic consciousness, there are commonalities between them that illuminate a phenomenology of negative symptoms – thus dispelling Jaspers' pessimistic view that the essential strangeness of schizophrenia renders it beyond understanding or comprehension. All three phenomenologists (and Sass himself) reject popular models of schizophrenia that regard the disorder as either a deficit state – 'usually involving decline of one or more of the higher cognitive faculties widely considered to define the human essence' – or, in psychoanalytic circles as a 'regression to infantile forms of experience and as dominance of instinct over intellect or more sophisticated emotional attitudes' (Sass 2001).

127

According to Sass, Minkowski was greatly influenced by another of his teachers, the philosopher Henri Bergson, in developing his conception of schizophrenia. Bergson described a basic opposition between intellect and intuition – the former 'associated with analysis and abstract reason and with geometrical or spatial modes of experience (and) the latter based on, and fundamentally attuned with, the vitality and temporal dynamism of experience as it is actually lived' (Sass 2001). Minkowski viewed schizophrenia as a rupture between these two aspects of experience so that there is a loss of the 'primal sense of vitality or vital connectedness with the world, often accompanied by a hypertrophy of intellectual tendencies' (Sass 2001). This causes the world around to appear perplexing and it seems colourless, neutral or dull (Minkowski 1999). Although patients with schizophrenia are often perfectly aware of more objective aspects of reality – 'though they register and know' – they do not 'feel' the reality of what they experience (Minkowski 1999). As Sass (2001) explains, 'Such patients sense that they are not fully *present* in their actions and experiences: Although they may appear to behave just like other people, they have the sense that nothing is real'.

Clearly influenced by Minkowski, Sass and Parnas (2003) argue that the basic disturbance in schizophrenia is a disturbance of *ipseity* – this is the experiential sense of being a vital and self-coinciding subject of awareness and experience; it encapsulates the first-person perspective on the world (*ipse* is Latin for 'self' or 'itself'). These authors explain that disturbed ipseity manifests as two distinct but complementary phenomena in schizophrenia: 'hyperreflexivity', which refers to 'exaggerated self-consciousness in which a subject or agent experiences itself, or what would normally be inhabited as an aspect or feature of itself, as a kind of external object'; and 'diminished self-affection', which is a diminished sense of basic self-presence or 'implicit sense of existing as a vital and self-possessed subject of awareness' (Sass & Parnas 2003).

Wolgang Blankenburg (b. 1928) describes the central abnormality in schizophrenia as a 'loss of natural self-evidence' (Blankenburg 1971). According to Sass (2001), this refers to: 'A loss of the usual common-sense orientation to reality, that is, of the unquestioned sense of familiarity and of the unproblematic background quality that normally enables a person to take for granted so many of the elements and dimensions of the social and practical world'. This phenomenon is borne out by research and shows that although patients with schizophrenia do well on many intellectual tasks requiring logical and abstract thought, they have particular difficulties with more common-sense or practical problems, especially problems relating to the social world (Cutting & Murphy 1990). Blankenburg (1971) maintains that these individuals fail to grasp the basic 'common-sense' coherence and meaning implicit in the world of the integrated person. For most people this sense of understanding or knowing is so familiar and taken for granted that it recedes into the background of awareness. He compares this to Heidegger's explanation of how 'being' announces itself precisely by retiring. The patient Anne, quoted by Blankenburg, (1971) describes her experience of loss of common sense as a lack of 'something small . . . but so important that without it one cannot live'. Normal people, she says, all have some sort of 'way', 'manner of thinking', or 'frame within which everything plays out'; whereas she finds 'everything, everything in general so problematic. No matter how, I don't understand anything at all . . . the only thing that remains for me is to rely upon rational grounds'.

Sass (2001) explains how this loss of natural self-evidence in patients with negative symptoms, leads to 'exaggerated forms of self-conscious awareness (hyperreflexivity) in which patients focus on aspects or processes of action and experience that, in normal experience, would simply go unnoticed'. Anne speaks of being 'hooked to' or 'hung up on' problems that, for most people, are obvious or self-evident; and Sass believes that this conscious preoccupation and attention to what is normally implicit and automatic, is both exhausting and distracting for patients – perhaps accounting for what Blankenburg called 'schizophrenic asthenia' as well as the apparent detachment of some patients from stimuli in the world around. It also has the effect of objectifying thoughts, feelings and impulses so that they are experienced as alien to the patient. Anne said, 'In my case everything is just an object of thought'.

In his extraordinary book *Madness and Modernism: insanity in the light of modern art, literature, and thought*, Sass argues that compensatory, hyperreflexive ruminations in patients who are experiencing a loss of contact with the social world will have the effect of further distancing them from any sense of real-world engagement and implicit contact (Sass 1992). This may exacerbate their sense of fragmentation and alienation from the embedded self and world. One of Sass's (1992) patients put it this way: 'My downfall was insight . . . Too much insight can be very dangerous, because you can tear your mind apart . . . Well, look at the word "analysis" . . . that means to break apart. When it turns in upon itself, the mind would rip itself apart . . . once I started destroying [my mind], I couldn't stop'. Sass explains that hyperreflexivity, besides referring to the actively directed forms of self-consciousness, also refers to a host of other, more passive, automatic, or 'pre-reflective' ways of focusing on self or self-functioning. Pre-reflective phenomena include unusual sensations, feelings and thoughts that 'pop-up' and acquire an object-like quality (Sass 2001). In most people, these may be perfectly normal sensations 'implicit in ongoing experience and action' that would normally not be attended to, but in schizophrenic patients are experienced as alien 'in the perfectly *abnormal* condition of hyperreflexivity and altered self-affection' (Sass 2001).

During the early or prodromal phases of disturbance, patients may experience these phenomena in a largely passive manner, as a kind of 'basal irritation' (Klosterkötter et al. 1997). Kodman (1983) reports that prodromal subjects describe many sensori-perceptual changes, such as clumsiness, loss of taste and changes in bodily awareness. This is often accompanied by irritability and confusion as well as mounting anxiety. In the Edinburgh High Risk Study, Eve Johnstone and colleagues found that situational anxiety, nervous tension, depression and changed perception were the commonest symptoms experienced by subjects who later became psychotic (Johnstone et al. 2005; Owens et al. 2005). Sass (2001) argues that, with ongoing hyperreflexivity and alienation from the embedded self and world, there follows a progression of these prodromal experiences to frank first-rank psychotic symptoms. This occurs through 'increasing objectification and externalization of normally tacit[4] inner phenomena'. These phenomena become thematized in the form of first-rank symptoms. As Sass explains:

> To have focal awareness of what would usually be tacit is to object-ify or alienate that phenomenon – to cause it to be experienced as existing at some kind of remove from what Husserl (1989) called the 'zero point' of orientation of ongoing experiential selfhood. At the extreme, the patient loses the sense of inhabiting his own actions, thoughts, or sensations and may feel that these are under the control of some alien being or force – as in the first rank symptoms.
>
> (Sass 2001)

Sass's (2001) discussion of the work of Kimura Bin (b. 1931) is complex and focuses on his basic distinction between two aspects of the 'self' – the subjective lived self ('noetic') and the objective position of self-scrutiny that involves taking oneself as the object of awareness ('noematic').[5] He reviews Kimura's view of schizophrenia as a disturbance of the relationship between these two forms of self-experience. The noetic self is embedded in the body and world of experience, it is the real or 'existing self', while the noematic self is the virtual or 'thinking self'. In schizophrenia, the hyperreflexive act of detached self-observation and self-consciousness draws the patient away from his noetic sense of being an embodied presence in the world.

If we reflect on Merleau-Ponty's (2002) concept of the mind as an 'embodied' phenomenon, constructed by and engaged in the physical world of the body and society – see our discussion in Chapter 5 – we can see the way in which all these viewpoints coincide. Merleau-Ponty described an 'intentional arc' that is the prereflective connection between body and world that is 'prior to any subject-object distinction' (Fuchs 2005). It is a 'preconscious or tacit layer of experience, namely a hidden texture of similarities that connects the body with the world' and exists 'beneath the intentionality of conscious perception' (Fuchs 2005). This, I would argue, describes the 'social mind' or social self that is the basis of lived human experience – to recall Bracken's (2002) statement (quoted in Chapter 5): 'Existence, in the sense of lived human existence, involved and embedded in the world, is the necessary precedent and the enabling condition of thought' (Bracken 2002).

Schizophrenia represents an alienation from the embodied self and world, a detachment from Minkowski's 'primal sense of vitality or vital connectedness with the world' (Sass 2001). In the same way and drawing on Blankenburg, we can say that schizophrenia represents a loss of 'natural self-evidence' or 'basic common sense' engagement in the lived world. And using Kimura's formulation, we might speak of the schizophrenic's detachment from the noetic sense of being an embodied presence in the world. Thus, all three authors describe the embodied nature of the self as a lived, 'felt' self, and they speak a common language (as Sass 2001 observed) when they consider the phenomenology of alienation that characterizes schizophrenia. One might therefore conclude that the weight of twentieth-century phenomenological efforts to capture the essential disturbance of schizophrenia supports the following statement: That the basic problem faced by these patients relates to their sense of detachment and disembodiment from 'social self' and 'social world'.

As Louis Sass, Joseph Parnas and others have so clearly articulated, all the 'symptoms' or experiences of people with schizophrenia can be explained in terms of this primary sense of alienation or 'loss of ipseity'. These authors' concept of 'hyperreflexive self-observation', Minkowski's 'hypertrophy of intellectual tendencies', and Kimura's expansion of the 'noematic self', all point to the same phenomenon that seems to account for many of the positive and disorganized symptoms of the disorder. But, in the tradition of Minkowski,[6] I would argue that this phenomenon of excessive self-consciousness manifests as a secondary and compensatory reaction to the primary experience of alienation from social self and social world.

Thus, 100 years later, it seems that Bleuler's conceptualization of the 'basic symptoms' of schizophrenia provides us with perhaps the most useful and accurate description of the core pathology of the disorder.[7] But how does this phenomenological description of schizophrenic social alienation coincide with the basic thesis of this book? In previous chapters I argued that *Homo sapiens* evolved a social brain and I provided anatomical and functional evidence for the existence of this highly socially attuned brain in modern humans. In fact, I have argued that it is this social character of our brains and consciousness that truly defines our 'humanness' and our humanity. In this chapter I have made a case for regarding the primary problem in schizophrenic experience as being a sense of alienation or detachment from or loss of natural embeddedness in the world. I have suggested that schizophrenic patients experience a kind of disembodiment from their social selves. One would therefore expect that these same patients, when subjected to clinical research, would demonstrate difficulties or even

131

'deficits' in multiple domains of social and interpersonal relatedness. In this next section I address research evidence pertaining to this issue – in particular the data emerging from contemporary neuropsychological and neuroimaging methods. Of course, a perennial problem for the reader, when we move from one academic framework to another, is the change in language and perspective. And so, from the worldview of philosophy of mind to the worldview of cognitive science!

SCHIZOPHRENIA AND THE SOCIAL BRAIN

I wish to recall our discussion of Erich Fromm in Chapter 5, in particular his claim that there exists what he termed an instinct or need – 'the need to be related to the world outside oneself, the need to avoid aloneness' (Fromm 1942/2003). In *Fear of Freedom*, he went on to state that the absence of such connectedness to others and to the world should be termed 'moral aloneness' and that this state led to insanity. It turns out that Fromm was entirely correct, for in schizophrenia (which is the archetypal manifestation of insanity) one finds numerous problems in comprehending and interacting in social discourse that lead to an absence of connectedness with the social world – so patients do, in fact, experience a kind of 'moral aloneness'.

It is perhaps the major objective in cognitive psychiatry to discover what functional brain processes are going wrong when an individual experiences abnormal mental functioning. Thus, in the case of 'moral aloneness' in schizophrenia, the task at hand is to ask what errors or changes are occurring at a cognitive level that give rise to the social alienation that characterizes the disorder? Social psychologists address this problem from the opposite perspective – they ask what social processes and conditions push the individual into a state of alienation. This latter concern is equally important in my opinion, but is not the focus of our current discussion. When addressing the problems of social interaction and social functioning in schizophrenia, the social cognitive scientist[8] begins by breaking down the moment of social interaction into its constituent phases and operational factors.

So, for example, Newman (2001), in his chapter contributed to the edited volume *Social Cognition in Schizophrenia* (editors: Corrigan and Penn), identifies the following components of social cognition: 'person perception'; 'person memory and representation'; 'representation of the self'; and 'affective influences on cognition'. This broadly corresponds to Adolphs' model, elucidated in Chapter 5, which included: 'social perception'; 'central processes of social cognition' (including recognition and emotional responses); and 'social behaviour' (Adolphs 2001). Leonhard and Corrigan (2001), in their chapter in the same volume (see above), argue that social perception differs from non-social perception in several important ways, rendering a simple information-processing approach unsatisfactory to the task of understanding the former. For example, *social perception* is usually affect-laden, personally relevant, interactive, dynamic and changing (as opposed to static), context dependent and conveys complex meanings. Penn et al. (2001), also writing in the same volume, note that, in addition to social perception, the individual needs to adequately *represent socially relevant information* and this requires: knowledge of social situations; knowledge of social conventions and judgement; and knowledge of self and others. In their research Penn et al. (1997) have shown that performance on measures of social cognition better predict the social competence of patients than tests of general cognitive deficits.

Before we now turn our attention to specific research on social cognition in schizophrenia, it is well worth noting some naturalistic observations of patients, dating back to Darwin himself, which were conducted in the spirit of ethological enquiry. The following are extracts from Darwin's *On the Expression of Emotions in Man and Animals*, published in 1872:

> In the second place, it occurred to me that the insane ought to be studied, as they are liable to the strongest passions, and give uncontrolled vent to them. I had, myself, no opportunity of doing this, so I applied to Dr. Maudsley and received from him an introduction to Dr. J. Crichton Browne, who has charge of an immense asylum near Wakefield, and who, as I found, had already attended to the subject . . .

> Although with the insane the grief-muscles often act persistently; yet in ordinary cases they are sometimes brought unconsciously into momentary action by ludicrously slight causes. A gentleman rewarded a young lady by an absurdly small present; she pretended to be offended, and as she upbraided him, her eyebrows became extremely oblique, with the forehead properly wrinkled . . .

> Dr. Browne further remarks that the bristling of the hair which is so common in the insane, is not always associated with terror. It is perhaps most frequently seen in chronic maniacs, who rave incoherently and have destructive impulses; but it is during their paroxysms of violence that the bristling is most observable. The fact of the hair becoming erect under the influence both of rage and fear agrees perfectly with what we have seen in the lower animals.
>
> (Darwin 1872)

In his excellent book, *The Social Brain: evolution and pathology* (Brüne et al. 2003), Brüne discusses some of the most important ethological studies of schizophrenia (Brüne 2003). For example, in a naturalistic observation of chronic female patients over 18 months, Staehelin (1953) noted 'that the patients' behavioural repertoire was severely restricted to the defence of a personal "territory", to maintaining a rigid social hierarchy, and to the avoidance of any body contact' (Brüne 2003). Brüne comments on the fact that Staehelin was particularly impressed at the apparent absence of friendships, mutual help and emotions of mercy or empathy in his patients. Other studies cited by Brüne point to multiple problems in social and interpersonal nonverbal behaviour including poor eye contact and less eyebrow raising[9] (Pitman et al. 1987); fewer upper face activities, fewer primary emotions and more negative emotions (Krause et al. 1989); and lower scores on pro-social behaviour, gesture and displacement activities (Troisi 1999, Troisi et al. 1998). In his study, Troisi (1999) noted that these findings were largely independent of psychopathological measures (i.e. negative and positive symptoms), suggesting that 'impaired social interaction reflects a separate dimension of schizophrenic disorders' (Brüne 2003). Thus, ethological insights point to pervasive problems in social cognitive ability in patients with schizophrenia, regardless of symptom or syndrome type. We may assume that these cognitive problems underlie the interpersonal difficulties experienced by patients with the disorder and contribute largely to their social alienation.

When subjected to neuropsychological testing, patients with schizophrenia demonstrate a range of impairments of social cognition. For example, judgement of the direction of eye gaze has been shown to be impaired in schizophrenia (Phillips & David 1997; Rosse et al. 1994). Furthermore, there is ample evidence that face processing is altered, both in the processing of neutral faces (Williams et al. 1999) and in the perception of emotional expressions on faces (Archer et al. 1994; Borod et al. 1993; Gaebel & Wölwer 1992; Kohler et al. 2000). Of interest are three studies that showed no correlation between emotional blunting in patients and their ability to either recognize or experience emotions (Shaw et al. 1999; Streit et al. 1997; Sweet et al. 1998). This seems to lend support to Bleuler's insistence that 'under no conditions has the affectivity disappeared altogether' (Bleuler 1923), as well as to my argument earlier in this chapter that affective disturbances in schizophrenia should be viewed in qualitative rather than quantitative terms.

Brüne (2003) addresses the issue of whether these emotion recognition problems experienced by schizophrenic patients are state or trait dependent – in other words, do these problems occur only during frank psychosis or are they in fact enduring 'deficits' that characterize the disorder itself? He cites well-replicated research, which indicates the latter (Bell et al. 1997; Gaebel & Wölwer 1992; Wölwer et al. 1996). Furthermore, a study of first-episode patients in partial remission confirmed the early manifestation of emotion-recognition deficits – the authors speculated that problems with recognizing emotional states in others might even precede the onset of the disorder (Edwards et al. 2001). In my view, this data supports Minkowski's belief that his patients' loss of 'vital connectedness to the world' pre-empted their retreat into what Sass (2001) terms 'hyperreflexive self-observation'. The first-rank symptoms of full-blown psychosis may indeed occur as a secondary compensation to the patient's difficulties with social perception and recognition and ensuing alienation from the social world.

Various studies have been conducted, examining the anatomical location of social cognitive deficits in schizophrenia. It is obvious from the discussion so far, that one would expect to find both anatomical and functional abnormalities in the regions and circuits of the social brain when individuals with schizophrenia perform tasks related to social cognition and behaviour. And this is indeed the case. For example, imaging experiments, using emotional faces as stimuli, have demonstrated reduced activity in the ventral lateral prefrontal cortex (PFC) for angry faces (Phillips et al. 1999) and reduced activity in the amygdala in response to fearful, happy and sad faces (Phillips et al. 1999; Schneider et al. 1998) in patients compared with healthy controls. And an fMRI study of facial emotion processing in schizophrenia demonstrated significantly reduced activation in the left amygdala and bilateral hippocampi (Gur et al. 2002). When patients with schizophrenia are asked to induce sad moods during fMRI scanning, the amygdala fails to activate compared with controls (Schneider et al. 1998), implying a functional abnormality of this structure in addition to the structural abnormalities that have been observed (Lawrie & Abukmeil 1998). Finally, deficits in response and conflict-monitoring (Mathalon et al. 2002; Yucel et al. 2002), decision-making (Paulus et al. 2002) and affiliative behaviour (Kirkpatrick 1997) have been observed in schizophrenia. Neuroanatomical regions implicated include the ACC and DLPFC during response and conflict monitoring (Mathalon et al. 2002; Yucel et al. 2002) and the PFC and inferior parietal cortex (IPC) during decision-making (Paulus et al. 2002).

Another strategy is to perform brain imaging on patients who have prominent 'negative symptoms' – those who classically exhibit deficits in volition, motivation and affect. As these are crucial components of social cognition and behaviour, it is especially useful to consider evidence from these particular patients. One of the most common findings pertains to the DLPFC, with evidence of both structural (Chua et al. 1997; Sanfilipo et al. 2000) and functional abnormalities (Frith et al. 1991; Liddle et al. 1992; Tamminga et al. 1992) reported in the literature. In addition, the OFC and its connections have similarly been implicated in negative symptoms with various studies showing structural (Baare et al. 1999; Gur et al. 2000; Sigmundsson et al. 2001) and functional abnormalities (Tamminga et al. 1992). Other regions that may be involved in the generation of negative symptoms include the temporal lobes (especially left-side and limbic structures) (Sanfilipo et al. 2000; Sigmundsson et al. 2001), the ACC and the IPC (Kirkpatrick et al. 1999; Ross & Pearlson 1996; Sigmundsson et al. 2001).

Finally, a word on the mirror neuron system and schizophrenia: In an fMRI study that tested 'emotional resonance' in schizophrenia, Fahim et al. (2004) demonstrated a relative failure to activate the PFC and they attribute this to 'failure or distortion in the development of the mirror neuron system'. Quintana et al. (2001) demonstrated increased compensatory mirror neuron function in schizophrenia on fMRI during facial affect processing. The links between abnormal social cognitive ability in schizophrenia and aberrant mirror neuron function are clearly an important avenue for further research, as a recent essay testifies (Arbib & Mundhenk 2005).

In concluding this section on the social brain in schizophrenia, I think it is fair to state that ethological, neuropsychological and imaging experiments indicate the following: It appears that the primary cognitive deficits in schizophrenia lie within the domain of social cognition, while the primary structural and functional abnormalities are located within the distributed FP and FT cortical networks of the social brain.

THEORY OF MIND IN SCHIZOPHRENIA

In Chapter 5, I introduced the concept of theory of mind (TOM) as a cognitive mechanism for inferring mental states in others and facilitating interpersonal communication. In Chapter 6, I reviewed the evidence supporting a limited degree of TOM ability in great apes and suggested that a 'full TOM' only emerged in the earliest *Homo sapiens* approximately 150,000 years ago. In this section, I address TOM in schizophrenia – recent research confirms our expectation: people suffering from schizophrenic disorders have great difficulty with a wide range of TOM tasks and consequently tend to misinterpret the mental states and inferences of others during interpersonal discourse.

Interestingly, within psychiatry, the concept of TOM is most commonly associated with autism rather than with schizophrenia. This is partly due to the historical focus on social dysfunction in autism, while in schizophrenia clinicians have always tended to become distracted by the more 'flamboyant' disturbances such as delusions and hallucinations. The seminal study of TOM in autism was conducted by Simon Baron-Cohen and colleagues in 1985. These authors demonstrated a specific difficulty with acknowledging false belief in autistic children (Baron-Cohen et al. 1985). Numerous subsequent studies employing a variety of novel tasks have confirmed this finding (Frith 1989; Leekam & Perner 1991; Leslie & Thaiss 1992; Perner et al. 1989). Baron-Cohen has examined the neural basis of autism and describes a circuit including the amygdala, OFC and superior temporal sulcus (STS) that mediates TOM ability and is dysfunctional in the disorder (Baron-Cohen 1995; Baron-Cohen et al. 2000). Frith argues that impaired mentalizing in autism probably relates to the failure of medial prefrontal–parietal attentional networks to effectively modulate connectivity in regions such as the extrastriate visual cortex and temporal lobes (Frith 2003).

Given that autistic individuals show TOM deficits, it is not surprising that the cardinal features of autism (autistic aloneness, poor communication and lack of pretend play (Wing & Gould 1979)) parallel some of the negative symptoms of schizophrenia (such as social withdrawal, poverty of speech and stereotyped rather than spontaneous behaviour). In addition, the language difficulties are similar in the two disorders, with pragmatic rather than syntactic or semantic aspects impaired (Frith & Allen 1988). Autism experts, Chris and Uta Frith, have argued that autism and schizophrenia may represent early and late acquired variations of a similar underlying process. They cite evidence presented by Murray and Lewis (1987) that there is a 'neurodevelopmental' subgroup of schizophrenics who exhibit features that closely resemble childhood autism, namely early onset, male dominant and defects in premorbid IQ, behaviour and sociability. They suggest that there may be greater comorbidity between the two conditions than is acknowledged.

In terms of TOM impairment and the specific symptomatology of schizophrenia, Frith (1994) has proposed several mechanisms within a cognitive framework. Negative symptoms such as flattening of affect and impoverishment of will are attributed to the individual's lack of awareness of his own mental and emotional states and a corresponding unawareness of personal goals and intentions. Incoherence of speech and language, Frith argues, is due to a failure to take account of the listener's lack of knowledge. Thus, the TOM-impaired individual uses speech that lacks referents (Rochester & Martin 1979), and assumes that the listener shares an understanding of his 'logical' train of thought. Similarly, there is a failure in discourse planning, with the omission of explicit links between different topics in the discourse. Positive symptoms in schizophrenia, argues Frith (1994) result from attempts to infer the mental states of others because, unlike the autistic patient, the person with schizophrenia has had an experience of using TOM abilities prior to onset of illness and knows that one must attempt to interpret the mental contents of others. However, the illness impairs mind-reading ability and errors result – this is the basis of some positive symptoms. Thus, false inferences about the intentions of others lead to paranoid delusions, while referential delusions are a consequence of falsely inferring that others are communicating with one.

TOM abnormalities have been demonstrated in people with schizophrenia using a range of experiments that seek to test their ability to attribute mental states and to detect deception and false beliefs. Using 'hinting' and 'false-belief' tasks Corcoran et al. (1995) and Frith and Corcoran (1996) have shown that patients with schizophrenia who have negative, disorganized or paranoid symptoms struggle to infer intentions behind indirect speech. Doody et al. (1998) have shown that, within the functional psychoses, TOM impairment is specific to schizophrenia. Subsequent studies have substantiated the specificity of TOM impairment to behaviourally disorganized

137

patients with schizophrenia and have argued that it reflects disturbance of a particular cognitive module rather than general cognitive impairment (Langdon et al. 2001; Mazza et al. 2001; Pickup & Frith 2001; Sarfati et al. 1999; Sarfati & Hardy-Baylé 1999). Pickup and Frith also reiterate earlier observations (Pilowsky et al. 2000) that TOM impairments in schizophrenia are less severe than in autism, probably as a result of earlier age of onset in the latter and some residual mind-reading skills in the former. The two functional imaging studies to date examining TOM in schizophrenia correlated poor mentational ability with abnormal activity in the PFC and the temporal lobes (Brünet et al. 2003; Russell et al. 2000).

PSYCHOPATHOLOGY AND THE SOCIAL BRAIN

In examining social brain function and TOM ability in schizophrenia, and the functional and structural bases for the deficits encountered in people with the disorder, we are forced to return to the following problem: Is abnormal social cognition unique to schizophrenia or do other mental disorders fall within the concept of 'social brain disorders'? At the beginning of this chapter, I quoted Martin Brüne's bold assertion that the entire spectrum of functional psychoses, and perhaps all forms of psychopathology, should be regarded as 'social brain disorders'. Is there empirical support for this claim, and if so, what are the consequences of this troublesome fact for the social brain hypothesis of schizophrenia?

It turns out that there is in fact good evidence for social brain dysfunction in a variety of psychiatric disorders, both psychotic and neurotic in nature. In the section above I have already discussed TOM deficits and general social brain problems in autism, arguing that this disorder is characterized by early failure to develop normal social cognitive skills. However, abnormalities of social cognition and TOM ability have also been demonstrated in bipolar disorder (Bora et al. 2005; Inoue et al. 2004; Kerr et al. 2003; Kinderman 2003), psychopathy (Mealey 1995; Mealey & Kinner 2003) and dementia (Garcia Cuerva et al. 2001; Gregory et al. 2002; Snowden et al. 2003); and in time further research may well demonstrate similar problems in other psychiatric disorders. In a study of bipolar disorder, Kerr et al. (2003) showed impaired TOM performance in symptomatic patients with either manic or depressive illness. Two subsequent studies indicated that even asymptomatic bipolar patients in remission may have difficulties with TOM tasks (Bora et al. 2005; Inoue et al. 2004).

Thus, as with schizophrenia, we may surmise that TOM dysfunction is a trait rather than a state marker in bipolar disorder. The study by Inoue et al. (2004) is interesting in that unipolar depressive patients in remission also showed TOM problems, suggesting that the entire spectrum of mood disorder is characterized by abnormalities of social cognition. Although, at the

138

time of writing, there are no published studies of TOM in anxiety disorders, we might speculate that patients within the anxiety spectrum similarly experience difficulties with mentalizing ability. This seems likely in view of the marked overlap in depressive and anxiety symptomatology.

If then deficits in social cognition and TOM ability are apparent across a range of mental disorders, how is it possible to conceptualize schizophrenia specifically as 'a disorder of the social brain'? The answer, I believe, lies in a simple model of psychopathology (see Figure 7.1) that illustrates the extensive overlap and continuity within the entire spectrum of mental disorder.

If indeed there is extensive biological and clinical overlap between anxiety, depression, manic depression, schizophrenia and autistic disorders (as the psychiatric literature and personal experience indicates), then it is no surprise that TOM problems are common to most forms of psychopathology. The conceptual shift that is necessary is to view all forms of mental illness as *disorders of the social brain*. In Chapter 5, I proposed a model of the social brain that included both *upper* and *lower* components, the former comprising cortical networks and the latter comprising the limbic system. And, functionally, I suggested that the social brain operated in terms of both top-down and bottom-up processes. I believe that an expanded model of the social brain, with both upper and lower components and top-down

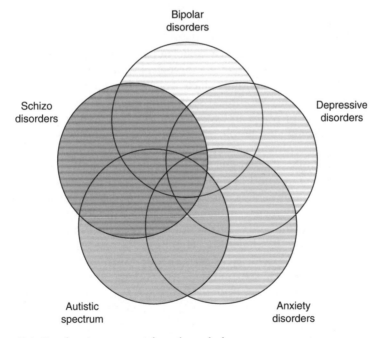

Figure 7.1 Overlapping spectra of psychopathology.

and bottom-up processes, provides us with a framework within which to explain most mental disorders in terms of a spectrum of social brain dysfunction. Clearly, the aetiological factors responsible for dysfunctional social cognition may vary according to specific expressions of psychopathology (see discussion in Brüne et al. 2003) but I would suggest that the anatomical and functional location of specific disorders within the structure of the social brain may also vary. Since the social brain is a broad system of interconnected cortical and subcortical structures, it is feasible that 'social brain disorders' manifest differently from one another according to where in the system their focal point of pathology lies.

For example, anxiety and depression are likely to be an expression of predominant lower social brain (LSB) dysfunction, based in a primary limbic and brainstem pathology with bottom-up processes leading to secondary cognitive disturbance. On the other hand, psychotic illness might be understood in terms of both lower and upper social brain (USB) pathology with bottom-up and top-down processes giving rise to a range of primitive (e.g. threat versus safety judgements) and recently evolved (e.g. paranoid delusion) symptoms. This model would accommodate and possibly help explain the subgroup of schizophrenia sufferers referred to by Gilbert (2004) where posttraumatic stress disorder is aetiological. Within the spectrum of 'schizophrenias', one might surmise that those individuals with prominent positive and affective symptoms (whose symptomatology may overlap with bipolar and unipolar mood disorders) have predominant LSB dysfunction, while those with negative schizophrenia have predominant USB dysfunction. Figure 7.2 illustrates the hypothesized model.

The many implications of such a model of psychopathology are important for our understanding of human psychological suffering. As I have argued, it provides a framework within which we can appreciate the dimensional and overlapping reality of clinical symptoms and syndromes encountered in practice. It also provides an explanation to a biological reality that perplexes me (and I am sure perplexes others in the mental health field); and that is the fact that physiological and anatomical entities such as serotonin, dopamine, the limbic system and the prefrontal cortex all seem to be disturbed in one way or another right across the spectrum of psychiatric disorders. Whether one is dealing with anxiety or mood disturbances or autism or psychosis, a brief review of neurobiological data concerning all these disorders reveals disturbances of the same areas of the brain and the same chemicals regardless of diagnosis. Highbrow lectures and pharmaceutical homilies on the specificity of serotonergic function in depression and dopaminergic function in schizophrenia are nothing more than reductionist and misleading generalizations.[10] In reality we find commonalities everywhere: common mechanisms; common areas of the brain and common clinical symptoms. The attempts within the DSM system to neatly box disorders as distinct biological entities is fraught with problems – hence the

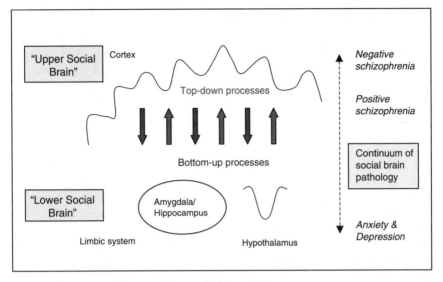

Figure 7.2 Model of the social brain showing different components, processes and the predominant location of pathology for a continuum of 'social brain pathology'.

regular reappearance of new editions of the diagnostic manual. With each new edition we find changes in the classification system, the appearance of new 'disorders' and the deletion of old concepts.

Politics and ethics have as much to do with the ever-evolving classification system as hard scientific data – witness the (appropriate) removal of homosexuality from the list of mental disorders in the 1980 edition. If then all mental disorders can be considered disorders of the social brain, what place does psychosis occupy in this spectrum of 'social brain disorders'? In my view, psychosis, and perhaps classic schizophrenia in particular, represents the 'ultimate' or 'arch' social brain disorder. In schizophrenia we find a disturbance of mind that epitomizes dysfunction in every sphere of social cognition and behaviour. Autistic alienation, social ambivalence and anxiety, misperception and misinterpretation of interpersonal signals, misattribution of internally generated stimuli and socially inappropriate behaviour characterize chronic psychosis and disable sufferers enormously. This 'special' place for schizophrenia among the spectrum of psychopathologies we might call 'social brain disorders' is supported by Giovanni Stanghellini of the Section on Clinical Psychopathology of the World Psychiatric Association:

The de-structuring of social life (Criterion B) is a basic diagnostic characteristic of the schizophrenic syndrome. While for other psychiatric disorders the impairment of social life is a direct consequence

141

of the clinical symptoms, in the case of schizophrenia it 'does not appear to be a direct result of any single feature' (APA 1994; 2000). Since it is not possible to find the pathognomonic character of schizophrenia in the clinical patterns (Criterion A), it is legitimate to ask if the basic psychopathological character of schizophrenia might not lie right there in Criterion B. What gives the character of schizophrenia to certain psychotic pictures is a particular form of impairment of social life.

(Stanghellini & Ballerini 2002)

I believe this social brain model is important not least because it high-lights the profoundly social nature of the disability accompanying psychotic illness. The individual afflicted with schizophrenia or indeed an affective psychosis is disadvantaged in what is arguably the most challenging and important functional human capability; that is, the ability to engage in and respond appropriately to the social world in which he or she lives. As Erich Fromm suggested: To fail in the most basic human psychological need to interconnect with others, is to risk 'mental disintegration'; and where there is no belonging or connectedness, but only aloneness and alienation, we witness insanity and intolerable suffering.

8

THE DYSCONNECTIVITY
HYPOTHESIS OF SCHIZOPHRENIA

Sejunction is a universal and cardinal psychopathological symptom that occurs prominently in most acute psychoses . . . Sejunction, in my sense, means a breakdown in consciousness of a particular type. It is the simultaneous collapse of several functionally separate series of associations. The most important component of the concept is that the activity of consciousness always has to be seen as the product of many simultaneously ongoing psychophysical processes. The unity of consciousness is never apparent to us in its entirety, but is produced by the synthesis of simultaneous processes. This synthesising activity can be suspended by functional disturbances of an unknown kind, and that is what I mean by the sejunction mechanism.

(Gross 1904)

'DISSOCIATION PSYCHOSIS'

Otto Gross (1877–1920) was an eccentric alcoholic and drug addict who consulted both Freud and Jung – the latter regarded him as schizophrenic. An anarchist in the years before World War I and an active participant in the socialist revolutions that wracked Germany and Austria after the war, Gross counted among his friends Max Brod and Franz Kafka in Prague. Although he suffered mental illness himself, Gross managed to contribute extensively to the turn-of-the-century debates around classification of the psychoses. His term *dementia sejunctiva* (literally 'insanity of dissociation') was one of many nosological efforts[1] to encapsulate the essence of what we now term schizophrenia. Gross borrowed the concept of *sejunction* from Carl Wernicke (1848–1905), who had earlier described a syndrome called *sejunktionspsychose* (or 'dissociation psychosis') (Wernicke 1899). Gross states:

My views on sejunction were derived from those of Wernicke, but

143

there are some differences in our two concepts ... Whereas in Wernicke's scheme, the sejunction mechanism is a 'closed circuit' of associative ties, in mine it is the work of synthesis which is affected. Wernicke's explanation of sejunction involves the loss of certain associations caused by an interruption in pathways. I invoke a general decline in some higher cerebral function. Wernicke's sejunction factors are theoretically localisable, whereas mine are diffuse. In summary, Wernicke is more concerned with a breakdown in the contents of consciousness, whereas my formulation emphasizes the processes involved.

(Gross 1904)

Thus, Wernicke attributed psychosis to disturbances of associative systems in the brain. He anticipated that the ' "splitting" of the different psychic functions', which Bleuler (1950) described in introducing the term 'schizophrenia', had an anatomical basis – the 'interruption of pathways' of the brain. Interestingly, Gross (and many others) disagreed with Wernicke's speculations regarding a structural basis for 'psychic splitting', on the grounds that it implied localization rather than a diffuse 'general decline in some higher cerebral function' (Gross 1904). In this chapter, I wish to resuscitate Wernicke and Gross's notion of *sejunction*, drawing on a model of schizophrenia that has emerged within the last 20 years as probably the most robust contemporary understanding of schizophrenic cognitive and neurological pathology. This model is succinctly called the *dysconnectivity hypothesis*.[2]

As we shall see later in this chapter, there is good evidence supporting the fact that patients with schizophrenia do indeed suffer, in terms of both their neuropsychological function and their neuropathology, from a form of *sejunction*. The dysconnectivity hypothesis focused initially on *functional* problems with the integration or synthesis of information, thus vindicating Bleuler and Gross and others who invoked a 'splitting' or dissociation of psychic functions. Latterly, however, new technologies for imaging and measuring the structural integrity of neural pathways have shown that those with the disorder have abnormalities in the actual *structure* of white matter connections within their brains. This *structural dysconnectivity*, only detectable with the aid of the most complex and recent twenty-first-century scientific methods, proves Carl Wernicke's 100-year-old claim that psychosis resulted from disruptions of the 'organs of connection' (Wernicke 1899). It also diminishes Bleuler's pessimism regarding the longevity of Wernicke's ideas – in his *Dementia Praecox*, Bleuler wrote:

At present ... we have no means of localizing psychic functions beneath the cortex; neither can we recognize the signs which indicate the difference between sub-cortical and cortical psychological

144

material. Therefore, we are unable to deal with such theories at this time. With his ideas of localization, Wernicke has attempted to give the most far-reaching explanation. However, the symptomatology of schizophrenia . . . provides no definite indications of localization . . . Wernicke's sejunction-hypothesis is . . . too mechanical for the purpose of explaining such complicated phenomena as sensory deceptions.

(Bleuler 1950: 388–9)

In Chapter 7 I argued that schizophrenia is a disorder of the social brain, characterized by a fundamental disturbance of social cognition that renders the psychotic individual disabled in interpersonal communication and alienated from the social world. In support of my argument I presented data from cognitive studies of social cognition in schizophrenia, demonstrating numerous errors in mental state attribution and theory of mind (TOM). Now, before proceeding with a discussion of the dysconnectivity hypothesis – which can be considered the modern evidence-based descendant of Wernicke's *sejunktionspsychose* or 'dissociation psychosis' – I think it is important to consider the following questions: First, how is social cognition disrupted in this disorder? Second, at a psychological level, can we explain these impairments of mental state attribution, 'mind-reading' and affective responsiveness in information-processing terms? And third, if we can, then would a 'cognitive model' of schizophrenia serve to inform our understanding of what is happening at a neural level? In the next section, I address these questions and draw upon the work of several authors in constructing a cognitive model of schizophrenia. As the reader will discover, this model describes schizophrenic psychopathology in terms of what I have called *cognitive malintegration* – a basic problem with the integration and synthesis of information or knowledge, particularly that of a social nature (Burns 2004). This model will set a background for our discussion of the dysconnectivity hypothesis later in this chapter.

A COGNITIVE MODEL OF SCHIZOPHRENIA

In my earlier discussion of theory of mind in schizophrenia, I referred to Frith's (1994) model of impaired mental state attribution and faulty self-monitoring and I believe this model is a good place to start in constructing a cognitive model of the disorder. To recap, Frith conceptualizes positive symptoms in terms of misattribution of intentions and beliefs of others, while he considers negative symptoms a result of inadequate awareness of one's own mental state. At the cognitive level, he argues that this failure in mental state attribution results from a deficiency in the 'central monitoring of action' (Mlakar et al. 1994). Thus, symptoms such as delusions of control and thought insertion arise when 'the monitor fails to receive information about intended actions generated by the patient on his own initiative. As a result, these actions are perceived as emanating from "outside" or from an alien force' (Frith 1987). In a later elaboration of this model, Frith (1992) suggests that central monitoring deficiency results from the patient's inability to reflect upon his own mental activity.

In normal everyday behaviour, we are aware of an action we are about to perform before actually performing it. We are also able to imagine an action without actually performing it. These abilities constitute forms of self-monitoring that enable us to distinguish self from other and discriminate between stimuli emanating from our own brains and those arising from the outside world. This discrimination process occurs unconsciously as a rapid error correction between different parts of the brain (usually prefrontal cortex and posterior cortices). The physiologist, Hermann von Helmholtz (1821–94), was the first to describe this rapid 'checking' system – he termed it the *corollary discharge system* – and he recognized that 'perception is a creative process dependent upon "unconscious inferences" made in the brain' (Frith & Johnstone 2003).

For example, when I am about to move my arm, my prefrontal cortex sends a corollary message to my parietal cortex (responsible for analysing sensations), 'warning' it that my intended movement will generate sensations from my arm (i.e. self-generated stimuli). This corollary discharge also serves to 'dampen down' my conscious perception of sensations generated during arm movement. This is what Frith and others mean by the term 'self-monitoring' in respect of the cognitive mechanisms operative in schizophrenia. What these authors propose is that in schizophrenia there is a failure of this corollary discharge system so that self-generated stimuli are not subject to 'damping' by the prefrontal cortex; instead they intrude into consciousness and are perceived as emanating from the environment. Where self-generated auditory stimuli processed in the temporal cortices are implicated, the person with schizophrenia misattributes them to an external source, that is, as auditory hallucinations or 'voices'. This is the basis of the dysconnectivity hypothesis, which posits that there is a disconnection between prefrontal and posterior cortices and a failure of integration of information between them.

In examining the integrative mechanisms at work within the cerebral cortex during conscious thought and behaviour, it is useful to consider a novel proposal by archaeologist, Steven Mithen (outlined in his book *The Prehistory of the Mind*) regarding the cognitive architecture of the modern mind (Mithen 1996). Mithen has critiqued the popular modular model of the mind (Fodor 1983) or 'Swiss army knife' model of evolutionary psychologists such as Cosmides and Tooby (1992), in which the mind is conceived as a collection of independently evolved and independently used 'modules', each 'hardwired' and adapted to the environment of the Pleistocene. Drawing upon his impressive grasp of the archaeological record, Mithen suggests that, much like extant apes such as chimpanzees, early hominids possessed a brain that was organized around a number of module-like processing systems. Similar to Gardner's (1983) 'multiple intelligences', Mithen includes modules for 'social intelligence', 'technical intelligence' and so on. However, he argues that humans became the creative and imaginary species they are because of a gradual breakdown in this modularization, producing increasing connections between modules and resulting in a 'cognitive fluidity' that first becomes apparent in the symbolic and religious art of early *Homo sapiens* 60–30,000 years ago.

I shall return to Mithen later, but what is extremely useful at this stage, I believe, is his conceptualization of the modern mind as a fluid and connected entity that allows for integration of specialized information in the 'formation' of abstract and symbolic thought. In respect of schizophrenia, one might surmise that intact mentational ability and self-monitoring relies upon healthy connections and 'cognitive fluidity', while impaired social cognition implies a breakdown in the normal integration of knowledge as a result of *cognitive malintegration* (Burns 2004).

Indeed, this is by no means a novel concept in the schizophrenia literature. Cleghorn and Albert (1990) argue that psychosis, and schizophrenia in particular, may be a problem in the integrated functioning of internal modular processing systems. They suggest that neural networks subserving cognitive and emotional modules are desynchronized in their activation and inactivation – a problem they term *cognitive disjunction* – and that this causes the symptoms of the disorder. They attribute both positive and negative symptoms to 'desynchronization of widely distributed neurocognitive systems'.

In terms of individual symptoms, a number of authors have suggested that the specific cognitive error that underlies hallucinations is the misattribution of internal cognitive events to an external source (Bentall 1990; Hemsley 1993, 2005; Hoffman & Rapaport 1994; Morrison & Haddock 1997; see discussion of Frith above). For example, Bentall has argued that this misattribution may reflect a bias, rather than a primary deficit, in the monitoring of internal events and that this bias may be influenced by 'top-down' processes such as a patient's beliefs and expectations about what events are likely to occur (Bentall 1990). And Morrison and Haddock (1997) have proposed 'metacognitive beliefs inconsistent with intrusive thoughts lead to their external attribution as auditory hallucinations'.

The work of Gilbert (2000) is helpful with respect to positive symptoms in schizophrenia. Gilbert has highlighted the importance of *dialogical reasoning* – the way in which people create dialogues within their own heads. For some authors, he says, this inner dialogue is at the centre of the development and construction of the self and is based on the internalization of social roles. As the early twentieth-century thinker George Herbert Mead (1913) eloquently

147

stated: 'There is a field, a sort of inner forum, in which we are the only spectators and the only actors. In that field each one of us confers with himself. We carry on something of a drama'. Gilbert describes how various 'selves' such as the 'aggressive', 'dominant', 'forgiving' and 'blaming' 'evolved to enact a plurality of social roles' and, at the cognitive level, he locates them in specialized modules for information-processing. With regard to schizophrenia, symptoms such as hostile, shaming voices represent the misinterpretation of signals from one's own dominant, blaming 'self', such that these signals are experienced as external. Gilbert et al. (2001) presents supporting empirical evidence and attributes such symptoms to 'problems in the integration of the modular processes underpinning self–other cognitions'.

Finally, returning to TOM, it would be an omission not to cite Bering (2002, 2003) who has questioned the suitability of domain-specific accounts of mind reading. As with Mithen, Bering has stressed the importance of emerging 'cognitive fluidity', or integrated cognitive functions, in the genesis of what he calls the 'existential TOM (ETOM)'. Bering defines ETOM as 'a biologically based, generic explanatory system that allows individuals to perceive meaning in certain life events'. A meaningful life event is one that implies purpose or intention as the causal force. Thus, natural events are interpreted as 'symbolic of the communicative attempts of some nondescript or culturally elaborated (e.g. God) psychological agency'. As he himself admits, Bering is not the first to suggest a link between TOM and theism (see Barrett & Keil 1996; Boyer 1994). Neither is he the first to propose that TOM becomes generalized to other domains (see Barrett & Keil 1996; Boyer 1994). However, his suggestion that ETOM occupies a domain different from the one occupied by the 'domain-specific module' of TOM proposed by these authors is novel. Bering (2002) states: 'The notion of domain specificity crumbles, and the very idea that theory of mind is modular suffers a serious blow, when one considers that intentional explanations can be evoked by entirely different classes of input: behaviour and experience'.

Thus, Bering is arguing that the case of flexible ETOM shows us that a modular concept of TOM is inappropriate, in that this highly evolved aspect of mentational ability (i.e. ETOM) is related to experiential rather than purely behavioural stimuli. Instead, he proposes that TOM ability as a whole has a cognitive architecture that is based on the integration of separate cognitive faculties related to intentionality. He goes on to suggest that TOM and ETOM evolved in modern *Homo sapiens*, not as 'exaptations' (Gould 1991) or useless by-products of a large brain, but rather as adaptive systems in their own right. Furthermore, he envisages a separate evolutionary history for ETOM specifically, arguing that some time after the human lineage split from the African apes 'the intentionality framework expanded to include those ambient life experiences that humans had little or no control over'. Thus, ETOM has been 'co-opted from a broad intentional stance taken by our ancestors, the primary adaptation of which was to explain and predict behaviour' (Bering 2002).

This analysis is helpful, both in terms of understanding the concept of perceived intentionality as a part of TOM competency, and because it echoes Mithen's proposal that the modern conceptual mind represents a breakdown of phylogenetically older modularization, allowing for integration of information. I certainly agree with Bering that TOM is the product of a gradual breakdown in cognitive modularity. As for an evolutionary time frame, it seems intuitively correct that ETOM should have evolved later than TOM, given Bering's argument that chimpanzees may be capable of 'secondary representation' (Suddendorf & Whiten 2001) (an immature aspect of TOM), while there is no convincing evidence that they are capable of representing intentionality (Heyes 1998; see discussion in Chapter 6). Finally, and importantly, Bering's analysis is useful in terms of understanding the role of misattribution of agency in the genesis of symptoms in schizophrenia. As I stated in the opening chapter of this book, patients with schizophrenia seek meaning in the bizarre phenomena of their psychoses. Theistic and philosophical phenomena populate their hallucinations, while the frantic search for, and misattribution of intentionality must lie at the heart of symptoms such as thought insertion, ideas of reference and paranoid delusions.

Thus, the unifying theme in all of these cognitive accounts of social communication, and TOM specifically, is one of integration of functionally distributed cognitive systems. Within the period between the divergence of hominid and chimpanzee lineages 5–6 mya, and the emergence of modern *Homo sapiens* 60–30,000 years ago, a process has occurred involving the gradual breakdown in the modular construction of the mind. This process was enabled as the brain reorganized and evolved increasing connectivity between previously independent regions of specialization (see discussion in Chapter 6). There is evidence that this process may have commenced prior to the last common ancestor but, if so, then it was still in its infancy. In hominids, I argue, these evolving changes in the brain provided a substrate for integration of previously modularized components of cognition, leading to 'cognitive fluidity' and a capacity for increasingly complex social cognition. A cognitive model of schizophrenia must take this process into account.

What we see in schizophrenia then, in cognitive terms, are multiple problems with the integration of information related to social behaviour, metarepresentation and the attribution of intentionality. In Mithen's (1996) terminology, we can infer that individuals with schizophrenia have a problem with *cognitive fluidity*; and this inability to adequately and appropriately integrate social information results in *cognitive disjunction* (Cleghorn & Albert 1990) or *cognitive malintegration* (Burns 2004). In the next section we see how this model informs and predicts some of the most robust research data emerging from functional and structural brain imaging in schizophrenia. This data has given rise to the dysconnectivity hypothesis. However, before proceeding to a discussion of this hypothesis, there is an important issue, touched upon in Chapter 7, which requires our renewed attention.

In my discussion of so-called 'negative symptoms', I drew upon the ideas of Sass and Parnas and suggested that Bleuler's 'autism', 'ambivalence' and 'affective disturbance' have been misrepresented in modern psychiatry as deficit or deficiency states. In the context of our present consideration of a cognitive model of schizophrenia, I think it is important to revisit this issue. I have been careful to talk about 'problems', 'alterations' and 'disturbances' of cognitive fluidity and integration, rather than 'deficits' and 'deficiencies'. This is because I do not believe we can assume that the differences we detect in schizophrenic information-processing are necessarily *losses* or *absences* of normal function. To recall Scharfetter's (2001) observation regarding early twentieth-century views of schizophrenia (see Note 3 of Chapter 7: p. 209 at the end of this book): most alienists viewed the disorder as a form of 'weakness of the psyche' or feeble-mindedness. We see echoes of this in contemporary phrases such as 'failure of self-monitoring' (Frith 1994) and 'deficiency in central monitoring of action' (Mlakar et al. 1994). We know that patients have alterations or differences in self-monitoring and central monitoring that indeed give rise to problems or even abnormalities of social cognition and behaviour. But to assume that these differences represent absolute deficiencies is to reinforce the age-old notion that psychosis is a degenerate condition characterized by 'a paucity of psychological activity or even a dimming of subjective life, perhaps especially of higher forms of consciousness or mental life' (Sass & Parnas 2001). In my view this serves to further stigmatize those unfortunates who attract a diagnosis of schizophrenia. As Porter (2002) put it, it 'spoils their identity'.

Finally, I think it is important to explore whether this cognitive model can be reconciled with the conclusion I reached in my discussion of phenomenology in the previous chapter: that 'the basic problem faced by these patients relates to their sense of detachment and disembodiment from "social self" and "social world"'. Is it possible to bridge these two paradigms: phenomenology and cognitive science? Of course, the answer I would offer is 'yes'. If we first consider the person with normal social cognition: in phenomenological terms we would say that her mental processes are 'embodied' in the healthy functioning of her soma (physical brain and body) that is interfaced directly with the social world. This mental embodiment allows her to distinguish stimuli emanating from her own soma from stimuli arising from the 'outside world'. This is because, in her brain, she has a normally functioning corollary discharge system that provides a warning of imminent self-generated stimuli. Thus, stimuli emanating from her own soma are understood as part of 'the self'.

If we now consider the psychotic individual: Phenomenologically, his mental life is disembodied from the physical – detached or alienated from his own corporality and the interaction of his body with the outside world. Even perception is separated from the psychotic mental world. In cognitive terms, there is a disconnection between prefrontal monitoring and posterior cortical generation of stimuli. Problems with the corollary discharge mechanism mean that there is no adequate warning of stimuli emanating from one's own soma – body and brain – and these stimuli are then misattributed to the outside world. Thus, in psychosis there is true alienation of mental life from the physical, whether it be the corporal physicality of one's own body and brain or the content of the social world around. And the 'hyper-reflexive' basis of positive symptoms, eschewed by Sass, can be understood in cognitive terms as a distortion of information-processing, resulting from a primary problem of dysconnectivity. Of course, it is this dysconnectivity that is in the first place responsible for the autistic alienation we recognize as 'negative symptoms'.

THE 'DYSCONNECTIVITY HYPOTHESIS' OF SCHIZOPHRENIA

The dysconnectivity hypothesis of schizophrenia has its roots, as I have already elaborated, in ideas of nineteenth- and early twentieth-century scientists and doctors of the mind/brain. As far back as 1881, Goltz (1881) had argued that higher brain function involves cooperative interactions between anatomically separate brain regions. Later, Camillo Golgi (1906), in his Nobel Prize acceptance speech stated: 'If one halts, to consider these connections, one becomes convinced that one single nerve fibre may have connections with an infinite number of nerve cells, as well as with completely different parts of nerve centres which may be a long way from each other'. With his concept of *sejunktionspsychose* or 'dissociation psychosis', Carl Wernicke anticipated the dysconnectivity hypothesis by 100 years, while others such as Otto Gross and Stransky followed closely with terms such as *dementia sejunctiva* (insanity of dissociation) and *dissoziationsprozess* (dissociation process). Of course, with the name 'schizophrenia', Bleuler had intended to capture the notion of dissociation or 'splitting of psychic functions'. Thus the concept of 'dysconnectivity' is not new to psychiatry but merely resuscitated. The term, as I have explained, refers to a disruption of interconnecting fibres that link spatially distributed regions in the brain. And, as we can see, this idea has been variously entertained for more than 100 years and by some very illustrious figures in the history of neuroscience.

In the modern age of high-technology research, a number of scientists such as Chris Frith, Eve Johnstone, Steve Lawrie and others have shown that the cognitive problems exhibited by patients with schizophrenia, can be linked to a breakdown in the functional integration of the PFC with the temporal and parietal cortices (Fletcher et al. 1998; Frith et al. 1995; Lawrie et al. 2002). We find that there is a host of evidence from structural and functional imaging studies supporting the notion that schizophrenia is a disorder of cortical connectivity. This has given rise to the so-called dysconnectivity hypothesis (Friston & Frith 1995) that reflects a shift in focus from the previously popular 'hypofrontality hypothesis'[3] (Weinberger et al. 1986).

In recent years, largely as a result of PET studies of neural activity during verbal fluency tasks, researchers in the field have begun to think in terms of *functional dysconnectivity* in schizophrenia. Friston et al. (1993) defines normal functional connectivity as 'the temporal correlation between spatially remote neurophysiological events'. As I have previously mentioned, this is in contrast to the classic theoretical framework informing concepts of higher brain function, namely 'functional segregation'. Functional segregation emphasizes a modular system in which different cognitive functions are localized to discrete anatomical regions. This classic framework has dominated much of neurology and also the early decades of brain imaging in psychiatry. However, with the recent re-emergence of interest in network models of the brain, functional connectivity is once again in vogue. There are two approaches that have been described by Friston et al. (1995) to measuring connectivity in the brain, the first being 'functional connectivity'. The second is 'effective connectivity' which is mechanistic, harder to measure and refers to the effect on a brain region of one or more extrinsic inputs to that region. To date, the vast majority of research into connectivity in schizophrenia has relied upon measures of functional connectivity.

Recent studies demonstrate abnormal frontotemporal (FT) activations on verbal fluency and verbal memory tasks, especially in the presence of auditory hallucinations, lending support to the hypothesis that the core feature of schizophrenia is a disruption of normal FT integration (Frith et al. 1995; Hoffman & McGlashan 1998; Lawrie et al. 2002; McGuire & Frith 1996; McGuire et al. 1995; Yurgelun-Todd et al. 1996a). For example, in normal subjects, Frith et al. demonstrated dorsolateral prefrontal cortex (DLPFC) activation during a verbal fluency task on PET scan (Frith et al. 1991). This activation is accompanied by a reduction of activity in the superior temporal gyrus (STG) with an inverse correlation between the prefrontal and temporal responses (Friston et al. 1991). Friston et al. (1991) concluded that the DLPFC modulates the responsivity of a neural system in the STG relating to willed action and intentional states. When the same analysis was applied to patients with chronic schizophrenia, it was found that this correlation between prefrontal and temporal activation was disturbed (Frith et al. 1995).

Patients demonstrated the same DLPFC activation during the verbal fluency task, but failed to show the normal decrease in blood flow in the left superior temporal cortex. One could say that there was a failure of 'dampening' of the temporal lobe activity by the PFC. In a review of their findings, these authors argue that this loss of correlation represents 'a profound disruption of large-scale prefronto-temporal interactions in schizophrenia' (Friston & Frith 1995). In other words, it reflects abnormal functional connectivity between frontal and temporal cortices. Of interest, this initial study also demonstrated these findings across three groups of patients with different symptoms, leading the authors to suggest that it might be a trait marker of the illness *per se*. Subsequently, there have been many replications of these findings (Dolan et al. 1999; Lawrie et al. 2002; Meyer-Lindenberg et al. 2001; Yurgelun-Todd et al. 1996b). Novel methods of analysis have also provided confirmation (Sigmundsson 2001; Woodruff et al. 1997; Wright et al. 1999), including electrophysiological techniques (Peled et al. 2001; Lee et al. 2003).

While the focus has undoubtedly been on connected DLPFC and temporal systems in schizophrenia, there is also evidence that other prefrontal-posterior cortical circuits exhibit similar deficits. In particular, the anterior cingulate cortex (ACC), the orbitofrontal cortex (OFC) and the inferior parietal cortex (IPC) and their interconnections are implicated. For example, in normal subjects, McIntosh (1999) used fMRI to demonstrate strong right hemisphere interactions between the ACC and the hippocampus during a working memory task, suggesting functional connectivity between these two regions. When similar tests are performed on patients with schizophrenia, one finds abnormal connectivity between the ACC and the temporal cortex (Dolan et al. 1995; Fletcher et al. 1999). A number of studies have highlighted the role played by the ACC in schizophrenia, both in terms of its own discrete functions as well as its role in modulating neural circuits.[4]

With respect to the OFC in schizophrenia: the majority of structural MRI studies correlate reduced OFC volume with negative symptoms (Baare et al. 1999; Gur et al. 2000) and some specifically correlate orbitofrontal white matter reductions with negative symptoms (Sanfilipo et al. 2000; Sigmundsson et al. 2001). While the functional imaging literature on OFC function in schizophrenia is scarce, there are a few studies and they tend to show reduced metabolism in the OFC (Andreasen et al. 1997; Clark et al. 1989; Kawasaki et al. 1996). For example, Kawasaki et al. (1996) used SPECT and correlated reduced cerebral blood flow (rCBF) in the left OFC with increased rCBF in the right temporal lobe in schizophrenics with delusions and hallucinations, suggesting that functional dysconnectivity between these regions may account in part for positive symptoms of the disorder.

As for the ACC and the OFC, the IPC and its connections have been relatively neglected in the dysconnectivity hypothesis of schizophrenia. This is surprising considering the prominent role of the parietal cortex, and the IPC in particular, in a variety of important cognitive functions; for example, attentional processes (Kastner & Ungerleider 2000; Mesulam & Geschwind

1978; Morecraft et al. 1993), working memory (McCarthy et al. 1997b), language processing (Aboitiz & Garcia 1997) and the attribution of agency (Farrer & Frith 2002; Ruby & Decety 2001). Both structural abnormalities (Bilder et al. 1994; Frederikse et al. 2000; Schlaepfer et al. 1994; Tien et al. 1996), and functional abnormalities (Cleghorn et al. 1989a, 1989b; Honey et al. 2002; Paulus et al. 2002) of the IPC have been demonstrated in schizophrenia. For example, Cleghorn et al. (1989a, 1989b) reported results from a resting PET study in which they found significantly reduced glucose metabolism in the IPC that correlated with increased metabolism in frontal lobes in schizophrenia. They suggest 'that the relation of frontal and parietal regions is altered in drug-naïve schizophrenics in episode' and further, 'that they may be reciprocally related'. It is surprising then, in the light of these early findings, that the dysconnectivity hypothesis of schizophrenia focused almost exclusively on FT interactions until very recently.

In summary, then, it appears that the predictions of Goltz and others were in fact correct: certain regions and structures in the brain (especially the cortex) are indeed functionally interconnected; and impairment of the functional relationship between these regions may well be the primary pathology in schizophrenia. These regions include: the DLPFC, OFC, ACC, amygdala, hippocampus, STG, anterior temporal pole and the IPC (i.e. prefrontal, temporal and parietal cortices).

STRUCTURAL CORRELATES OF FUNCTIONAL DYSCONNECTIVITY

Given that there is evidence for abnormal functional connectivity between these regions in schizophrenia, it is logical to consider whether there might be a structural basis for this finding. Does physiological dysconnectivity have an anatomical basis in structural dysconnectivity? Was Wernicke (1899) correct with his prediction that the fundamental pathology characterizing *sejunktionspsychose* is a disruption of the 'organs of connection'?

In terms of our modern knowledge of the brain, these organs of connection must refer to the white matter fasciculi or tracts that reciprocally connect different cortical regions to each other. We know that the human brain is largely comprised of grey matter and white matter – the former consisting of regions dense in neuronal cell bodies and the latter comprised of bundles of axons travelling between spatially separated regions, carrying information from one region to another. White matter tracts can be classified in terms of their directional course: Some connect the overlying cortex with deep brain structures (e.g. the internal capsule); others cross the midline, connecting cortical regions in one hemisphere with corresponding regions in the opposite hemisphere ('inter-hemispheric', e.g. the corpus callosum); and yet others run along an anterior–posterior axis within a hemisphere, connecting areas of the frontal cortex with posterior cortical regions ('intra-hemispheric', e.g. the arcuate fasciculus). In essence, all these fibres serve a communicating and integrating function. By linking electrical 'data' from spatially separate regions, these connections allow for the synthesis of complex information, which is the basis of consciousness.

Now in order for us to arrive at an answer to the question posed earlier (Is there a structural basis for functional dysconnectivity in schizophrenia?), we clearly need to examine the anatomical integrity of white matter tracts linking the cortical regions we have identified as 'functionally dysconnected' in the disorder. Earlier in this chapter I presented evidence for functional dysconnectivity in frontal–temporal (FT) and frontal–parietal (FP) circuits; and thus it is to the white matter tracts connecting prefrontal, temporal and parietal cortices that we must turn our attention to if we are to answer this question. In other words, we must examine the intra-hemispheric fasciculi that run along the anterior–posterior axis. What are these fasciculi?

FT white matter tracts have been studied in non-human primates[5] and inform our understanding of the likely comparable anatomy in humans. The OFC and ACC (Brodman area 24) have robust reciprocal connections with the medial and anterior temporal lobes via the *uncinate fasciculus* (UF), which constitutes much of the white matter of the anterior temporal stem. The UF carries reciprocal fibres from the OFC and the ACC via the anterior temporal stem to the rostral STG, the anterior temporal pole, the entorhinal cortex and the amygdala (Morris et al. 1999; Pandya & Yeterian 1996; Petrides & Pandya 1988; Seltzer & Pandya 1989).

In addition, the *anterior cingulum* bundle (AC) runs within the anterior cingulate gyrus and connects the DLPFC and the ACC with the para-hippocampal gyrus (PHG) and hippocampal formation (Morris et al. 1999; Pandya et al. 1981). There are also connections via the *arcuate fasciculus* (AF) (or *superior longitudinal fasciculus*) between the DLPFC and the STG and temporal association cortex (Ban et al. 1991; Petrides & Pandya 1988). Other smaller tracts that carry FT fibres include the *extreme capsule* and the *external capsule* (Petrides & Pandya 1988).

Importantly, human anatomical studies confirm that these connections in non-human primates are paralleled in the human brain (Dejérine 1895; Makris et al. 1999) (see Figure 8.1). In particular, the UF in humans is the most substantial of the FT tracts, forming a tight bundle as it hooks around the temporal stem and fanning out at either end into the frontal and tem-poral lobes. In the temporal lobes some of its fibres become continuous with the fibres of the *inferior longitudinal fasciculus*.

If we now consider FP connections, we find that there are a number of FP white matter tracts, however, for the sake of brevity and relevance to this discussion, I focus on the two major tracts. The *arcuate fasciculus* (AF), referred to above, is a highly connected structure, regarded as the principal association tract linking the DLPFC to cortical regions of the parietal,

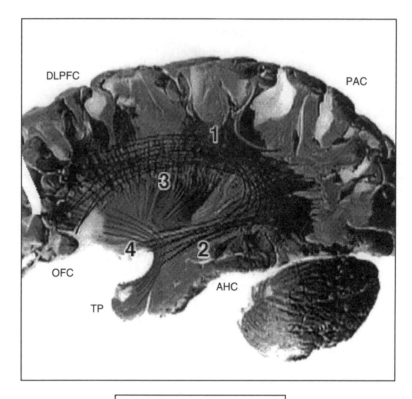

1	Arcuate fasciculus
2	Inferior longitudinal fasciculus
3	Fronto-occipital fasciculus
4	Uncinate fasciculus

Figure 8.1 Left hemisphere dissected to reveal major association tracts including those implicated in the social brain. Relevant cortical regions are also labelled: dorsolateral prefrontal cortex (DLPFC); orbitofrontal cortex (OFC); parietal association cortex (PAC); amygdalo-hippocampal complex (AHC); temporal pole (TP).

temporal and occipital lobes. In particular, after tracking posteriorly as a well-defined bundle parallel to the cingulum, it fans out with fibres connecting to the parietal association cortex in the region of the temporoparietal junction (Dejérine 1895; Makris et al. 1999). It also forms the main cortical connection between the language areas of Wernicke and Broca.

The *anterior cingulum* (AC), also discussed in relation to FT tracts, connects the DLPFC and the ACC to parietal, temporal and occipital cortex. In particular, its parietal connections include the medial aspect of the parietal cortex (Dejérine 1895; Makris et al. 1999).

At this point, I think it is important to summarize my line of argument.

First, I have established that functional abnormalities of FT and FP neural networks underlie many of the predominant features of schizophrenia. I have also raised the question as to whether 'functional dysconnectivity' implies 'structural dysconnectivity' in the disorder. In order to address this question, I have argued that, in the first instance, white matter tracts constituting these FT and FP connections need to be identified. Here, several such tracts have been identified. In terms of the pathology of schizophrenia, it is now possible to propose the following hypothesis: the *uncinate fasciculus*, the *anterior cingulum* and the *arcuate fasciculus*, constituting the main FT and FP white matter connections in the brain, are likely to show structural abnormalities in schizophrenia. In other words, this is a hypothesis aimed at proving Wernicke's claim regarding the 'organs of connection'. But if we are to set about testing such a hypothesis, we need a method for investigating the structural integrity of these tracts. A hundred years ago, as Bleuler stated, there was no such method, but do we have one today in the twenty-first century?

STRUCTURAL DYSCONNECTIVITY IN SCHIZOPHRENIA

Examining the structure of human white matter tracts *in vivo* is a challenging task. This is because, on standard structural brain imaging with MRI, the resolution of white matter is poor and analysis is difficult. Until recently most data regarding human white matter was obtained post-mortem; but this is obviously unhelpful when it comes to identifying correlates of behavioural and cognitive functioning in the 'here-and-now'. However, newer MRI methodologies, developed within the last decade, are providing researchers with novel means of exploring anatomical connections in the human brain and relating their findings to current mental functioning. *Diffusion tensor magnetic resonance imaging* (DT-MRI) is one such methodology; and with its advent it seems that we might now have a method for identifying the structural correlates of impaired FT and FP functional connectivity in schizophrenia.

DT-MRI is a relatively new structural MRI technique that to date has been used mostly within the neurological and neurosurgical disciplines, with a fair degree of success. DT-MRI measures the mobility of brain water molecules *in vivo* (Basser et al. 1994; Jones et al. 1999). Most MR visible water is enclosed within axons. Structures such as myelin sheaths, axonal membranes and microfilaments cause the water diffusion to be slower perpendicular to axons than parallel to them. Thus, within tissue with an oriented structure (such as white matter) the diffusion of water is higher in the direction of the fibre tracts. This directional dependence of water diffusion is called 'diffusion anisotropy'. In this technique, the deviation from

157

pure isotropic diffusion along axons is measured, and described in terms of the 'fractional anisotropy' (**FA**). This parameter is thought to provide a useful marker of white matter fibre integrity, with high levels of **FA** indicating healthy neurons (O'Sullivan et al. 2001). Obviously, where fibre tracts are disrupted (either developmentally or due to acquired insult), water diffusion within the axons is obstructed and reduced levels of **FA** are recorded during scanning. Data obtained during DT-MRI can be analysed using two different methods: *voxel-based morphometry* (VBM)[6] and *region-of-interest* (ROI)[7] analysis.

Between 1998 and 2003, several research centres published a number of studies using DT-MRI in schizophrenia. Of ten studies published, reporting mainly ROI analyses of structures including the corpus callosum (CC), ACC and frontotemporal white matter, six found reductions in **FA** in patients relative to controls (Agartz et al. 2001; Ardekani et al. 2003; Buchsbaum et al. 1998; Foong et al. 2000; Lim et al. 1999; Sun et al. 2003). Structures most commonly exhibiting reduced **FA** were the ACC (Ardekani et al. 2003; Sun et al. 2003) and the splenium of the CC (Agartz et al. 2001; Foong et al. 2000).

Against this background of exploratory studies using DT-MRI in schizophrenia, my colleagues and I (in Edinburgh, Scotland) conducted a study designed to investigate the issue of structural dysconnectivity in schizophrenia (Burns et al. 2003). Working under Professor Eve Johnstone (who published the first CT study in schizophrenia in 1976 (Johnstone et al. 1976)), we wanted to address the question of whether indeed there is a *structural* basis for *functional dysconnectivity* in the disorder. With DT-MRI, we had a method for measuring the integrity of FT and FP white matter connections (such as the *uncinate fasciculus* (UF), the *anterior cingulum* (AC) and the *arcuate fasciculus* (AF)). We recruited 30 patients with schizophrenia and 30 matched control subjects and performed whole brain DT-MRI and structural MRI on all 60 individuals. Then, using voxel-based morphometry (VBM) with a small volume correction tool, we compared **FA** values between groups in the UF, the AF and the AC bilaterally. The results were quite conclusive: There was a significant reduction in **FA** in the left UF and left AF, suggesting that there are indeed structural correlates for 'functional dysconnectivity' in schizophrenia and that these changes affect specifically FT and FP tracts.[8]

Before considering the implications of this finding for our understanding of the neurobiology, phenomenology and evolutionary history of schizophrenia, it is necessary to contextualize our study within subsequent DT-MRI findings since 2003. At the time of writing, there have been a further nine published DT-MRI studies of schizophrenia – giving a total of 20 studies to date. Almost all these later studies have used ROI analyses and all except one have found reductions of **FA** in schizophrenia. Again the ACC white matter (*cingulum*) was the most common structure implicated, although Hubl et al. (2004) replicated our findings of reduced **FA** in the UF and AF; and Nestor et al. (2004) found reduced **FA** in the left UF in schizophrenia. Thus, if we consider all 20 DT-MRI studies of schizophrenia to date, we find that the following white matter tracts more commonly demonstrate structural dysconnectivity:

- *ACC/cingulum* – four studies (Ardekani et al. 2003; Kubicki et al. 2003; Sun et al. 2003; Wang et al. 2004)
- *CC* – four studies (Agartz et al. 2001; Ardekani et al. 2003; Foong et al. 2000; Hubl et al. 2004)
- *UF* – three studies (Burns et al. 2003; Hubl et al. 2004; Nestor et al. 2004)
- *AF* – two studies (Burns et al. 2003; Hubl et al. 2004)
- *PHG/hippocampus* – two studies (Ardekani et al. 2003; Kalus et al. 2004)

Furthermore, there are two DT-MRI studies that yield important additional data on the UF in the schizophrenias. The first is a study by Kubicki et al. (2002) where the authors looked at diffusion anisotropy in the UF and found a group-by-side interaction in the patient group with relatively reduced **FA** on the left side, thus suggesting asymmetry of this important frontotemporal tract. In the second study, Nakamura et al. (2005) used DT-MRI to examine the structural integrity of the UF and ACC in schizotypal personality disorder (SPD). Their findings of bilaterally reduced **FA** in the UF of schizotypal patients have important implications for my evolutionary formulation of schizophrenia. This study supports my argument throughout this book that psychosis exists as a spectrum of anatomical dysconnectivity of white matter tracts linking the prefrontal cortex with posterior cortical regions.

In Chapter 4, I elaborated a genetic model of psychosis, which identified increasing numbers of susceptibility alleles (SAs) up to a threshold as corresponding to increased cortical connectivity and increasing risk for psychosis. Beyond the 'cliff-edge' threshold, excess developmental pruning of these 'social brain circuits' results in increasing dysconnectivity, reduced reproductive fitness and 'schizotypal' vulnerability to full-blown psychosis. Therefore, in terms of this model, one would expect some degree of functional and structural dysconnectivity of FT and FP tracts in SPD. Nakamura et al.'s (2005) DT-MRI study confirms that this is the case: patients with SPD do in fact have reduced integrity of the *uncinate fasciculus* – arguably the main FT white matter tract of the social brain. And, as we can see from schizophrenia research using DT-MRI, patients with full-blown schizophrenia, show evidence of both FT and FP structural dysconnectivity – thus supporting the notion that psychosis is a disorder of the social brain in our species.

REVISITING CEREBRAL ASYMMETRY
IN SCHIZOPHRENIA

In their commentary response to my 2004 *BBS* paper, André Aleman and René S. Kahn complain that I have ignored the abnormalities of transcallosal white matter connectivity demonstrated in some studies of schizophrenia. And indeed, in the 20 DT-MRI studies of schizophrenia to date, we see that 'structural dysconnectivity' has been demonstrated in the corpus callosum (CC) in four of these studies (Agartz et al. 2001; Ardekani et al. 2003; Foong et al. 2000; Hubl et al. 2004).[9] So these authors' complaint is justified and I agree that any theory of schizophrenia must acknowledge and account for the findings of both *inter-hemispheric dysconnectivity* (as evidenced by reduced **FA** in the CC) and *intra-hemispheric dysconnectivity* (as evidenced by reduced **FA** in the UF, ACC and AF).

In my discussion of the evolution of cerebral asymmetry in Chapter 6, I argued that asymmetry has ancient roots within the hominoid lineage and that it emerged as a result of decreasing inter-hemispheric connectivity and increasingly lateralized specialization of functions. Thus, there seems to have been a reciprocal relationship between inter- and intra-hemispheric connectivity. If, as I have suggested, the elaboration of intra-hemispheric tracts was associated with an increase in developmental vulnerability of these emerging networks, then it is no surprise that inter-hemispheric tracts would be similarly vulnerable to developmental insults. Thus, in schizophrenia where we find abnormal FT and FP connectivity, it follows logically that there should also be some differences in transcallosal white matter (i.e. in the CC). I would suggest that FT and FP abnormalities are primary and are genetically determined, and that transcallosal abnormalities are a secondary developmental consequence of faulty wiring within the hemispheres. This relationship between inter- and intra- hemispheric connectivity accounts too for the findings of reduced asymmetry in the disorder, since aberrant wiring within the hemispheres means that discrete functions are inadequately lateralized during development. In summary, therefore, I am suggesting that intra-hemispheric dysconnectivity is primary in schizophrenia and that the findings of both inter-hemispheric dysconnectivity and reduced asymmetry are a secondary developmental consequence.

CONCLUSION

So with the advent of DT-MRI and its application in schizophrenia over the last seven years, we have confirmation of the hypothesis offered earlier in this chapter: The UF, the ACC and the AF – constituting the major FT and FP white matter cortical connections – do indeed show structural abnormalities in schizophrenia. And 100 years later, Wernicke's prediction regarding 'the organs of connection' has been proven correct. Furthermore, as I have argued, the schizophrenias can be considered a disorder of the FT and FP circuits that have evolved in our species as a substrate for the social brain. In this sense, psychosis is indeed a costly by-product of social brain evolution in *Homo sapiens*!

And, finally, in terms of my cognitive model of schizophrenia, we can assume that FT and FP dysconnectivity (both functional and structural) accounts for the problems these patients have with the integration of information related to social behaviour, metarepresentation and the attribution of intentionality. As Mithen (1996) has suggested, *cognitive fluidity* depends on healthy functioning of our evolved social brain circuitry in adequately and appropriately integrating social information. Functional and structural dysconnectivity of these same circuits in schizophrenia results in *cognitive disjunction* (Cleghorn & Albert 1990) or *cognitive malintegration* (Burns 2004). In phenomenological terms, these disturbances of biological function render the individual vulnerable to partial or complete mental disembodiment from the physical. Psychotic phenomena represent a detachment or alienation from the 'embodied self' – a disturbance of one's natural sense of corporality and embeddedness in the social world.

9

EVOLUTIONARY ONTOGENY
OF SCHIZOPHRENIA

Ontogeny is the brief and rapid recapitulation of phylogeny, dependent on the physiological functions of heredity (reproduction) and adaptation (nutrition).

(Haeckel 1866)

Although a prolonged period of juvenile helplessness and dependency would, by itself, be disadvantageous to a species because it endangers the young and handicaps their parents, it is a help to man because the slow development provides time for learning and training, which are far more extensive and important in man than in any other animal.

(From Dobzhansky 1962. Reprinted with permission.)

In this penultimate chapter, I wish to consider the subject of *development*, specifically human brain development, and relate this to my thesis regarding the evolutionary origins of psychosis. So far I have argued that psychosis, and schizophrenia in particular, should be considered a costly by-product of social brain evolution in *Homo sapiens*. Furthermore, I have identified the evolution of complex cortical circuits as the key to both modern human social cognition and behaviour, and our species' capacity for psychotic illness. Any discussion of cerebral connectivity must include a review of the mechanisms involved in the development and maturation of the brain itself. Specifically, any evolutionary discourse on cerebral connectivity must include an analysis of how neurodevelopmental processes have changed during evolution. Such discussion and analysis will illustrate the mechanism by which the hominoid brain might have become larger and more connected. It will also allow us to speculate about abnormal developmental processes in the genesis of the schizophrenic brain.

THE 'MISSING LINK' IN THE
'MODERN SYNTHESIS'

When we consider the history of evolutionary theory since Darwin made his extraordinary ideas public with the publication of *The Origin of Species* in 1859, it becomes apparent that our present-day concept of evolution has itself evolved significantly. In fact, many evolutionists term their field 'neo-Darwinism'. The unit of natural selection, the gene, was only identified after Darwin's death; and so concepts such as *mutation, gene flow* and *genetic drift* only entered the evolutionary language during the twentieth century. In his book *Shapes of Time*, the Australian palaeontologist, Kenneth McNamara, argues that:

> ... In this modern synthesis a critical factor in the equation [was] left out: a missing link in evolutionary studies, the role that changes in the patterns of development of an organism play in evolution. In other words, how do variations in the genetic makeup of species influence development and produce the changes in shape and size of animals and plants to allow them to be susceptible to natural selection? This missing link is the third, and central, factor in the triumvirate of evolution: genetic changes in the timing and rate of development producing variation that is acted upon by natural selection.
>
> (McNamara 1997)

So, according to McNamara, 'changes in developmental patterns' is as important an element in evolutionary theory as 'the genes' themselves and the mechanism of 'natural selection'. But this element has been neglected for 100 years – as McNamara (1997) explains: 'Any attempt to write about the relationship between organisms' developmental histories and their evolutionary histories will forever be constrained by the tyranny of the past'. Why is this so? It all boils down to the statement (quoted at the beginning of this chapter) by the German anatomist, Ernst Haeckel, in his 1866 book *Generelle Morphologie der Organismen* – the statement which coined the phrase 'Ontogeny recapitulates phylogeny'. 'Ontogeny' refers to the developmental history of the individual from embryo to adult, while 'phylogeny' refers to the evolutionary history of a species. Haeckel's 'biogenetic law' thus suggested that the development of the individual passes through, or repeats, the same sequences as the evolutionary development of the species. The term *heterochrony* (literally 'changing time') was introduced by Haeckel to describe the general process whereby new features of a species may originate from an evolutionary change in the rate or timing of development.[1] Regarding the controversial concept of 'biogenetic law', McNamara (1997) argues that Haeckel's original meaning was lost as 'recapitulation theory'

163

was simplified or reduced to a 'strait-jacketed approach, which saw all the change as being a progressive addition of morphological complexity of the entire organism'. As Bjorklund and Pellegrini (2002) have explained: Interpreted in its most reduced form, 'biogenetic law' meant that, '. . . (T)he entire phylogenetic past of a species can be discerned by looking at (primarily) embryological development, which is essentially a much speeded-up version of evolutionary history. What is new in evolution is what is added to the end states of ontogeny'.

Unfortunately for developmental theory in the evolutionary discourse of the next 100 years, such highly literal interpretations of recapitulation theory soon raised scepticism regarding its role. By the 1920s 'recapitulation' was well and truly discredited. In its place, however, another heterochronic theory emerged with the Dutch anatomist, Louis Bolk (1926), its most ardent champion: the theory of *neoteny* or *fetalization* as Bolk himself termed it. Derived from the Greek word *neteinein*, meaning 'holding onto youth', the term 'neoteny' described the retention of juvenile features of an ancestor in adult forms of the descendant. This occurred through slowing of the rate of growth (*retardation*) and delayed maturation. Thus, in some senses, neoteny represented the reverse of recapitulation – in neoteny there is a prolongation into adult life of some features of infant ancestors, while in recapitulation there is the appearance early in development of adult forms of ancestors.

Bolk's main interest was human evolution and he maintained that all the defining characteristics of modern humans were neotenous – in his view, adult humans were no more than apes arrested in a juvenile stage of development. He claimed that 'man, in his bodily development, is a primate fetus that has become sexually mature' (Bolk 1926). Among the anatomical features Bolk identified as neotenous in humans are the enlarged skull and brain, reduced facial structure and jaw, curvature of the pelvis and relative hairlessness of the body. In support of neoteny as the major developmental mechanism in hominid evolution, the relative similarity of the adult human form to that of the juvenile chimpanzee is often cited. Bolk himself, as well as later proponents of the theory such as Montagu (1962, 1989) and Gould (1977), have emphasized the role of neoteny in human brain evolution, with a delay in the plateau of brain growth responsible for the large and complex brain of modern *Homo sapiens*. Gould (1977) has argued, 'human beings are "essentially" neotenous . . .'. Furthermore, both Gould (1977, 1981) and Montagu (1962, 1989) have expanded the heterochronic paradigm to the cognitive, emotional and behavioural characteristics of our species. They have suggested that a sort of 'behavioural neoteny' is responsible for the persistence of curiosity, emotional attachment and playfulness into human adulthood. As Brüne (2000) has explained: 'These attributes were supposed to cause the uniquely human "*Weltoffenheit*" (cosmopolitanism; Gehlen 1940; Lorenz 1973)'.

164

Despite the apparent decline in popularity of recapitulation theory and the relative ascendance of neoteny during the twentieth century, there are increasing voices of dissent – developmental psychologists, primatologists and neuroscientists, who are challenging neoteny as the overriding mechanism in human evolution (Langer 1998; McKinney & McNamara 1991; Parker & McKinney 1999; Shea 1989, 2000). For example, McKinney and McNamara (1991) argue, 'There is no single heterochronic process that accounts for all of human evolutionary change . . .'. These authors then go on to suggest that 'there is one process that accounts for much of it . . . It is hypermorphosis . . .'. So here we encounter another heterochronic term. Lock and Peters (1999) define *hypermorphosis* as the 'phyletic extension of ontogeny beyond its ancestral termination, such that adult ancestral stages become preadult stages of descendants'. They argue that it is a misconception that human development is generally retarded or slow across the lifespan: 'Humans do not grow more slowly than other primates but grow for a longer time in each phase of growth'. Figure 9.1 graphically demonstrates this phylogenetic increase in each phase of development.

In *Shapes of Time*, McNamara (1997) explains in detail how this relative expansion in each phase of human development has been misunderstood as retardation or neoteny. Instead, he argues that this phenomenon is better described in terms of the heterochronic mechanism hypermorphosis and offers the following reasons for this misunderstanding of the human developmental process:

> Much of the confusion that has arisen concerning the role of heterochrony in human evolution has done so for more than one reason.

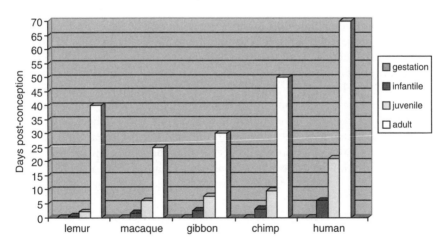

Figure 9.1 Comparison of growth stages in five primate species (in years of age). (Adapted from Smith 1992.)

Not only do we desire to distance ourselves as much as possible from any possible connotations of recapitulation (and the resultant assumption that we must therefore be the most complex and therefore the best), but I believe there has been a basic mistake in equating delays in transition from one growth phase to another with reduction in growth rate. They are nothing of the sort. Had humans been the product of reduced, neotenic growth we would be vastly different beasts, small of stature, small of limb, and, significantly, small of brain. Delays in transition from one growth phase to the next and neoteny are empirically different processes, yielding fundamentally different results. In the case of humans the product of our pattern of development, which is characterized by long, drawn-out growth phases, is overwhelmingly not one of paedomorphosis[2] but one dominated by peramorphosis[3]. In many important ways we have developed 'beyond' our ancestors and all other primates.

(McNamara 1997)

This renewed interest in the delay or extension of growth phases during human evolution has clearly touched upon some old anxieties surrounding Haeckel's 'biogenetic law'. Terms such as 'hypermorphosis' and 'peramorphosis' signal, in many people's minds, a return to the largely discredited notion of recapitulation. However, as McNamara (1997) is quick to reassure, this is not the case – they are different processes: 'However, fear not. There is no need to raise the spectre of recapitulation, for, as I will show, the peramorphic nature of our species is the product of much more than simple terminal addition to our ontogenetic development'.

Ultimately, the subtle differences in meaning of these terms are somewhat irrelevant in view of the following conclusion reached by most students of human evolution. While most authors would reject the idea that recapitulation (or hypermorphosis) occurs as an all-encompassing process in human evolution, the increasing recognition of *mosaic evolution* – that is the evolution of different components of a phenotype at highly unequal rates (Lock & Peters 1999) – has helped to rehabilitate recapitulation as a possible phenomenon. Mosaic evolution implies that some aspects of the phenotype may have evolved through developmental retardation while others have been accelerated. Thus, most participants in the ongoing debate around heterochrony in human evolution would accept that there is room for accepting both neotenic and hypermorphotic processes (Chaline 1998; Rice 1997).

NORMAL HUMAN BRAIN DEVELOPMENT

Before proceeding with a discussion of the heterochronic processes that may underlie the evolution of the social brain and the origins of psychosis in

166

Homo sapiens, it is necessary to consider briefly the normal ontogeny of the brain. Histological and molecular study of the developing brain from early foetal life through to adulthood has provided us with new insights into the mechanisms controlling each stage of development. We find that there are species-specific regulatory processes that ensure the correct patterning of the cerebral cortex as it emerges from embryonic precursors, proceeds through a cascade of predictable stages of maturation, before finally attaining its full adult complexity. Importantly, we discover that healthy neurodevelopment depends critically on specific timing of phases and coordination of events. Furthermore, we shall see that contemporary evidence supports the claim that it is the differences in timing of phases that separates species such as chimpanzees, bonobos and humans. Thus, data emerging from modern scientific methods is confirming the central role played by heterochrony in the evolution of modern humans.

If we consider the human embryo, we discover that during the fifth week of gestation the anterior end of the embryonic neural tube balloons outwards, forming the telencephalon, the precursor of the cerebral hemispheres. Progenitors of cortical neurons are confined to the ventricular zone (VZ) where they divide symmetrically during the process of *neurogenesis* (Rakic & Kornack 2001). Early pattern formation and neurogenesis are under the genetic control of homeobox genes such as POU (e.g. Brn, Oct-6 and SCIP), Dlx, Emx, BF-1 and -2 and MADS box (e.g. MEF2 class genes) (Allman 2000). Asymmetric division occurs in cells originating in the VZ with *migration* in radial columns or units towards the pial surface. Postmitotic cells settle in an inside-out temporospatial gradient such that later 'born' cells settle in more superficial layers. Radial migration is facilitated by glial cells that span the embryonic cerebral wall and is therefore 'gliophilic' (Rakic 2000). Other cells are 'neurophilic' and migrate tangentially along axons, for example GABA interneurons from the basal ganglia.

Migration is regulated by a host of cell adhesion molecules (CAMs, e.g. NCAM), cadherins, Reelin and various chemoattractant molecules. Axonal *arborization* follows with the outgrowth of axonal cones along pathways, mediated by molecules such as limbic associated membrane protein (LAMP), GAP 43 and ephrins (e.g. Eph-A5) (Rubenstein et al. 1999). *Synaptogenesis* involves the interaction of dendritic filipodia and axonal spinous processes in the formation of connections (Cohen-Cory 2002). A variety of CAMs and tyrosine kinases are involved in synaptogenesis and maintenance including synaptophysin, cadherins and neurotrophins (e.g. BDNF, NGF and NT-3). Both synapse formation and *myelination* continue well into adolescence in highly interconnected regions such as the association cortices. Simultaneously, there is a normal process of pruning or *apoptosis* that results in fine-tuning of connections. This fine-tuning is necessary for specialization of cognitive skills (Bock & Braun 1999; Casey 1999; Changeux

& Danchin 1976; Chechik et al. 1998). Apoptosis involves a number of molecules including Caspases 3 and 9, Jnk1 and 2 and BCL-2 gene family (Kuan et al. 2000; Kuida et al. 1998).

Thus, in summary, neurodevelopment proceeds according to specific stages: neurogenesis; migration; arborization; synaptogenesis; and apoptosis. Each phase is itself divided into consecutive microscopic events. Notably, this temporal sequence is essential, since subsequent processes depend on and build upon preceding processes. It follows that any disturbance of one phase upstream will completely disrupt the ensuing cascade downstream, amplifying the resultant disorganization of neural tissue. Thus, the importance of neuroregulatory molecules – both genes (such as homeobox) and protein chemicals – cannot be overemphasized in the healthy genesis of the human brain.

HETEROCHRONY IN SOCIAL BRAIN EVOLUTION

If we were able to compare all the phases of neurodevelopment outlined above across a range of primate species, we would be in a position to determine whether heterochronic mechanisms have indeed been operative during human brain evolution. Although data on the timing of development of specific brain structures is sparse in primates as a whole – especially data from great apes – there are some research findings supporting the role of heterochronic processes. For example, Clancy et al. (2000) compared embryological development in the macaque with human embryogenesis. They identified the timing of neurogenesis of various brain structures in the limbic system, the cortex and the rest of the brain in both species. They reported the first appearance, the peak and the end of this embryological phase in terms of the 'day post-conception'. Their results are shown graphically in Figure 9.2.

For each limbic or cortical structure whose peak day of neurogenesis is identified in the macaque, we see that the corresponding timing is later in the human embryo. Clearly, neurogenesis in the primate brain follows a specific geographical sequence with limbic structures appearing earlier than cortical layers – and this sequence is preserved between the species. However, human neurogenesis is characterized by a uniform delay in the timing of this phase relative to phylogenetically ancestral simians. To my mind, this suggests a heterochronic shift during the evolutionary history of primate neurogenesis. Specifically, the appearance of corresponding structures later in humans (than in macaques) suggests that limbic and cortical development has been subject to hypermorphotic change. Sean Rice of Yale University has compared brain growth curves for the chimpanzee and human and has shown that 'sequential hypermorphosis' characterizes the developmental shift from the former to the latter (Rice 2002). Every stage of neurodevelopment from

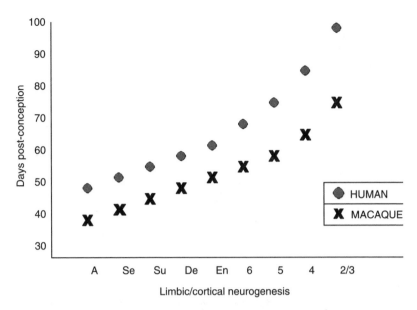

Figure 9.2 Comparison of macaque and human neurogenesis. The post-conception day when neurogenesis peaks is noted for a range of limbic and cortical structures. (A = amygdala; Se = septal nuclei: Su = subiculum; De = dentate gyrus; En = entorhinal cortex; 6 = cortical layer 6; 5 = cortical layer 5; 4 = cortical layer 4; 2/3 = cortical layers 2 and 3.) (Adapted from Clancy et al. 2000.)

conception to adulthood is delayed and continues for longer in humans compared with chimpanzees.

Although it is difficult to separate specific 'social brain' structures and circuits from the brain as a whole, for the purposes of identifying hetero-chronic shifts during human evolution, it is in my view likely that similar patterns would apply to both entities. Thus, regarding the evolution of the social brain, in particular, I would tentatively suggest that it resulted from a process of sequential hypermorphotic development (see Figure 9.3). In a review of heterochronic speculations regarding brain evolution and psychi-atric disorders, Brüne (2000) has previously suggested that hypermorphosis may have played a role in the evolution of the social brain. And in his discussion of evolving neurodevelopment, McKinney (2000) states: 'Many of our mental abilities are largely attributable to extension of brain devel-opment to produce a proportionately scaled-up version of the ancestral ape brain. Sequential hypermorphosis of behavioural and cognitive develop-ment is accompanied by prolonged stages of neurogenesis, dendritogenesis (and dendritic pruning), synaptogenesis and myelination'.

Thus, ontogeny may recapitulate phylogeny as far as the social brain and social cognition are concerned.[4] From our earlier discussion of both brain

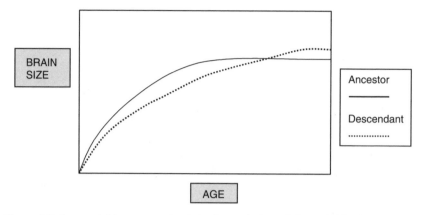

Figure 9.3 Sequential hypermorphosis in the evolution of the social brain.

development and evolution, it appears that the trend towards increasingly complex connectivity in subsequently more sophisticated regions of the cortex during development reflects the trend during our evolutionary history towards increasingly complex cortical connectivity, social cognition and metarepresentation (Brüne 2000; Deacon 1990; Finlay & Darlington 1995; Gibson 1991). McKinney (2000) stresses that it is 'terminal extension' (of connectivity and cognitive function) that occurs, rather than 'terminal addition'. Furthermore, he traces the prolonged stages of neurodevelopment back to 'our originally larger endowment of embryonic neurons'. Finlay and Darlington (1995) have argued that it is developmentally easier to generate a larger brain by extending prenatal brain growth than by altering the rate of growth. McKinney (2000) suggests that this delay in foetal brain growth in humans (25 days longer than in extant monkeys) '... seems to have cascading effects on neuronal complexity by prolonging the development of individual neurons, allowing more complex dendritic and synaptic outgrowths and connections'.

If, then, delaying foetal brain growth is the basis of increasing brain complexity, then what mechanism causes this prolongation? Drawing upon Deacon and others, we have seen that it is the timing and duration of neuronal generation that determines adult brain size and complexity (Deacon 2000; Finlay & Darlington 1995). Thus, the later the onset of neurogenesis and the longer its duration, the larger and more complex the resulting structure. This is because the longer period of time before neuron production commences allows more mitotic cycles for the production of stem cells to occur. Moreover, the later a neuron's birth date, the further it migrates, the higher the laminar position it finally occupies and the more complex its connectivity (McKinney 2000). Therefore, we may conclude that it all seems to hinge upon timing – timing of the onset, timing of the duration

170

and timing of the termination of these earliest developmental events. And this 'timing' is determined principally by *regulatory genes* that direct and coordinate the sequence of embryological brain formation.

We know that these regulatory genes, such as homeobox genes, have been largely conserved during the course of mammalian evolution. Thus, actual mutation of regulatory genes is unlikely to be the principal cause of heterochronic change in primates. However, *evolutionary change in the expression of regulatory genes* is certainly likely to have altered the trajectory of neurodevelopment from ancestor to descendant. For example, a simple change in regulatory gene expression would alter the proportion of late-maturing embryonic stem neurons and therefore alter the entire cascade of migration, arborization, synaptogenesis and apoptosis (Chaline 1998). In this case, '. . . the ultimate heterochronic event underlying human brain evolution would be traceable to mutations in (or altered expression of) homeotic genes' (McKinney 2000).

An additional factor of great importance is the following: It is well recognized that within primates the period of postnatal brain growth relative to prenatal is progressively lengthened, with humans having the most prolonged postnatal period of continued maturation (Deacon 2000; Finlay & Darlington 1995). Bogin has even argued that childhood and adolescence are developmental stages unique to humans (Bogin 1999). Importantly, this delay in brain maturation results in both a larger brain (Finlay & Darlington 1995), and in the extension of dendritic and synaptic growth, so that the human brain has more interconnections among neurons than the brains of other primates (Gibson 1991). Langer (2000) points out that, relative to other primates, humans, as well as having prolonged and accelerated cognitive and intellectual development (hypermorphosis), have largely retarded motor and physiological development (neoteny), allowing for a longer period of dependency and cognitive and social learning and maturation. Deacon argues that both of these changes could result from a heterochronic shift in the time course of the expression of segmental genes.

Is this model compatible with epigenetic theories of evolution? In Chapter 4, I discussed the role of epigenetic mechanisms in the evolution of the brain and the origins of psychosis. To recap briefly: these theories emphasize the continuous interaction of the environment with the biology of the individual. Epigenetic theories view a developing organism's response to environmental changes as a mechanism for phylogenetic change (Bjorklund & Pellegrini 2002). This is important both in terms of the social brain hypothesis and the argument for evolving cortical connectivity upon which it is based. Synaptic plasticity is an inherent feature of the modern human brain and increasingly research is suggesting that behavioural novelty may influence brain evolution (Bateson 1988; Gottlieb 1987, 2000; see Bjorklund & Pellegrini 2002 for a review). As I explained in Chapter 4, the advocates of epigenetic theory are at pains to point out that the mechanisms they propose are not Lamarckian, but are in keeping with the 'modern synthesis' in that evolution is still conceived as changes in gene frequencies in populations of individuals.

If, as these authors argue, the benefits accrued by the individual in terms of synaptic reorganization can lead to adaptive genetic changes in descendants, then one could hypothesize that heterochronic prolongation of brain maturation has served to escalate the potential for epigenetic change in brain evolution. In other words, a longer period of synaptogenesis and remodelling allows for increasing plasticity of networks, and this in turn increases the degree to which epigenetic effects can play a role. This might explain how the social environment became the driving force in the evolution of cortical connectivity and the social brain. One might speculate that such a process might have latterly been responsible for the explosion in neural, cognitive and cultural complexity during the last 60–100,000 years.

Before concluding this section, I must sound a note of caution. It may be that heterochronic mechanisms are too blunt an instrument to explain the evolution of cortical connectivity and the social brain. It may be that sequential hypermorphosis can account for the increase in primate brain size and cortical surface area as demonstrated by Finlay and Darlington (1995), but that the evolution of connectivity involved more complex mechanisms. Grove and others have shown that there is a morphogenic gradient of growth factors across the cortex which is translated into distinct fields of gene expression (Fukuchi-Shimogori & Grove 2001). These 'patterning' genes may include Emx and Pax6 (Mallamaci et al. 2000).

Jack Price of the Institute of Psychiatry (London, UK) has suggested that evolutionary changes in the extent of corticocortical connectivity may have resulted from changes in the sequential nature of cortical wiring (Price, personal communication). He points out that in mammalian non-primates cortical areas develop and connect more or less synchronously (e.g. in the rodent embryo, the hippocampus and the neocortex and their connections develop almost synchronously), while in primates – and in humans in particular – developmental events become asynchronous (e.g. in the 19-week human embryo, the hippocampus is highly differentiated in contrast to the neocortex, which is still undifferentiated (Hevner & Kinney 1996)). Thus, he argues, within the primate lineage, the development of some corticocortical connections could become contingent upon others. Finally, Price stresses the point that the emergence of asynchrony and contingent events in neurodevelopment pre-dated the first humans, appearing first in earlier primate ancestors. Thus, asynchrony and contingent events were not unique to hominid ancestors and cannot alone account for the massive advances that characterized human cognitive descent.

In terms of the evolution of cortical connectivity, one might speculate whether heterochronic mechanisms may have played a role (at a molecular level) in the timing of expression of individual developmental genes, thereby altering the sequencing of cortical wiring. Is it possible, for example, that a relative delay in the expression of genes determining neocortical development might account for the differences in differentiation between the neocortex and hippocampus in the 19-week embryo? If so, then the emergence of asynchrony and contingent events within the primate ancestry may also have depended on heterochronic mechanisms. And the fact that these features pre-dated the first hominids is consistent with the hypothesis that the social brain began to evolve earlier during primate descent.

Finally, one might speculate that the emergence of asynchrony and contingent events during primate cortical evolution was associated with increasing degrees of vulnerability and increasing potential for insult. Since these mechanisms of change were most radically manifest in the human line, it was in the hominid brain that insults were most likely to occur.

SCHIZOPHRENIA IS A DISORDER OF NEURODEVELOPMENT

In the rest of this chapter, I return to the principal subject of this book – psychosis and, in particular, schizophrenia – and seek to ascertain whether our discussion of the evolutionary ontogeny of the brain can inform our understanding of this mental disease. Can concepts such as heterochrony and sequential hypermorphosis enhance our understanding of psychosis? And are they useful concepts in terms of an evolutionary theory of schizophrenia? These are clearly important questions and the reader will have already guessed that the answer to all of them is 'yes'. It is my belief that heterochronic theory must be scrutinized in relation to the origins of psychosis since schizophrenia is widely accepted as a disorder of neurodevelopment (Weinberger 1987). Indeed, the prevailing neuropathological theory regarding the disorder is termed the *neurodevelopmental hypothesis of schizophrenia*.[5]

In previous chapters, I outlined the evidence for abnormal cortical connectivity in schizophrenia. But I did not address the matter of the underlying pathological processes that give rise to this macroscopic finding, which is characteristic of the brains of those afflicted with the disorder. Furthermore, I argued that schizophrenia lies on a genetic continuum with schizotypy and schizotaxia (see Chapter 3) and entails a variation in normal white matter connectivity. But I did not ask how this schizophrenic genetic spectrum could translate into altered anatomy? Clearly, none of these subjects can be addressed without first taking a close look at the neuropathology of schizophrenia and the developmental mechanisms giving birth to them. In reviewing the evidence, we need to consider at which phase/s of ontogeny the genetic defect becomes manifest. Does the schizophrenic genotype disturb normal neurogenesis, cell migration, arborization, synaptogenesis, myelination (Randall 1983; Randall 1998) or pruning (Feinberg 1983) or a combination of several phases? We must remember that it is also possible that the disturbance involves either an increase or decrease in one or more of these processes. Thus, abnormal connectivity may, for example, reflect either reduced pruning of abnormal connections or increased pruning of healthy connections or reduced dendritic arborization in the 'right' places or increased arborization in the 'wrong' places and so on. There are numerous possibilities, and different processes may be implicated to varying extents in particular sub-populations of schizophrenics.

Harrison (1999) has reviewed the evidence regarding the neuropathology of schizophrenia and the abnormalities for which he finds strong evidence are tabulated in Table 9.1. Harrison (1999) concludes that the evidence points towards later processes in ontogeny, namely arborization, synaptogenesis and pruning. Conversely, the evidence for migratory processes (such as neuronal disarray, maldistribution and dysplasia) is inconclusive and unsubstantiated. Abnormalities in Reelin protein and Reelin mRNA have been demonstrated in the PFC, temporal cortex and hippocampi (Impagnatiello et al. 1998); however, this may relate more to its role in synaptic function than in migration (Weeber et al. 2002). In terms of the timing of insults, Harrison argues that the evidence points to the second trimester. First trimester insults affecting neurogenesis are unlikely as gross structural defects (such as schizencephaly and polymicrogyria) would be expected. However, the increased findings of abnormal dermatoglyphics, craniofacial dysplasias and abnormal septum pellucida in people with

Table 9.1 Neuropathology of schizophrenia

Hippocampus/ DLPFC	Hippocampus	DLPFC	ACC
Normal number neurons	↓ synaptophysin	↓ synaptophysin	↑ synaptophysin
↓ size of neurons	↓↓ SNAP 25	↓ dentritic spines on layer III pyramidal neurons	↑ glutamatergic axons
↑ packing density	↓↓ complexin II		↑ axospinous synapses
↓ neuropil	↓↓ GAP 43 mRNA		↓ inhibitory (GABA) neurons
↓ pre/postsynaptic markers	↓/aberrant expression of MAP 2 (in dendrites)		
↓ arborization ↓ inhibitory neurons ↓ NAA ↑ synaptic pruning no gliosis			

schizophrenia do suggest early insults and thus the first trimester cannot be ignored.

A perennial problem for the neurodevelopmental hypothesis is the adolescent or early adult onset of the disorder. If schizophrenia is a disorder of neurodevelopment, why does it typically not manifest earlier on? And how do we account for the obvious role played by psychosocial factors in its onset? The explanation favoured by most schizophrenia researchers is that genetic (and possibly foetal and perinatal) insults disturb neurodevelopmental processes resulting in abnormal cortical circuitry. This manifests clinically as a spectrum of minor behavioural and psychological problems in childhood (or as normal). However, with the hormonal and neurodevelopmental changes of adolescence (including late synaptogenesis and myelination in association cortices as well as the onset of pruning) and the possibility of multiple 'hits', vulnerability to psychosis increases and, in some cases, the disorder manifests.

As we have seen, there is sound pathological evidence for disturbances of neurogenesis, arborization, synaptogenesis and pruning in schizophrenia. One scenario that integrates these findings is the following: abnormal neurogenesis results in small cortical neurons with reduced axospinous processes and arborization; subsequently, abnormal synapses develop; and finally, pruning in adolescence results in mass loss of synapses, loss of neuropil, denser packing of neurons and a decrease in synaptic marker proteins. Reduced and dysfunctional synapses would also account for the disturbed neurotransmitter levels described in schizophrenia. Of course, it is also possible that neurogenesis is normal and that the primary gene effects disrupt arborization or synaptogenesis, leading to a similar array of neuropathological findings. Regardless of the exact mechanisms, it seems that these disturbances predominate in regions comprising the social brain and result in functional and structural abnormalities of neuronal connectivity.

Finally, in terms of the pathological basis for the notion of a schizotypal spectrum, McGlashan and Hoffman have used computer-simulated pruning to demonstrate enhanced cognition by means of pruning and refinement (Hoffman & McGlashan 1997; McGlashan & Hoffman 2000). They hypothesize that: with excess pruning (beyond normal apoptosis) certain cognitive skills might be further refined, giving rise to creative genius in, for example, the schizotypal individual, and to possible select genius in the autistic savant; and that schizophrenia may represent an overshoot of the pruning process, resulting in severely abnormal connectivity. This is certainly a useful model since one might envisage a 'mild' degree of dysconnectivity in the schizotype and more severe dysconnectivity in the person with schizophrenia, relating to the respective 'dose' of the genotype.

EVOLUTIONARY ONTOGENY
OF SCHIZOPHRENIA

I am now in a position to formulate the following hypothesis: if schizophrenia is a disorder of neurodevelopment; and we know that heterochronic changes in the timing of neurodevelopment were largely responsible for human social brain evolution; then is it not highly likely that the origins of psychosis are in some way related to evolutionary changes in the timing of hominid neurodevelopment? In other words, the heterochronic mechanism that gave rise to a bigger and better connected brain in *Homo sapiens* may also have been responsible for psychotic illness in our species. I am by no means the first person to invoke heterochronic processes in the origins of psychosis – a brief review of previous suggestions will follow. But first, we must take a look at the candidate regulatory genes involved in the timing of neurodevelopment.

According to Harrison (1999), the main findings of smaller cortical neurons, reduced axospinous processes and arborization, reduced neuropil, denser packing of neurons and decreased synaptic marker proteins, all point towards later ontogenic processes such as arborization, synaptogenesis and apoptosis. However, the high occurrence of morphological defects such as abnormal dermatoglyphics and craniofacial dysplasias suggest that, in fact, neurogenesis may be disturbed. Earlier in this chapter I proposed a scenario where abnormal neurogenesis led to a cascade of disturbances in subsequent ontogenic phases. Most authors would agree that speculations about the molecular basis of abnormal neurogenesis are premature as we have little idea of potential candidates. For example, we cannot exclude the Emx-1 and Emx-2 homeobox genes on the grounds that mutations result in gross structural defects such as agenesis of the corpus callosum and schizencephaly. This is because schizophrenia may be a consequence of gene sequence variants that result in changes in gene expression (rather than mutations).

There are others such as BF-1, Caspases-3 and -9, and POU 111 gene family (including Brn-1 and -2, SCIP and Oct-6 genes) that could also be implicated. Indeed, Oct-6 gene, usually expressed in embryonic stem cells, has shown increased expression in the temporal lobes and hippocampi in patients with schizophrenia (Ilia et al. 2002). Weickert and Weinberger (1998) have identified POU 111 class genes as candidate molecules. I would also consider Caspase-1 and -3, both involved in founder cell apoptosis and thus influential in neurogenesis (Haydar et al. 1999; Kuida et al. 1998). Interestingly, certain caspases map to chromosome 11q22, which is adjacent to a known schizophrenia gene locus, 11q23. In the event that neurogenesis is the 'site' of initial insult, it would seem intuitive that pathologies of the synapse and neuropil represent secondary effects of the primary disturbance. However, it is just as likely that a number of genes regulating different

176

phases of development might be implicated in different individuals, given the extraordinary heterogeneity of pathological, morphological and clinical findings in this disorder. New methods such as microarray technology are providing powerful research strategies for identifying genes involved in synaptic processing in schizophrenia (Bunney et al. 2003; Mirnics et al. 2001). Thus, it is likely we shall arrive at a better understanding of the molecular basis of this disorder in the not too distant future.

If genes regulating neurogenesis were implicated in the evolutionary origins of schizophrenia, one would anticipate that the disorder might be characterized by an altered trajectory of neurodevelopment. Is there evidence for this? A number of authors have suggested that there is delayed brain maturation in schizophrenia (James et al. 1999; Saugstad 1994; Saugstad 1998). Delayed motor and language development (Cannon et al. 2002; Isohanni et al. 2001), earlier male onset and preponderance of pathomorphological changes (in accordance with the male slower rate of maturation) (Flaum et al. 1995; Saugstad 1999) and high levels of fluctuating asymmetry (Gruzelier 1999; Mellor 1992) all suggest a relative delay in neurodevelopment. Later developmental milestones increase risk for schizophrenia (Isohanni et al. 2001), while late maturing male adolescents have been shown to score higher than early maturers on measures of schizotypy (Gruzelier & Kaiser 1996). Several authors have shown that the average age of puberty has been declining over the last few centuries (Bogin 1999; Kaplan et al. 2000) and Saugstad relates this to the reduction in 'the most malignant non-paranoid forms [of schizophrenia]' (Saugstad 1998). She argues that this relationship is to be expected if schizophrenia is conceptualized as a disorder of delayed brain development.

Several authors have responded to these observations (about delayed brain development in schizophrenia) by attempting to invoke heterochrony in the genesis of the disorder (Bemporad 1991; Crow 1995a; Feierman 1994). In particular, they have suggested that schizophrenia may be related to a *failure of neoteny*. Notably, there are models for the role of heterochrony in other neurodevelopmental disorders (Wilson 1988). Brüne (2000) has examined the evidence for and against heterochronic mechanisms in schizophrenia and concludes that neither neoteny nor sequential hypermorphosis alone sufficiently explains the aetiology of schizophrenic disorders. However, I think there is some worth in considering certain morphological observations in schizophrenia which may, I would argue, suggest a disturbance of heterochronic mechanisms during cortical evolution. Specifically, data on head and brain size across the developmental life cycle are intriguing.

A meta-analysis of brain and cranial size in adults with schizophrenia found that there is a small but significant reduction in brain size compared with controls, while extracranial size is non-significantly *increased* (Ward et al. 1996). In another study, Bassett et al. (1996) found significantly increased head circumference (HC) in male patients and as one possible explanation, state 'head size increases may be due to overgrowth, secondary to pleiotropic expression of a developmental gene'. While reduced brain size is likely to reflect the effects of excessive pruning of abnormal synapses, increased HC reflects the limit of brain growth during development (and prior to onset of pruning). In terms of earlier development, the only data on cranial and brain size in schizophrenia are those from measures of HC at birth (Cantor-Graae et al. 1998; Kunugi et al. 1996; McNeil et al. 1993). These studies show significantly reduced HC at birth in those who subsequently develop schizophrenia. In the study by Cantor-Graae et al. (1998), the patient group showed smaller HC at birth, but increased HC in adulthood compared with controls.

Most authors conclude that these findings point towards delayed cerebral development *in utero*. Taken in conjunction with findings of craniofacial dysmorphogenesis and abnormal dermatoglyphics, Waddington et al. (1999) identify foetal weeks 9 to 15 as the likely timing of insult. Importantly, if HC is smaller at birth but bigger in adulthood compared with controls, and if maximal brain size determines HC, we can surmise that *sometime prior to the onset of pruning the schizophrenic brain was larger than normal*. Of course, larger size does not imply normal architecture. In this light, the finding in the Edinburgh High Risk Study of relatively increased brain size premorbidly in male high risk subjects who later developed psychosis is not surprising (Johnstone et al. 2002).

Figure 9.4 attempts to graphically illustrate the hypothesized neurodevelopmental trajectory, based upon these data, in schizophrenia compared with normal. I would argue that this trajectory is reminiscent of the pattern that characterizes *sequential hypermorphosis*. Is this merely coincidence or is it feasible that the disorder represents a disturbance of heterochronic processes implicated in the evolution of the social brain? If the answer is 'yes', then, in the light of comments made earlier in this chapter, it would seem logical that these disturbances served to alter the pattern of expression of individual developmental genes across the cortical plate. This may be possible to test if future methods of research allow us to map the sequence of gene expression in the developing cortex of individuals destined to have schizophrenia compared with normal individuals.

In summary, then, I would argue that the hominid social brain evolved in part through heterochronic processes including sequential hypermorphosis. I would also speculate that the neurodevelopmental pattern that characterizes schizophrenia represents a disturbance of normal heterochronic processes; and that therefore it seems likely that the genetic basis of the disorder involves a disturbance of regulatory genes governing the timing of neurodevelopment. Clearly, this disturbance results in a cascade of abnormal developmental events that interact with epigenetic factors, leading to abnormal synapses and gross pruning during adolescence. The circuits most severely

178

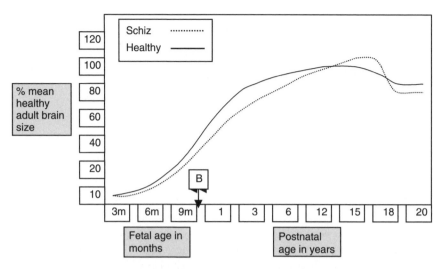

Figure 9.4 Graphic illustration of hypothesized trajectory of brain development (size) from fetus to adult in schizophrenia compared with healthy individuals. (Adapted from Lemire et al. 1975.) (**B** = birth.)

affected are those that evolved most recently and they comprise the connected regions of the social brain. Finally, I think it is sobering to consider that the mechanism 'employed' by evolution to allow for the expansion and reorganization of the social brain, which itself was demanded by an increasingly complex social environment, also rendered the organism extremely vulnerable to both genetic and environmental insult and subsequent disorder.

179

10

THE COSTLY LEGACY OF AN EVOLVED SOCIAL BRAIN

Darwin published the Origin of Species fifty years ago . . . the argument for natural selection has long been won, and its basic tenet is that only that which confers an advantage on the species is continually selected by the environment and therefore . . . perpetuated in the 'genes'. Nature never selects against the benefit of the species; it cannot. Furthermore, these poor schizophrenic people have self-inflicted losses in reproduction . . . Yet they survive at a constant level in the population. How can this be? It breaks the first law of Darwin! It can only be that a variant of that inheritance – the same units, but differently combined, so that they do not express themselves as illness – confers huge advantages. So huge that they compensate both for the misery of the illness, against the species' interests, and the reproductive failure of the afflicted! And what are the advantages? They are superior brain power, language, creative ability; and, consequently, divine dissatisfaction, a yearning for the absolute . . . the very things that distinguish us from the animals. The same 'genes' that drive us mad have made us human: in different combinations, I admit, but precisely, and in my view unarguably, the same particles of inheritance. You cannot have humanity without psychosis; they are indivisible . . .

. . . The truth is, we have always, from the moment of our origination, been a profoundly flawed species – mad in the basic particles of our being, radically insane – and the building of the great asylums only served to show us the magnitude of our madness . . . psychosis, ladies and gentlemen, is the price we pay for being what we are . . .

. . . Whatever you believe in your hearts, ladies and gentlemen, I ask you to believe with me that either conclusion must logically lead you to see that we are the most fortunate species ever to have lived or that it is possible to conceive of existing – ever, in this universe or in any other; and that it is our duty each day therefore to appreciate our astonishing good fortune by caring for the insane who pay the price for all of us, and by turning our own healthy lives, so near as we can manage it, day by day, into an extended rapture.

(From Faulks 2005. Reprinted with permission.)

These are the rousing words of Dr Thomas Midwinter, English psychiatrist and hero of Sebastian Faulks' latest novel, *Human Traces* (Faulks 2005). Set in late nineteenth-century Europe, this is a saga of two friends, both psychiatrists, whose lifelong quest is for a true understanding of what it means to be human. In his construction of Thomas Midwinter, Faulks has drawn on the thinking of another English psychiatrist – this time contemporary – Professor Timothy Crow of Oxford University. Midwinter is a thinly veiled disguise for this giant of modern psychiatry and evolutionary thought. To Crow goes the real credit for linking the origins of psychosis to the very origins of *Homo sapiens* him- or herself. In fiction, Faulks has recreated Crow's odyssey – a journey that includes painstaking analysis of the schizophrenic brain; immersion in Darwinian theory and debate; and rigorous appraisal of contemporary evidence regarding brain evolution in our species. Following Crow, Midwinter concludes that psychosis emerged as a costly consequence of cerebral laterality and the capacity for language in humans. Furthermore, it emerged sometime prior to the migration of the earliest *Homo sapiens* out of Africa and the successful dispersal of this fledgling species across the planet. Due to its inextricable 'linkage' to the core human capacity for language and, therefore, culture, psychosis survived the relentless purges of natural selection. As Midwinter (Faulks 2005) states: 'The same "genes" that drive us mad have made us human'.

As I have argued throughout this book, I differ from Tim Crow on a number of points – regarding language, laterality and his protocadherin gene – but in his fundamental claim that madness constitutes a costly price paid by our species for our extraordinary cognitive superiority, I concur wholeheartedly. Conceptually, I am with Crow – it is in the detail and emphasis that we differ. And our differences boil down to a basic philosophical divergence on the issue of what specific quality defines us as human. What anatomical and cognitive transformation 100,000 or 150,000 years ago signalled the arrival of the first modern human? What is the essence of humanness itself? This question is one that is debated and has been debated for centuries in disciplines as diverse as religious studies, archaeology, biology, law, medicine and philosophy. And there are factions that transcend these disciplinary boundaries. Some would say that 'language' defines humanness; some say 'art'; some say 'consciousness' or 'self-consciousness'; some say 'culture'; and some say 'spirituality'.

Personally, I subscribe to the faction that defines *humanness* in terms of 'a capacity for complex social and interpersonal relationship'. In this view, all of the abilities routinely cited as uniquely human are, in fact, secondary to the fundamental human capacity for complex social cognition. Thus, what makes language unique to our species is the 'elevation' of generic animal communication by a highly social human mind. (In other words: communication + social cognition = language.) Likewise, I would argue that individual self-consciousness is only possible in the context of existing interpersonal consciousness. The developing child forms his or her individual concept of the self on the basis of first becoming conscious of others to whom he or she relates (Brothers 1997; Mead 1913; Vygotsky 1978). As I quoted Brothers (1997) in Chapter 5, '. . . only brains in a social field can generate the kind of consciousness that includes "I" '.

It is generally common knowledge that many species other than humans are social and engage in impressive social repertoires to the point that we question the existence of non-human forms of consciousness. Termites exhibit remarkable social cooperation, cohesion, self-sacrifice and communication. Migrating birds seem to possess a profound knowledge of shared intention and interdependence. Bat-eared foxes in the Kalahari Desert will deliberately risk their lives in the face of a predator in order to distract it from others in the pack. And many primates – not just the highly social chimpanzee – engage in complex 'interpersonal' behaviours such as deception, reciprocal altruism and conflict resolution. However, no other species besides *Homo sapiens* relies so dramatically and consistently on highly complex metarepresentational ability and interpersonal 'dynamics' in order to survive within its species-specific environment or society. The human condition is fundamentally social – every aspect of human function and behaviour is rooted in social life. The modern preoccupation with individuality – individual expression, individual achievement and individual freedom – is really just a fantasy, a form of self-delusion, since all individual expressions, achievements and freedoms depend primarily on social expressions, achievements and freedoms. As in the African notion of *ubuntu*, 'A person is a person through other persons'.

We have seen that the Cartesian construct of an ethereal mind separated from the physical matter of brain, body and world has failed to represent the reality of embodied human consciousness. The philosophies of Heidegger, Merleau-Ponty and Fromm constitute a valiant and largely successful movement against Cartesianism. These thinkers have provided us with a better conceptualization of the social mind and a phenomenology that is truer to our everyday experience of human emotion and thought that derives from 'being-in-the-world'. It is no longer possible to describe 'the mind' as some kind of free-floating, disembodied, isolated and uniquely personal entity, hidden from view within the depths of each person. Individual consciousness emerges from and is reciprocally connected to the electrochemical shifts within and between brain cells, somatic cells of the body and stimuli arising from the environment outside the body. This is what these and other philosophers are describing when they use terms such as 'the embodied mind'. And contemporary evidence from developmental psychology confirms that this mystical 'thing' we call 'the mind' is, in fact, the outward manifestation of brain function – derived from the continuous two-way interaction of genes with neural tissue with the physical, social and cultural world around (the 'environment'). The best attempt within mainstream psychiatry to encapsulate this dynamic process lies within the 'biopsychosocial model', but I would argue that this retains the Cartesian split and that there is a real need for a new model that better describes the embodied mind.

A great portion of this book is dedicated to evolutionary theory and, in particular, to the evolutionary origins of the human mind/brain both in health and disease. I have argued that the brain and cognitive behaviour of modern *Homo sapiens* is but a point on a path forged by means of natural selection through millions of years of systematic 'pressure' to survive and succeed in a social world. While factors such as tool use (Wynn 1988), foraging behaviour (Milton 1988), meat-eating (Stanford 1999) and climactic change (Calvin 2002) have been postulated as ultimate causes for human brain evolution, I believe the accumulated evidence from disciplines across the breadth of behavioural science better supports the so-called social brain hypothesis. Over the last 60 million years of primate evolution, social selective pressures have steered subsequent generations of lemurs, then monkeys, then apes and then hominids along a course of progressively more complex and sophisticated social cognitive ability.

In Chapter 6, I outlined both the neuroanatomical and neuropsychological evidence for this phylogenetic emergence of the social brain and corresponding increase in social cognition. The evidence at our disposal supports an evolutionary process of progressive enlargement and reorganization of neural circuits governing social behaviour, social cognition and theory of mind (TOM). With each phylogenetic step down (or up) the primate family tree, we see an advance in this social brain structure and an advance in social cognitive ability. Prefrontal, temporal and parietal association cortices have undergone significant enlargement, reorganization and connectedness during primate evolution, producing a cortical network that interacts in both a top-down and bottom-up manner with deeper limbic structures – this complex we describe as the evolved social brain. In my view, it is this highly complex social brain that defines us as a species. While many other creatures are undoubtedly social in nature, none exhibits a level of interpersonal relationship and interdependence as sophisticated and indispensable as modern *Homo sapiens*. We have no idea as to whether non-human species possess consciousness in a way similar to humans. Many would argue that it is our self-consciousness that sets us apart from the beasts – if this is so, then we possess it because we have evolved, over millions of years, the ability to become aware and responsive to other 'minds'.

Generating awareness of the minds of others in our social environment has allowed us to formulate an internal world we call 'the self'. In the development of each new individual, we witness again and again the process by which a young child first begins to interact with the world around, building a platform of interpersonal relationship, before embarking on a journey of self-discovery, identity formation and consolidation of the 'self'. Aided by high-powered microscopes, we are now discovering cells in the brain that mediate social exchanges, understanding of the mental states of others and a capacity for empathy. These 'mirror neurons' are located, not surprisingly, in the anatomical regions that comprise the social brain. Perhaps it is to these socially sensitive cells then that we should turn our attention, if we wish to understand the physical seat of 'the self'.

How then did we as a species come to experience a capacity for madness? Why do some humans become psychotic, 'out of touch with reality', travellers in a world of delusion, fragmentation and alienation from society? The key lies, I believe, in the genetic mechanism by which the human brain evolved into its extant form. In Chapter 9, I discussed the heterochronic mechanism termed 'sequential hypermorphosis'. This mechanism entailed evolutionary changes in genes that regulate the timing of neurodevelopment in the growing individual. Specifically, in response to selective pressure to evolve a brain well adapted to the complex social environment in which they lived, our ancestors experienced changes in regulatory genes that resulted in the progressive prolongation of brain maturation. A relative delay in and extension of each phase of neurodevelopment gave rise to increasing intra-hemispheric cortical connectivity – providing a substrate for complex social cognition that we now call 'the social brain'. Evidence of an early 'metamind', as well as a trend towards increasing specialization of FT and FP circuits in our nearest relatives, the apes, suggests that these changes evolved during the period 18–0.5 mya. Importantly, the emergence of the social brain over nearly 20 million years involved changes in multiple neuroregulatory genes. These included genes regulating neurogenesis, cell migration, arborization, synaptogenesis, myelination and apoptosis (pruning). For some reason, these changes were accompanied by a particular sensitivity or vulnerability in the developmental processes of these cortical circuits. In the apes, this process occurred too, but to a much lesser degree, leaving their ancestors' brains less vulnerable to insult.

It is against this evolutionary developmental backdrop that events took place, giving rise to the psychotic genotype. Sometime during the period 500–100,000 years ago, prior to the migration of *Homo sapiens* out of Africa, a series of specific but as yet unknown changes occurred in neuroregulatory genes. Importantly, these changes occurred gradually and thus did not represent a speciation event. In some individuals, changes in the morphology or expression of regulatory genes involved in the timing of neurodevelopment may have altered the developmental trajectory of vulnerable FT and FP cortical circuits, resulting in aberrant connectivity in the social brain. This was/is expressed phenotypically as schizophrenia and

184

related disorders. It is likely that those individuals with the greatest expression of the genotype perished quickly in the ancestral environment. The presence of a continuum of variation in the expression of the genotype meant that some individuals (with perhaps a milder degree of dysconnectivity and subsequent pruning that actually enhanced cognition) manifested special cognitive abilities, while others manifested schizophrenia. The psychotic genotype itself was unlikely to have conferred a reproductive advantage on the schizotype, but because of its association with genes that code for the development of the social brain in the species, the disorder persisted in the human genome. Thus, as Thomas Midwinter (Faulks 2005) proclaims 'The same "genes" that drive us mad have made us human'.

Psychosis is therefore one, and maybe the greatest, of the prices paid by humans for evolving complex cognitive and social abilities. It is precisely because we have the capacity to have a TOM and function in a socially appropriate manner that we also have the capacity for aberrant cortical connectivity and an illness such as schizophrenia. One benefit of harbouring this potentially disastrous genotype in our human gene pool is that in some cases individuals, occupying a 'tamer' position in the spectrum, may exhibit unusual creativity, brilliance and iconoclasm. It is quite likely that these individuals are among those responsible for pioneering and creating the great artistic, technological and cultural advances of human history. Henry Maudsley (1908), one of the fathers of British psychiatry, toyed briefly with eugenic principles (Crow 1995b), but later admitted: 'To forbid the marriage of a person sprung from an insanely disposed family might be to deprive the world of a singular genius or talent, and so be an irreparable injury to the race of men . . . If, then, one man of genius were produced at the cost of one thousand or fifty thousand insane persons, the result might be a compensation for the terrible cost.'

In the final part of this section I wish to propose a number of ways in which this evolutionary hypothesis might inform future schizophrenia research and clinical practice:

- In terms of molecular research, regulatory genes that control the timing of neurodevelopment, and in particular the timing of neurogenesis and stem cell differentiation, should be considered as candidates in schizophrenia. So too should genes known to interact with and modulate these regulatory genes. Furthermore, it may transpire that the disorder is caused by altered expression rather than mutation of genes. Thus, the search for the genes for schizophrenia is sure to be a Herculean task. It is also likely that if such a genotype is identified, it will be implicated in only some people with schizophrenia – the phenotypic heterogeneity suggests that multiple factors, both genetic and environmental, may disturb neurodevelopmental processes thus giving rise to psychosis.

- More speculatively, since I have argued that the social brain and schizophrenia emerged gradually from an evolutionary process already present in hominoid ancestors, I would anticipate that both human-specific cognition (e.g. language) and schizophrenia have a molecular basis in genes we already share with extant apes. I would predict that what separates us cognitively are differences in gene expression rather than differences in gene composition. For this reason the search for both the genes that make us human and for those that cause schizophrenia is likely to be far more complicated than a mere contrasting of human and chimpanzee genomes in the not too distant future (see Gagneux & Varki 2001 for a review).

- In terms of future imaging in schizophrenia, more studies are needed of the social brain and the exact nature of its impairment in the disorder. Techniques such as DT-MRI and fMRI may help us to identify both structural and functional deficits within the FT and FP circuitry. fMRI studies using paradigms that activate different components of social cognition should be a priority. For example, further studies examining the neural basis of self-recognition may help increase our understanding of the neurology of social cognition. Also, specific cortical connections (such as the UF and AF) merit further attention and new methods of scanning and data processing may help unravel the core pathologies that characterize the brain in schizophrenia.

- New imaging techniques could also be used effectively in comparative primate studies to further our understanding of brain evolution and specifically the changes I have hypothesized in the social brain. In this endeavour, I would suggest that DT-MRI studies of extant apes might be particularly informative, providing critical data on white matter connectivity, hitherto inaccessible with standard MRI methods. In terms of the social brain hypothesis, I would predict such data would show a progressive phylogenetic increase in the density of FT and FP tracts in primates.

- And lest we forget that all meaningful research should have direct clinical implications for those whom we find intellectually interesting, I would suggest that this model can inform our management of patients in two important ways. First, if the pathologies we see in the brain have their origins as early as mid-gestation, and if subsequent ontogenic events constitute a cascade of aberrant developmental processes all sensitive to epigenetic factors, then surely, as many authors have suggested, *prevention* is the main avenue for intervention. We cannot hope to prevent early genetic effects (unless genes can be identified *in utero*) but later damaging developmental events could be retarded and the trajectory of aberrant neurodevelopment corrected by means of early detection and intervention. These interventions might include dietary, pharmacological and psychosocial measures and may serve to reduce or even abolish vulnerability to subsequent disorder. And second, this model highlights the importance of social deficits in schizophrenia, and consequently a large part of our clinical and research effort should be dedicated to understanding and confronting the social, cultural, economic and political obstacles that face our patients. If these vulnerable individuals, who have particular difficulties with comprehending and responding to the social world, are isolated, stigmatized and subjected to societal prejudices, then they have no hope of averting a lifelong struggle with incapacitating mental illness.

REVISITING THE BOUNDARIES OF HUMANITY AND SANITY

The scope of this book is undoubtedly wide – I have touched on a number of important issues, some controversial and some almost speculative. In constructing an evolutionary theory of schizophrenia based upon the emergence of the social brain in primates, I have drawn on various academic lines of inquiry as diverse as the archaeology of shamanism and the neuropathology of psychosis. In this section I wish to revisit several themes that might otherwise get lost; and which I believe can now be viewed differently in the light of the social brain hypothesis. These are large philosophical questions that no brief discussion can hope to answer; and yet perhaps there are small insights that can be gained from the perspective I have developed in the pages of this book.

The boundaries of humanity

In his concise but profoundly intellectual little book *So You Think You're Human*, Felipe Fernández-Armesto, Professor of Global Environmental History at Queen Mary, University of London, reviews the development and challenges the scientific veracity of our modern definition of humanity (Fernández-Armesto 2004). One should not be put off by the rather frivolous title of this book – it comprises an erudite discourse on human nature that is highly intellectual and thought-provoking. Fernández-Armesto questions our traditional assumptions around what it means to be human and the ways in which historically we have moved the boundaries to include or exclude certain groups from the human family. For example, at certain periods in our history, great apes such as orang-utans have been regarded as human – the red ape's very name is translated as 'man of the forest' – while in the modern era they are, of course, excluded. With new scientific data on apes and closer observation of their habits and behaviour both in the wild and in captivity, we find that once again the gap between them and us is narrowing. Today, there is a significant lobby for 'human rights' for great apes: The Great Ape Project aims to extend moral, ethical and legal rights to great apes.[1] Fernández-Armesto argues that most human specializations, which are often cited as defining of our species, are really no more than novel compensations for human frailty and weakness relative to other species in our environment. He states:

> Most of the attributes on which we humans congratulate ourselves seem, in short, to be evolutionary compensations for physical feebleness. Well-developed brain power is a competitive advantage in a struggle for survival with more powerful rival predators. Tool-making suits species under-equipped in tooth and claw. Language is useful for creatures compelled to huddle in large groups for security and for hairless apes who need a substitute for grooming. Cooking is the obvious recourse for a species short of ruminative skills and reliant on foods which bipedalism makes hard to digest. Against this background, the struggle for human self-definition has been understandably hard and long.
>
> (Fernández-Armesto 2004)

This author addresses each of the so-called defining characteristics of humanity and dismantles them by drawing on contemporary research that shows mere qualitative differences between human and ape ability. For example, regarding language, Fernández-Armesto (2004) points out that: 'Apes have brains that seem well suited to develop human-style language'; chimps, on the whole, are better at mastering human language than humans are at understanding chimp communication; chimps and bonobos in captivity have learnt to understand and sign up to 150–200 words in human vocabulary; and great apes show an extraordinary range and complexity of non-verbal communication. Similarly, in regard to our human capacity for creativity in art, Fernández-Armesto makes the following case against a human monopoly in this area:

> Art is the realization of what is imagined (for even a relatively uncontrived photograph or one of Duchamp's *objets trouvés* is changed by appropriation by the artist) and we can be sure that many non-human animals have powers of imagination similar to our own: imagination is a vital mechanism in obtaining food and shelter, reading the weather, anticipating predators and rivals. So potentially, at least, such animals are artists ... It is commonly and correctly said that apes never adorn themselves in the wild with the kind of bijouterie favoured by humans ... However, at the Yerkes Institute of Primatology in Atlanta, female bonobos sometimes put dead rats or cockroaches on their heads and keep them there all day, deriving apparent gratification from the fact. The parallel with behatted human ladies at Ascot is hard to resist. The transformation

of dead vermin into items of *haute couture* is not, after all, unintelligible even in human terms, as any wearer of squirrel-skin or fox-fur will be obliged to admit. To see a dead cockroach and reimagine it as headgear requires a mind capable of inventive transformations.

(Fernández-Armesto 2004)

In a similarly forthright and amusing manner, Fernández-Armesto takes on claims of human uniqueness with regard to our capacities for tool-making, fire-making, ritual behaviour and culture. None of these attributes, he argues, define us as unique – these are not the features by which we can identify what it means to be human. What then does this mean in terms of establishing the position of *Homo sapiens* within Nature? Is there nothing special about being human?

I believe that any attempt to answer this question must take cognizance of the fact that there is a fundamental *difference* between scientific and religious enquiry. I use the word 'difference' intentionally – to indicate that these two paradigms cannot really be compared or substituted for one another. Science and religion ask different questions, operate on separate planes and invoke entirely unrelated 'forces' in reaching answers to the big questions about existence. In my view, and in the view of the contemporary philosopher, Michael Ruse (2001), religious belief or faith and scientific belief or 'faith' are not mutually exclusive. One can hold both a religious and scientific view of the world contemporaneously. The battle between science and religion for the hearts and minds of humanity is, in fact, a battle between fundamentalist believers in both camps who seek to usurp the role of 'the other side' with exclusive interpretations from their own perspective. So, for example, when creationists insist on a literal interpretation of Genesis and seek to date the beginning of the world to 5000 years ago, they are usurping the authority of science – where science has clearly established that the earth is billions of years old and that life evolved over countless millions of years. Ruse argues that a Darwinian model of the origins of life is quite compatible with a metaphorical interpretation of Genesis. Similarly, when science attempts to explain such nebulous and unpredictable human idiosyncrasies as morality, selflessness and compassion in terms of biological laws, science is overreaching its mandate.

Thus, in my opinion, evolutionary game theory cannot truly provide us with satisfactory explanations for why some humans die for others, go to jail as conscientious objectors or show compassion for the poor. By definition true altruism, as Clark (2002) argues, cannot be a consequence of the individual calculating the relative costs and reciprocal rewards of his or her actions. If an act of altruism is no more than a disguised strategy to reap later benefits for the individual concerned, then it is not truly altruistic. Real altruism is sacrificial and occurs in the absence of potential reward. The historical and ongoing conflict between science and religion is bigoted and unintelligent. When any faith, religious or scientific, becomes exclusivist and intolerant of the explanatory value of the other, then meaningless conflict results. That is why the current political manoeuvring in America to make compulsory the teaching of so-called 'intelligent design' theory in schools is intellectually pathetic. This is a twenty-first-century example of fundamentalist religion (by means of a wholly contrived fable) attempting to usurp the authority of science in accounting for the origins of life on our planet.

So, when it comes to the question I posed earlier – 'Is there nothing special about being human?' – I believe we need to be clear as to which perspective we are adopting in arriving at an answer. This book is a scientific work, based in its entirety on data and theoretical discourse emerging from the behavioural and social sciences. I am therefore asking this question in scientific terms only – I am not engaging in a religious debate around the essence of humanity. And, as I have stated above, I do not believe that a scientific answer to this question is necessarily mutually exclusive of a religious answer to the same question. In fact, the respective answers may prove to be compatible.

In my view there is one unique and defining characteristic that makes us 'human' and separates us from other life forms. And that characteristic is summarized within a term we commonly use to describe others: *humanity*. 'Humanity' not in the sense of the collective species of modern *Homo sapiens*, but 'humanity' in the sense that an individual displays humanity towards another person – kindness, compassion, altruism, caring, love. It is in our capacity to show humanity towards others that we set ourselves apart from the rest of Nature. So, in place of the popular maxim 'Human is as human does' we should rather state, 'Human is as human does to others'. Being humane means looking outwards from our selves and engaging with the needs, welfare and concerns of others in our social world. It means that we are socially attuned and responsive – responsive not because there is some gain in it for ourselves or our immediate kin, but responsive because we recognize our common humanity with others and our fundamental interconnectedness. This is the essence of *ubuntu* – that my well-being and life course is integrally tied up in the well-being and life course of others.

I would argue that acts of selflessness, altruism and self-sacrifice can be wholly understood if we think in terms of human consciousness being rooted in a social mind and a social brain. If our individual thoughts and feelings and development as beings are embedded in the social world that is our environment, then we cannot help but feel the suffering of others and respond with our humanity. Following Mary E. Clark and the Dalai Lama, the spiritual leader of Tibet, I have an optimistic view of human nature. What defines us as *human* is the fundamentally social origin and character of our individual minds that are the outward manifestation of our evolved social brains. The Dalai Lama states:

It is still my firm conviction that human nature is essentially compassionate, gentle. That is the predominant feature of human nature. . . . I believe that our underlying or fundamental nature is gentleness, and intelligence is a later development. And I think that if human ability, that human intelligence, develops in an unbalanced way, without being properly counterbalanced with compassion, then it can become destructive. It can lead to disaster.

(His Holiness, the Dalai Lama, 1998)

The boundaries of sanity

In this book I have attempted to understand why some humans suffer a loss of reason, become immersed in worlds of delusion and fear and experience a sense of alienation from their social world. I have presented a case that represents psychosis, madness, schizophrenia – call it what you will – as a state of disturbed social cognitive function and resulting interpersonal alienation that has its basis in disrupted development of the social brain. I have suggested that psychosis represents a costly consequence or by-product of social brain evolution in modern *Homo sapiens*. We encounter madness in some of our neighbours because we are the benefactors of a gradual process spanning millions of years that gave rise to our capacity to be socially complex and interdependent beings. Before going on to consider the implications of this thesis – and I believe there are many profound implications – I first wish to reconsider the question of the boundaries of sanity and insanity. What constitutes a sane man or woman? Are some fortunate people spared any hint of insanity? When did the first hominids experience true insanity? And are we humans truly the only creatures that experience madness?

It is logical to approach these questions from the periphery of humanity first – with our living primate relatives. In Chapter 2, I examined the evidence for psychosis or psychotic-like behaviour in great apes, specifically chimpanzees. I argued that, owing to their lack of language, chimps obviously could not display many of the positive features of psychosis. Rather, it is in their behaviour that we might detect abnormalities reminiscent of human psychosis. I proposed that some chimps might exhibit a *psychotic behavioural syndrome* (PBS), characterized by stereotypies, changes in dominance/submission behaviour and inappropriate social interactions. This kind of syndrome has certainly been identified, if only anecdotally, in captive chimps. Because some authorities remain sceptical about observed behaviours in captive primates – arguing that such behaviours may be the product of artificial conditions and human proximity – it is important to seek further and look for evidence of spontaneous psychosis in wild individuals. Drawing on descriptions by Jane Goodall in Gombe, Tanzania, I suggested that there is indeed evidence for a 'naturally occurring' PBS in wild chimps.

Does this finding conflict with the social brain hypothesis I have developed throughout this book? If we consider the evolution of social cognition and the cortical circuits of the social brain as a gradual process spanning perhaps 30 million years, then there is no conflict with the claim that extant apes such as chimpanzees may exhibit a PBS in certain circumstances. The evidence we have considered in Chapter 6 supports a gradualist process of emerging metarepresentational or theory of mind (TOM) ability in hominid ancestors. We know, for example, that monkeys are able to orchestrate alliances, engage in reconciliatory behaviours and make use of deception in social contexts. Great apes, on the other hand, demonstrate some elements of TOM, comparable with a human child of four or five years old – arguably, chimps and orang-utans show a limited ability to attribute mental states and intentionality to others.

Thus, if we accept that human psychosis is essentially a problem of altered social brain function and subsequent alienation from the social world, then it follows that chimps, who have some mind-reading ability, would be likely to exhibit a PBS in their species. However, given the large gap between human and chimp social cognitive ability, as well as the absence in chimps of anything approaching the human capacity for humane interpersonal behaviour, we can safely assume that chimps and other great apes will never exhibit a disorder as complex and socially disabling as schizophrenia. Interestingly, reports of 'psychotic' chimps have sometimes reported some degree of social disability in these individuals, in the form of a drop in social rank. This loss of status, and the reduction in reproductive potential that accompanies it, is reminiscent of the well-recognized 'social drift' and severe social disability that is characteristic of schizophrenia.

Making use of cladistic analysis, we are able to make an educated guess as to when true madness first manifested in human ancestors. As I elaborated in Chapter 2, the last common ancestor of chimps and humans lived approximately 5–6 million years ago. It is possible, therefore, that this early ancestor experienced a PBS similar to the modern chimp. Later hominids, such as the *Australopithecines*, *Homo habilis* and *Homo erectus*, may have encountered conspecific individuals who suffered psychotic symptoms more reminiscent of human psychosis. However, the absence of a full TOM and 'mature' social cognitive ability, comparable to modern human ability, means that these hominids did not have the capacity for true human psychosis as we recognize it today. Furthermore, the expression of psychosis in these prehuman species would have been modified into unique forms by the cultural environment in which they lived. It was only with the emergence of a full TOM and a capacity for truly humane interpersonal cognitions approximately 150,000 years ago that early *Homo sapiens* began to manifest psychotic illness of the complexity we encounter today.

Our knowledge of the mental capacity of early *Homo sapiens* is derived from the discoveries of archaeology and anthropology – the ritual burial sites, the cave art of Palaeolithic Europe and sub-Saharan Africa and the records and observations of psychotropic substance use in the induction of altered states of consciousness (ASCs). From these surviving sources, some of which date to 80,000 years ago, we can draw certain conclusions about the cognitive capacity of the earliest fully modern humans. We can also quite comfortably assert that these individuals experienced a wide range of abnormal psychological phenomena, some of which we now recognize as psychotic. For example, in the entoptic phenomena, widely depicted in both European and African cave art, we can assume that hallucinations were a common experience – whether induced by ritual use of psychotropic plants, rhythmic drumming and dance or other shamanic group practices.

Similarly, mood alterations, divergent thoughts and dissociative phenomena such as depersonalization and derealization were experienced widely, if only in the context of shamanic rituals. In Chapter 2, I argued that, although ASCs and psychosis share a number of experiential phenomena, they are not one and the same. The shamanic ASC differs from the functional psychosis in terms of its organizational structure – the former does not manifest the disorganization and chaotic quality of the latter. Similarly, I argued that the prominent social role and able functioning of the shaman differs markedly from the social disability and dysfunction of the schizophrenic individual. Thus, evidence of ASCs in prehistory is not evidence for psychosis in prehistory. But it is evidence for the emergence of complex brain reorganization and the cognitive potential for psychotic-like experience in early *Homo sapiens*.

From Biblical times we have written records of modern human experience. From these records, whether they are religious historical documents or the emerging literature of the second millennium, we learn of individuals afflicted with bizarre and wonderful disturbances of mind. The written descriptions of these disturbances were constructed in terms of the dominant philosophy of each age – thus the ravings of Nebuchadnezzar and the destructive rampage of Ajax were evidence of supernatural punishment and alienation from God. Later, in the ages of Aristotle, Hippocrates and Aretaeus, insanity was located in derangements of the bodily humours and the brain. The medieval period witnessed a return to supernatural explanations of psychosis while the succeeding Enlightenment which swept Europe from the seventeenth to the nineteenth centuries brought with it the 'restoration of reason' and the predominant model of insanity as a form of degeneration or loss of reason. Identifying evidence of what we now recognize as psychosis in the historical record of the last 5000 years requires a conceptual shift.

As postmodern thinkers such as Foucault and Derrida have illustrated in their work, we need to deconstruct the language and dominant concepts of history in terms of the specific social, cultural, political and religious attitudes and philosophy of each era. Deconstructing madness therefore requires an awareness of the lenses through which we experience the world and construct our truths about it. It also requires an awareness and sensitivity to other lenses through which people in other times and places experience the world and construct their truths about it. If we are successful in this exercise of 'decoding' our historical record, then we shall, without any difficulty, realize that psychosis has existed as a human experience for as long as our ancestors have cared to document it.

In concluding this section on the boundaries of sanity, I wish to return to a central theme of this book. Within psychiatry we have tried desperately to model our science (and art) on other medical disciplines such as internal medicine and surgery. Rather cynically, I believe this may have something to do with our collective hang-up as a profession. We regard ourselves and fear that other medical professionals regard us as a 'Cinderella' profession – not real medicine, the poor cousin of hard rigorous medical science. In our efforts to gain respectability (after the 'phantastic' musings of neo-Freudism) and respect from our colleagues, we resorted to a grand pro-gramme of categorizing mental distress. With the DSM and ICD systems we constructed boxes, each containing a specific mental condition or disorder. I have debated the relative merits and pitfalls of this categorical approach to psychopathology earlier in this book. The functional psychoses, which are the focus of this book, are broadly categorized within our current nosology as the schizophrenias and the affective psychoses. The implication of this rigid system is that either you have psychosis, schizophrenia, bipolar dis-order, or you do not. Practically speaking, there is no room for recognizing degrees of psychosis in a categorical system. Thus, the boundary between sanity and insanity is clear, unambiguous and easy to define. You are either sane or insane.

There is comfort in this system for psychiatrists, psychologists and other professionals working within the field of mental health and ill health. Such clarity and universal allegiance to these definitions provides a comforting feeling of scientific objectivity to the clinician and researcher alike. (It also is very convenient and satisfactory for pharmaceutical companies and managed health care consortiums whose profits depend upon 'scientific objectivity!) As we shall see in the final section of this chapter and book, however, such certainty in defining who is mad and who is not has many negative and destructive implications for those poor unfortunates who are 'defined' onto the wrong side of the fence. As we are only too aware from our messy history of racial, ethnic, gender-based, socioeconomic, religious and political division of 'us' from 'them', such rigid categorization lends itself to the rampant growth of stigma, prejudice and persecution. One of the greatest problems that confronts those who treat, those who live with, and those who suffer mental illness is stigma and social discrimination. In my view, as the insane were burnt as witches in the Dark Ages, so in part we create suffering for the mentally ill in this modern age through our insistence on defining them as disordered, defective and abnormal in relation to us – who are, of course, normal.

The reality of course is that there is no easy-to-define boundary between sanity and insanity. Emotional, cognitive and behavioural traits exist on continua of variation. Some individuals experience mild anxiety or a degree of obsessionality or a bout of depression at some point in their lives. Others experience repeated episodes of depression or anxiety with protracted periods of wellness intervening between these episodes. And still others live their entire lives in the grip of chronic mood or anxiety disturbance. Similarly, with psychosis, we encounter a spectrum of symptomatology, both between different individuals and within the same individual at different points in his or her life. Within our classification systems we have attempted to capture this variation in the expression of psychosis – those with few or subtle symptoms may be classified as having 'schizotypal personality disorder' or, for those experiencing short-lived episodes, we have categories such as 'brief psychotic disorder' and 'schizophreniform disorder'. And if we are really perplexed as to where to fit in our psychotic patient, we can always make use of that wonderful opt-out category 'psychotic disorder not otherwise specified'! Interestingly, those of us who work in the developing world seem to encounter many people who end up in this last box. The clinical reality, acknowledged by more and more professionals working within mental health, is that the protean manifestation of psychosis cannot be neatly sorted into tightly defined diagnostic categories. Psychosis, as with anxiety or depression, exists as a continuum of variation. In this sense there is, I believe, truth in the aphorism: 'everyone has a touch of madness'.

Thankfully, there is a growing voice within psychiatry lobbying for and working to develop a system of describing individual mental suffering in terms that better reflect reality. There are efforts under way to revise our psychiatric nomenclature, away from categorical and towards a dimensional approach to mental disorder. This task is not as easy as it seems, since a dimensional approach does not lend itself easily to use in the research and therapeutic settings. Personally, I do not believe that a move to dimensional thinking will weaken or discredit psychiatry as a medical science. In other branches of medicine we have many well-respected examples of dimensionally conceived ill-health. Diabetes mellitus, for example, is viewed in terms of a spectrum of glucose intolerance. Some individuals have mild glucose intolerance, easily managed through dietary changes; others have moderate disease and require oral antihyperglycaemics; and others have full-blown diabetes requiring regular insulin injections. In malnourished children we recognize degrees of malnutrition from discrete vitamin deficiencies to life-threatening marasmus and kwashiorkor. Of course, it goes without saying that some individuals quite clearly have a mental illness and others quite clearly do not – but it is the vast expanse of variable and ambiguous symptoms and altered experience in between these extremes that concerns me here.

It is bizarre that within psychiatry we have tried to be so rigid and definite regarding the absolute presence or absence of a mental disorder. We have moved beyond the levels of certainty practised by many of our non-psychiatric medical colleagues – and now think of ourselves as almost more objective than anyone else. But this is a contrived sort of objectivity, and our day-to-day experience with patients – in all their array of variable, atypical and overlapping mental and behavioural symptoms – reminds us constantly of the insufficiencies of our psychiatric understanding of human distress. When we begin to recognize and acknowledge the only real certainty about madness – that, in fact, there is no boundary between sanity and insanity – then we will have ourselves a much easier time in our work with those who suffer. Then also we will begin to provide a genuine role model for wider society of how to understand and respond to the mentally ill among us. Bringing an end to the stigmatization of the mentally afflicted depends, in the main, on our public confession as a profession that we have got it wrong. We need to be explicit about the fact that sanity and insanity exist on a spectrum, and that each one of us lies somewhere on that spectrum.

THE MARK OF CAIN: STIGMA, SUFFERING AND THE FUTURE

In Genesis, Chapter 4, we find the first Biblical account of fratricide. Cain, jealous of God's favouring of Abel, lures his brother into the fields and kills him. God punishes Cain by exiling him into the Land of Nod, east of Eden. But, as an act of apparent mercy, God puts a mark on Cain to protect him from death at the hands of others. 'The mark of Cain' is thus, according to the author of Genesis (some believe this was Moses), a sign of God's love and forgiveness; and some scholars argue that this is prophetic of Christ's role as the sacrificial lamb offered to redeem a sinful world. However, in popular usage over the centuries, 'the mark of Cain' has come to symbolize the stigmatization of an individual or group of individuals by virtue of some characteristic borne by that individual or those individuals. To bear 'the mark of Cain' is to carry some stigmata or blemish that signifies and bears testimony to one's guilt or culpability. To be 'marked' is to be identified as different, isolated or alienated from normal society and thus set apart as an object of stigma and societal prejudice.

Over the centuries there have been many groups of individuals who one could claim have been branded with 'the mark of Cain'. Among these groups are, of course, people of colour, those not of European descent, women, sufferers of leprosy or tuberculosis, religious minorities, gypsies,

196

homosexuals, conscientious objectors, the poor and, of course, the mentally ill. Attracting a diagnosis of mental disorder is almost invariably associated with some degree of stigmatization – either overt or covert. Although mental illnesses like depression and anxiety are universally common, individuals presenting for treatment often speak of feeling unique in their suffering. Everyone else around them in their daily lives seems to be so relaxed and happy, coping with life and making the most of their circumstances. The reality is, of course, that many people are privately suffering disabling symptoms and are wearing a 'brave face' to the world around. The vast majority of mental anguish is hidden, concealed, covered up from society because most people feel embarrassment, shame and a sense of personal failure in their experience of psychological ill health. Furthermore, they perceive society as intolerant and judgemental of those experiencing mental illness. Either in their workplace or in their home or in their social circle, they believe that they will be regarded as weak, complaining, unreliable or just crazy. This perception is sadly not just a symptom of being depressed or anxious or disturbed in some other manner. Feeling judged and even discriminated against because one is suffering a mental illness is not just being paranoid or oversensitive or delusional. The fact is, this widespread perception among patients is quite justified and is based entirely on the real-life existence of stigma against the mentally ill that pervades most societies. This stigma is most commonly encountered in the workplace; and mentally ill people almost invariably experience prejudice and discrimination from colleagues and employers alike.

Our twenty-first-century liberal capitalist societies are generally intolerant of frank racism and are increasingly inclusive regarding the rights of women, the physically disabled, those of homosexual orientation and even those exiting penal institutions. However, these rights are rarely extended to the mentally ill and there is little in the way of state or societal sanction against the use of pejorative terms such as 'loony', 'fruitcake', 'nutter', 'whacko', 'spastic', 'moron', 'psycho' and so on. Few modern institutions explicitly assert the rights of and equal opportunities available to mentally ill people seeking employment in these institutions. While the civil service, private companies and academic institutions are increasingly careful to present themselves as open and unprejudiced towards many previously disadvantaged and stigmatized groups in society, they do not on the whole extend the same welcome to those with mental illness. In some societies the mentally ill are not just recipients of stigma and prejudice, but are actually victimized and persecuted in ways reminiscent of dark medieval Europe. Stigma has always shadowed the mentally afflicted, and widely continues to in this 'civilized' modern age.

In the context of the main thesis of this book – that is, that psychosis is a state of social alienation, based in altered functioning of the evolved social brain – one can readily appreciate that the experience of stigma is, for those suffering psychotic illness, particularly devastating and destructive. The following pages make clear that social and economic stressors both contribute to the onset and exacerbate the course of psychosis. Stigma and prejudice constitute powerful social forces in the domestic and work environments of those vulnerable to psychosis and the psychotically ill. It thus follows that our collective social attitudes to and treatment of the mentally ill (and the psychotic in particular) impact profoundly upon the clinical expression of their illness and their hopes and possibilities of recovery.

The links between psychosis and social class have long been recognized. In his seminal study of the links between poverty, low socioeconomic status and schizophrenia, the psychiatrist Richard Warner argues that the political and economic dynamics of 'Western Society' are particularly damaging for the seriously mentally ill (Warner 1985). In *Recovery from Schizophrenia*, he acknowledges the physiological basis of schizophrenia, but maintains that many social, economic and political factors have a significant bearing on whether individuals experience psychosis in their lives. So, an individual may be predisposed to schizophrenia by their genetic makeup; and they may become vulnerable to the disorder by virtue of childhood factors (such as birth trauma, infections and toxic family environment). However, the actual manifestation of the illness in the form of a psychotic episode largely depends on social and economic environmental factors. In Western society, with its emphasis on wage-earning and social class, some of these factors include unemployment, poverty, poor living conditions, greater mortality and sickness among family and friends, greater exposure to crime and less access to medical and social services. All these environmental stressors are common in the lives of those people occupying the lower social classes, and they impact negatively on their mental health.[2]

Two hypotheses have been offered to explain the well-established finding that there is a greater than expected incidence of schizophrenia in the lower social classes.[3] The 'social drift hypothesis' (Eaton 1980) maintains that the illness itself causes individuals to 'drift' down the social ladder, since ongoing symptoms and repeated hospitalizations result in difficulties holding down a job and competing in the labour market. The alternative hypothesis, which we might term the 'social stress hypothesis', reverses the direction of causality, suggesting that the stresses of lower socioeconomic status give rise to increased rates of schizophrenia. The sociologist, Melvin Kohn (1973), who has reviewed the evidence on social class and schizophrenia, concludes: 'The weight of evidence lies against the drift hypothesis providing a sufficient explanation of the class-schizophrenia relationship. In all probability, lower class families produce a disproportionate number of schizophrenics.'

Warner (1985) notes that for many years mainstream psychiatry did not take too favourably to the proposal that low social class might cause schizophrenia. Furthermore, he explains that the two theories are not necessarily mutually exclusive. It is quite likely that both 'social stress' and 'social drift' hypotheses are correct and relevant in the origin and course of most patients' illnesses. In other words, the stressors of low socioeconomic status play a role in the initial manifestation of psychosis; and the course of the illness is characterized by a reciprocal relationship between psychosis and social status. Thus, a vicious cycle ensues, where social stress contributes to the onset of psychosis, which in turn leads to increasing social hardship, which in turn aggravates and impacts negatively upon the course of the illness (see Figure 10.1).

This social stress-schizophrenia cycle fits neatly with the 'stress-vulnerability model' of psychosis. As Warner (1985) is careful to emphasize, recognizing the role of low socioeconomic variables such as poverty, unemployment and social alienation in the onset and course of psychosis does not diminish the obvious significance of biological factors in the disease. We know that genetic predisposition and biological vulnerability does not in itself dictate manifestation of the disorder. Environmental stressors including major life events act as precipitants of psychosis in biologically vulnerable individuals. Carl Cohen, Professor of Psychiatry at the State University of New York, argues that 'being poor contributes disproportionately to having more untoward life events and may lead to increased exacerbations of symptoms among persons with schizophrenia' (Cohen 1993). Furthermore, poor education, social disempowerment and the relative inaccessibility of health services to the poor in modern industrial societies means that individuals with incipient psychosis often access treatment later than those in higher social classes. Since there is now clear evidence that longer duration of untreated psychosis results in a more chronic and debilitating course of the illness, we may conclude that low social status

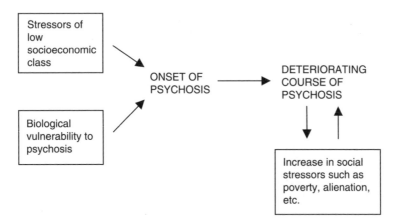

Figure 10.1 The reciprocal relationship between the stressors of low socioeconomic status and the onset and course of psychosis.

contributes directly to a less favourable outcome and prognosis. Cohen also highlights the fact that the negative effects of poverty are felt more acutely by psychotic individuals 'because of their reported heightened sensitivity to the social environment' (Cohen 1993).

In the light of the social brain hypothesis of schizophrenia this assertion rings true. In this book I have argued that psychosis is a state of social alienation and impaired social cognitive ability. It thus follows that socially sensitive or disabled individuals are likely to 'feel' and react to the stressors of socioeconomic deprivation to a far greater extent than those with more interpersonal resilience.[4] Indeed, the links between chronic poverty and chronic poor-prognosis schizophrenia are difficult to ignore, causing some authors to consider 'persons with schizophrenia as primarily indigent rather than primarily mentally ill' (Cohen 1993). And Zubin has suggested that the negative symptoms of schizophrenia may be, in part, a side-effect of the 'noxious niche' occupied by individuals with schizophrenia after an overt psychotic episode (Zubin 1985). Stephen Pattison, a theologian at the Open University, UK, highlights the special position occupied by the mentally ill person in Western society as equivalent to 'the poorest of the poor' (Pattison 1997). In his book *Pastoral Care and Liberation Theology*, Pattison (1997) writes: 'Those regarded as mentally disordered (a substantial, if often unnoticed, minority in the population) can be seen as the poor in our society. They should be regarded as among the poorest of the poor . . . this situation is integrally linked to the nature and structure of our society'.

Pattison believes that an analysis of the social and political factors impinging on the experience of mental disorder, '. . . exposes the situation of mentally ill people as being broadly one of injustice, exploitation, power-lessness, and oppression in society as a whole, and within the various contexts in which they are "cared" for' (Pattison 1997).

This leads me to a brief consideration of the politics of psychosis, the plight of psychotic individuals in our modern society and, perhaps most importantly, the nature of our responsibility as citizens of these societies in the face of such obvious injustice and suffering. Professor Paul Farmer of Harvard University and founder of Partners in Health, an organization involved in health development and human rights on several continents, has examined the role of 'structural violence' in the physical, material and psychological suffering of the poor. Derived from the liberation theology movement in Latin America, the term 'structural violence' is a 'broad rubric that includes a host of offensives against human dignity: extreme and relative poverty, social inequalities ranging from racism to gender inequality, and the more spectacular forms of violence that are uncontestedly human rights abuses . . .' (Farmer 2005). Farmer's work as a doctor, anthropologist and human rights activist over the last 25 years in Haiti (the poorest country in the western hemisphere) has focused largely on infectious diseases such as tuberculosis and HIV/AIDS.[5]

However, Farmer's passionate analysis of the social, economic and political forces that 'shape both the landscape of risk for developing [these illnesses] and the context in which health-care is provided' (Kelly 2005) is of great relevance and importance for our understanding of mental illness and schizophrenia in particular. In a remarkably insightful paper entitled *Structural violence and schizophrenia*, Kelly has argued that the social, economic and political forces that impact on the development and course of schizophrenic illness, constitute a form of structural violence. He draws attention to the fact that individuals with schizophrenia are overrepresented in the homeless, migrant and prison populations. He states:

> The adverse effects of these social, economic and political factors, along with enduring stigma about mental illness (Byrne 1999), constitute a form of structural violence that acts to impair access to psychiatric care and social services and to amplify the effects of schizophrenia in the lives of sufferers. As a result of these over-arching social and economic circumstances, individuals with schizophrenia are systematically excluded from full participation in civic and social life, and are constrained to live lives that are shaped, in large part, by stigma, isolation, homelessness and the denial of basic human rights.
>
> (Kelly 2005)

How do we respond to this realization that mentally ill people, and those with schizophrenia in particular, are among the most oppressed and marginalized in our modern Western societies? What is our responsibility, as citizens of these societies, given that our forms of government, economic systems and societal structures all contribute to the structural violence that characterizes the lives of the mentally ill? And, for those of us that work with the mentally ill, what are our specific responsibilities in striving to maximize psychological well-being in our patients and in our society?

I believe that we are all 'called' to be activists for change: social change, economic change and political change. Our humanity is inextricably tied up in the humanity of others. Where fellow citizens face dehumanizing stigma, victimization, economic deprivation and social alienation, our own personal humanity is diminished. My individual sense of human dignity and freedom is stunted and prevented its fullest expression within a society that undermines the dignity and constrains the freedom of even one of its citizens. For those of us whose task it is to treat the depressed, the anxious and the psychotic, we have no choice but to confront and struggle to dismantle the harmful forces within society that wreak such havoc in the lives of our patients. Pills alone will never alleviate the psychological suffering that results from discriminatory laws, unfair labour practices and social and institutional stigmatization of the mentally ill.

If we really want to be 'healers', we must become advocates for social, economic and political conditions that are best conducive to healing. And for all of us who are relatively sane, healthy and happy in our lives and experience a sense of belonging within the communities we live in, it is my firm belief that we have a particular duty towards those who suffer madness. As a species we have evolved an astonishing capacity for social interconnectedness and interdependence. The cost of this legacy is manifest in the suffering of those few individuals afflicted with psychosis. They bear the cost of our humanity. As Thomas Midwinter puts it: 'They pay the price for us all'. And so we, who are of sound mind, owe something of a debt to the mad. Instead of paying this debt by patronizing and feeling sorry for them, I believe we should strive as best we can in our everyday lives to forge the kind of conditions in our society that maximize their chances of recovery and social acceptance.

GLOSSARY

Clade   A group of species that share a common ancestor.

Cladistic analysis   Comparing species that share a common ancestor in order to surmise characteristics of that common ancestor.

Environment of evolutionary adaptedness   The environment in which our species evolved and in which it is adapted to live. Period: 2 million to 40 thousand years ago.

Genotype   The genetic constitution of the individual.

Heterochrony   Changes in the timing of development or maturation of an organ or organism with respect to the timing in its ancestors.

Hominids   Members of the Homo genus, which led to modern humans (within the last 5 million years).

Hominoids   All members of the ape family and their ancestors, (including *Hylobatid* or gibbon, *Pongo* or orang-utan, *Gorilla* or gorilla, *Pan troglodytes* or common chimpanzee, *Pan paniscus* or bonobo and *Homo* or human.)

Hypermorphosis   The evolutionary process whereby juvenile forms of the descendant resemble adult forms of the ancestor.

(Inclusive) fitness   Refers to the number of copies of an individual's genetic material that survive him or herself (including indirect descendants).

Metarepresentation   Synonymous with 'theory of mind' (TOM), 'mind-reading ability' and 'mentational ability'. Refers to one's ability to appreciate and attribute to others a mental state or mind similar to one's own.

Natural selection   The principle mechanism of evolutionary change, originally proposed by Darwin (1859), by which those individuals possessing certain advantageous characteristics contribute more offspring to the next generation than those who don't.

Neoteny   The evolutionary process whereby adult forms of the descendant resemble juvenile forms of the ancestor.

Ontogeny   The development of an organism through the course of its life cycle.

Paleolithic   Pertaining to the earlier part of the prehistoric Stone Age.

Phenotype The characteristics of an organism as a manifestation of the genes possessed by it. Note: Two organisms possessing the same genotype may have different phenotypes as a result of environmental factors.

Phylogeny The evolutionary origin and development of a species.

Pleistocene The geological period that covers the last 2 million years.

Proximate causation Aetiological factors that operate on and through the constitution and life experience of the individual.

Schizotaxia Non-psychotic manifestations of the schizophrenic genotype.

Schizotypy A genetic or developmental predisposition to withdrawal and alienation from members of the group, often accompanied by eccentric magical thinking, odd idiosyncratic speech, referential thinking and occasional auditory hallucinations.

Sexual selection A mechanism of evolutionary change in which certain individuals possess features that make them attractive to members of the opposite sex or help them compete with members of the same sex for access to mates (e.g. peacock's tail; antlers).

Ultimate causation Factors contributing to the structure of the human genome over millions of years of selection pressure.

NOTES

1 INTRODUCTION

1 Sequential hypermorphosis is an evolutionary process whereby descendant generations exhibit extended development relative to ancestors. Lock and Peters describe it as the 'phyletic extension of ontogeny beyond its ancestral termination, such that adult ancestral stages become preadult stages of descendants' (Lock & Peters 1999). This process occurs through changes in genes regulating the timing of development.

2 A 'balanced polymorphism' model postulates that heterozygotes have a selective advantage that compensates for gene loss in maladaptive homozygotes. The heterozygote has two different alleles while the homozygote has two identical alleles at the gene locus.

3 Alleles are variant forms of genes found at the gene locus. Each locus has two alleles, one inherited from each parent. If both alleles are identical the individual is homozygous at that locus, but if the alleles differ the individual is heterozygous. A 'susceptibility allele' is an allele that increases an individual's vulnerability to a specific disorder. In disorders due to multiple gene effects, increasing numbers of SAs increases the likelihood of disorder in the individual.

2 A HISTORY AND PRE-HISTORY OF MADNESS

1 Negative symptoms closely resemble the criteria specified by Eugen Bleuler, a German psychiatrist, as constituting the fundamental symptoms of schizophrenia. These criteria became known as 'Bleuler's four A's' and include: affective disturbance; associational disturbances; autism; and ambivalence.

2 Major field studies of great apes in Africa are at the following sites: Tiwai Island, Sierra Leone (chimpanzee); Taï National Park, Côte d'Ivoire (chimpanzee); Bossou, Guinea (chimpanzee); Douala-Edéa Forest Reserve, Cameroon (chimpanzee and gorilla); Lopé Forest Reserve and Forêt des Abeilles-Makandé, Gabon (chimpanzee and gorilla); M'Passa Reserve, Gabon (chimpanzee and gorilla); Lomako Forest, DRC (bonobo); Wamba, DRC (bonobo); Ituri Forest, DRC (chimpanzee); Nouabalé-Ndoki National Park, DRC (chimpanzee and gorilla); Kibale National Park, Uganda (chimpanzee); Budongo Forest Reserve, Uganda (chimpanzee); Karisoke Research Centre, Rwanda (gorilla); Gombe, Tanzania (chimpanzee); Mahale Mountains National Park, Tanzania (chimpanzee). Major field studies of orang-utans in SE Asia include Tanjung Puting National Park, Kalimantan; Kutai National Park, Kalimantan; Ulu Segama, Sabah; Gunung Leuser National Park, Sumatra (McGrew et al. 1996).

3 Resilience is a concept from the developmental literature and refers to a child's constitutional resistance to psychological disorder. A number of factors contribute to resilience including genetic profile, obstetric history and quality of early attachment. Variation in individual resilience is apparent when two individuals are exposed to the same stressor and have differing outcomes. The individual with greater resilience would be expected to fare better than the other who may manifest symptoms of psychopathology.

4 The 'dop system' was a notorious method of payment by employers to their workers that was practised on vineyards and other farms as well as by the South African Defence Force whereby workers were given free alcohol in lieu of a large portion of their salary. This encouraged alcohol abuse and dependence and yoked many an alcoholic to their source of drink.

5 Erika Bourguignon carried out a survey of 488 societies and found that 90 per cent were reported to have 'culturally patterned forms of altered states of consciousness' (Bourguignon 1973).

6 See Bahn (1988, 1997a, 1997b) for critiques and Pearson (2002) for a discussion of the controversy.

7 For the interested reader there is an extensive bibliography on psychedelic research and experience: *LSD, My Problem Child*, Albert Hofmann's account of his self-experimentation with LSD (Hofmann 1983); *The Doors of Perception*, Aldous Huxley on his use of Peyote (Mescaline) (Huxley 1954); *Acid Dreams*, a reflection on the political and social impact of LSD during the 1960s (Lee and Shlain 1985); *Plants of the Gods* (Schultes & Hofmann 1979), *Flesh of the Gods* (Furst 1972), *Hallucinogens: Cross-Cultural Perpectives* (Dobkin de Rios 1984); and *The Varieties of Psychedelic Experience* (Masters & Houston 1966) document the historical use of psychedelics; for a bold defence of the centrality of natural psychedelics in shaping human evolution see Terence McKenna's *Food of the Gods* (McKenna 1992). Scientific studies of the neuropsychological effects of hallucinogens include: *Mescal and the Mechanisms of Hallucinations* (Klüver 1966); *LSD Hallucinations* (Siegel 1985); *Drug-induced Hallucinations in Animals and Man* (Siegel & Jarvik 1975); for a review of current experimental research see the entire supplement of: *Pharmacopsychiatry* 31 (1998) (Suppl).

8 See Winkelman (2000: 127–133), for a comprehensive discussion of the neurophysiology of ASCs.

9 For an in-depth and up-to date review of the neurochemical effects of hallucinogens as well as a discussion of their clinical relevance see Nichols (2004).

10 Interestingly the *Prayer of Nabonidus* ends with: '. . . I prayed to the gods of silver and gold, bronze and iron, wood, stone and lime, because I thought and considered them gods . . .'. This phrase returns in Daniel, just 22 lines below the account of Nebuchadnezzar's madness, supporting the idea that the two characters were one individual and that Daniel's report of royal insanity was accurate.

11 Hippocratic medicine was based upon four humours or body fluids that balanced each other in health. Blood, choler (or yellow bile), phlegm and black bile were present within the skin envelope and shifts in balance gave rise to illness, both physical and mental. The humours corresponded to four basic temperaments: sanguine (blood); choleric (choler); phlegmatic (phlegm); and melancholic (black bile).

3 EVOLUTIONARY PRINCIPLES OF THE ORIGINS OF PSYCHOSIS

1 According to Gould and Lewontin (1979), '"spandrels" are the tapering triangular spaces formed by the intersection of two rounded arches at right angles [that] are necessary architectural by-products of mounting a dome on rounded arches'.

2 The French cleric and palaeontologist, Pierre Teilhard de Chardin, maintained that evolution was progressive, with human advancement towards moral and spiritual perfection the ultimate consequence of natural selection. His philosophy drew strong opposition from both the church (who objected to his belief in human material progress) and from evolutionists (who rejected the teleological basis of his philosophy).

3 Darwin's final sentence of his introduction to the first edition of *Origin of Species* was: 'I am convinced that Natural Selection has been the main, but not the exclusive means of modification'. Gould and Lewontin (1979) drew on this phrase as evidence that the 'master' himself did not regard natural selection as the *only* evolutionary mechanism, but rather viewed it as the *most important* mechanism.

4 Huxley et al. (1964) and later Carter and Watts (1971) suggested that schizophrenia might confer resistance against infection but there is little empirical support for this hypothesis. Although Brüne (2004b) draws our attention to new research in psychoneuroimmunology (Yovel et al. 2000) that may require us to reconsider this issue.

5 A classic clinical example of heterozygous advantage is found in the genetic disease, sickle-cell anaemia. The individual who possesses two copies of the abnormal haemoglobin S gene (HbS) is described as 'homozygous' and will manifest sickle-cell anaemia (SSA), often dying young of anaemia and heart failure. Interestingly, HbS is common in the tropics and one might ask why this is so, given that SSA commonly kills before reproductive age. The answer lies in the advantage gained by 'heterozygote' carriers of HbS, individuals who have only one copy of the abnormal gene and one normal haemoglobin gene. These lucky people are resistant to malaria, since their haemoglobin molecules kill invading malarial parasites.

6 The list of authors who have written about this association between mental illness and creativity/genius is long and includes Andreasen (1987), Horrobin (1998, 2001), Maudsley (1908), Nettle (2001), O'Reilly et al. (2001), Post (1994) and Prentky (1980). For books examining this subject see: *Touched with Fire* by Kay Redfield Jamison (1993); a chapter, *Creativity and Madness* by Gordon Claridge (1998) in A. Steptoe (ed.) (1998), *Genius and the Mind*, A. Steptoe. *The Madness of Adam and Eve* by David Horrobin (2001); *The Origin of Consciousness in the Breakdown of the Bicameral Mind* by Julian Jaynes (1976); *The Price of Greatness* by Arnold Ludwig (1995); *Strong Imagination* by Daniel Nettle (2001); *Madness and Modernism* by Louis Sass (1992); *Origins of Genius* by Dean Keith Simonton (1999).

7 Kay Jamison is Professor of Psychiatry at Johns Hopkins University School of Medicine and has a personal experience of living with bipolar disorder. She is the author of several books including *An Unquiet Mind* (1995a) (an account of her own struggle with bipolar disorder), *Touched With Fire* (1993) (a history of the links between artistic genius and bipolar disorder), as well as a standard textbook on bipolar disorder.

8 In particular, G.C. Williams' 1966 book, *Adaptation and Natural Selection*, was influential in turning evolutionists against group selection theory.

9 For a fascinating discussion of the psychology of cult leaders or gurus and their followers, see *Feet of Clay* by Anthony Storr (1997).

10 The 'out of Africa' hypothesis maintains that all living humans originated from common ancestors that evolved in East Africa and dispersed over several thousand years into Europe, Asia, Australasia and the Americas. In contrast, the theory of 'multiregional continuity' argues that modern humans emerged from different populations of early hominids, evolving separately (or with some degree of interbreeding) in separate continents or regions.

4 EVOLUTIONARY GENETICS OF PSYCHOSIS

1 Epistatic interaction or epigenetics refers to the regulation of gene activity and the control of the degree of gene expression. Inactivation of the X-chromosome in females is an example of epigenetic regulation, but in most cases the regulation is far subtler and represents fine-tuning of expression of genes. Epigenetic regulation of the genome is dynamic and changes markedly during embryogenesis, infant life and aging and may be substantially modified by both intracellular and extracellular events or influences (e.g. hormonal changes). Thus, epigenetics helps explain the complex contribution and interaction of multiple genetic and environmental factors in the genesis of complex traits.

5 A SOCIAL BRAIN FOR A SOCIAL WORLD

1 Dietrich Bonhoeffer was a theologian in Germany during the rise and rule of the Nazi dictatorship. He became an outspoken voice for justice and freedom against the regime and was finally executed during the final days of the war for his alleged involvement in a plot to overthrow Hitler. His writings have inspired and guided many who have felt morally challenged to oppose unjust regimes in South and Central America, in Southeast Asia and in Southern Africa.
2 Konrad Lorenz and Nico Tinbergen shared the Nobel Prize in 1973 for their contributions to the field of ethology. Some of their most important discoveries were the identification of *imprinting, fixed action patterns* (FAPs) and *innate releasing mechanisms* (IRMs), all of which have informed the understanding of infant attachment behaviour. Lorenz classically described imprinting in ducklings and Greylag goslings, the phenomenon where young animals form an immediate and irreversible social bond with the first moving object they encounter. The phenomena of FAPs and IRMs were first observed in the herring gull and the stickleback, and formed a basis for understanding the complex innate mechanisms that facilitate mother–infant bonding during the first weeks.
3 Elliot Sober and David Sloan Wilson have argued that altruistic behaviour in humans and non-humans has an innate biological basis and that altruism has evolved and is maintained by means of group selection.
4 Jean-Baptiste de Lamarck (1744–1829), a French biologist, introduced the hugely influential evolutionary theory of the inheritance of acquired characteristics. This much decried theory maintains that an organism develops according to the needs of the environment; and adaptive traits that consequently develop in the individual can be passed on to its offspring. He wrote: 'Inasmuch as an individual is capable of intelligent thought it is that alone which guides the actions [of that individual].'
5 At the molecular level, this primarily involves the modulation of expression of regulatory genes. These genes regulate the timing, pattern and magnitude of expression of other genes involved in neurodevelopment.
6 The late neuroscientist Paul MacLean conceived of the brain as three separate components, each with a different phylogenetic history. The *reptilian brain* is the

most primitive component and evolved in reptilian ancestors approximately 300 million years ago. In modern humans this is represented by the basal ganglia and is principally responsible for basic instincts or drives. The *paleo-mammalian brain* evolved in early mammals, includes the subcortical structures of the limbic system, and functions to control homeostasis, emotion and memory. The most recently evolved component is the *neo-mammalian brain*, which comprises the neocortex and is the site of higher cognitive functions.

7 The intriguing cognitive profile of individuals with Williams syndrome, in which social cognition is preserved despite significant intellectual disability, seems to support Brothers' notion of a module for 'social cognition'.

8 Perhaps, rather disturbingly, a number of studies have shown increased amygdala activation when subjects view faces of another race (compared with their own), suggesting that there are primitive neural mechanisms that mediate racial out-group responses (Hart et al. 2000; Phelps et al. 2000).

9 ACC damage may in extreme cases result in the neurological condition known as 'akinetic mutism'. In this state, the awake patient is mute, often incontinent and exhibits extreme apathy.

6 THE EVOLUTION OF THE SOCIAL BRAIN

1 It was this kind of reasoning that also gave rise to the notion of 'sexual selection' in evolutionary biology. In that case, the classic question to be answered was 'Why does the peacock have its tail?' Of course, the elaborate tail of the male bird serves no advantage in the classic struggle for survival – instead the advantage that accrues to the 'most elegant fowl' manifests in the contest for a mate.

2 A clade is formed by all the extant (living) and extinct species that, at some time in the past, shared a common ancestor.

3 The *Uncinate Fasciculus* (UF) is a white matter tract connecting the orbitofrontal cortex (OFC) to the anterior temporal pole in a bidirectional manner. The *Arcuate Fasciculus* (AF) is a large white matter tract extending from the prefrontal cortex to the temporoparietal junction. It is well known for its role as the main connecting tract between the receptive (Wernicke's) and expressive (Broca's) language areas of the brain. The language areas are lateralized to the left hemisphere in most humans and lesions of the AF classically give rise to aphasia. The *Anterior Cingulum* (AC) is the white matter tract that extends from the anterior cingulate cortex (ACC) to the temporal, parietal and limbic cortices.

4 'Petalia' describes the extension of one cerebral hemisphere beyond the other.

7 SCHIZOPHRENIA AND THE SOCIAL BRAIN

1 In fact, Bleuler (1923) qualifies this 'psychological' use of the term 'affective dementia' when he states: 'Hence it may be assumed that the morbid process as such does not attack the affects, but they are functionally only prevented from appearing, somewhat in the same manner as a child that is suddenly placed in a strange environment may merge into a stupor without an affect'.

2 Bentall addresses a concern about the reliability of a symptom-oriented approach raised in the *British Journal of Psychiatry* by American psychiatrists, Mojtabai and Rieder (1998).

3 Scharfetter (2001) explains that early alienists (psychiatrists) considered 'weakness of the psyche' or *psychasthenia* a core aspect of psychosis. This weakness accounted for the poor integrative functions of the patient's mind that led to splitting or dissociation of the psychic properties and subsequent psychosis.

Turn-of-the-century alienists coined a variety of terms for this 'debility of cohesion' – for example, Evensen's *amblynoia* (1903) and Berze's *hypophrenia* (1903). Scharfetter (2001) states 'This low synthetic capacity of the psyche kept some personalities vulnerable to insanity. The term *psychic vulnerability* was first used in 1841 by Canstatt (1841). It is close to earlier concepts of predisposition'.

4 The term 'tacit', as used by Sass, means 'all the taken-for-granted that we have forgotten once it has become our second nature and part of our bodily habits' (Fuchs 2001). The philosopher Michael Polanyi (1967) used the term 'tacit knowledge' to describe the knowledge that lies at the roots of 'common sense' and, according to Thomas Fuchs, 'is based on processes of Gestalt formation that enable us to grasp unified wholes through their constituting elements without still being aware of the latter' (Fuchs 2001).

5 The terms 'noesis' and 'noema' are derived from Husserl and respectively refer to 'the act of consciousness' and its intentional correlate, namely, 'the object and world of which we are aware' (Sokolowski 2000).

6 Minkowski (1927) describes the decline of the 'intimate dynamism of our life' and of vital contact with reality, as the 'essential', 'fundamental', 'initial' and 'generative disturbance' (*'trouble initial, trouble genérateur'*).

7 Significantly, Maj (1998), one of the leading psychiatrists pursuing a reformulation of our classification systems in psychiatry, 'proposes a recovery of the broad psychopathological organisers of the continental tradition, such as autism, advancing the hypothesis that the basic phenomenon of schizophrenic pictures lies in a disturbance of social relationships' (Stanghellini & Ballerini 2002).

8 Isen and Hastorf (1982) described the approach of the social cognitive scientist as 'an approach that stresses understanding of cognitive processes as a key to understanding complex, purposive, social behaviour'.

9 Brüne notes that this human behaviour 'corresponds to staring as an agonistic behavioural correlate' (Brüne 2003). Note also Darwin's description of inappropriate frowning (in the quote above). Perhaps we should say that inappropriate use of facial muscles during social discourse is a feature of schizophrenia.

10 Recently, during an industry-sponsored meeting, I heard a colleague assert, 'It's the Dopamine 4 receptor that causes psychosis isn't it?' Such absurdity is common and reflects the extent to which many practitioners have been swayed towards an unswerving faith in psychopharmacology as the answer to every aspect of madness.

8 THE DYSCONNECTIVITY HYPOTHESIS OF SCHIZOPHRENIA

1 The idea of dissociation of mental functions had its roots early in the nineteenth century with Herbart (1816) who referred to *dissoziation von komplexen* (dissociation of complexes). Others who invoked dissociation include: Esquirol (1838) – *spaltung psychischer funktionen* (split of psychic functions); Griesinger (1845) – *abspaltung aus dem bewusstsein* (splitting from the field of consciousness); Janet (1889) – *dissociation, désagrégation* (dissociation of consciousness); Stransky (1903) – *dissoziationsprozess* (process of dissociation); and Zweig (1908) – *dementia dissecans* (insanity of dissociation). The early uses of the word 'dissociation', prior to the establishment of Kraepelin's dichotomy of psychoses, incorporated a much wider range of psychopathology than today. In fact, the term referred to a variety of clinical pictures from hysteria to conversion to dissociative states to psychosis. Scharfetter (2001) argues that, following Kraepelin, the concept of schizophrenia was 'dissociated from one of its roots, namely the model of dissociation, separation, segregation, a split of certain

psychic functions from the main complexes of the psyche'. Even though Kraepelin (1913) himself acknowledged the dissociative aspects of psychosis – he wrote of 'the peculiar destruction of the inner coherence of the psychic personality with dominant damage of the emotional life' – the consequences of his new formulation of schizophrenia were for twentieth-century psychiatry: to regard it henceforth as a discrete degenerative disease of the brain; and to lose touch with a core building-block in the historical construction of the disorder. Scharfetter (2001) suggests that this omission may well in part account for the present problems we encounter with the DSM system of classification.

2 The importance of this hypothesis is demonstrated by the fact that the World Psychiatric Association chose as a 'special article' in only the second edition of its new publication *World Psychiatry*, a paper entitled 'Dysfunctional connectivity in schizophrenia' by 'connectivity guru', Karl Friston (2002) of the Institute of Neurology, London.

3 The 'hypofrontality hypothesis' emerged from functional studies of the prefrontal cortex (PFC) that showed relative hypofunction in schizophrenia during tasks activating the PFC. For example, Weinberger et al. (1986) showed reduced blood flow to the dorsolateral prefrontal cortex (DLPFC) while performing the Wisconsin Card Sorting Test (WCST) in schizophrenics as compared with controls. The earliest work, performed by Ingvar and Franzen (1974), using arterial injection of Xe 133, suggested that subjects with schizophrenia had a relative reduction of blood flow to the frontal cortex (i.e. 'hypofrontality'). Although hypofrontality has been replicated many times, the hypothesis has been challenged on the basis that positive rCBF data may reflect artefactual differences in patient performance (Ebmeier et al. 1995).

4 In Cambridge (UK), researchers have demonstrated both a segregated abnormality of ACC function in that there was a relative failure of activation in the ACC with a verbal fluency task, and an integrative abnormality in that there was a relative failure of corresponding deactivation in the left STG and inferior parietal lobe (Dolan et al. 1995; Fletcher et al. 1999). They have argued that schizophrenia is associated with a disruption of normal ACC modulation of FT integration. Abnormal ACC function has also been shown in schizophrenia in the resting state (Tamminga et al. 1992), during attentional tasks (Yucel et al. 2002), during self-monitoring tasks (Carter et al. 2001; Nordahl et al. 2001) and during working memory tasks (Artiges et al. 2000; Meyer-Lindenberg et al. 2001).

5 These tracts are investigated using horseradish peroxidase or radioactively labelled compounds injected into the tracts and then analysed autoradiographically.

6 VBM analysis entails statistical comparison of each corresponding voxel (or three-dimensional portion of brain) between two groups of subjects – patients and controls. Corresponding voxels that show significant differences in FA are identified, thus one can derive a complete map detailing areas of reduced or increased diffusion anisotropy.

7 ROI analysis entails the a priori selection of a specific region to be compared between patients and controls. The region is traced on the scans and a statistical comparison of relative FA is then calculated.

8 Furthermore, the fact that structural changes were lateralized to the left hemisphere suggested that future work on connectivity must somehow incorporate Crow's cerebral asymmetry hypothesis into a cohesive theory that accounts for both the FT and FP and the asymmetry findings.

9 It is important to note that the patient subjects in these four DT-MRI studies

211

were predominantly male. Out of a combined total of 80 patients, 53 were male and 27 female – a gender ratio of 2:1. As males with schizophrenia are known to have an excess of soft neurological signs, negative symptoms and positive radiological findings, the male predominance in the combined sample may constitute a confounding factor. It may, for example, be that CC dysconnectivity is a feature of the male rather than the female schizophrenic brain.

9 EVOLUTIONARY ONTOGENY OF SCHIZOPHRENIA

1 Thus, 'heterochrony' implies that, compared with their ancestors, certain features may arise in descendants at a different phase of development. In other words, there may be acceleration or deceleration of maturation of an organ relative to its developmental timing in an ancestor (McKinney & McNamara 1991).
2 'Paedomorphosis' is a term introduced by Walter Garstang in 1922 to describe the outcome of neoteny in the evolution of a species.
3 'Peramorphosis' is a term introduced by Gould and colleagues (Alberch et al. 1979) to describe the outcome of increased growth or development, for example through the mechanism of hypermorphosis.
4 Sue Taylor Parker in California has advocated a form of cognitive recapitulation – a concept popularized by the late-nineteenth-century psychologist, James Baldwin. As McNamara (1997) explains, Baldwin 'suggested that the stages of mental development of humans recapitulated the stages of human and primate evolution'. In this present age, where talk of recapitulation is once again 'semi-acceptable', Parker (1994) has compared the relative cognitive capacity of the major orders of primates with Jean Piaget's lifespan stages of human cognitive development. Piaget identified four main stages, with subdivisions within each: the *sensorimotor stage* (from birth to two years); the *preoperations stage* (from two to six years); the *concrete operations stage* (from six to twelve years); and the *formal operations stage* (from twelve years to adulthood). Parker states that, according to their level of cognitive development, primates correspond to the following Piagetian stages of ontological development: prosimians = early sensorimotor; simians = late sensorimotor; apes = early preoperations. Thus, human cognitive ontogeny recapitulates primate cognitive phylogeny.
    Parker and Gibson (1979) have also estimated, by examining the sophistication of tool use (from the archaeological record), the approximate cognitive capacity of extinct hominids. They have suggested that human ancestors achieved a level of cognitive ability corresponding to the following Piagetian stages: Australopithecus = early preoperations; Homo habilis = late preoperations; Homo erectus = early concrete operations; Early Homo sapiens = late concrete operations; Modern Homo sapiens = formal operations. Thus, human cognitive ontogeny recapitulates human cognitive phylogeny.
5 The neurodevelopmental hypothesis of schizophrenia is principally based upon the following pathological and clinical findings: the brain is already structurally abnormal at the first onset of psychosis; there is an absence of cellular gliosis (which suggests that the pathology commences *in utero*); schizophrenic patients have an excess of dysmorphic and dermatoglyphic features (again suggesting foetal origins); there is an excess of obstetric complications in those who develop the disorder; and affected individuals have motor and cognitive problems, which precede the onset of illness (Semple et al. 2005).

10 THE COSTLY LEGACY OF AN EVOLVED SOCIAL BRAIN

1 For discussions of the Great Ape Project and the wider debate around moral, ethical and legal rights for great apes, see Arluke (2001), Cavalieri and Singer (1994), Warren (2001) and Wise (2001).

2 For more on the relationship between social class, poverty and mental health, see Cohen (1993), Hill (1983), Ingleby (1983), Navarro (1978) and Pattison (1997).

3 For example in New Haven, Hollingshead and Redlich (1958) demonstrated a gradient of increasing schizophrenia as one moved down the social classes. The lowest social class had a prevalence 11 times greater than that of the highest social class. This gradient has been demonstrated in countries as diverse as Canada (Leighton et al. 1963), Norway (Ödegard 1956) and England (Stein 1957).

4 In a discussion paper for the World Bank and the Australian Government, Cullen and Whiteford (2001) have examined the links between 'social capital' and mental health. 'Social capital' is a concept that refers to 'networks of people deriving benefit from common interaction with each other' (Cullen & Whiteford 2001). In their paper, these authors illustrate vividly the benefits that good social capital has for the individual's mental health. Conversely, relative absence or poverty of social capital in a person's life is associated with higher risk for mental disorder. Thus, the socially deprived, alienated and disabled person with schizophrenia, who is by definition 'low in social capital', finds him or herself in a vicious cycle where increasing socioeconomic deprivation and alienation leads to worsening psychosis, which in turn results in enhanced sensitivity to social stressors and even greater social and economic deprivation.

5 Farmer's involvements have also seen him centrally involved in managing epidemics of multi-drug-resistant tuberculosis in Russian prisons and the slums of Lima, Peru, as well as HIV-related disease in the Americas and in Africa.

REFERENCES

Aboitiz, F. (1996) 'Does bigger mean better? Evolutionary determinants of brain size and structure', *Brain and Behavioural Evolution*, 47: 225–45.

Aboitiz, F. and Garcia, R. (1997) 'The anatomy of language revisited', *Biological Research*, 30: 171–83.

Adolphs, R. (1999) 'Social cognition and the human brain', *Trends in Cognitive Sciences*, 3: 469–79.

Adolphs, R. (2001) 'The neurobiology of social cognition', *Current Opinion in Neurobiology*, 11: 231–39.

Adolphs, R., Tranel, D., Damasio, H. and Damasio, A. (1994) 'Impaired recognition of emotion in facial expressions following bilateral damage to the human amygdala', *Nature*, 372: 669–72.

Adolphs, R., Cahill, L., Schul, R. and Babinsky, R. (1997) 'Impaired declarative memory for emotional material following bilateral amygdala damage in humans', *Learning and Memory*, 4: 291–300.

Adolphs, R., Damasio, H., Tranel, D., Cooper, G. and Damasio, A.R. (2000) 'A role for somatosensory cortices in the visual recognition of emotion as revealed by three-dimensional lesion mapping', *Journal of Neuroscience*, 20 (7): 2683–90.

Adovasio, J.M. and Fry, G.F. (1976) 'Prehistoric psychotropic drug use in Northeastern Mexico and Trans-Pecos Texas', *Economic Botany*, 30: 94–96.

Agartz, I., Andersson, J.L. and Skare, S. (2001) 'Abnormal brain white matter in schizophrenia: a diffusion tensor imaging study', *Neuroreport*, 12 (10): 2251–54.

Aggleton, J.P. (ed.) (1992) *The Amygdala: neurobiological aspects of emotion, memory and mental dysfunction*, New York: Wiley-Liss.

Aghajanian, G.K. and Marek, G.J. (1999) 'Serotonin and hallucinogens', *Neuropsychopharmacology*, 21 (2): 16s–23s.

Aghajanian, G.K. and Marek, G.J. (2000) 'Serotonin model of schizophrenia: emerging role of glutamate mechanisms', *Brain Research and Brain Research Reviews*, 31 (2–3): 302–12.

Alberch, P., Gould, S.J., Oster, G.F. and Wake, D.B. (1979) 'Size and shape in ontogeny and phylogeny', *Paleobiology*, 5: 296–317.

Aleman, A. and Kahn, R.S. (2004) 'Genes can disconnect the social brain in more way than one', *Behavioral and Brian Sciences*, 27: 855.

Allen, J.S. and Sarich, V.M. (1988) 'Schizophrenia in an evolutionary perspective', *Perspectives in Biology and Medicine*, 32: 132–53.

Allen, R.E. (1990) *The Concise Oxford Dictionary, 8th ed.*, Oxford: Clarendon Press.

Allman, J. (2000) *Evolving Brains*, New York: Scientific American Library.

Amaral, D.G. (2002) 'The primate amygdala and the neurobiology of social behaviour: implications for understanding social anxiety', *Biological Psychiatry*, 51: 11–17.

Amaral, D.G., Price, J.L., Pitkanin, A. and Carmichael, T. (1992) 'Anatomical organization of the primate amygdaloid complex', in J. Aggleton (ed.) *The Amygdala: neurobiological aspects of emotion, memory, and mental dysfunction*, New York: Wiley-Liss, pp. 1–66.

American Psychiatric Association (APA) (1994) *Diagnostic and Statistical Manual of Mental Disorders*, 4th edn, Washington, DC: APA.

American Psychiatric Association (APA) (2000) *Diagnostic and Statistical Manual of Mental Disorders*: TR, 4th edn, Washington, DC: APA.

Andreasen, N.C. (1987) 'Creativity and mental illness: prevalence rates in writers and their first-degree relatives', *American Journal of Psychiatry*, 144: 1288–92.

Andreasen, N.C. and Carpenter Jnr., W.T. (1993) 'Diagnosis and classification of schizophrenia', *Schizophrenia Bulletin*, 19 (2): 199–214.

Andreasen, N.C., O'Leary, D.S., Flaum, M., Nopoulos, P., Watkins, G.L., Boles Ponto, L.L. and Hichwa, R.D. (1997) 'Hypofrontality in schizophrenia: distributed dysfunctional circuits in neuroleptic-naive patients', *Lancet*, 349: 1730–34.

Arbib, M.A. and Mundhenk, T.N. (2005) 'Schizophrenia and the mirror system: an essay', *Neuropsychologia*, 43: 268–80.

Archer, J., Hay, D.C. and Young, A.W. (1994) 'Movement, face processing and schizophrenia: evidence of a differential deficit in expression analysis', *British Journal of Clinical Psychology*, 33 (4): 517–28.

Ardekani, B.A., Nierenberg, J., Hoptman, M.J., Javitt, D.C. and Lim, K.O. (2003) 'MRI study of white matter diffusion anisotropy in schizophrenia', *Neuroreport*, 14 (16): 2025–29.

Arluke, A. (2001) 'Perspectives on the ethical status of great apes', in B.B. Beck, T.S. Stoinski, M. Hutchins, T.L. Maple, B. Norton, A. Rowan, E.F. Stevens, A. Arluke (eds) *Great Apes and Humans: the ethics of coexistence*, Washington, DC: Smithsonian Institution Press, pp. 367–78.

Artiges, E., Salame, P., Recasens, C., Poline, J.B., Attar-Levy, D., De La, R.A., Paillere-Martinot, M.L., Danion, J.M., Martinot, J.L. (2000) 'Working memory control in patients with schizophrenia: a PET study during a random number generation task'. *American Journal of Psychiatry*, 157: 1517–19.

Aureli, F. and de Waal, F.B. (2000) *Natural Conflict Resolution*, Berkeley: University of California Press.

Avila, M., Thaker, G. and Adami, H. (2001) 'Genetic epidemiology and schizophrenia: a study of reproductive fitness', *Schizophrenia Research*, 47: 233–41.

Avis, J. and Harris, P. (1991) 'Belief-desire reasoning among Baka children: evidence for a universal conception of mind', *Child Development*, 62: 460–67.

Baare, W.F., Hulshoff Pol, H.E., Hijman, R., Mali, W.P., Viergever, M.A. and Kahn, R.S. (1999) 'Volumetric analysis of frontal lobe regions in schizophrenia: relation to cognitive function and symptomatology', *Biological Psychiatry*, 45: 1597–1605.

Bachevalier, J., Alvarado, M.C. and Malkova, L. (1999) 'Memory and socioemotional behaviour in monkeys after hippocampal damage incurred in infancy or in adulthood', *Biological Psychiatry*, 46: 329–39.

Bahn, P.G. (1988) 'Comment on "The Sign of All Times: Entopic Phenomena in Upper Palaeolithic Art", by J.D. Lewis-Williams and T.A. Dowson', *Current Anthropology*, 29: 217–18.

Bahn, P.G. (1997a) *Journey Through the Ice Age*, London: Weidenfeld and Nicolson.

Bahn, P.G. (1997b) 'Membrane and numb brain: a close look at a recent claim for shamanism in Palaeolithic art', *Rock Art Research*, 14: 1.

Bailey, J.M. (2000) 'How can psychological adaptations be heritable?' *Novartis Foundation Symposium*, 233: 171–80.

Baker, J.R. (1938) 'The evolution of breeding seasons', in G.R. de Beer (ed.) *Evolution: essays on aspects of evolutionary biology*, Oxford: Oxford University Press, pp. 161–77.

Ban, T., Shiwa, T. and Kawamura, K. (1991) 'Cortico-cortical projections from the prefrontal cortex to the superior temporal sulcal area (STs) in the monkey studied by means of HRP method', *Archives of Italian Biology*, 129: 259–72.

Barbas, H. (2000) 'Connections underlying the synthesis of cognition, memory, and emotion in primate prefrontal cortices', *Brain Research Bulletin*, 52: 319–30.

Baron-Cohen, S. (1995) *Mindblindness: an essay on autism and theory of mind*, Cambridge, MA: MIT Press.

Baron-Cohen, S. (1999) 'The evolution of a theory of mind', in M.C. Corballis and S.E.G. Lea (eds) *The Descent of Mind: psychological perspectives on hominid evolution*, Oxford: Oxford University Press, pp. 261–77.

Baron-Cohen, S., Leslie, A.M. and Frith, U. (1985) 'Does the autistic child have a "theory of mind"?' *Cognition*, 21: 37–46.

Baron-Cohen, S., Ring, H., Moriarty, J., Schmitz, B., Costa, D. and Ell, P. (1994) 'Recognition of mental state terms: clinical findings in children with autism and a functional neuroimaging study of normal adults', *British Journal of Psychiatry*, 165: 640–49.

Baron-Cohen, S., Ring, H.A., Bullmore, E.T., Wheelwright, S., Ashwin, C. and Williams, S.C. (2000) 'The amygdala theory of autism', *Neuroscience and Biobehavioural Reviews*, 24: 355–64.

Baron-Cohen, S., Wheelwright, S., Skinner, R., Martin, J. and Clubley, E. (2001) 'The autism-spectrum quotient (AQ): evidence from Asperger syndrome/high-functioning autism, males and females, scientists and mathematicians', *Journal of Autism and Developmental Disorders*, 31: 5–17.

Barrett, J.L. and Keil, F.C. (1996) 'Conceptualizing a nonnatural entity: anthropomorphism in God concepts', *Cognitive Psychology*, 31: 219–47.

Barton, R. and Aggleton, J. (2000) 'Primate evolution and the amygdala', in J. Aggleton (ed.) *The Amygdala: neurobiological aspects of emotion, memory, and mental dysfunction*, New York: Wiley-Liss, pp. 479–508.

Basser, P.J., Mattiello, J. and Le Bihan, D. (1994) 'Estimation of the effective self-diffusion tensor from the NMR spin echo', *Journal of Magnetic Resonance (Series B)*, 103: 247–54.

Bassett, A.S., Chow, E.W., Bury, A., Ali, F., Haylock, C.A., Smith, G.N., Lapointe, J.S. and Honer, W.G. (1996) 'Increased head circumference in schizophrenia', *Biological Psychiatry*, 40: 1173–75.

Bates, E. and Elman, J. (2000) 'The ontogeny and phylogeny of language: a neural network perspective', in S. Taylor Parker, J. Langer and M.L. McKinney (eds) *Biology, Brains and Behaviour*, Sante Fe: School of American Research Press/ Oxford: James Curry Ltd, pp. 89–130.

Bateson, P.P.G. (1988) 'The active role of behaviour in evolution', in M.W. Ho and S. Fox (eds) *Process and Metaphors in Evolution*, Chichester: Wiley, pp. 191–207.

Bechara, A., Damasio, H., Tranel, D. and Damasio, A.R. (1997) 'Deciding advantageously before knowing the advantageous strategy', *Science*, 275: 1293–95.

Bell, M., Bryson, G. and Lysaker, P. (1997) 'Positive and negative affect recognition in schizophrenia: a comparison with substance abuse and normal control subjects', *Psychiatric Research*, 73: 73–82.

Bemporad, J.R. (1991) 'Dementia praecox as a failure of neoteny', *Theoretical Medicine*, 12: 45–51.

Bentall, R.P. (1990) 'The illusion of reality: a review and integration of psychological research on hallucinations', *Psychological Bulletin*, 107: 82–95.

Bentall, R.P. (2003) *Madness Explained: psychosis and human nature*, London: Allen Lane.

Bentall, R.P., Claridge, G.S. and Slade, P.D. (1989) 'The multidimensional nature of schizotypal traits: a factor-analytic study with normal subjects', *British Journal of Clinical Psychology*, 28: 363–75.

Bering, J.M. (2002) 'The existential theory of mind', *Review of General Psychology*, 6: 3–24.

Bering, J.M. (2003) 'Towards a cognitive theory of existential meaning', *New Ideas in Psychology*, 21: 101–20.

Berner, P. (1997) 'Conceptualization of schizophrenia: the symptom-oriented approach', *Psychopathology*, 30 (5): 251–56.

Berze, J. (1903) *Über das Primärsymptom der Paranoia*, Halle: Marhold.

Bilder, R.M., Wu, H., Bogerts, B., Degreef, G., Ashtari, M., Alvir, J.M., Snyder, P.J. and Lieberman, J.A. (1994) 'Absence of regional hemispheric volume asymmetries in first-episode schizophrenia', *American Journal of Psychiatry*, 151: 1437–47.

Bjorklund, D.F. and Pellegrini, A.D. (2002) *The Origins of Human Nature: evolutionary developmental psychology*, Washington, DC: American Psychological Association.

Blankenburg, W. (1971) *Der Verlust der Naturlichen Selbstverstandlichkeit: ein beitrag zur psychopathologie symptomarmer schizophrenien*, Stuttgart: Ferdinand Enke Verlag.

Bleuler, E. (1923) *Textbook of Psychiatry*, translated by A.A. Brill, London: George Allen and Unwin.

Bleuler, E. (1950) *Dementia Praecox or the Group of Schizophrenias*, translated by J. Zinkin, New York: International Universities Press.

Bock, J. and Braun, K. (1999) 'Filial imprinting in domestic chicks is associated with spine pruning in the associative area, dorsocaudal neostriatum', *European Journal of Neuroscience*, 11: 2566–70.

Bogin, B. (1999) 'Evolutionary perspective on human growth', *Annual Review of Anthropology*, 28: 109–53.

Bolk, L. (1926) *Das Problem der Menschwerdung*, Jenna: Gustav Fischer.

Bonhoeffer, D. (1971) *Letters and Papers from Prison*, enlarged edition by Eberhard Bethge (ed.) London: SCM Press Ltd.

Bora, E., Vahip, S., Gonul, A.S., Akdeniz, F., Alkan, M., Ogut, M. and Eryavuz, A.

(2005) 'Evidence for theory of mind deficits in euthymic patients with bipolar disorder', *Acta Psychiatrica Scandinavica*, 112 (2): 110–16.

Borod, J.C., Martin, C.C., Alpert, M., Brozgold, A. and Welkowitz, J. (1993) 'Perception of facial emotion in schizophrenic and right brain-damaged patients', *Journal of Nervous and Mental Diseases*, 181: 494–502.

Bourguignon, E. (ed.) (1973) *Religion, Altered States of Consciousness and Social Change*, Columbus: Ohio State University Press.

Bowlby, J. (1969) *Attachment and Loss, vol. 1, Attachment*, London: Hogarth Press and the Institute of Psycho-Analysis.

Bowlby, J. (1973) *Attachment and Loss, vol. 2, Separation: anxiety and anger*, London: Hogarth Press and the Institute of Psycho-Analysis.

Boyer, P. (1994) *The Naturalness of Religious Ideas: a cognitive theory of religion*, Berkeley: University of California Press.

Bracken, P. (2002) *Trauma: culture, meaning and philosophy*, London: Whurr Publishers.

Bracken, P. and Thomas, P. (2001) 'Postpsychiatry: a new direction for mental health', *British Medical Journal*, 322: 724–27.

Breiter, H.C., Etcoff, N.L., Whalen, P.J., Kennedy, W.A., Rauch, S.L., Buckner, R.L., Strauss, M.M., Hyman, S.E. and Rosen, B.R. (1990) 'Response of neurons in the macaque amygdala to complex social stimuli', *Behavioral and Brain Research*, 41: 199–213.

Broks, P. (1997) 'Brain, self, and others: the neuropsychology of social cognition', in G. Claridge (ed.) *Schizotypy: implications for illness and health*, Oxford: Oxford University Press, pp. 98–123.

Brothers, L. (1990) 'The social brain: a project for integrating primate behavior and neurophysiology in a new domain', *Concepts in Neuroscience*, 1: 27–51.

Brothers, L. (1997) *Friday's Footprint: how society shapes the human mind*, Oxford: Oxford University Press.

Brothers, L., Ring, B. and Kling, A.S. (1990) Response of neurons in the macaque amygdala to complex social stimuli. *Behavioural Brain Research*, 41: 199–213.

Brothers, L. and Ring, B. (1993) Mesial temporal neurons in the macaque monkey with responses selective for aspects of social stimuli', *Behavioural Brain Research*, 57: 53–61.

Brown, S. (1997) 'Excess mortality of schizophrenia: a meta-analysis', *British Journal of Psychiatry*, 171: 502–08.

Brüne, M. (2000) 'Neoteny, psychiatric disorders and the social brain: hypotheses on heterochrony and the modularity of the mind', *Anthropology and Medicine*, 7: 301–18.

Brüne, M. (2001) 'Social cognition and psychopathology in an evolutionary perspective: current status and proposals for research', *Psychopathology*, 34: 85–94.

Brüne, M. (2003) 'Social cognition and behaviour in schizophrenia', in M. Brüne, H. Ribbert and W. Schiefenhövel (eds) *The Social Brain: evolution and pathology*, Chichester: Wiley, pp. 253–76.

Brüne, M. (2004a) 'Schizophrenia – an evolutionary enigma?', *Neuroscience and Biobehavioural Reviews*, 28: 41–53.

Brüne, M. (2004b) 'Understanding the symptoms of "schizophrenia" in evolutionary terms', *Behavioral and Brain Sciences*, 27: 857.

Brüne, M., Ribbert, H. and Schiefenhövel, W. (2003) *The Social Brain: evolution and pathology*, Chichester: Wiley.

Brünet, E., Sarfati, Y., Hardy-Baylé, M.C. and Decety, J. (2000) 'A PET investigation of the attribution of intentions with a nonverbal task', *Neuroimage*, 11: 157–66.

Brünet, E., Sarfati, Y., Hardy-Baylé, M.C. and Decety, J. (2003) 'Abnormalities of brain function during a nonverbal theory of mind task in schizophrenia', *Neuropsychologia*, 41 (12): 1574–82.

Buccino, G., Binkofski, F., Fink, G.R., Fadiga, L., Fogassi, L. and Gallese, V. (2001) 'Action observation activates premotor and parietal areas in a somatotopic manner: an fMRI study', *European Journal of Neuroscience*, 13: 400–04.

Buchsbaum, M.S., Trestman, R.L., Hazlett, E., Siegel, B.V., Schaefer, C.H., Luu-Hsia, C., Tang, C., Herrera, S., Solimando, A.C., Losonczy, M., Serby, M., Silverman, J. and Siever, L.J. (1997a) 'Regional cerebral blood flow during the Wisconsin Card Sort Test in schizotypal personality disorder', *Schizophrenia Research*, 27: 21–28.

Buchsbaum, M.S., Yang, S., Hazlett, E., Siegel, B.V., Germans, M., Haznedar, M., O'Flaithbheartaigh, S., Wei, T., Silverman, J. and Siever, L.J. (1997b) 'Ventricular volume and asymmetry in schizotypal personality disorder and schizophrenia assessed with magnetic resonance imaging', *Schizophrenia Research*, 27: 45–53.

Buchsbaum, M.S., Tang, C.Y., Peled, S., Gudbjartsson, H., Lu, D., Hazlett, E.A., Downhill, J., Haznedar, M., Fallon, J.H. and Atlas, S.W. (1998) 'MRI white matter diffusion anisotropy and PET metabolic rate in schizophrenia', *Neuroreport*, 9 (3): 425–30.

Bunney, W.E., Bunney, B.G., Vawter, M.P., Tomita, H., Evans, S.J., Choudary, P.V., Myers, R.M., Jones, E.G., Watson, S.J. and Akil, H. (2003) 'Microarray technology: a review of new strategies to discover candidate vulnerability genes in psychiatric disorders', *American Journal of Psychiatry*, 160: 657–66.

Burns, J.K. (2004) 'An evolutionary theory of schizophrenia: cortical connectivity, metarepresentation and the social brain', *Behavioral and Brain Sciences*, 27: 831–55.

Burns, J.K., Job, D.E., Bastin, M.E., Whalley, H.C., McGillivray, T., Johnstone, E.C. and Lawrie, S.M. (2003) 'Structural dysconnectivity in schizophrenia: a diffusion tensor MRI study', *British Journal of Psychiatry*, 182: 439–43.

Bush, G., Luu, P. and Posner, M.I. (2000) 'Cognitive and emotional influences in anterior cingulate cortex', *Trends in Cognitive Sciences*, 4: 215–22.

Buss, D.M. (1991) 'Evolutionary personality psychology', *Annual Review of Psychology*, 45: 459–91.

Butter, C.M. and Snyder, D.R. (1972) 'Alterations in aversive and aggressive behaviours following orbital frontal lesions in rhesus monkeys', *Acta Neurobiologiae Experimentalis*, 32: 525–65.

Buxhoeveden, D.P., Switala, A.E., Litaker, M., Roy, E. and Casanova, M.F. (2001) 'Lateralization of minicolumns in human planum temporale is absent in nonhuman primate cortex', *Brain and Behavioural Evolution*, 57: 349–58.

Byrne, M., Hodges, A., Grant, E., Owens, D.C. and Johnstone, E.C. (1999) 'Neuropsychological assessment of young people at high genetic risk for developing schizophrenia compared with controls: preliminary findings of the Edinburgh High Risk Study (EHRS)', *Psychological Medicine*, 29: 1161–73.

Byrne, P. (1999) 'Stigma of mental illness', *British Journal of Psychiatry*, 174: 1–2.

Byrne, R.W. (1996) 'Relating brain size to intelligence in primates', in P.A. Mellars and K.R. Gibson (eds) *Modelling the Early Human Mind*, Cambridge: Macdonald Institute for Archaeological Research, pp. 49–56.

Byrne, R.W. (1997) 'The technical intelligence hypothesis: an additional evolutional stimulus to intelligence?' in A. Whiten and R.W. Byrne (eds.) *Machiavellian Intelligence* II: *evaluations and extensions*, Cambridge: Cambridge University Press, pp. 289–311

Byrne, R.W. (1999) 'Human cognitive evolution', in M.C. Corballis and S.E.G. Lea (eds) *The Descent of Mind: psychological perspectives on hominid evolution*, Oxford: Oxford University Press, pp. 147–59.

Byrne, R.W. (2000) 'Evolution of primate cognition', *Cognitive Science*, 24: 543–70.

Byrne, R.W. (2001) 'Social and technical forms of primate intelligence', in F.B.M. de Waal (ed.) *Tree of Origin*, Cambridge: Harvard University Press, pp. 145–72.

Byrne, R.W. and Russon, A.E. (1998) 'Learning by imitation: a hierarchical approach', *Behavioural and Brain Sciences*, 21: 667–84.

Byrne, R.W. and Whiten, A. (1985) 'Tactical deception of familiar individuals in baboons (*Papio ursinus*)', *Animal Behaviour*, 33: 669–73.

Byrne, R.W. and Whiten, A. (eds) (1988) *Machiavellian Intelligence: social expertise and the evolution of intellect in monkeys, apes and humans*, Oxford: Clarendon Press.

Byrne, R.W. and Whiten, A. (1991) 'Computation and mind-reading in primate tactical deception', in A. Whiten (ed.) *Natural Theories of Mind*, Oxford: Blackwell pp. 127–41.

Byrne, R.W. and Whiten, A. (1992) 'Cognitive evolution in primates: evidence from tactical deception', *Man*, 27: 609–27.

Byrne, R.W. and Whiten A. (1999) 'Tactical deception in primates: the 1990 database', *Primate Report*, 27: 1–101.

Cadenhead, K.S., Perry, W., Shafer, K. and Braff, D.L. (1999) 'Cognitive functions in schizotypal personality disorder', *Schizophrenia Research*, 37: 123–32.

Cahill, L., Haier, R.J., Fallon, J., Alkire, M.T., Tang, C., Keator, D., Wu, J. and McGaugh, J.L. (1996) 'Amygdala activity at encoding correlated with long-term, free recall of emotional information', *Proceedings of the National Academy of Sciences of the USA*, 93: 8016–21.

Calder, A.J., Lawrence, A.D., Keane, J., Scott, S.K., Owen, A.M., Christoffels, I. and Young, A.W. (2002) 'Reading the mind from eye gaze', *Neuropsychologia*, 40: 1129–38.

Calvert, G.A., Bullmore, E.T., Brammer, M.J., Campbell, R., Williams, S.C., McGuire, P.K., Woodruff, P.W., Iverson, S.D. and David, A.S. (1997) 'Activation of auditory cortex during silent lipreading', *Science*, 276: 593–96.

Calvin, W.H. (2002) *A Brain For All Seasons: human evolution and abrupt climate change*, Chicago: University of Chicago Press.

Cannon, M., Caspi, A., Moffitt, T.E., Harrington, H., Taylor, A., Murray, R.M. and Poulton, R. (2002) 'Evidence for early-childhood, pan-developmental impairment specific to schizophreniform disorder: results from a longitudinal birth cohort', *Archives of General Psychiatry*, 59: 449–56.

Canstatt, C. (1841) *Handbuch der Medicinischen Klinik. Bd. 1: die spezielle pathologie und therapie vom klinischen standpunkte aus bearbeitet*, Stuttgart: Enke.

Cantalupo, C. and Hopkins, W.D. (2001) 'Asymmetric Broca's area in great apes', *Nature*, 414: 505.

Cantalupo, C., Pilcher, D.L. and Hopkins, W.D. (2003) 'Are plenum temporale and sylvian fissure asymmetries directly related? A MRI study in great apes', *Neuropsychologia*, 41 (14): 1975–81.

Cantor-Graae, E., Ismail, B. and McNeil, T.F. (1998) 'Neonatal head circumference and related indices of disturbed fetal development in schizophrenic patients', *Schizophrenia Research*, 32: 191–99.

Capitanio, J.P. (1986) 'Behavioural pathology', in G. Mitchell and J. Erwin (eds) *Comparative Primate Biology, vol. 2A: behaviour, conservation and ecology*, New York: Allan R. Liss, pp. 411–54.

Carter, C.S., MacDonald III, A.W., Ross, L.L. and Stenger, V.A. (2001) 'Anterior cingulate cortex activity and impaired self-monitoring of performance in patients with schizophrenia: an event-related fMRI study', *American Journal of Psychiatry*, 158: 1423–28.

Carter, M. and Watts, C.A. (1971) 'Possible biological advantages among schizophrenics' relatives', *British Journal of Psychiatry*, 118: 453–60.

Casey, B.J. (1999) 'Images in neuroscience. Brain development. XII. Maturation in brain activation', *American Journal of Psychiatry*, 156: 504.

Castelli, F., Happé, F., Frith, U. and Frith, C. (2000) 'Movement and mind: a functional imaging study of perception and interpretation of complex intentional movement patterns', *Neuroimage*, 12: 314–25.

Castillo, R.J. (2003) 'Trance, functional psychosis and culture', *Psychiatry*, 66 (1): 9–21.

Castner, S.A. and Goldman-Rakic, P.S. (1999) 'Long-lasting psychotomimetic consequences of repeated low-dose amphetamine exposure in rhesus monkeys', *Neuropsychopharmacology*, 20: 10–28.

Cavalieri, P. and Singer, P. (eds) (1994) *The Great Ape Project: equality beyond humanity*, New York: St Martin's Press.

Celsus. (1935) *Volume 111. De Medicina*, translated by W.G. Spencer, London: William Heinemann Ltd.

Chaline, J. (1998) 'Vers une approche globale de l'evolution des hominids/Towards an all-round approach to hominid evolution', *C.R. Académie Science Paris*, 326: 307–18.

Chance, M.R.A. and Mead, A.P. (1953) 'Social behaviour and primate evolution', *Symposia of the Society of Experimental Biology*, 7: 395–439.

Changeux, J.P. (1997) *Neuronal Man: the biology of the mind*, Princeton: Princeton University Press.

Changeux, J.P. and Danchin, A. (1976) 'Selective stabilisation of developing synapses as a mechanism for the specification of neuronal networks', *Nature*, 264: 705–12.

Chapais, B. (1992) 'The role of alliances in social inheritance of rank among female primates', in A.H. Harcourt and F.B.M. de Waal (eds) *Coalitions and Alliances in Humans and Other Primates*, Oxford: Oxford University Press, pp. 29–59.

Chapman, L.J., Chapman, J.P., Kwapil, T.R., Eckblad, M. and Zinser, M.C. (1994) 'Putatively psychosis-prone subjects 10 years later', *Journal of Abnormal Psychology*, 103: 171–83.

Charlesworth, B. (1987) 'The heritability of fitness', in J.W. Bradbury and M.B. Andersson (eds) *Sexual Selection: testing the alternatives*, Chichester: Wiley, pp. 21–40.

Charlesworth, B. (1994) *Evolution in Age-Structured Populations*, 2nd edn, Cambridge: Cambridge University Press.

Charlton, B. (2000) *Psychiatry and the Human Condition*, Oxford: Radcliffe Medical Press.

Chechik, G., Meilijson, I. and Ruppin, E. (1998) 'Synaptic pruning in development: a computational account', *Neural Computation*, 10: 1759–77.

Cheney, D.L. and Seyfarth, R.M. (1990) *How Monkeys See the World: inside the mind of another species*, Chicago: University of Chicago Press.

Cheney, D.L., Seyfarth, R.M. and Smuts, B.B. (1986) 'Social relationships and social cognition in nonhuman primates', *Science*, 234: 1361–66.

Chomsky, N. (1972) *Language and Mind*, New York: Harcourt Brace Jovanovich.

Chua, S.E., Wright, I.C., Poline, J.B., Liddle, P.F., Murray, R.M., Frackowiak, R.S., Friston, K.J. and McGuire, P.K. (1997) 'Grey matter correlates of syndromes in schizophrenia: a semi-automated analysis of structural magnetic resonance images', *British Journal of Psychiatry*, 170: 406–10.

Clancy, B., Darlington, R.B. and Finlay, BL. (2000) 'The course of human events: predicting the timing of primate neural development', *Developmental Science*, 3: 57–66.

Claridge, G.S. (1998) 'Creativity and madness: clues from modern psychiatric diagnosis', in A. Steptoe (ed.) *Genius and the Mind*, Oxford: Oxford University Press, pp. 227–50.

Claridge, G.S. and Beech, T. (1995) 'Fully and quasi-dimensional constructions of schizotypy', in A. Raine, T. Lencz and S.A. Mednick (eds) *Schizotypal Personality*, Cambridge: Cambridge University Press, pp. 192–216.

Clark, C., Klonoff, H., Tyhurst, J.S., Li, D., Martin, W. and Pate, B.D. (1989) 'Regional cerebral glucose metabolism in three sets of identical twins with psychotic symptoms', *Canadian Journal of Psychiatry*, 34: 263–70.

Clark, M.E. (2002) *In Search of Human Nature*, London: Routledge.

Cleghorn, J.M. and Albert, M.L. (1990) 'Modular disjunction in schizophrenia: a framework for a pathological psychophysiology', in A. Kales, C.M. Stefanis and J.A. Talbott (eds) *Recent Advances in Schizophrenia*, New York: Springer-Verlag.

Cleghorn, J.M., Garnett, E.S., Nahmias, C., Firnau, G., Brown, G.M., Kaplan, R., Szechtman, H. and Szechtman, B. (1989a) 'Increased frontal and reduced parietal glucose metabolism in acute untreated schizophrenia', *Psychiatry Research*, 28: 119–33.

Cleghorn, J.M., Kaplan, R.D., Nahmias, C., Garnett, E.S., Szechtman, H. and Szechtman, B. (1989b) 'Inferior parietal region implicated in neurocognitive impairment in schizophrenia', *Archives of General Psychiatry*, 46: 758–60.

Clottes, J. (1996) 'Epilogue', in J.-M. Chauvet, E.B. Deschamps and C. Hillaire (eds) *Dawn of Art: the Chauvet Cave*, New York: Harry N. Abrams, pp. 89–127.

Cohen, C.I. (1993) 'Poverty and the course of schizophrenia: implications for research and policy', *Hospital and Community Psychiatry*, 44 (10): 951–58.

Cohen-Cory, S. (2002) 'The developing synapse: construction and modulation of synaptic structures and circuits', *Science*, 298: 770–76.

Conrad, M. (1989) 'The brain-machine disanalogy', *Biosystems*, 22 (3): 197–213.

Corballis, M.C. (1992) 'On the evolution of language and generativity', *Cognition*, 44: 197–226.

Corcoran, R., Mercer, G. and Frith, C.D. (1995) 'Schizophrenia, symptomatology and social inference: investigating "theory of mind" in people with schizophrenia', *Schizophrenia Research*, 17: 5–13.

Cords, M. (1997) 'Friendships, alliances, reciprocity and repair', in A. Whiten and R.W. Byrne (eds) *Machiavellian Intelligence 11: extensions and evaluations*, Cambridge: Cambridge University Press, pp. 24–49.

Cosmides, L. and Tooby, J. (1992) 'Cognitive adaptations for social exchange', in J.H. Barkow, L. Cosmides and J. Tooby (eds) *The Adapted Mind: evolutionary psychology and the generation of culture*, Oxford: Oxford University Press, pp. 163–228.

Crow, T.J. (1980) 'Molecular pathology of schizophrenia: more than one disease process?', *British Medical Journal*, 280 (6207): 66–68.

Crow, T.J. (1990) 'Temporal lobe asymmetries as the key to the etiology of schizophrenia', *Schizophrenia Bulletin*, 16: 433–43.

Crow, T.J. (1995a) 'A Darwinian approach to the origins of psychosis', *British Journal of Psychiatry*, 167: 12–25.

Crow, T.J. (1995b) 'A theory of the evolutionary origins of psychosis', *European Neuropsychopharmacology*, 5, Suppl: 59–63.

Crow, T.J. (1997) 'Is schizophrenia the price that Homo sapiens pays for language?', *Schizophrenia Research*, 28: 127–41.

Crow, T.J. (1998) 'From Kraepelin to Kretschmer leavened by Schneider: the transition from categories of psychosis to dimensions of variation intrinsic to Homo sapiens', *Archives of General Psychiatry*, 55: 502–4.

Crow, T.J. (ed.) (2002) *The Speciation of Modern Homo Sapiens*, Oxford: Oxford University Press.

Cullen, M. and Whiteford, H. (2001) 'The interrelations of social capital with health and mental health', Commonwealth of Australia, http://www.mentalhealth.gov.au

Cutting, J. and Dunne, F. (1989) 'Subjective experience of schizophrenia', *Schizophrenia Bulletin*, 15: 217–31.

Cutting, J. and Murphy, D. (1990) 'Impaired ability of schizophrenics, relative to manics or depressives, to appreciate social knowledge about their culture', *British Journal of Psychiatry*, 157: 355–58.

Dalai Lama the, His Holiness and Cutler, H.C. (1998) *The Art of Happiness: a handbook for living*, New York: Riverhead Books/Penguin Putnam.

Daly, M. and Wilson, M. (1994) 'Evolutionary psychology: adaptationist, selectionist and comparative', *Psychological Inquiry*, 6: 34–38.

Damasio, A.R. (1994) *Descartes' Error: emotion, reason and the human brain*, New York: Putnam.

Darwin, C. (1859) *The Origin of Species by Means of Natural Selection*, London: John Murray.

Darwin, C. (1871) *The Descent of Man and Selection in Relation to Sex*, London: John Murray.

Darwin, C. (1872) *The Expression of the Emotions in Man and Animals*, London: John Murray.

Darwin, C. (1960) 'Darwin's Notebooks on Transmutation of Species', *Bulletin of the British Museum (Natural History), Historical Series*, 2: 163–228.

Davenport, R.K. and Menzel, E.W. (1963) 'Stereotyped behaviour of the infant chimpanzee', *Archives of General Psychiatry*, 8: 99–104.

Davis, M. (1992) 'The role of the amygdala in fear and anxiety', *Annual Review of Neuroscience*, 15: 353–75.

Dawkins, R. (1976) *The Selfish Gene*, Oxford: Oxford University Press.

Deacon, T.W. (1990) 'Problems of ontogeny and phylogeny in brain size evolution', *International Journal of Primatology*, 11: 237–82.

Deacon, T.W. (1998) *The Symbolic Species: the co-evolution of language and the human brain*, New York: W.W. Norton & Company.

Deacon, T.W. (2000) 'Heterochrony in brain evolution: cellular versus morpho-logical analyses', in S. Taylor Parker, J. Langer and M.L. McKinney (eds) *Biology, Brains and Behaviour*, Sante Fe: School of American Research Press/Oxford: James Curry Ltd, pp. 41–88.

Decety, J. and Grèzes, J. (1999) 'Neural mechanisms subserving the perception of human actions', *Trends in Cognitive Science*, 3: 172–78.

Decety, J. and Jackson, P.L. (2004) 'The functional architecture of human empathy', *Behavioral and Cognitive Neurosciences Review*, 3 (2): 71–100.

Dejérine, J. (1895) *Anatomie des Centres Nerveux*, Paris: Rueff et Cie.

De Lisi, L.E. (2001) 'Speech disorder in schizophrenia: review of the literature and exploration of its relation to the uniquely human capacity for language', *Schizophrenia Bulletin*, 27: 481–96.

Dennett, D.C. (1987) *The Intentional Stance*, Cambridge, MA: Bradford Books/ MIT Press.

Devereaux, G. (1956) 'Normal and abnormal: the key problem in psychiatric anthropology', in J.B. Casagrande and T. Gladwin (eds) *Some Uses of Anthropol-ogy: theoretical and applied*, Washington, DC: Anthropological Society of Washington, pp. 23–48.

Devinsky, O., Morrell, M.J. and Vogt, B.A. (1995) 'Contributions of anterior cingulate cortex to behaviour', *Brain*, 118: 279–306.

De Waal, F.B. (1982) *Chimpanzee Politics*, London: Jonathan Cape.

De Waal, F.B. (2000) 'Primates: a natural heritage of conflict resolution', *Science*, 289: 586–90.

De Waal, F.B.M. and Roosmalen, A. (1979) 'Reconciliation and consolation among chimpanzees', *Behavioral Ecology and Sociobiology*, 5: 55–56.

Dewsbury, D.A. (1999) 'The proximate and the ultimate: past, present, and future', *Behavioural Processes*, 46 (3): 189–99.

Dickey, C.C., McCarley, R.W. and Shenton, M.E. (2002) 'The brain in schizotypal personality disorder: a review of structural MRI and CT findings', *Harvard Review of Psychiatry*, 10: 1–15.

Dicks, D., Myers, R.E. and Kling, A. (1969) 'Uncus and amygdala lesions: effects on social behaviour in the free-ranging rhesus monkey', *Science*, 165: 69–71.

Dienske, H. and Griffin, R. (1978) 'Abnormal behaviour patterns developing in chimpanzee infants during nursery care: a note', *Journal of Child Psychology and Psychiatry*, 19 (4): 387–91.

Dietrich, A. (2003) 'Functional neuroanatomy of altered states of consciousness: the transient hypofrontality hypothesis', *Consciousness and Cognition*, 12: 231–56.

Di Pellegrino, G., Fadiga, L., Fogassi, L., Gallese, V. and Rizzolatti, G. (1992)

'Understanding motor events: a neurophysiological study', *Experimental Brain Research*, 91 (1): 176–80.

Dobkin de Rios, M. and Winkelman, M. (1989) 'Shamanism and altered states of consciousness: an introduction', *Journal of Psychoactive Drugs*, 21: 1–7.

Dobzhansky, T. (1937) *Genetics and the Origin of Species*, New York: Columbia University Press.

Dobzhansky, T. (1956) 'What is an adaptive trait?' *American Naturalist*, 90: 337–47.

Dobzhansky, T. (1962) *Mankind Evolving: the evolution of the human species*, New Haven: Yale University Press.

Dolan, R.J., Fletcher, P., Frith, C.D., Friston, K.J., Frackowiak, R.S. and Grasby, P.M. (1995) 'Dopaminergic modulation of impaired cognitive activation in the anterior cingulate cortex in schizophrenia', *Nature*, 378: 180–82.

Dolan, R.J., Fletcher, P.C., McKenna, P., Friston, K.J. and Frith, C.D. (1999) 'Abnormal neural integration related to cognition in schizophrenia', *Acta Psychiatrica Scandinavica (Supplement)*, 395: 58–67.

Doody, G.A., Gotz, M., Johnstone, E.C., Frith, C.D. and Owens, D.G. (1998) 'Theory of mind and psychoses', *Psychological Medicine*, 28: 397–405.

Dowson, T.A. (1988) 'Revelations of religious reality: the individual in San rock art', *World Archaeology*, 20: 116–28.

Dubrovsky, B. (2002) 'Evolutionary psychiatry: adaptationist and nonadaptationist conceptualizations', *Progress in Neuropsychopharmacology and Biological Psychiatry*, 26: 1–19.

Dunbar, R.I.M. (1988) *Primate Social Systems*, London: Croom Helm.

Dunbar, R.I.M. (1992) 'Neocortex size as a constraint on group size in primates', *Journal of Human Evolution*, 20: 469–93.

Dunbar, R.I.M. (2001) 'Brains on two legs: group size and the evolution of intelligence', in F.B.M. de Waal (ed.) *Tree of Origin*, Cambridge: Harvard University Press, pp. 173–92.

Durrant, R. and Haig, B.D. (2001) 'How to pursue the adaptationist program in psychology', *Philosophical Psychology*, 14: 357–80.

Eaton, W.W. (1980) *The Sociology of Mental Disorders*, New York: Praeger.

Ebmeier, K.P., Lawrie, S.M., Blackwood, D.H., Johnstone, E.C. and Goodwin, G.M. (1995) 'Hypofrontality revisited: a high resolution single photon emission computed tomography study in schizophrenia', *Journal of Neurology, Neurosurgery, and Psychiatry*, 58: 452–56.

Edwards, L., Pattison, P.E., Jackson, H.J. and Wales, R.J. (2001) 'Facial affect and affective prosody recognition in first-episode schizophrenia', *Schizophrenia Research*, 48: 235–53.

Eibl-Eibefeldt, I. (1971) *Love and Hate*, London: Methuen.

Eliade, M. (1989) *Shamanism: archaic techniques of ecstasy*, Harmondsworth, Middlesex: Penguin Books Ltd.

Ellison, G.D. (1979) 'Animal models of psychopathology: studies in naturalistic colony environments', in J.D. Keehn (ed.) *Psychopathology in Animals: research and clinical implications*, New York: Academic Press, pp. 81–101.

Emery, N.J. (2000) 'The eyes have it: the neuroethology, function and evolution of social gaze', *Neuroscience and Biobehavioural Reviews*, 24: 581–604.

Engel, G.L. (1980) 'The clinical application of the biopsychosocial model', *The American Journal of Psychiatry*, 137: pp. 535–544.

Erwin, J. and Deni, R. (1979) 'Strangers in a strange land', in J. Erwin, T. Maple and G. Mitchell (eds) *Captivity and Behaviour*, New York: Van Nostrand Reinhold, pp. 1–28.

Eslinger, P.J. and Damasio, A.R. (1985) 'Severe disturbance of higher cognition after bilateral frontal lobe ablation: patient EVR', *Neurology*, 35: 1731–41.

Esquirol, J.E.D. (1838) *Des Maladies Mentales*, Paris: Baillière.

Evans, K., McGrath, J. and Milns, R. (2003) 'Searching for schizophrenia in ancient Greek and Roman literature: a systematic review', *Acta Psychiatrica Scandinavica*, 107: 323–30.

Evensen, H. (1903) 'Die psychologische grundlage der katatonischen krankheitszeichen', *Neurologia*, 2 (5): 6.

Fábrega Jr., H. (2002) *Origins of Psychopathology*, Piscataway: Rutgers University Press.

Fadiga, L., Fogassi, L., Pavesi, G. and Rizzolatti, G. (1995) 'Motor facilitation during action observation: a magnetic simulation study', *Journal of Neurophysiology*, 73: 2608–11.

Fahim, C., Stip, E., Mancini-Marïe, A., Boualem, M., Malaspina, D. and Beauregard, M. (2004) 'Negative socio-emotional resonance in schizophrenia: a functional magnetic resonance imaging hypothesis', *Medical Hypotheses*, 63: 467–75.

Falk, D. (1980) 'A reanalysis of the South African australopithecine natural endocasts', *American Journal of Physical Anthropology*, 53: 525–39.

Falk, D. (1985) 'Hadar AL 162–28 endocast as evidence that brain enlargement preceded cortical reorganization in hominid evolution', *Nature*, 313: 45–47.

Falk, D. (1986) 'Reply to Holloway and Kimble', *Nature*, 321: 536–37.

Farley, J.D. (1976) 'Phylogenetic adaptations and the genetics of psychosis', *Acta Psychiatrica Scandinavica*, 53: 173–92.

Farmer, P. (2005) *Pathologies of Power: health, human rights, and the new war on the poor*, Berkeley and Los Angeles: University of California Press.

Farrer, C. and Frith, C.D. (2002) 'Experiencing oneself vs another person as being the cause of an action: the neural correlates of the experience of agency', *Neuroimage*, 15: 596–603.

Farrow, T.F., Zheng, Y., Wilkinson, I.D., Spence, S.A., Deakin, J.F., Tarrier, N., Griffiths, P.D. and Woodruff, P.W. (2001) 'Investigating the functional anatomy of empathy and forgiveness', *Neuroreport*, 12: 2433–38.

Faulks, S. (2005) *Human Traces*, London: Hutchinson/Random House Group Ltd.

Feierman, J.R. (1994) 'A testable hypothesis about schizophrenia generated by evolutionary theory', *Ethology and Sociobiology*, 15: 263–82.

Feinberg, I. (1983) 'Schizophrenia: caused by a fault in programmed synaptic elimination during adolescence?' *Journal of Psychiatric Research*, 17: 319–34.

Fernández-Armesto, F. (2004) *So You Think You're Human?* Oxford: Oxford University Press.

Finlay, B.L. and Darlington, R.B. (1995) 'Linked regularities in the development and evolution of mammalian brains', *Science*, 268: 1578–84.

Fisher, R.A. (1930) *The Genetical Theory of Natural Selection*, New York: Dover.

Flaum, M., Swayze, V.W., O'Leary, D.S., Yuh, W.T., Ehrhardt, J.C., Arndt, S.V. and Andreasen, N.C. (1995) 'Effects of diagnosis, laterality, and gender on brain morphology in schizophrenia', *American Journal of Psychiatry*, 152: 704–14.

Fletcher, P.C., Happé, F., Frith, U., Baker, S.C., Dolan, R.J., Frackowiak, R.S. and

Frith, C.D. (1995) 'Other minds in the brain: a functional imaging study of "theory of mind" in story comprehension', *Cognition*, 57: 109–28.

Fletcher, P.C., McKenna, P.J., Frith, C.D., Grasby, P.M., Friston, K.J. and Dolan, R.J. (1998) 'Brain activations in schizophrenia during a graded memory task studied with functional neuroimaging', *Archives of General Psychiatry*, 55: 1001–8.

Fletcher, P.C., McKenna, P.J., Friston, K.J., Frith, C.D. and Dolan, R.J. (1999) 'Abnormal cingulate modulation of fronto-temporal connectivity in schizophrenia', *Neuroimage*, 9: 337–42.

Fodor, J. (1983) *The Modularity of Mind*, Cambridge, MA: MIT Press.

Foong, J., Maier, M., Clark, C.A., Barker, G.J., Miller, D.H. and Ron, M.A. (2000) 'Neuropathological abnormalities of the corpus callosum in schizophrenia: a diffusion tensor imaging study', *Journal of Neurology, Neurosurgery and Psychiatry*, 68 (2): 242–44.

Foucault, M. (2001) *Madness and Civilization*, London: Routledge.

Frecska, E., White, K.D. and Luna, L.E. (2003) 'Effects of the Amazonian psychoactive beverage Ayahuasca on binocular rivalry: interhemispheric switching or interhemispheric fusion?' *Journal of Psychoactive Drugs*, 35 (3): 367–74.

Frederikse, M., Lu, A., Aylward, E., Barta, P., Sharma, T. and Pearlson, G. (2000) 'Sex differences in inferior parietal lobule volume in schizophrenia', *American Journal of Psychiatry*, 157: 422–27.

Friston, K.J. (2002) 'Dysfunctional connectivity in schizophrenia', *World Psychiatry*, 1 (2): 66–71.

Friston, K.J. and Frith, C.D. (1995) 'Schizophrenia: a disconnection syndrome?', *Clinical Neuroscience*, 3: 89–97.

Friston, K.J., Frith, C.D., Liddle, P.F. and Frackowiak, R.S. (1991) 'Investigating a network model of word generation with positron emission tomography', *Proceedings of the Royal Society of London Brain and Biological Sciences*, 244: 101–6.

Friston, K.J., Frith, C.D., Liddle, P.F. and Frackowiak, R.S. (1993) 'Functional connectivity: the principal-component analysis of large (PET) data sets', *Journal of Cerebral Blood Flow Metabolism*, 13: 5–14.

Friston, K.J., Ungerleider, L.G., Jezzard, P. and Turner, R. (1995) 'Characterizing modulatory interaction between areas V1 and V2 in human cortex: a new treatment of functional MRI data', *Human Brain Mapping*, 2: 211–24.

Frith, C.D. (1987) 'The positive and negative symptoms of schizophrenia reflect impairments in the perception and initiation of action', *Psychological Medicine*, 17: 631–48.

Frith, C.D. (1992) *The Cognitive Neuropsychology of Schizophrenia*, Hove, UK: Lawrence Erlbaum Associates Ltd.

Frith, C.D. (1994) 'Theory of mind in schizophrenia', in A.S. David and J.C. Cutting (eds) *The Neuropsychology of Schizophrenia*, Hove, UK: Lawrence Erlbaum Associates Ltd.

Frith, C. D. (2002) 'What do imaging studies tell us about the neural basis of autism?' *Novartis Foundation Symposium*, 25: 149–66.

Frith, C.D. and Allen, H.A. (1988) 'Language disorders in schizophrenia and their implications for neuropsychology', in P. Bebbington and P. McGuffin (eds) *Schizophrenia: the major issues*, Oxford: Heinemann.

Frith, C.D. and Corcoran, R. (1996) 'Exploring "theory of mind" in people with schizophrenia', *Psychological Medicine*, 26: 521–30.

Frith, C. and Johnstone, E. (2003) *Schizophrenia: a very short introduction*, Oxford: Oxford University Press.

Frith, C.D., Friston, K., Liddle, P.F. and Frackowiak, R.S. (1991) 'Willed action and the prefrontal cortex in man: a study with PET', *Proceedings of the Royal Society of London Brain and Biological Sciences*, 244: 241–46.

Frith, C.D., Friston, K.J., Herold, S., Silbersweig, D., Fletcher, P., Cahill, C., Dolan, R.J., Frackowiak, R.S. and Liddle, P.F. (1995) 'Regional brain activity in chronic schizophrenic patients during the performance of a verbal fluency task', *British Journal of Psychiatry*, 167: 343–49.

Frith, U. (1989) 'A new look at language and communication in autism', *British Journal of Disorders of Communication*, 24: 123–50.

Fritzsche, M. (2002) 'Impaired information processing triggers altered states of consciousness', *Medical Hypotheses*, 58 (4): 352–58.

Fromm, E. (1942) *Fear of Freedom*, London: Routledge and Kegan Paul (Reprint 2003, Routledge Classics).

Fromm, E. (2000) *The Art of Loving*, New York: Perennial Classics.

Fuchs, T. (2001) 'The tacit dimension', *Philosophy, Psychiatry and Psychology*, 8 (4): 323–26.

Fuchs, T. (2002) 'The challenge of neuroscience: psychiatry and phenomenology today', *Psychopathology*, 35 (6): 319–27.

Fuchs, T. (2005) 'Delusional mood and delusional perception: a phenomenological analysis', *Psychopathology*, 38: 133–39.

Fukuchi-Shimogori, T. and Grove, E.A. (2001) 'Neocortex patterning by the secreted signalling molecule FGF8', *Science*, 294: 1071–74.

Futuyma, D.J. (1998) *Evolutionary Biology*, 3rd edn, Sunderland, MA: Sinauer Associates, Inc.

Gaebel, W. and Wölwer, W. (1992) 'Facial expression and emotional face recognition in schizophrenia and depression', *European Archives of Psychiatry and Clinical Neurosciences*, 242: 46–52.

Gagneux, P. and Varki, A. (2001) 'Genetic differences between humans and great apes', *Molecular Phylogenetics and Evolution*, 18: 2–13.

Gallagher, H.L., Happé, F., Brunswick, N., Fletcher, P.C., Frith, U. and Frith, C.D. (2000) 'Reading the mind in cartoons and stories: an fMRI study of "theory of mind" in verbal and nonverbal tasks', *Neuropsychologia*, 38: 11–21.

Gallese, V. (2003a) 'The roots of empathy: the shared manifold hypothesis and the neural basis of intersubjectivity', *Psychopathology*, 36: 171–80.

Gallese, V. (2003b) 'The manifold nature of interpersonal relations: the quest for a common mechanism', *Philosophical Transactions of the Royal Society of London*, 5 (358): 517–28.

Gallese, V., Keysers, C. and Rizzolatti, G. (2004) 'A unifying view of the basis of social cognition', *Trends in Cognitive Science*, 8 (9): 396–403.

Galton, F. (1869) *Hereditary Genius: an inquiry into its laws and consequences*, London: Macmillan.

Gannon, P.J., Broadfield, D.C., Kheck, N.M., Hof, P., Braun, A.R. and Erwin, J.M. (1998a) 'Brain language area evolution 1: anatomic expression of Heschl's gyrus and planum temporale asymmetry in great apes, lesser apes and Old World monkeys', *Society for Neuroscience Abstracts*, 24 (1): 60.

Gannon, P.J., Holloway, R.L., Broadfield, D.C. and Braun, A.R. (1998b) 'Asymmetry of chimpanzee planum temporale: humanlike pattern of Wernicke's brain language area homolog', *Science*, 279: 220–22.

Gannon, P.J., Kheck, N.M. and Hof, P.R. (2001) 'Language areas of the hominoid brain: a dynamic communicative shift on the upper east side planum', in D. Falk and K.R. Gibson (eds) *Evolutionary Anatomy of the Primate Cerebral Cortex*, Cambridge: Cambridge University Press, pp. 216–40.

Garcia Cuerva, A., Sabe, L., Kuzis, G., Tiberti, C., Dorrego, F. and Starkstein, S.E. (2001) '"Theory of mind" and pragmatic abilities in dementia', *Neuropsychiatry, Neuropsychology and Behavioral Neurology*, 14: 153–58.

Gardner, H. (1983) *Frames of the Mind: the theory of multiple intelligences*, New York: Basic Books.

Garstang, W. (1922) 'The theory of recapitulation: a critical restatement of the biogenetic law', *Journal of the Linnaean Society*, 35: 81–101.

Gehlen, A. (1940) *Der Mensch, seine Natur und seine Stellung in der Welt*, Berlin: Athenaion.

Geshwind, N. and Galaburda, A.M. (eds) (1984) *Cerebral Dominance: the biological foundations*, Cambridge: Harvard University Press.

Gibson, K.R. (1991) 'Myelination and brain development: a comparative perspective on questions of neoteny, altriciality, and intelligence', in K.R. Gibson and A.C. Peterson (eds) *Brain Maturation and Cognitive Development: comparative and cross-cultural perspectives*, New York: Aldine de Gruyter, pp. 29–63.

Gibson, K.R., Rumbaugh, D. and Beran, M. (2001) 'Bigger is better: primate brain size in relationship to cognition', in D. Falk and K.R. Gibson (eds) *Evolutionary Anatomy of the Primate Cerebral Cortex*, Cambridge: Cambridge University Press, pp. 79–97.

Gilbert, P. (2000) 'Social mentalities: internal "social" conflicts and the role of inner warmth and compassion in cognitive therapy', in P. Gilbert and K.G. Bailey (eds) *Genes on the Couch: explorations in evolutionary psychotherapy*, Hove, UK: Brunner-Routledge, pp. 118–50.

Gilbert, P. (2004) 'Threat, safeness and schizophrenia: hidden issues in an evolutionary story', *Behavioural and Brain Sciences*, 27: 858–59.

Gilbert, P. and Bailey, K.G. (eds) (2000) *Genes on the Couch: explorations in evolutionary psychotherapy*, Hove, UK: Brunner-Routledge.

Gilbert, P., Birchwood, M., Gilbert, J., Trower, P., Hay, J., Murray, B., Meaden, A., Olsen, K. and Miles, J.N. (2001) 'An exploration of evolved mental mechanisms for dominant and subordinate behaviour in relation to auditory hallucinations in schizophrenia and critical thoughts in depression', *Psychological Medicine*, 31: 1117–27.

Gilissen, E. (2001) 'Structural symmetries and asymmetries in human and chimpanzee brains', in D. Falk and K.R. Gibson (eds) *Evolutionary Anatomy of the Primate Cerebral Cortex*, Cambridge: Cambridge University Press, pp. 187–215.

Glantz, K. and Pearce, J. (1989) *Exiles from Eden: psychotherapy from an evolutionary perspective*, New York: Norton.

Goel, V., Grafman, J., Sadato, N. and Hallett, M. (1995) 'Modeling other minds', *Neuroreport*, 6: 1741–46.

Golgi, C. (1906) *Neuron Doctrine: theory and facts*, Nobel Institute, 215, Nobel Lecture.

Goltz, F. (1881) *Transactions of the Seventh International Medical Congress*, London: J.W. Kolkmann.

Goodall, J. van Lawick (1971) *In the Shadow of Man*, London: William Collins Sons and Co Ltd.

Goodall, J. (1990) *Through a Window: thirty years with the chimpanzees of Gombe*, London: Weidenfeld and Nicolson.

Goosen, C. (1981) 'Abnormal behaviour patterns in rhesus monkeys: symptoms of mental disease', *Biological Psychiatry*, 16 (8): 697–716.

Gorno-Tempini, M.L., Price, C.J., Josephs, O., Vandenberghe, R., Cappa, S.F., Kapur, N., Frackowiak, R.S. and Tempini, M.L. (1998) 'The neural systems sustaining face and proper-name processing', *Brain*, 121: 2103–18.

Gottesman, I.I. (1991) *Schizophrenia Genesis: the origins of madness*, New York: W.H. Freeman and Co.

Gottlieb, G. (1987) 'The developmental basis of evolutionary change', *Journal of Comparative Psychology*, 101: 262–71.

Gottlieb, G. (1991a) 'Experiential canalization of behavioral development: theory', *Developmental Psychology*, 27: 4–13.

Gottlieb, G. (1991b) 'Experiential canalization of behavioral development: results', *Developmental Psychology*, 27: 35–39.

Gottlieb, G. (1992) *Individual Development and Evolution: the genesis of novel behaviour*, New York: Oxford University Press.

Gottlieb, G. (2000) 'Environmental and behavioral influences on gene activity', *Current Directions in Psychological Science*, 9: 93–102.

Gould, S.J. (1977) *Ontogeny and Phylogeny*, Cambridge: Harvard University Press.

Gould, S.J. (1981) *The Mismeasure of Man*, New York: Norton.

Gould, S.J. (1982) 'Darwinism and the expansion of evolutionary theory', *Science*, 216: 380–87.

Gould, S.J. (1991) 'Exaptation: a crucial tool for evolutionary psychology', *Journal of Social Issues*, 47: 43–65.

Gould, S.J. and Lewontin, R.C. (1979) 'The spandrels of San Marco and the Panglossian paradigm: a critique of the adaptationist programme', *Proceedings of the Royal Society of London*, Series B, 205 (1161): 581–98.

Gouzoulis-Mayfrank, E., Schreckenberger, M., Sabri, O., Arning, C., Thelen, B., Spitzer, M., Kovar, K-A., Hermle, L., Büll, U. and Sass, H. (1999) 'Neurometabolic effects of psilocybin, 3,4-methylenedioxyethylamphetamine (MDE) and d-methamphetamine in healthy volunteers: a double-blind, placebo-controlled PET study with [18F]FDG', *Neuropsychopharmacology*, 20 (6): 565–81.

Grady, C.L. and Keightley, M.L. (2002) 'Studies of altered social cognition in neuropsychiatric disorders using functional neuroimaging', *Canadian Journal of Psychiatry*, 47: 327–36.

Grafton, S.T., Arbib, M.A., Fadiga, L. and Rizzolatti, G. (1996) 'Localization of grasp representations in humans by PET: 2. Observation compared with imagination', *Experimental Brain Research*, 112: 103–11.

Gregory, C., Lough, S., Stone, V., Erzinclioglu, S., Martin, L., Baron-Cohen, S. and Hodges, J.R. (2002) 'Theory of mind in patients with frontal variant frontotemporal dementia and Alzheimer's disease: theoretical and practical implications', *Brain*, 125: 752–64.

Griesinger, W. (1845) *Die Pathologie und Therapie der Psychische Krankheiten*, Stuttgart: A. Krabbe.

Gross, O. (1904) 'Dementia sejunctiva', *Neurologisches Centralblatt*, 23: 1144–66. (Translated from J. Cutting and M. Shepherd (eds) 1987 *The Clinical Roots of the Schizophrenia Concept*, Cambridge: Cambridge University Press.

Gruzelier, J.H. (1999) 'Functional neuropsychophysiological asymmetry in schizophrenia: a review and reorientation', *Schizophrenia Bulletin*, 25: 91–120.

Gruzelier, J.H. and Kaiser, J. (1996) 'Syndromes of schizotypy and timing of puberty', *Schizophrenia Research*, 21: 183–94.

Gur, R.E., Cowell, P.E., Latshaw, A., Turetsky, B.I., Grossman, R.I., Arnold, S.E., Bilker, W.B. and Gur, R.C. (2000) 'Reduced dorsal and orbital prefrontal gray matter volumes in schizophrenia', *Archives of General Psychiatry*, 57: 761–68.

Gur, R.E., McGrath, C., Chan, R.M., Schroeder, L., Turner, T., Turetsky, B.I., Kohler, C., Alsop, D., Maldjian, J., Ragland, J.D. and Gur, R.C. (2002) 'An fMRI study of facial emotion processing in patients with schizophrenia', *American Journal of Psychiatry*, 159: 1992–99.

Gusnard, D.A., Akbudak, E., Shulman, G.L. and Raichle, M.E. (2001) 'Medial prefrontal cortex and self-referential mental activity: relation to a default mode of brain function', *Proceedings of the National Academy of Sciences of the U.S.A*, 98: 4259–64.

Haeckel, E. (1866) *Generelle Morphologie der Organismen, 2 Vols. 1. Allgemeine Anatomie der Organismen; 11. Allgemeine Entwicklungsgeschichte der Organismen*, Berlin: Georg Reimer Verlag.

Hamann, S.B., Ely, T.D., Grafton, S.T. and Kilts, C.D. (1999) 'Amygdala activity related to enhanced memory for pleasant and aversive stimuli', *Nature Neuroscience*, 2: 289–93.

Harcourt, A. (1988) 'Alliances in contests and social intelligence', in R.W. Byrne and A. Whiten (eds) *Machiavellian Intelligence: social expertise and the evolution of intellect in monkeys, apes, and humans*, Oxford: Clarendon Press, pp. 132–52.

Hardcastle, V.G. (2004) 'Schizophrenia: a benign trait?' *Behavioural and Brain Sciences*, 27: 859–60.

Harlow, H.F. and Harlow, M.K. (1962) 'Social deprivation in monkeys', *Scientific American*, 207: 136–46.

Harlow, H.F. and Novak, M.A. (1973) 'Psychopathological perspectives', *Perspectives in Biology and Medicine*, 16 (3): 461–78.

Harrison, P.J. (1999) 'The neuropathology of schizophrenia: a critical review of the data and their interpretation', *Brain*, 122: 593–624.

Hart, A.J., Whalen, P.J., Shin, L.M., McInerney, S.C., Fischer, H. and Rauch, S.L. (2000) 'Differential response in the human amygdala to racial outgroup vs ingroup face stimuli', *Neuroreport*, 11: 2351–55.

Haukka, J., Suvisaari, J. and Lönnqvist, J. (2003) 'Fertility of patients with schizophrenia, their siblings, and the general population: a cohort study from 1950–1959 in Finland', *American Journal of Psychiatry*, 160: 460–63.

Haxby, J.V., Horwitz, B., Ungerleider, L.G., Maisog, J.M., Pietrini, P. and Grady, C.L. (1994) 'The functional organization of human extrastriate cortex: a PET-rCBF study of selective attention to faces and locations', *Journal of Neurosciences*, 14: 6336–53.

Haxby, J.V., Gobbini, M.I., Furey, M.L., Ishai, A., Schouten, J.L. and Pietrini, P.

(2001) 'Distributed and overlapping representations of faces and objects in ventral temporal cortex', *Science*, 293: 2425–30.

Haxby, J.V., Hoffman, E.A. and Gobbini, M.I. (2002) 'Human neural systems for face recognition and social communication', *Biological Psychiatry*, 51: 59–67.

Haydar, T.F., Kuan, C.Y., Flavell, R.A. and Rakic, P. (1999) 'The role of cell death in regulating the size and shape of the mammalian forebrain', *Cerebral Cortex*, 9: 621–26.

Hedrick, P.W. (1999) 'Antagonstic pleitropy and genetic polymorphism: a perspective', *Heredity*, 82, 126–32.

Hemsley, D.R. (1993) 'A simple (or simplistic?) cognitive model for schizophrenia', *Behavioral Research and Therapeutics*, 31 (7): 633–45.

Hemsley, D.R. (2005) 'The development of a cognitive model of schizophrenia: placing it in context', *Neuroscience and Biobehavioral Reviews*, 29 (6): 977–88.

Henshilwood, C.S., D'Errico, F., Yates, R., Jacobs, Z., Tribolo, C., Duller, G.A.T., Mercier, N., Sealy, J.C., Valladas, H., Watts, I. and Wintle, A.G. (2002) 'Emergence of modern human behaviour: Middle Stone Age engravings from South Africa', *Science*, 295: 1278–80.

Herbart, J.F. (1816) *Herbarts Sämtliche Werke. Kehrbach K, Hrsg*. Aalen: Scienta.

Hermle, L., Funfgeld, M., Oepen, G., Botsch, H., Borchardt, D., Gouzoulis, E., Fehrenbach, R.A. and Spitzer, M. (1992) 'Mescaline-induced psychopathological, neuropsychological, and neurometabolic effects in normal subjects: experimental psychosis as a tool for psychiatric research', *Biological Psychiatry*, 32 (11): 976–91.

Hevner, R.F. and Kinney, H.C. (1996) 'Reciprocal entorhinal-hippocampal connections established by human fetal midgestation', *Journal of Comparative Neurology*, 372: 384–96.

Heyes, C.M. (1998) 'Theory of mind in nonhuman primates', *Behavioral and Brain Sciences*, 21: 101–14.

Hill, D. (1983) *The Politics of Schizophrenia*, Lanham, MD: University Press of America.

Hippocrates (1931) 'The sacred disease', in *Volume 11. Prognostic. Regimen in acute diseases. The sacred disease. The art. Breaths. Law. Decorum. Physician (Ch1). Dentition* (translated by W.H.S. Jones), London: William Heinemann Ltd.

Hof, P.R., Nimchinsky, E.A., Perl, D.P. and Erwin, J.M. (2001) 'An unusual population of pyramidal neurons in the anterior cingulate cortex of hominids contains the calcium-binding protein calretinin', *Neuroscience Letters*, 307: 139–42.

Hoffman, E.A. and Haxby, J.V. (2000) 'Distinct representations of eye gaze and identity in the distributed human neural system for face perception', *Nature Neuroscience*, 3: 80–84.

Hoffman, R.E. and McGlashan, T.H. (1997) 'Synaptic elimination, neurodevelopment and the mechanism of hallucinated "voices" in schizophrenia', *American Journal of Psychiatry*, 154: 1683–9.

Hoffman, R.E. and McGlashan, T.H. (1998) 'Reduced corticocortical connectivity can induce speech perception pathology and hallucinated "voices"', *Schizophrenia Research*, 30: 137–41.

Hoffman, R.E. and Rapaport, J. (1994) 'A psycholinguistic study of auditory/verbal hallucinations: preliminary findings', in A.S. David and J.C. Cutting (eds) *The*

Neuropsychology of Schizophrenia, Hove, UK: Lawrence Erlbaum Associates Ltd, pp. 255–67.

Hoffman R.E., Hampson, M., Varanko, M. and McGlashan, T.H. (2004) 'Auditory hallucinations, network connectivity and schizophrenia', *Behavioral and Brain Sciences*, 27: 860–61.

Hofman, M.A. (1989) 'On the evolution and geometry of the brain in mammals', *Progress in Neurobiology*, 32: 137–58.

Hollingshead, A.B. and Redlich, F.C. (1958) *Social Class and Mental Illness*, New York: Wiley.

Holloway, R.L. (1966) 'Cranial capacity and neuron number: critique and proposal', *American Journal of Physical Anthropology*, 52: 305–14.

Holloway, R.L. (1967) 'The evolution of the human brain: some notes toward a synthesis between neural structure and the evolution of complex behaviour', *General Systems*, 12: 3–20.

Holloway, R.L. (1968) 'The evolution of the primate brain: some aspects of quantitative relations', *Brain Research*, 7: 121–72.

Holloway, R.L. (1972) 'Australopithecine endocasts, brain evolution in the Hominoidea and a model of human evolution', in R. Tuttle (ed.) *The Functional and Evolutionary Biology of Primates*, Chicago: Aldine Press, pp. 185–204.

Holloway, R.L. (1974) 'On the meaning of brain size: a review of H.J. Jerison's 1973 *Evolution of the Brain and Intelligence*', *Science*, 184: 677–79.

Holloway, R.L. (1975) 'The role of human social behavior in the evolution of the brain', *43rd James Arthur Lecture on the Evolution of the Human Brain 1973*, The American Museum of Natural History.

Holloway, R.L. (1976) 'Paleoneurological evidence for language origins', *Annals of the New York Academy of Sciences*, 280: 330–48.

Holloway, R.L. (1983a) 'Cerebral brain endocast pattern of Australopithecus afarensis hominid', *Nature*, 303: 420–22.

Holloway, R.L. (1983b) 'Human paleontological evidence relevant to language behavior', *Human Neurobiology*, 2: 105–14.

Holloway, R.L. (1984) 'The Taung endocast and the lunate sulcus: a rejection of the hypothesis of its anterior position', *American Journal of Physical Anthropology*, 64: 285–87.

Holloway, R.L. (1985) 'The past, present, and future significance of the lunate sulcus in early hominid evolution', in P.V. Tobias (ed.) *Hominid Evolution: past, present, and future*, New York: A.R. Liss, pp. 47–62.

Holloway, R.L. (1995) 'Toward a synthetic theory of human brain evolution', in J-P. Changeux and J. Chavaillon (eds) *Origins of the Human Brain*, Oxford: Oxford University Press, pp. 42–54.

Holloway, R.L. (1996) 'Evolution of the human brain', in A. Lock and C.R. Peters (eds) *Handbook of Human Symbolic Evolution*, Oxford: Oxford University Press, pp. 74–116.

Holloway, R.L. and de la Costelareymondie, M.C. (1982) 'Brain endocast asymmetry in pongids and hominids: some preliminary findings on the paleontology of cerebral dominance', *American Journal of Physical Anthropology*, 58: 101–10.

Holy Bible New International Version (1984) 'Daniel 4', Colorado Springs, CO: International Bible Society.

Honey, G.D., Bullmore, E.T. and Sharma, T. (2002) 'De-coupling of cognitive performance and cerebral functional response during working memory in schizophrenia', *Schizophrenia Research*, 53: 45–56.

Hook, M.A., Lambeth, S.P., Perlman, J.E., Stavisky, R., Bloomsmith, M.A. and Shapiro, S.J. (2002) 'Inter-group variation in abnormal behaviour in chimpanzees (*Pan troglodytes*) and rhesus macaques (*Macaca mulatto*)', *Applied Animal Behaviour Science*, 76: 165–76.

Hopkins, W.D. and Rilling, J.K. (2000) 'A comparative MRI study of the relationship between neuroanatomical asymmetry and interhemispheric connectivity in primates: implication for the evolution of functional asymmetries', *Behavioural Neurosciences*, 114: 739–48.

Hopkins, W.D., Marino, L., Rilling, J.K. and MacGregor, L.A. (1998) 'Planum temporale asymmetries in great apes as revealed by magnetic resonance imaging (MRI)', *Neuroreport*, 9: 2913–18.

Hopkins, W.D., Pilcher, D.L. and MacGregor, L.A. (2000) 'Sylvian fissure asymmetries in nonhuman primates revisited: a comparative MRI study', *Brain and Behavioural Evolution*, 56: 293–99.

Horrobin, D.F. (1998) 'Schizophrenia: the illness that made us human', *Medical Hypotheses*, 50: 269–88.

Horrobin, D. (2001) *The Madness of Adam and Eve: how schizophrenia shaped humanity*, London: Bantam Press.

Houle, D., Morikawa, B. and Lynch, M. (1996) 'Comparing mutational variabilities', *Genetics*, 143: 1467–83.

Hrdy, S.B. (1999) *Mother Nature: a history of mothers, infants, and natural selection*, New York: Pantheon Books.

Hubl, D., Koenig, T., Strik, W., Federspiel, A., Kreis, R., Boesch, C., Maier, S.E., Schroth, G., Lovblad, K. and Dierks, T. (2004) 'Pathways that make voices: white matter changes in auditory hallucinations', *Archives of General Psychiatry*, 61 (7): 658–68.

Humphrey, N.K. (1976) 'The social function of intellect', in P.P.G. Bateson and R.A. Hinde (eds) *Growing Points in Ethology*, Cambridge: Cambridge University Press, pp. 303–17.

Husserl, E. (1989) *Ideas Pertaining to a Pure Phenomenology and to a Phenomenological Philosophy: second book*, translated by R. Rojcewicz and A. Schuwer, Dordrecht, Holland: Kluwer.

Huxley, J. (1916) 'Bird-watching and biological science', *Auk*, 33: 142–61.

Huxley, J. and Kettlewell, H.B.D. (1965) *Charles Darwin and His World*, London: Thames and Hudson Ltd.

Huxley, J., Mayr, E., Osmond, H. and Hoffer, A. (1964) 'Schizophrenia as a genetic morphism', *Nature*, 204: 220–21.

Ilia, M., Beasley, C., Meijer, D., Kerwin, R., Cotter, D., Everall, I. and Price, J. (2002) 'Expression of Oct-6, a POU III domain transcription factor, in schizophrenia', *American Journal of Psychiatry*, 159: 1174–82.

Impagnatiello, F., Guidotti, A.R., Pesold, C., Dwivedi, Y., Caruncho, H., Pisu, M.G., Uzunov, D.P., Smalheiser, N.R., Davis, J.M., Pandey, G.N., Pappas, G.D., Tueting, P., Sharma, R.P. and Costa, E. (1998) 'A decrease of reelin expression as a putative vulnerability factor in schizophrenia', *Proceedings of the National Academy of Sciences of the U.S.A.*, 95: 15718–23.

Ingleby, D. (1983) 'Mental health and social order', in S. Cohen and A. Scull (eds) *Social Control and the State*, Oxford: Blackwell, pp. 141–88.

Ingvar, D.H. and Franzen, G. (1974) 'Abnormalities of cerebral blood flow distribution in patients with chronic schizophrenia', *Acta Psychiatrica Scandinavica*, 50: 425–62.

Inoue, Y., Tonooka, Y., Yamada, K. and Kanba, S. (2004) 'Deficiency of theory of mind in patients with remitted mood disorder', *Journal of Affective Disorders*, 82 (3): 403–9.

Isen, A.M. and Hastorf, A.H. (1982) 'Some perspectives on cognitive social psychology', in A. Hastorf and A. Isen (eds) *Cognitive Social Psychology*, New York: Elsevier/North Holland, pp. 1–33.

Isohanni, M., Jones, P.B., Moilanen, K., Rantakallio, P., Veijola, J., Oja, H., Koiranen, M., Jokelainen, J., Croudace, T. and Jarvelin, M. (2001) 'Early developmental milestones in adult schizophrenia and other psychoses: a 31-year follow-up of the Northern Finland 1966 Birth Cohort', *Schizophrenia Research*, 52: 1–19.

Jablensky, A. (1988) 'Epidemiology of schizophrenia', in P. Bebbington and P. McGuffin (eds) *Schizophrenia: the major issues*, London: Heinemann Professional Publishing, pp. 19–34.

Jacobson, R. (1986) 'Disorders of facial recognition, social behaviour and affect after combined bilateral amygdalotomy and subcaudate tractotomy: a clinical and experimental study', *Psychological Medicine*, 16: 439–50.

James, A.C., Crow, T.J., Renowden, S., Wardell, A.M., Smith, D.M. and Anslow, P. (1999) 'Is the course of brain development in schizophrenia delayed? Evidence from onsets in adolescence', *Schizophrenia Research*, 40: 1–10.

James, W. (1890) *Principles of Psychology*, New York: Holt.

Jamison, K.R. (1993) *Touched with Fire: manic-depressive illness and the artistic temperament*, New York: Free Press.

Jamison, K.R. (1995a) *An Unquiet Mind: a memoir of moods and madness*, London: Picador.

Jamison, K.R. (1995b) 'Manic-depressive illness and creativity', *Scientific American*, 272: 62–7.

Janet, P. (1889) *L'Automatisme Psychologique*, Paris: Alcan.

Jaspers, K. (1963) *General Psychopathology*, translated by J. Hoenig and M.W. Hamilton, Chicago: University of Chicago Press.

Jaynes, J. (1976) *The Origin of Consciousness in the Breakdown of the Bicameral Mind*, Boston: Houghton Mifflin Company.

Jeannerod, M. (1994) 'The representing brain: neural correlates of motor intention and imagery', *Behavioral and Brain Sciences*, 17: 187–245.

Jelik, W. (1982) 'Altered states of consciousness in North American Indian ceremonials', *Ethos*, 10 (4): 326–43.

Jensen, P.S., Mrazek, D., Knapp, P.K., Steinberg, L., Pfeffer, C., Schwalter, J. and Shapiro, T. (1997) 'Evolution and revolution in child psychiatry: ADHD as a disorder of adaptation', *Journal of the American Academy of Child and Adolescent Psychiatry*, 36: 1672–81.

Jerison, H.J. (1973) *Evolution of the Brain and Intelligence*, New York: Academic Press.

Jevning, R., Wallace, R.K. and Beidebach, M. (1982) 'The physiology of meditation:

a review. A wakeful hypometabolic integrated response', *Neuroscience and Biobehavioral Reviews*, 16: 415–24.

Johnstone, E.C., Crow, T.J., Frith, C.D., Husband, J. and Kreel, L. (1976) 'Cerebral ventricular size and cognitive impairment in chronic schizophrenia', *Lancet*, 2: 924–26.

Johnstone, E.C., Lawrie, S.M. and Cosway, R. (2002) 'What does the Edinburgh high-risk study tell us about schizophrenia?' *American Journal of Medical Genetics*, 114: 906–12.

Johnstone, E.C., Ebmeier, K.P., Miller, P., Owens, D.G. and Lawrie, S.M. (2005) 'Predicting schizophrenia: findings from the Edinburgh High-Risk Study', *British Journal of Psychiatry*, 186: 18–25.

Jolly, A. (1966) 'Lemur social behaviour and primate intelligence', *Science*, 153: 501–6.

Jones, D.K., Simmons, A., Williams, S.C. and Horsfield, M.A. (1999) 'Non-invasive assessment of axonal fiber connectivity in the human brain via diffusion tensor MRI', *Magnetic Resonance in Medicine*, 42: 37–41.

Kalus, P., Buri, C., Slotboom, J., Gralla, J., Remonda, L., Dierks, T., Strik, W.K., Schroth, G. and Kiefer, C. (2004) 'Volumetry and diffusion tensor imaging of hippocampal subregions in schizophrenia', *Neuroreport*, 15 (5): 867–71.

Kanwisher, N., McDermott, J. and Chun, M.M. (1997) 'The fusiform face area: a module in human extrastriate cortex specialized for face perception', *Journal of Neurosciences*, 17: 4302–11.

Kaplan, H.I. and Sadock, B.J. (1998) *Synopsis of Psychiatry, 8th ed.*, Baltimore, MD: Lippincott Williams and Wilkins.

Kaplan, H., Hill, K., Lancaster, J. and Hurtado, A.M. (2000) 'A theory of human life history evolution: diet, intelligence, and longevity', *Evolutionary Anthropology*, 9: 156–85.

Karlsson, J.L. (1970) 'Genetic association of giftedness and creativity with schizophrenia', *Hereditas*, 66: 177–81.

Karlsson, J.L. (1984) 'Creative intelligence in relatives of mental patients', *Hereditas*, 100: 83–86.

Karlsson, J.L. (2001) 'Mental abilities of male relatives of psychotic patients', *Acta Psychiatrica Scandinavica*, 104: 466–68.

Kasanin, J. (1933) 'The acute schizoaffective psychoses', *American Journal of Psychiatry*, 151: 144–54.

Kastner, S. and Ungerleider, L.G. (2000) 'Mechanisms of visual attention in the human cortex', *Annual Review of Neurosciences*, 23: 315–41.

Kato, C., Petronis, A., Okazaki, Y., Tochigi, M., Umekage, T. and Sasaki, T. (2002) 'Molecular genetic studies of schizophrenia: challenges and insights', *Neuroscience Research*, 43: 295–304.

Kawasaki, H., Kaufman, O., Damasio, H., Damasio, A.R., Granner, M., Bakken, H., Hori, T., Howard, M.A. III and Adolphs, R. (2001) 'Single-neuron responses to emotional visual stimuli recorded in human ventral prefrontal cortex', *Nature Neuroscience*, 4: 15–16.

Kawasaki, Y., Maeda, Y., Sakai, N., Higashima, M., Yamaguchi, N., Koshino, Y., Hisada, K., Suzuki, M. and Matsuda, H. (1996) 'Regional cerebral blood flow in patients with schizophrenia: relevance to symptom structures', *Psychiatry Research*, 67: 49–58.

Keller, M.C. (2004) 'Evolutionary theories of schizophrenia must ultimately explain the genes that predispose to it', *Behavioral and Brain Sciences*, 27: 861–62.

Kellett, J.M. (1973) 'Evolutionary theory for the dichotomy of the functional psychoses', *Lancet*, 21 April, 1973.

Kelly, B.D. (2005) 'Structural violence and schizophrenia', *Social Sciences and Medicine*, 61: 721–30.

Kendell, R.E. and Brockington, I.F (1980) 'The identification of disease entities and the relationship between schizophrenic and affective psychoses', *British Journal of Psychiatry*, 137: 324–31.

Kendell, R.E. and Gourlay, J. (1970) 'The clinical distinction between the affective psychoses and schizophrenia', *British Journal of Psychiatry*, 117: 261–66.

Kendler, K., Karkowski, L. and Walsh, D. (1998) 'The structure of psychosis: latent class analysis of probands from the Roscommon family study', *Archives of General Psychiatry*, 55: 492–99.

Kendler, K.S., Myers, J.M., O'Neill, F.A., Martin, R., Murphy, B., MacLean, C.J., Walsh, D. and Straub, R.E. (2000) 'Clinical features of schizophrenia and linkage to chromosomes 5q, 6p, 8p, and 10p in the Irish Study of High-Density Schizophrenia Families', *American Journal of Psychiatry*, 157: 402–8.

Kerr, N., Dunbar, R.I. and Bentall, R.P. (2003) 'Theory of mind deficits in bipolar affective disorder', *Journal of Affective Disorders*, 73 (3): 253–59.

Kety, S., Rosenthal, D., Wender, P.H., Schulsinger, F. and Jacobsen, B. (1975) 'Mental illness in the biological and adoptive families of adopted individuals who have become schizophrenic: a preliminary report based on psychiatric interviews', in R. Fieve, D. Rosenthal and H. Brill (eds) *Genetic Research in Psychiatry*, Baltimore, MD: The Johns Hopkins University Press, pp. 147–65.

Kimura, M. (1968) 'Evolutionary rate at the molecular level', *Nature*, 217: 624–26.

Kinderman, P. (2003) 'Social cognition in paranoia and bipolar affective disorder', in M. Brüne, H. Ribbert and W. Schiefenhövel (eds) *The Social Brain: evolution and pathology*, Chichester: Wiley, pp. 339–54.

King James Holy Bible Version (1997) 'Deuteronomy 28', Gary, SD: King James.

Kirkpatrick, B. (1997) 'Affiliation and neuropsychiatric disorders: the deficit syndrome of schizophrenia', *Annals of the New York Academy of Sciences*, 807: 455–68.

Kirkpatrick, B., Conley, R.C., Kakoyannis, A., Reep, R.L. and Roberts, R.C. (1999) 'Interstitial cells of the white matter in the inferior parietal cortex in schizophrenia: an unbiased cell-counting study', *Synapse*, 34: 95–102.

Kling, A. and Steklis, H.D. (1976) 'A neural substrate for affiliative behaviour in nonhuman primates', *Brain and Behavioural Evolution*, 13: 216–38.

Klosterkötter, J., Schultze-Lutter, F., Gross, G., Huber, G. and Steinmeyer, E.M. (1997) 'Early self-experienced neuropsychological deficits and subsequent schizophrenic diseases: an 8-year average follow-up prospective study', *Acta Psychiatrica Scandinavica*, 95: 396–404.

Klüwer, H. (1966) *Mescal and Mechanisms of Hallucination*, Chicago: University of Chicago Press.

Kodman, F. (1983) 'The acute schizophrenic break: a phenomenological description', *Psychological Reports*, 53 (3 Pt 1): 960–62.

237

Kohler, C.G., Bilker, W., Hagendoorn, M., Gur, R.E. and Gur, R.C. (2000) 'Emotion recognition deficit in schizophrenia: association with symptomatology and cognition', *Biological Psychiatry*, 48: 127–36.

Kohler, E., Keysers, C., Umiltà, M.A., Fogassi, L., Gallese, V. and Rizzolatti, G. (2002) 'Hearing sounds, understanding actions: action representation in mirror neurons', *Science*, 297: 846–48.

Kohn, M.L. (1973) 'Social class and schizophrenia: a critical review and a reformulation', *Schizophrenia Bulletin*, 7: 60–79.

Kraepelin, E. (1896) *Psychiatrie. Ein Lehrbuch für Studirende und Aerzte*, 5th edn, Leipzig: Johann Ambrosius Barth.

Kraepelin, E. (1913) *Psychiatrie. Ein Lehrbuch für Studirende und Aerzte*, 8th edn, Leipzig: Johann Ambrosius Barth.

Krause, R., Steimer, E., Sänger-Alt, C. and Wagner, G. (1989) 'Facial expression of schizophrenic patients and their interaction partners', *Psychiatry*, 52: 1–12.

Krippner, S. and Winkler, M. (1995) 'Studying consciousness in the postmodern age', in W.T. Anderson (ed.) *The Truth About the Truth*, New York: G.P. Putnam's Sons, pp. 161–69.

Kuan, C.Y., Roth, K.A., Flavell, R.A. and Rakic, P. (2000) 'Mechanisms of programmed cell death in the developing brain', *Trends in Neuroscience*, 23: 291–97.

Kubicki, M., Westin, C.F., Maier, S.E., Frumin, M., Nestor, P.G., Salisbury, D.F., Kikinis, R., Jolesz, F.A., McCarley, R.W. and Shenton, M.E. (2002) 'Uncinate fasciculus findings in schizophrenia: a magnetic resonance diffusion tensor imaging study', *American Journal of Psychiatry*, 159: 813–20.

Kubicki, M., Westin, C.F., Nestor, P.G., Wible, C.G., Frumin, M., Maier, S.E., Kikinis, R., Jolesz, F.A., McCarley, R.W. and Shenton, M.E. (2003) 'Cingulate fasciculus integrity disruption in schizophrenia: a magnetic resonance diffusion tensor imaging study', *Biological Psychiatry*, 54 (11): 1171–80.

Kudo, H. and Dunbar, R.I.M. (2001) 'Neocortex size and social network size in primates', *Animal Behaviour*, 62: 711–22.

Kuida, K., Haydar, T.F., Kuan, C.Y., Gu, Y., Taya, C., Karasuyama, H., Su, M.S., Rakic, P. and Flavell, R.A. (1998) 'Reduced apoptosis and cytochrome c-mediated caspase activation in mice lacking caspase 9', *Cell*, 94: 325–37.

Kummer, H. (1967) 'Tripartite relations in hamadryas baboons', in S.A. Altmann (ed.) *Social Communication Among Primates*, Chicago: University of Chicago Press, pp. 63–71.

Kunugi, H., Takei, N., Murray, R.M., Saito, K. and Nanko, S. (1996) 'Small head circumference at birth in schizophrenia', *Schizophrenia Research*, 20: 165–70.

Kuttner, R.E., Lorincz, A.B. and Swan, D.A. (1967) 'The schizophrenia gene and social evolution', *Psychological Reports*, 20: 407–12.

La Barre, W. (1970) *The Ghost Dance: origins of religion*, London: George Allen and Unwin.

Lack, D. (1954) *The Natural Regulation of Animal Numbers*, Oxford: Oxford University Press.

Langdon, R., Coltheart, M, Ward, P.B. and Catts, S.V. (2001) 'Mentalising, executive planning and disengagement in schizophrenia', *Cognitive Neuropsychiatry*, 6: 81–108.

Langer, J. (1998) 'Phylogenetic and ontogenetic origins of cognition: classification', in J. Langer and M. Killen (eds) *Piaget, Evolution, and Development*, Mahwah, NJ: Lawrence Erlbaum Associates, Inc., pp. 257–77.

Langer, J. (2000) 'The heterochronic evolution of primate cognitive development', in S. Taylor Parker, J. Langer and M.L. McKinney (eds) *Biology, Brains and Behaviour*, Sante Fe: School of American Research Press/Oxford: James Curry Ltd, pp. 215–36.

Langfeldt, T.G. (1939) *The Schizophreniform States*, Copenhagen: Munksgaard.

Larson, C.A. and Nyman, G.E. (1973) 'Differential fertility in schizophrenia', *Acta Psychiatrica Scandinavica*, 49: 272–80.

Lauren, P.G. (1998) *The Evolution of International Human Rights: visions seen*, Philadelphia: University of Pennsylvania Press.

Lawrie, S.M. and Abukmeil, S.S. (1998) 'Brain abnormality in schizophrenia: a systematic and quantitative review of volumetric magnetic resonance imaging studies', *British Journal of Psychiatry*, 172: 110–20.

Lawrie, S.M., Whalley, H.C., Abukmeil, S.S., Kestelman, J.N., Donnelly, L., Miller, P., Best, J.J., Owens, D.C. and Johnstone, E.C. (2001) 'Brain structure, genetic liability, and psychotic symptoms in subjects at high risk of developing schizophrenia', *Biological Psychiatry*, 49: 811–23.

Lawrie, S.M., Buechel, C., Whalley, H.C., Frith, C., Friston, K. and Johnstone, E.C. (2002) 'Reduced fronto-temporal functional connectivity in schizophrenia associated with auditory hallucinations', *Biological Psychiatry*, 51: 1008–11.

Leckman, J.F. and Herman, A.E. (2002) 'Maternal behaviour and developmental psychopathology', *Biological Psychiatry*, 51: 27–43.

Le Doux, J.E. (1994) 'Emotion, memory and the brain', *Scientific American*, 270: 50–57.

Lee, K.H., Williams, L.M., Breakspear, M. and Gordon, E. (2003) 'Synchronous gamma activity: a review and contribution to an integrative neuroscience model of schizophrenia', *Brain Research and Brain Research Reviews*, 41: 57–78.

Leekam, S.R. and Perner, J. (1991) 'Does the autistic child have a metarepresentational deficit?' *Cognition*, 40: 203–18.

Leighton, D.C., Harding, J.S., Macklin, D.B., Macmillan, A.M. and Leighton, A.H. (1963) *The Character of Danger: psychiatric symptoms in selected communities*, New York: Basic Books.

Le May, M. (1976) 'Morphological cerebral asymmetries of modern man, fossil man, and nonhuman primate', *Annals of the New York Academy of Sciences*, 280: 349–66.

Le May, M., Billig, M.S. and Geschwind, N. (1982) 'Asymmetries of the brains and skulls of nonhuman primates', in E. Armstrong and D. Falk (eds) *Primate Brain Evolution*, New York: Plenum Press, pp. 263–77.

Lemire, R.J., Loeser, J.D., Leech, R.W. and Alvord, E.C. (1975) *Normal and Abnormal Development of the Human Nervous System*, London: Harper and Row.

Leonard, C.M., Rolls, E.T., Wilson, F.A. and Baylis, G.C. (1985) 'Neurons in the amygdala of the monkey with responses selective for faces', *Behavioral and Brain Research*, 15: 159–76.

Leonhard, C. and Corrigan, P.W. (2001) 'Social perception in schizophrenia', in P.W. Corrigan and D.L. Penn (eds) *Social Cognition and Schizophrenia*, Washington, DC: American Psychological Association, pp. 73–96.

Leroi-Gourhan, A. (1975) 'The flowers found with Shanidar IV, a Neanderthal burial in Iraq', *Science*, 190: 562–64.

Leslie, A.M. and Thaiss, L. (1992) 'Domain specificity in conceptual development: neuropsychological evidence from autism', *Cognition*, 43: 225–51.

Levine, B., Freedman, M., Dawson, D., Black, S. and Stuss, D.T. (1999) 'Ventral frontal contribution to self-regulation: convergence of episodic memory and inhibition', *Neurocase*, 5: 263–75.

Lewis-Williams, J.D. (1981) *Believing and Seeing: symbolic meanings in southern San rock paintings*, London: Academic Press.

Lewis-Williams, J.D. (1997) 'Agency, art and altered consciousness: a motif in French (Quercy) Upper Palaeolithic parietal art', *Antiquity*, 71: 810–30.

Lewis-Williams, J.D. (2002) *The Mind in the Cave: consciousness and the origins of art*, London: Thames and Hudson Ltd.

Lewis-Williams, J.D. and Dowson, T.A. (1988) 'The signs of all times: entoptic phenomena in Upper Palaeolithic art', *Current Anthropology*, 29: 201–45.

Lewis-Williams, J.D. and Dowson, T.A. (1999) *Images of Power: understanding Southern African rock art*, 2nd edn, Cape Town: Struik.

Lewontin, R.C. (1998) 'The evolution of cognition: questions we will never answer', in D. Scarborough and S. Sternberg (eds) *An Invitation to Cognitive Science: methods, models and conceptual issues*, Cambridge, MA: The MIT Press, pp. 107–32.

Liddle, P.F., Friston, K.J., Frith, C.D. and Frackowiak, R.S. (1992) 'Cerebral blood flow and mental processes in schizophrenia', *Journal of the Royal Society of Medicine*, 85: 224–27.

Lillard, A. (1998) 'Ethnopsychologies: cultural variations in theories of mind', *Psychological Bulletin*, 123: 3–32.

Lim, K.O., Hedehus, M., Moseley, M., de Crespigny, A., Sullivan, E.V. and Pfefferbaum, A. (1999) 'Compromised white matter tract integrity in schizophrenia inferred from diffusion tensor imaging', *Archives of General Psychiatry*, 56 (4): 367–74.

Limongelli, L., Boysen, S.T. and Visalberghi, E. (1995) 'Comprehension of cause-effect relations in a tool-using task by chimpanzees (Pan troglodytes)', *Journal of Computational Psychology*, 109: 18–26.

Lock, A. and Peters, C.R. (1999) *Handbook of Human Symbolic Evolution*, Oxford: Blackwell Publishers Ltd.

Lorberbaum, J.P., Newman, J.D., Dubno, J.R., Horwitz, A.R., Nahas, Z., Teneback, C.C., Bloomer, C.W., Bohning, D.E., Vincent, D., Johnson, M.R., Emmanuel, N., Brawman-Mintzer, O., Book, S.W., Lydiard, R.B., Ballenger, J.C. and George, M.S. (1999) 'Feasibility of using fMRI to study mothers responding to infant cries', *Depression and Anxiety*, 10: 99–104.

Lorenz, K. (1973) *Die Rückseite des Spiegels*, München: Piper.

Luchins, D.J., Weinberger, D.R. and Wyatt, R.J. (1979) 'Schizophrenia: evidence of a subgroup with reversed cerebral asymmetry', *Archives of General Psychiatry*, 36: 1309–11.

Ludwig, A. (1995) *The Price of Greatness: resolving the creativity and madness controversy*, New York: Guilford Press.

Lutz, C., Well, A. and Novak, M. (2003) 'Stereotypic and self-injurious behaviour in rhesus macaques: a survey and retrospective analysis of environment and early experience', *American Journal of Primatology*, 60 (1): 1–15.

McCabe, K., Houser, D., Ryan, L., Smith, V. and Trouard, T. (2001) 'A functional imaging study of cooperation in two-person reciprocal exchange', *Proceedings of the National Academy of Sciences of the U.S.A.*, 98: 11832–35.

McCarthy, G., Puce, A., Gore, J. and Allison, T. (1997a) 'Face-specific processing in the human fusiform gyrus', *Journal of Cognitive Neuroscience*, 9: 605–10.

McCarthy, G., Luby, M., Gore, J. and Goldman-Rakic, P. (1997b) 'Infrequent events transiently activate human prefrontal and parietal cortex as measured by functional MRI', *Journal of Neurophysiology*, 77: 1630–34.

MacDonald III, A.W., Cohen, J.D., Stenger, V.A. and Carter, C.S. (2000) 'Dissociating the role of the dorsolateral prefrontal and anterior cingulate cortex in cognitive control', *Science*, 288: 1835–38.

McGlashan, T.H. and Hoffman, R.E. (2000) 'Schizophrenia as a disorder of developmentally reduced synaptic connectivity', *Archives of General Psychiatry*, 57: 637–48.

McGrew, W.C. (1992) *Chimpanzee Material Culture: implications for human evolution*, Cambridge: Cambridge University Press.

McGrew, W.C., Marchant, L.F. and Nishida, T. (eds) (1996) *Great Ape Societies*, Cambridge: Cambridge University Press.

McGuire, M.T. and Fairbanks, L.A. (eds) (1977) *Ethological Psychiatry: psychopathology in the context of evolutionary biology*, New York: Grune and Stratton.

McGuire, M.T. and Troisi, A. (1998) *Darwinian Psychiatry*, New York: Oxford University Press.

McGuire, P.K. and Frith, C.D. (1996) 'Disordered functional connectivity in schizophrenia', *Psychological Medicine*, 26: 663–67.

McGuire, P.K., Silbersweig, D.A., Wright, I., Murray, R.M., David, A.S., Frackowiak, R.S. and Frith, C.D. (1995) 'Abnormal monitoring of inner speech: a physiological basis for auditory hallucinations', *Lancet*, 346 (8975): 596–600.

McIntosh, A.R. (1999) 'Mapping cognition to the brain through neural interactions', *Memory*, 7 (5–6): 523–48.

McKenna, T. (1992) *Food of the Gods*, New York: Bantam Books.

McKinney, M.L. (2000) 'Evolving behavioural complexity by extending development', in S. Taylor Parker, J. Langer and M.L. McKinney (eds) *Biology, Brains and Behaviour*, Sante Fe: School of American Research Press/Oxford: James Curry Ltd, pp. 25–40.

McKinney, M.L. and McNamara, K.J. (1991) *Heterochrony: the evolution of ontogeny*, New York: Plenum Press.

McKinney, W.T. Jnr. (1974) 'Primate social isolation: psychiatric implications', *Archives of General Psychiatry*, 31 (3): 422–26.

MacLean, P.D. (1973) *A Triune Concept of the Brain and Behavior*, Toronto: University of Toronto Press.

McNamara, K.J. (1997) *Shapes of Time: the evolution of growth and development*, Baltimo and London: Johns Hopkins University Press.

McNeil, T.F., Cantor-Graae, E., Nordstrom, L.G. and Rosenlund, T. (1993) 'Head circumference in "preschizophrenic" and control neonates', *British Journal of Psychiatry*, 162: 517–23.

Machiavelli, N. (1532/1979) *The Prince*, Harmondsworth, Middlesex: Penguin Books.

Maddock, R.J. (1999) 'The retrosplenial cortex and emotion: new insights from functional neuroimaging of the human brain', *Trends in Neurosciences*, 22: 310–16.

Maj, M. (1998) 'Critique of the DSM-IV operational diagnostic criteria for schizophrenia', *British Journal of Psychiatry*, 172: 458–60.

Makris, N., Meyer, J.W., Bates, J.F., Yeterian, E.H., Kennedy, D.N. and Caviness, V.S. (1999) 'MRI-based topographic parcellation of human cerebral white matter and nuclei II: rationale and applications with systematics of cerebral connectivity', *Neuroimage*, 9: 18–45.

Málková, L., Mishkin, M., Suomi, S.J. and Bachevalier, J. (1997) 'Socio-emotional behaviour in adult rhesus monkeys after early versus late lesions of the medial temporal lobe', in C.S. Carter, I.I. Lederhendler and B. Kirkpatrick (eds) *Annals of the New York Academy of Sciences, vol. 807: the integrative neurobiology of affiliation*, New York: New York Academy of Sciences, pp. 538–40.

Mallamaci, A., Muzio, L., Chan, C.H., Parnavelas, J. and Boncinelli, E. (2000) 'Area identity shifts in the early cerebral cortex of Emx2: mutant mice', *Nature Neuroscience*, 3: 679–86.

Malthus, T.R. (1798) *An Essay on the Principle of Population*, London: Everyman.

Mandell, A.J. (1980) 'Toward a psychobiology of transcendence: God in the brain', in J.M. Davidson and R.J. Davidson (eds) *The Psychobiology of Consciousness*, New York: Plenum, Press, pp. 379–464.

Mandell, A.J (1985) 'Interhemispheric fusion', *Journal of Psychoactive Drugs*, 17 (4): 257–66.

Marino, L. (2002) 'Convergence of complex cognitive abilities in cetaceans and primates', *Brain and Behavioural Evolution*, 59: 21–32.

Markow, T.A. and Gottesman, I.I. (1994) 'Behavioural phenodeviance: a Lernersque conjecture', in T.A. Markow (ed.) *Developmental Instability: its origins and evolutionary implications*, Dordrecht: Kluwer Academic Press, pp. 299–307.

Marks, I.M. (1969) *Fears and Phobias*, London: Heinemann.

Mathalon, D.H., Fedor, M., Faustman, W.O., Gray, M., Askari, N. and Ford, J.M. (2002) 'Response-monitoring dysfunction in schizophrenia: an event-related brain potential study', *Journal of Abnormal Psychology*, 111: 22–41.

Maudsley, H. (1908) *Heredity, Variation and Genius*, London: Bale and Daniellson.

Maxfield, M. (1994). 'The journey of the drum', *ReVision*, 16 (4): 157–63.

Mayr, E. (1961) 'Cause and effect in biology', *Science*, 134: 1501–06.

Mayr, E. (1983) 'How to carry out the adaptationist program?' *The American Naturalist*, 121: 324–33.

Mazza, M., De Risio, A., Surian, L., Roncone, R. and Casacchia, M. (2001) 'Selective impairments of theory of mind in people with schizophrenia', *Schizophrenia Research*, 47: 299–308.

Mead, G.H. (1913) 'The social self', *Journal of Philosophy, Psychology and Scientific Methods*, 10: 374–80.

Mealey, L. (1995) 'The socio-biology of sociopathy: an integrated evolutionary model', *Behavioral and Brain Sciences*, 18: 523–99.

Mealey, L. and Kinner, S. (2003) 'Psychopathy, Machiavellianism and theory of mind', in M. Brüne, H. Ribbert and W. Schiefenhövel (eds) *The Social Brain: evolution and pathology*, Chichester: Wiley, pp. 355–72.

Meehl, P. (1962) 'Schizotaxia, schizotypia, schizophrenia', *American Psychologist*, 17: 827–38.

Mellor, C.S. (1992) 'Dermatoglyphic evidence of fluctuating asymmetry in schizophrenia', *British Journal of Psychiatry*, 160: 467–72.

Menninger, K., Ellenberger, H., Pruyser, P. and Mayman, M. (1958) 'The unitary concept of mental illness', *Bulletin of the Menninger Clinic*, 22: 4–12.

Merleau-Ponty, M. (2002) *Phenomenology of Perception*, London: Routledge.

Mesulam, M. (2000) 'Brain, mind, and the evolution of connectivity', *Brain and Cognition*, 42: 4–6.

Mesulam, M.M. and Geschwind, N. (1978) 'On the possible role of neocortex and its limbic connections in the process of attention and schizophrenia: clinical cases of inattention in man and experimental anatomy in monkey', *Journal of Psychiatric Research*, 14: 249–59.

Metzner, R. (1998) 'Hallucinogenic drugs and plants in psychotherapy and shamanism', *Journal of Psychoactive Drugs*, 30: 333–41.

Meyer-Lindenberg, A., Poline, J.B., Kohn, P.D., Holt, J.L., Egan, M.F., Weinberger, D.R. and Berman, K.F. (2001) 'Evidence for abnormal cortical functional connectivity during working memory in schizophrenia', *American Journal of Psychiatry*, 158: 1809–17.

Milton, K. (1981) 'Distribution patterns of tropical plant foods as a stimulus to primate mental development', *American Anthropologist*, 83: 534–48.

Milton, K. (1988) 'Foraging behaviour and the evolution of primate intelligence', in R.W. Byrne and A. Whiten (eds) *Machiavellian Intelligence: social expertise and the evolution of intellect in monkeys, apes, and humans*, Oxford: Clarendon Press, pp. 285–306.

Minkowski, E. (1926) *La notion de perte de contact vital avec la réalite et ses applications en psychopathologie*, Paris: Jouve et Cie.

Minkowski, E. (1927) *La Schizophrenie: psychopathologie des schizoides et des schizophrènes*, Paris: Payot.

Minkowski, E. (1999) *Traité de Psychopathologie*, Paris: Institut Sythelabo.

Mirnics, K., Middleton, F.A., Lewis, D.A. and Levitt, P. (2001) 'Analysis of complex brain disorders with gene expression microarrays: schizophrenia as a disease of the synapse', *Trends in Neurosciences*, 24: 479–86.

Mithen, S. (1996) *The Prehistory of the Mind*, London: Thames and Hudson Ltd.

Mlakar, J., Jensterle, J. and Frith, C.D. (1994) 'Central monitoring deficiency and schizophrenic symptoms', *Psychological Medicine*, 24: 557–64.

Montagu, M.F.A. (ed.) (1962) 'Time, morphology, and neoteny in the evolution of man', in A. Montagu and A. Montagu (eds) *Culture and the Evolution of Man*, New York: Oxford University Press, pp. 324–42.

Montagu, M.F.A. (1989) *Growing Young*, 2nd edn, New York: Bergin and Garvey.

Morecraft, R.J., Geula, C. and Mesulam, M.M. (1993) 'Architecture of connectivity within a cingulo-fronto-parietal neurocognitive network for directed attention', *Archives of Neurology*, 50: 279–84.

Morris, J.S., Frith, C.D., Perrett, D.I., Rowland, D., Young, A.W., Calder, A.J. and Dolan, R.J. (1996) 'A differential neural response in the human amygdala to fearful and happy facial expressions', *Nature*, 383: 812–15.

Mojtabai, R. and Reider, R.O. (1998) 'Limitations of the system-oriented approach to psychiatric research', *British Journal of Psychiatry*, 173: 198–202.

243

Morris, R., Pandya, D.N. and Petrides, M. (1999) 'Fiber system linking the mid-dorsolateral frontal cortex with the retrosplenial/presubicular region in the rhesus monkey', *Journal of Computational Neurology*, 407: 183–92.

Morrison, A.P. and Haddock, G. (1997) 'Cognitive factors in source monitoring and auditory hallucinations', *Psychological Medicine*, 27: 669–79.

Morton, A. (1980) *Frames of Mind: constraints on the common-sense conception of the mental*, Oxford: Clarendon Press.

Mountford, D.D. (1968) 'The significance of litter size', *Journal of Animal Ecology*, 37: 363–67.

Muir Gray, J.A. (1999) 'Postmodern medicine', *Lancet*, 354: 1550–53.

Murray, R.M. and Lewis, S.W. (1987) 'Is schizophrenia a neurodevelopmental disorder?' *British Medical Journal (Clinical Research Edition)*, 295: 681–82.

Nakamura, K., Mikami, A. and Kubota, K. (1992) 'Activity of single neurons in the monkey amygdala during performance of a visual discrimination task', *Journal of Neurophysiology*, 67: 1447–63.

Nakamura, K., Kawashima, R., Sato, N., Nakamura, A., Sugiura, M., Kato, T., Hatano, K., Ito, K., Fukuda, H., Schormann, T. and Zilles, K. (2000) 'Functional delineation of the human occipito-temporal areas related to face and scene processing: a PET study', *Brain*, 123: 1903–12.

Nakamura, M., McCarley, R.W., Kubicki, M., Dickey, C.C., Niznikiewicz, M.A., Voglmaier, M.M., Seidman, L.J., Maier, S.E., Westin, C.F., Kikinis, R. and Shenton, M.E. (2005) 'Fronto-temporal disconnectivity in schizotypal personality disorder: a diffusion tensor imaging study', *Biological Psychiatry*, 58 (6): 468–78.

Nash, L.T., Fritz, J., Alford, P.A. and Brent, L. (1999) 'Variables influencing the origins of diverse abnormal behaviours in a large sample of captive chimpanzees (Pan troglodytes)', *American Journal of Primatology*, 48 (1): 15–29.

Navarro, V. (1978) *Class Struggle, the State and Medicine*, London: Martin Robertson.

Nesse, R.M. (1999) 'Proximate and evolutionary studies of anxiety, stress and depression: synergy at the interface', *Neuroscience and Biobehavioral Reviews*, 23: 895–903.

Nesse, R.M. (2004) 'Cliff-edged fitness functions and the persistence of schizophrenia', *Behavioral and Brain Sciences*, 27: 862–63.

Nesse, R.M. and Williams, G.C. (1995) *Evolution and Healing: the new science of Darwinian medicine*, New York: Vintage.

Nestor, P.G., Kubicki, M., Gurrera, R.J., Niznikiewicz, M., Frumin, M., McCarley, R.W. and Shenton, M.E. (2004) 'Neuropsychological correlates of diffusion tensor imaging in schizophrenia', *Neuropsychology*, 18 (4): 629–37.

Nettle, D. (2001) *Strong Imagination: madness, creativity and human nature*, Oxford: Oxford University Press.

Neville, H.J., Bavelier, D., Corina, D., Rauschecker, J., Karni, A., Lalwani, A., Braun, A., Clark, V., Jezzard, P. and Turner, R. (1998) 'Cerebral organization for language in deaf and hearing subjects: biological constraints and effects of experience', *Proceedings of the National Academy of Sciences of the U.S.A*, 95: 922–29.

Newman, L.S. (2001) 'What is "social cognition"? Four basic approaches and their implications for schizophrenia research', in P.W. Corrigan and D.L. Penn (eds) *Social Cognition and Schizophrenia*, Washington, DC: American Psychological Association, pp. 41–72.

Nichols, C.D., Garcia, E.E. and Sanders-Bush, E. (2003) 'Dynamic changes in prefrontal cortex gene expression following lysergic acid diethylamide administration', *Molecular Brain Research*, 3 (1–2): 182–88.

Nichols, D.E. (2004) 'Hallucinogens', *Pharmacology and Therapeutics*, 101: 131–81.

Nielsen, E.B., Lyon, M. and Ellison, G. (1983) 'Apparent hallucinations in monkeys during around-the-clock amphetamine for seven to fourteen days: possible relevance to amphetamine psychosis', *Journal of Nervous and Mental Diseases*, 171 (4): 222–33.

Nimchinsky, E.A., Gilissen, E., Allman, J.M., Perl, D.P., Erwin, J.M. and Hof, P.R. (1999) 'A neuronal morphologic type unique to humans and great apes', *Proceedings of the National Academy of Sciences of the U.S.A*, 96: 5268–73.

Noll, R. (1983) 'Shamanism and schizophrenia: a state-specific approach to the "schizophrenia metaphor" of shamanic states', *American Ethnologist*, 10: 443–59.

Nordahl, T.E., Carter, C.S., Salo, R.E., Kraft, L., Baldo, J., Salamat, S., Robertson, L. and Kusubov, N. (2001) 'Anterior cingulate metabolism correlates with stroop errors in paranoid schizophrenia patients', *Neuropsychopharmacology*, 25: 139–48.

O'Connor, T.G., Rutter, M., Beckett, C., Keaveney, L., Kreppner, J.M. and the English and Romanian Adoptees Study Team (2000) 'The effects of global severe privation on cognitive competence: extension and logitudinal followup', *Child Development*, 71: 376–90.

Ödegard, Ö. (1956) 'The incidence of psychosis in various occupations', *International Journal of Social Psychiatry*, 2: 85–104.

O'Reilly, T., Dunbar, R.I.M. and Bentall, R. (2001) 'Schizotypy and creativity an evolutionary connection?' *Personality and Individual Differences*, 31: 1067–78.

O'Sullivan, M., Jones, D.K., Summers, P.E., Morris, R.G., Williams, S.C. and Markus, H.S. (2001) 'Evidence for cortical "disconnection" as a mechanism of age-related cognitive decline', *Neurology*, 57: 632–38.

Owens, D.G., Miller, P., Lawrie, S.M. and Johnstone, E.C. (2005) 'Pathogenesis of schizophrenia: a psychopathological perspective', *British Journal of Psychiatry*, 186: 386–93.

Palha, A.P. and Esteves, M.F. (1997) 'The origin of dementia praecox', *Schizophrenia Research*, 28: 99–103.

Pandya, D.N., Van Hoesen, G.W. and Mesulam, M.M. (1981) 'Efferent connections of the cingulate gyrus in the rhesus monkey', *Experimental Brain Research*, 42: 319–30.

Pandya, D.N. and Yeterian, E.H. (1996) 'Comparison of prefrontal architecture and connections', *Philosophical Transactions of the Royal Society of London Behavioural and Biological Sciences*, 351: 1423–32.

Panksepp, J. (1998) *Affective Neuroscience*, Oxford: Oxford University Press.

Panksepp, J. and Moskal, J. (2004) 'Schizophrenia: the elusive disease', *Behavioral and Brain Sciences*, 27: 863–64.

Parker, S.T. (1994) 'Using cladistic analysis of comparative data to reconstruct the evolution of cognitive development in hominids', paper presented at the *Animal Behavior Society Meeting's Symposium on Phylogenetic Comparative Methods*, Seattle, Washington, July.

Parker, S.T. (1996) 'Apprenticeship in tool-mediated extractive foraging: the origins of imitation, teaching and self-awareness in great apes', in A.E. Russon, K. Bard and S.T. Parker (eds) *Reaching Into Thought*, Cambridge: Cambridge University Press, pp. 348–70.

Parker, S.T. and Gibson, K.R. (1977) 'Object manipulation, tool use, and sensori-motor intelligence as feeding adaptations in early hominids', *Journal of Human Evolution*, 6: 623–41.

Parker, S.T. and Gibson, K.R. (1979) 'A developmental model for the evolution of language and intelligence in early hominids', *Behavioral and Brain Science*, 2: 367–408.

Parker, S.T. and McKinney, M.L. (1999) *Origins of Intelligence: the evolution of cognitive development in monkeys, apes, and humans*, Baltimore: Johns Hopkins University Press.

Parnas, J. and Handest, P. (2003) 'Phenomenology of anomalous self-experience in early schizophrenia', *Comprehensive Psychiatry*, 44 (2): 121–34.

Pattison, S. (1997) *Pastoral Care and Liberation Theology*, London: SPCK.

Paulus, M.P., Hozack, N.E., Zauscher, B.E., Frank, L., Brown, G.G., McDowell, J. and Braff, D.L. (2002) 'Parietal dysfunction is associated with increased outcome-related decision-making in schizophrenia patients', *Biological Psychiatry*, 51: 995–1004.

Pearson, J.L. (2002) *Shamanism and the Ancient Mind: a cognitive approach to archaeology*, Walnut Creek, CA: AltaMira Press.

Peffer-Smith, P.G., Smith, E.O. and Byrd, L.D. (1983) 'Effects of d-amphetamine on self-aggression and posturing in stumptail macaques', *Journal of Experimental and Analytical Behaviour*, 40 (3): 313–20.

Peled, A., Geva, A.B., Kremen, W.S., Blankfeld, H.M., Esfandiarfard, R. and Nordahl, T.E. (2001) 'Functional connectivity and working memory in schizo-phrenia: an EEG study', *International Journal of Neuroscience*, 106: 47–61.

Penn, D.L., Corrigan, P.W., Bentall, R.P., Racenstein, J.M. and Newman, L. (1997) 'Social cognition in schizophrenia', *Psychological Bulletin*, 121: 114–32.

Penn, D.L., Combs, D. and Mohamed, S. (2001) 'Social cognition and social functioning in schizophrenia', in P.W. Corrigan and D.L. Penn (eds) *Social Cognition and Schizophrenia*, Washington, DC: American Psychological Association, pp. 97–122.

Perner, J. (1991) *Understanding the Representational Mind*, Cambridge, MA: MIT Press.

Perner, J., Frith, U., Leslie, A.M. and Leekam, S.R. (1989) 'Exploration of the autistic child's theory of mind: knowledge, belief, and communication', *Child Development*, 60: 688–700.

Perrett, D.I., Smith, P.A., Potter, D.D., Mistlin, A.J., Head, A.S., Milner, A.D. and Jeeves, M.A. (1985) 'Visual cells in the temporal cortex sensitive to face view and gaze direction', *Proceedings of the Royal Society of London Behavioural and Biological Sciences*, 223: 293–317.

Perrett, D.I., Hietanen, J.K., Oram, M.W. and Benson, P.J. (1992) 'Organization and functions of cells responsive to faces in the temporal cortex', *Philosophical Transactions of the Royal Society of London Behavioural and Biological Sciences*, 335: 23–30.

Peters, E., Day, S., McKenna, J. and Orbach, G. (1999) 'Delusion ideation in religious and psychotic populations', *British Journal of Clinical Psychology*, 38: 83–96.

Petrides, M. and Pandya, D.N. (1988) 'Association fiber pathways to the frontal cortex from the superior temporal region in the rhesus monkey', *Journal of Computational Neurology*, 273: 52–66.

Phelps, E.A., O'Connor, K.J., Cunningham, W.A., Funayama, E.S., Gatenby, J.C., Gore, J.C. and Banaji, M.R. (2000) 'Performance on indirect measures of race evaluation predicts amygdala activation', *Journal of Cognitive Neuroscience*, 12: 729–38.

Phillips, M.L. and David, A.S. (1997) 'Viewing strategies for simple and chimeric faces: an investigation of perceptual bias in normals and schizophrenic patients using visual scan paths', *Brain and Cognition*, 35: 225–38.

Phillips, M.L., Williams, L., Senior, C., Bullmore, E.T., Brammer, M.J., Andrew, C., Williams, S.C. and David, A.S. (1999) 'A differential neural response to threatening and non-threatening negative facial expressions in paranoid and non-paranoid schizophrenics', *Psychiatry Research*, 92: 11–31.

Pickup, G.J. and Frith, C.D. (2001) 'Theory of mind impairments in schizophrenia: symptomatology, severity and specificity', *Psychological Medicine*, 31: 207–20.

Pilowsky, T., Yirmiya, N., Arbelle, S. and Mozes, T. (2000) 'Theory of mind abilities of children with schizophrenia, children with autism, and normally developing children', *Schizophrenia Research*, 42: 145–55.

Pinker, S. (1994) *The Language Instinct*, New York: HarperCollins.

Pitkånen, A. and Kemppainen, S. (2002) 'Comparison of the distribution of calcium-binding proteins and intrinsic connectivity in the lateral nucleus of the rat, monkey, and human amygdala', *Pharmacology, Biochemistry and Behavior*, 71 (3): 369–77.

Pitman, R.K., Kolb, B., Orr, S.P. and Singh, M.M. (1987) 'Ethological study of facial behaviour in non-paranoid and paranoid schizophrenic patients', *American Journal of Psychiatry*, 144: 99–102.

Polanyi, M. (1967) *The Tacit Dimension*, Garden City, NY: Anchor Books.

Polimeni, J. and Reiss, J.P. (2002) 'How shamanism and group selection may reveal the origins of schizophrenia', *Medical Hypotheses*, 58: 244–48.

Polimeni, J. and Reiss, J.P. (2003) 'Evolutionary perspectives on schizophrenia', *Canadian Journal of Psychiatry*, 48: 34–39.

Porter, R. (2002) *Madness: a brief history*, Oxford: Oxford University Press.

Post, F. (1994) 'Creativity and psychopathology: a study of 291 world-famous men', *British Journal of Psychiatry*, 165: 22–34.

Post, R.M., Kopanda, R.T. and Black, K.E. (1976) 'Progressive effects of cocaine on behaviour and central amine metabolism in rhesus monkeys: relationship to kindling and psychosis', *Biological Psychiatry*, 11 (4): 403–19.

Povinelli, D.J. and Eddy, T.J. (1996) 'Chimpanzees: joint visual attention', *Psychological Science*, 7: 135.

Power, M. (1991) *The Egalitarians – Human and Chimpanzee: an anthropological view of social organization*, New York: Cambridge University Press.

Premack, D. (1988) '"Does the chimpanzee have a theory of mind?" revisited', in R.W. Byrne and A. Whiten (eds) *Machiavellian Intelligence: social expertise and the evolution of intellect in monkeys, apes and humans*, Oxford: Clarendon Press, pp. 160–79.

Premack, D. and Woodruff, G. (1978) 'Does the chimpanzee have a "theory of mind"?', *Behavioral and Brain Sciences*, 4: 515–26.

Prentky, R.A. (1980) *Creativity and Psychopathology: a neurocognitive perspective*, New York: Praeger.

Preuss, T.M. (2000) 'What's human about the human brain?' in M.S. Gazzaniga (ed.) *The New Cognitive Neurosciences*, Cambridge, MA: MIT Press, pp. 1219–34.

Price, J., Sloman, L., Gardner, R, Gilbert, P. and Rhode, P. (1994) 'The social competition hypothesis of depression', *British Journal of Psychiatry*, 164: 309–15.

Prout, T. (1999) 'How well does opposing selection maintain variation?' in R.S. Singh and C.B. Krimbas (eds) *Evolutionary Genetics from Molecules to Morphology*, Cambridge: Cambridge University Press, pp. 369–92.

Puce, A., Allison, T., Bentin, S., Gore, J.C. and McCarthy, G. (1998) 'Temporal cortex activation in humans viewing eye and mouth movements', *Journal of Neuroscience*, 18: 2188–99.

Quintana, J., Davidson, T., Kovalik, E., Marder, S.R. and Mazziotta, J.C. (2001) 'A compensatory mirror cortical mechanism for facial affect processing in schizophrenia', *Neuropsychopharmacology*, 25 (6): 915–24.

Rakic, P. (2000) 'Radial unit hypothesis of neocortical expansion', *Novartis Foundation Symposia*, 228: 30–42.

Rakic, P. and Kornack, D.R. (2001) 'Neocortical expansion and elaboration during primate evolution: a view from neuroembryology', in D. Falk and K.R. Gibson (eds) *Evolutionary Anatomy of the Primate Cerebral Cortex*, Cambridge: Cambridge University Press, pp. 30–56.

Raleigh, M.J., McGuire, M., Melega, W., Cherry, S., Huang, S.-C. and Phelps, M. (1996) 'Neural mechanisms supporting successful social decisions in simians', in Y. Christen, A. Damasio and H. Damasio (eds) *Neurobiology of Decision Making*, Berlin: Springer-Verlag, pp. 63–82.

Randall, P.L. (1983) 'Schizophrenia, abnormal connection, and brain evolution', *Medical Hypotheses*, 10: 247–80.

Randall, P.L. (1998) 'Schizophrenia as a consequence of brain evolution', *Schizophrenia Research*, 30: 143–48.

Rice, S.H. (1997) 'The analysis of ontogenetic trajectories: when a change in size or shape is not heterochrony', *Proceedings of the National Academy of Sciences of the U.S.A*, 94: 907–12.

Rice, S. (2002) 'Heterochrony', http://www.eeb.yale.edu/faculty/rice/hetero.html

Ridley, R.M., Baker, H.F., Owen, F., Cross, A.J. and Crow, T.J. (1982) 'Behavioural and biochemical effects of chronic amphetamine treatment in the vervet monkey', *Psychopharmacology*, 78 (3): 245–51.

Rilling, J.K. and Insel, T.R. (1998) 'Evolution of the cerebellum in primates: differences in relative volume among monkeys, apes and humans', *Brain and Behavioural Evolution*, 52: 308–14.

Rilling, J.K. and Insel, T.R. (1999a) 'The primate neocortex in comparative perspective using magnetic resonance imaging', *Journal of Human Evolution*, 37: 191–223.

Rilling, J.K. and Insel, T.R. (1999b) 'Differential expansion of neural projection systems in primate brain evolution', *Neuroreport*, 10: 1453–59.

Rilling, J.K. and Seligman, R.A. (2002) 'A quantitative morphometric comparative analysis of the primate temporal lobe', *Journal of Human Evolution*, 42: 505–33.

Ripinsky-Naxon, M. (1993) *The Nature of Shamanism: substance and function of a religious metaphor*, Albany: State University of New York Press.

Rizzolatti, G., Fadiga, L., Gallese, V. and Fogassi, L. (1996) 'Premotor cortex and the recognition of motor actions', *Brain Research and Cognitive Brain Research*, 3: 131–41.

Rochester, S. and Martin, J.R. (1979) *Crazy Talk: a study of the discourse of schizophrenic speakers*, New York: Plenum Press.

Rose, M.R. (1982) 'Antagonistic pleiotropy, dominance, and genetic variation', *Heredity*, 48: 63–78.

Ross, C.A. and Pearlson, G.D. (1996) 'Schizophrenia, the heteromodal association neocortex and development: potential for a neurogenetic approach', *Trends in Neurosciences*, 19: 171–76.

Rosse, R.B., Kendrick, K., Wyatt, R.J., Isaac, A. and Deutsch, S.I. (1994) 'Gaze discrimination in patients with schizophrenia: preliminary report', *American Journal of Psychiatry*, 151: 919–21.

Roth, G. (2001) 'The evolution of consciousness', in G. Roth and M.F. Wulliman (eds) *Brain Evolution and Cognition*, New York: John Wiley and Sons, Inc/ Heidelberg: Spektrum Akademischer Verlag, pp. 555–82.

Rubenstein, J.L., Anderson, S., Shi, L., Miyashita-Lin, E., Bulfone, A. and Hevner, R. (1999) 'Genetic control of cortical regionalization and connectivity', *Cerebral Cortex*, 9: 524–32.

Ruby, P. and Decety, J. (2001) 'Effect of subjective perspective taking during simulation of action: a PET investigation of agency', *Nature Neuroscience*, 4: 546–50.

Ruse, M. (2001) *Can a Darwinian be a Christian? The Relationship between Science and Religion*, Cambridge: Cambridge University Press.

Russell, T.A., Rubia, K., Bullmore, E.T., Soni, W., Suckling, J., Brammer, M.J., Simmons, A., Williams, S.C. and Sharma, T. (2000) 'Exploring the social brain in schizophrenia: left prefrontal underactivation during mental state attribution', *American Journal of Psychiatry*, 157: 2040–42.

Russon, A.E. (1999) 'Orangutans' imitation of tool use: a cognitive interpretation', in S. Taylor Parker, R.W. Mitchell and H.L. Miles (eds) *The Mentalities of Gorillas and Orangutans: comparative perspectives*, Cambridge: Cambridge University Press, pp. 117–46.

Sackett, G.P. (1969) 'The persistence of abnormal behaviour in monkeys following isolation rearing', *International Psychiatric Clinics*, 6 (1): 3–37.

Sanfilipo, M., Lafargue, T., Rusinek, H., Arena, L., Loneragan, C., Lautin, A., Feiner, D., Rotrosen, J. and Wolkin, A. (2000) 'Volumetric measure of the frontal and temporal lobe regions in schizophrenia: relationship to negative symptoms', *Archives of General Psychiatry*, 57: 471–80.

Sapolsky, R.M. (2002) *A Primate's Memoir: a neuroscientist's unconventional life among the baboons*, New York: Touchstone/Simon and Schuster.

Sarfati, Y. and Hardy-Baylé, M.C. (1999) 'How do people with schizophrenia explain the behaviour of others? A study of theory of mind and its relationship to thought and speech disorganization in schizophrenia', *Psychological Medicine*, 29: 613–20.

Sarfati, Y., Hardy-Baylé, M.C., Brunet, E. and Widlöcher, D. (1999) 'Investigating theory of mind in schizophrenia: influence of verbalization in disorganized and non-disorganized patients', *Schizophrenia Research*, 37: 183–90.

Sass, L. (1992) *Madness and Modernism: insanity in the light of modern art, literature, and thought*, New York: Basic Books.

Sass, L.A. (1994) *The Paradoxes of Delusion: Wittgenstein, Schreber, and the schizophrenic mind*, Ithaca: Cornell University Press.

Sass, L.A. (2001) 'Self and world in schizophrenia: three classic approaches', *Philosophy, Psychiatry and Psychology*, 8 (4): 251–70.

Sass, L.A. and Parnas, J. (2001) 'Phenomenology of self-disturbance in schizophrenia: some research findings and directions', *Philosophy, Psychiatry and Psychology*, 8 (4): 347–56.

Sass, L.A. and Parnas, J. (2003) 'Schizophrenia, consciousness and the self', *Schizophrenia Bulletin*, 29 (3): 427–44.

Saugstad, L.F. (1994) 'The maturational theory of brain development and cerebral excitability in the multifactorially inherited manic-depressive psychosis and schizophrenia', *International Journal of Psychophysiology*, 18: 189–203.

Saugstad, L.F. (1998) 'Cerebral lateralisation and rate of maturation', *International Journal of Psychophysiology*, 28: 37–62.

Saugstad, L.F. (1999) 'A lack of cerebral lateralization in schizophrenia is within the normal variation in brain maturation but indicates late, slow maturation', *Schizophrenia Research*, 39: 183–96.

Savage-Rumbaugh, E.S. (1990) 'Language acquisition in a nonhuman species: implications for the innateness debate', *Developmental Psychobiology*, 23: 599–620.

Savage-Rumbaugh, E.S., Rumbaugh, D.M. and Boysen, S. (1978) 'Symbolic communication between two chimpanzees (Pan troglodytes)', *Science*, 201: 641–44.

Scharfetter, C. (2001) 'Eugen Bleuler's schizophrenias: synthesis of various concepts', *Schweizer Archiv für Neurologie und Psychiatrie*, 152 (1): 34–37.

Schlaepfer, T.E., Harris, G.J., Tien, A.Y., Peng, L.W., Lee, S., Federman, E.B., Chase, G.A., Barta, P.E. and Pearlson, G.D. (1994) 'Decreased regional cortical gray matter volume in schizophrenia', *American Journal of Psychiatry*, 151: 842–48.

Schneider, F., Weiss, U., Kessler, C., Salloum, J.B., Posse, S., Grodd, W. and Müller-Gärtner, H.W. (1998) 'Differential amygdala activation in schizophrenia during sadness', *Schizophrenia Research*, 34: 133–42.

Schoenemann, P.T., Sheehan, M.J. and Glotzer, L.D. (2005) 'Prefrontal white matter volume is disproportionately larger in humans than in other primates', *Nature Neuroscience*, 8 (2): 242–52.

Schultes, R.E. (1998) 'Antiquity of the use of New World hallucinogens', *Heffter Review of Psychedelic Research*, 1: 1–7.

Schuman, M. (1980) 'The psychophysiological model of meditation and altered states of consciousness: a critical review', in J.M. Davidson and R.J. Davidson (eds) *The Psychobiology of Consciousness*, New York: Plenum Press, pp. 333–78.

Schwartz, J.H. (1999) *Sudden Origins: fossils, genes and the emergence of species*, New York: John Wiley and Sons, Inc.

Selten, J.-P. (1995) *The subjective experience of negative symptoms*, PhD dissertation, University of Groningen, Holland.

Selten, J.-P., van den Bosch, R.J. and Sijben, A.F.S. (1998) 'The subjective experience of negative symptoms', in X.F. Amador and A.S. David (eds) *Insight and Psychosis*, New York: Oxford University Press, pp. 78–90.

Selten, J.-P., Wiersma, D. and van den Bosch, R.J. (2000) 'Discrepancy between subjective and objective ratings for negative symptoms', *Journal of Psychiatric Research*, 34: 11–13.

Seltzer, B. and Pandya, D.N. (1989) 'Frontal lobe connections of the superior temporal sulcus in the rhesus monkey', *Journal of Computational Neurology*, 281: 97–113.

Semendeferi, K. (1994) *Evolution of the hominoid prefrontal cortex: a quantitative and image analysis of areas 13 and 10*, dissertation, University of Iowa.

Semendeferi, K. (1999) 'The frontal lobes of the great apes with a focus on the gorilla and the orangutan', in S. Taylor Parker, R.W. Mitchell and H.L. Miles (eds) *The Mentalities of Gorillas and Orangutans: comparative perspectives*, Cambridge: Cambridge University Press, pp. 70–98.

Semendeferi, K. (2001) 'Advances in the study of hominoid brain evolution: magnetic resonance imaging (MRI) and 3-D reconstruction', in D. Falk and K.R. Gibson (eds) *Evolutionary Anatomy of the Primate Cerebral Cortex*, Cambridge: Cambridge University Press, pp. 257–89.

Semendeferi, K. and Damasio, H. (2000) 'The brain and its main anatomical subdivisions in living hominoids using magnetic resonance imaging', *Journal of Human Evolution*, 38: 317–32.

Semendeferi, K., Damasio, H. and Van Hoesen, G.W. (1994) 'Evolution of frontal lobes: an MRI study on apes and humans', *Society for Neurosciences Abstracts*, 20: 1415.

Semendeferi, K., Damasio, H., Frank, R. and Van Hoesen, G.W. (1997) 'The evolution of the frontal lobes: a volumetric analysis based on three-dimensional reconstructions of magnetic resonance scans of human and ape brains', *Journal of Human Evolution*, 32: 375–88.

Semendeferi, K., Armstrong, E., Schleicher, A., Zilles, K. and Van Hoesen, G.W. (2001) 'Prefrontal cortex in humans and apes: a comparative study of area 10', *American Journal of Physical Anthropology*, 114: 224–41.

Semendeferi, K., Lu, A., Schenker, N. and Damasio, H. (2002) 'Humans and great apes share a large frontal cortex', *Nature Neuroscience*, 5: 272–76.

Semple, D., Smyth, R., Burns, J., Darjee, R. and McIntosh, A. (1995) *Oxford Handbook of Clinical Psychiatry*, Oxford: Oxford University Press.

Seyfarth, R. and Cheney, D. (1984) 'Grooming alliances and reciprocal altruism in vervet monkeys', *Nature*, 308: 541–42.

Shapiro, G.L. (1982) 'Sign acquisition in a home-reared/free-ranging orangutan: comparisons with other signing apes', *American Journal of Primatology*, 3: 121–29.

Shapiro, G.L. and Galdikas, B.M.F. (1999) 'Early sign performance in a free-ranging, adult orangutan', in S. Taylor Parker, R.W. Mitchell and H.L. Miles (eds) *The Mentalities of Gorillas and Orangutans: comparative perspectives*, Cambridge: Cambridge University Press, pp. 265–82.

Shaw, R.J., Dong, M., Lim, K.O., Faustman, W.O., Pouget, E.R. and Alpert, M. (1999) 'The relationship between affect expression and affect recognition in schizophrenia', *Schizophrenia Research*, 37: 245–50.

Shea, B.T. (1989) 'Heterochrony in human evolution: the case for neoteny reconsidered', *Yearbook of Physical Anthropology*, 32: 69–101.

Shea, B. (2000) 'Current issues in the investigation of evolution by heterochrony, with emphasis on the debate over human neoteny', in S. Taylor Parker, J. Langer and M.L. McKinney (eds) *Biology, Brains and Behaviour*, Sante Fe: School of American Research Press/Oxford: James Curry Ltd, pp. 181–214.

Shutte, A. (1993) *Philosophy for Africa*, Cape Town: University of Cape Town Press.

Sigmundsson, T., Suckling, J., Maier, M., Williams, S., Bullmore, E., Greenwood, K., Fukuda, R., Ron, M. and Toone, B. (2001) 'Structural abnormalities in frontal, temporal, and limbic regions and interconnecting white matter tracts in schizophrenic patients with prominent negative symptoms', *American Journal of Psychiatry*, 158: 234–43.

Silverman, J. (1967) 'Shamans and acute schizophrenia', *American Anthropologist*, 69: 21–31.

Simonton, D.K. (1999) *Origins of Genius: Darwinian perspectives on creativity*, New York: Oxford University Press.

Smith, B.H. (1992) 'Life history and the evolution of human maturation', *Evolutionary Anthropology*, 1 (4): 134–42.

Smuts, B.B. (1983) 'Special relationships between adult male and female olive baboons: selective advantages', in R.A. Hinde (ed.) *Primate Social Relationships*, Oxford: Blackwell, pp. 262–66.

Smuts, B.B. (1985) *Sex and Friendship in Baboons*, New York: Aldine Hawthorn.

Snowden, J.S., Gibbons, Z.C., Blackshaw, A., Doubleday, E., Thompson, J., Craufurd, D., Foster, J., Happe, F. and Neary, D. (2003) 'Social cognition in frontotemporal dementia and Huntington's disease', *Neuropsychologia*, 41 (6): 688–701.

Sober, E. (1984) *The Nature of Selection: evolutionary theory in philosophical focus*, Cambridge, MA: MIT Press.

Sober, E. (1993) *Philosophy of Biology*, Boulder, CO: Westview Press.

Sober, E. and Wilson, D.S. (1998) *Unto Others: the evolution and psychology of unselfish behaviour*, Cambridge: Harvard University Press.

Sokolowski, R. (2000) *Introduction to Phenomenology*, Cambridge: Cambridge University Press.

Sophocles. (1893) *The Ajax of Sophocles*, edited with introduction and notes by Sir Richard Jebb, Cambridge: Cambridge University Press.

Spencer, H. (1862) *First Principles*, London: Williams and Norgate, 6th edn revised, 1904 [*A System of Synthetic Philosophy, vol. 1*].

Spitzer, C., Haug, H.J. and Freyberger, H.J. (1997) 'Dissociative symptoms in schizophrenic patients with positive and negative symptoms', *Psychopathology*, 30 (2): 67–75.

Staehelin, B. (1953) 'Gesetzmäßigkeiten im gemeinschaftsleben schwer geisteskranker', *Schweizer Archiv für Neurologie Psychiatrie*, 72: 277–98.

Stanford, C. (1999) *The Hunting Apes*, Princeton: Princeton University Press.

Stanghellini, G. (2001) 'Psychopathology of common sense', *Philosophy, Psychiatry and Psychology*, 8: 201–18.

Stanghellini, G. and Ballerini, M. (2002) 'Dis-sociality: the phenomenological approach to social dysfunction in schizophrenia', *World Psychiatry*, 1 (2): 102–06.

Stein, L. (1957) '"Social class" gradient in schizophrenia', *British Journal of Preventive and Social Medicine*, 11: 181–95.

Stephen, M. and Suryani, L.K. (2000) 'Shamanism, psychosis and autonomous imagination', *Culture, Medicine and Psychiatry*, 24: 5–40.

Stevens, A. and Price, J. (1996) *Evolutionary Psychiatry: a new beginning*, London: Routledge.

Stevens, A. and Price, J. (2000) *Prophets, Cults and Madness*, London: Gerald Duckworth and Co. Ltd.

Storr, A. (1997) *Feet of Clay: a study of gurus*, London: HarperCollins.

Stransky, E. (1903) 'Zur kenntnis gewisser erworbener blödsinnsformen (zugleich ein beitrag zur lehre von der dementia praecox)', *Jahrbuch der Psychiatrie und Neurologie*, 24: 1–149.

Streit, M., Wölwer, W. and Gaebel, W. (1997) 'Facial affect recognition and visual scanning behaviour in the cause of schizophrenia', *Schizophrenia Research*, 24: 311–17.

Streit, M., Ioannides, A.A., Liu, L., Wölwer, W., Dammers, J., Gross, J., Gaebel, W. and Müller-Gärtner, H.W. (1999) 'Neurophysiological correlates of the recognition of facial expressions of emotion as revealed by magnetoencephalography', *Brain Research and Cognitive Brain Research*, 7: 481–91.

Striedter, G.F. (2005) *Principles of Brain Evolution*, Sunderland, MA: Sinauer Associates, Inc.

Stringer, C.B. and Andrews, P. (1988) 'Genetic and fossil evidence for the origin of modern humans', *Science*, 239: 1263–68.

Stringer, C. and Gamble, C. (1993) *In Search of the Neanderthals: solving the puzzle of human origins*, London: Thames and Hudson.

Suddendorf, T. (1999) 'The rise of the metamind', in M.C. Corballis and S.E.G. Lea (eds) *The Descent of Mind: psychological perspectives on hominid evolution*, Oxford: Oxford University Press, pp. 218–60.

Suddendorf, T. and Corballis, M.C. (1997) 'Mental time travel and the evolution of the human mind', *Genetic, Social and General Psychology Monographs*, 123: 133–67.

Suddendorf, T. and Whiten, A. (2001) 'Mental evolution and development: evidence for secondary representation in children, great apes, and other animals', *Psychological Bulletin*, 127: 629–50.

Sullivan, R.J., and Allen, J.S. (1999) 'Social deficits associated with schizophrenia defined in terms of interpersonal Machiavellianism', *Acta Psychiatrica Scandinavica*, 99: 148–54.

Sullivan, R.J. and Allen, J.S. (2004) 'Natural selection and schizophrenia', *Behavioral and Brain Sciences*, 27: 865–66.

Sullivan, R.J. and Hagen, E.H. (2002) 'Psychotropic substance-seeking: evolutionary pathology or adaptation?' *Addiction*, 97: 389–400.

Sun, Z., Wang, F., Cui, L., Breeze, J., Du, X., Wang, X., Cong, Z., Zhang, H., Li, B., Hong, N. and Zhang, D. (2003) 'Abnormal anterior cingulum in patients with schizophrenia: a diffusion tensor imaging study', *Neuroreport*, 14 (14): 1833–36.

Suomi, S.J. (1997) 'Long-term effects of different early rearing experiences on social, emotional and physiological development in non-human primates', in M.S. Keshavan and R.M. Murray (eds) *Neurodevelopment and Adult Psychopathology*, Cambridge: Cambridge University Press, pp. 104–16.

Suzuki, M., Yuasa, S., Minabe, Y., Murata, M. and Kurachi, M. (1993) 'Left superior temporal blood flow increases in schizophrenic and schizophreniform patients with auditory hallucination: a longitudinal case study using 123I-IMP SPECT', *European Archives of Psychiatry and Clinical Neuroscience*, 242: 257–61.

Sweet, L.H., Primeau, M., Fichtner, C.G. and Lutz, G. (1998) 'Dissociation of affect recognition and mood state from blunting in patients with schizophrenia', *Psychiatric Research*, 81: 301–8.

Tamminga, C.A., Thaker, G.K., Buchanan, R., Kirkpatrick, B., Alphs, L.D., Chase, T.N. and Carpenter, W.T. (1992) 'Limbic system abnormalities identified in schizophrenia using positron emission tomography with fluorodeoxyglucose and neocortical alterations with deficit syndrome', *Archives of General Psychiatry*, 49: 522–30.

Tien, A.Y., Eaton, W.W., Schlaepfer, T.E., McGilchrist, I.K., Menon, R., Powers, R., Aylward, E., Barta, P., Strauss, M.E. and Pearlson, G.D. (1996) 'Exploratory factor analysis of MRI brain structure measures in schizophrenia', *Schizophrenia Research*, 19: 93–101.

Tinbergen, N. (1951) *The Study of Instinct*, London: Oxford University Press.

Tomasello, M. and Call, J. (1997) *Primate Cognition*, New York: Oxford University Press.

Tooby, J. and de Vore, I. (1987) 'The reconstruction of hominid behavioural evolution through strategic modelling', in W.G. Kinzey (ed.) *The Evolution of Human Behaviour: primate models*, Albany, NY: SUNY Press, pp. 183–237.

Traub, R. (1980) 'Some adaptive modifications in fleas', in R. Traub and H. Starcke (eds) *Fleas*, Rotterdam: A.A. Baldema, pp. 33–67.

Trevarthen, C. and Aitken, K.J. (2001) 'Infant intersubjectivity: research, theory, and clinical applications', *Journal of Child Psychology and Psychiatry*, 42 (1): 3–48.

Trinkaus, E. (1983) *The Shanidar Neanderthals*, New York: Academic Press.

Trinkaus, E. and Shipman, P. (1993) *The Neandertals*, New York: Knopf.

Troisi, A., Spalletta, G. and Pasini, A. (1998) 'Non-verbal behaviour deficits in schizophrenia: an ethological study of drug-free patients', *Acta Psychiatrica Scandinavica*, 97: 109–15.

Troisi, A. (1999) 'Ethological research in clinical psychiatry: the study of non-verbal behaviour during interviews', *Neuroscience and Biobehavioral Reviews*, 23: 905–13.

Turner, C.H., Davenport, R.K. and Rogers, C.M. (1969) 'The effects of early deprivation on the social behaviour of adolescent chimpanzees', *American Journal of Psychiatry*, 125 (11): 1531–36.

Tutu, D.M. (1999) *No Future Without Forgiveness*, New York: Doubleday/Random House.

Vanduffel, W., Fize, D., Peuskens, H., Denys, K., Sunaert, S., Todd, J.T. and Orban, G.A. (2002) 'Extracting 3D from motion: differences in human and monkey intraparietal cortex', *Science*, 298: 413–15.

van Schaik, C.P. and van Hoof, J.A. (1996) 'Towards an understanding of the orangutan's social system', in W.C. McGrew, L.F. Marchant and T. Nishida (eds) *Great Ape Societies*, Oxford: Oxford University Press, pp. 3–15.

van Schaik, C.P., Fox, E.A. and Sitompul, A.F. (1996) 'Manufacture and use of tools in wild Sumatran orangutans. Implications for human evolution', *Naturwissenschaften*, 83: 186–88.

Vetulani, J. (2001) 'Drug addiction. Part 1. Psychoactive substances in the past and presence', *Polish Journal of Pharmacology*, 53: 201–14.

Vogeley, K., Bussfeld, P., Newen, A., Herrmann, S., Happé, F., Falkai, P., Maier, W.,

Shah, N.J., Fink, G.R. and Zilles, K. (2001) 'Mind reading: neural mechanisms of theory of mind and self-perspective', *Neuroimage*, 14: 170–81.

Vollenweider, F.X., Leenders, K.L., Scharfetter, C., Antonini, A., Maguire, P., Missimer, J. and Angst, J. (1997a) 'Metabolic hyperfrontality and psychopathology in the ketamine model of psychosis using positron emission tomography (PET) and [18F]fluorodeoxyglucose (FDG)', *European Neuropsychopharmacology*, 7 (1): 9–24.

Vollenweider, F.X., Leenders, K.L., Scharfetter, C., Maguire, P., Stadelmann, O. and Angst, J. (1997b) 'Positron emission tomography and fluorodeoxyglucose studies of metabolic hyperfrontality and psychopathology in the psilocybin model of psychosis', *Neuropsychopharmacology*, 16 (5): 357–72.

Vollenweider, F.X., Vontobel, P., Hell, D. and Leenders, K.L. (1999) '5-HT modulation of dopamine release in basal ganglia in psilocybin-induced psychosis in man: a PET study with [11C]raclopride', *Neuropsychopharmacology*, 20 (5): 424–33.

Von Bonin, G. (1948) 'The frontal lobe of primates: cytoarchitectural studies', *Research Publications Association for Research in Nervous and Mental Disease*, 27: 67–83.

Von Bonin, G. (1950) *Essay on the Cerebral Cortex*, Springfield, IL: Charles C. Thomas.

Vygotsky, L.S. (1978) *Mind in Society: the development of higher psychological processes*, Cambridge: Harvard University Press.

Waddell, P.J. and Penny, D. (1996) 'Evolutionary trees of apes and humans from DNA sequences', in A. Lock and C.R. Peters (eds) *Handbook of Human Symbolic Evolution*, Oxford: Oxford University Pres, pp. 53–73.

Waddington, J.L., Lane, A., Larkin, C. and O'Callaghan, E. (1999) 'The neurodevelopmental basis of schizophrenia: clinical clues from cerebrocraniofacial dysmorphogenesis, and the roots of a lifetime trajectory of disease', *Biological Psychiatry*, 46: 31–39.

Wallace, A.R. (1858) 'On the tendency of varieties to depart indefinitely from the original type', *Proceedings of the Linnean Society of London*, 3: 53–62, http://www.wku.edu/~smithch/wallace/S043.htm

Walsh, S., Bramblett, C.A. and Alford, P.L. (1982) 'A vocabulary of abnormal behaviours in restrictively reared chimpanzees', *American Journal of Primatology*, 3 (1): 315–19.

Wang, F., Sun, Z., Cui, L., Du, X., Wang, X., Zhang, H., Cong, Z., Hong, N. and Zhang, D. (2004) 'Anterior cingulum abnormalities in male patients with schizophrenia determined through diffusion tensor imaging', *American Journal of Psychiatry*, 161: 573–75.

Ward, K.E., Friedman, L., Wise, A. and Schulz, S.C. (1996) 'Meta-analysis of brain and cranial size in schizophrenia', *Schizophrenia Research*, 22: 197–213.

Warner, R. (1985) *Recovery from Schizophrenia: psychiatry and political economy*, London: Routledge and Kegan Paul.

Warren, M.A. (2001) 'The moral status of great apes', in B.B. Beck, T.S. Stoinski, M. Hutchins, T.L. Maple, B. Norton, A. Rowan, E.F. Stevens and A. Arluke (eds) *Great Apes and Humans: the ethics of coexistence*, Washington, DC: Smithsonian Institution Press.

Wasson, V.P. and Wasson, R.G. (1957) *Mushrooms, Russia and History*, New York: Pantheon Books.

Weeber, E.J., Beffert, U., Jones, C., Christian, J.M., Förster, E., Sweatt, J.D. and Herz, J. (2002) 'Reelin and ApoE receptors cooperate to enhance hippocampal synaptic plasticity and learning', *Journal of Biological Chemistry*, 277 (42): 39944–52.

Weickert, C.S. and Weinberger, D.R. (1998) 'A candidate molecule approach to defining developmental pathology in schizophrenia', *Schizophrenia Bulletin*, 24: 303–16.

Weil, A.T. (1972) *The Natural Mind: an investigation of drugs and the higher consciousness*, Boston, MA: Houghton Mifflin.

Weinberger, D.R., Berman, K.F. and Zec, R.F. (1986) 'Physiologic dysfunction of dorsolateral prefrontal cortex in schizophrenia. I. Regional cerebral blood flow evidence', *Archives of General Psychiatry*, 43: 114–24.

Weinberger, D.R. (1987) 'Implications of normal brain development for the pathogenesis of schizophrenia', *Archives of General Psychiatry*, 44: 660–69.

Weisfeld, G.E. (1999) *Evolutionary Principles of Human Adolescence*, New York: Basic Books.

Weisfeld, G.E. (2004) 'Some ethological perspectives on the fitness consequences and social emotional symptoms of schizophrenia', *Behavioral and Brain Sciences*, 27: 867.

Wellman, H.M. (1991) 'From desires to beliefs: acquisition of a theory of mind', in A. Whiten (ed.) *Natural Theories of Mind: evolution, development and simulation of everyday mindreading*, Oxford: Basil Blackwell, pp. 19–38.

Wernicke, C. (1899) *Psychiatrie*, 1st edn, Leipzig: Barth.

Whiten, A. (1991) *Natural Theories of Mind: evolution, development and simulation of everyday mindreading*, Oxford: Basil Blackwell.

Whiten, A. (1999) 'The evolution of deep social mind in humans', in M.C. Corballis and S.E.G. Lea (eds) *The Descent of Mind: psychological perspectives on hominid evolution*, Oxford: Oxford University Press, 342–66.

Whiten, A. and Byrne, R.W. (1988) 'Tactical deception in primates', *Behavioral and Brain Sciences*, 11: 233–73.

Whitley, D.S. (1994) 'Shamanism, natural modelling and the rock art of far western North America', in S. Turpin (ed.) *Shamanism and Rock Art in North America*, Special Publication I, San Antonio, TX: Rock Art Foundation, pp. 1–43.

Whitley, D.S. (1998) 'Meaning and metaphor in the Coso petroglyphs: understanding Great Basin rock art', in E. Younkin (ed.) *Coso Rock Art: a new perspective*, Ridgecrest, CA: Maturango Museum Press, pp. 109–74.

Whitley, D.S. (2000) *The Art of the Shaman: the rock art of California*, Salt Lake City: University of Utah Press.

Williams, G.C. (1966) *Adaptation and Natural Selection*, Princeton: Princeton University Press.

Williams, L.M., Loughland, C.M., Gordon, E. and Davidson, D. (1999) 'Visual scanpaths in schizophrenia: is there a deficit in face recognition?' *Schizophrenia Research*, 40: 189–99.

Williams, R. (2002) *Lost Icons: reflections on cultural bereavement*, London: Continuum.

Wilson, E.O. (1975) *Sociobiology: the new synthesis*, Cambridge: Belknap Press of Harvard University Press.

Wilson, G.N. (1988) 'Heterochrony and human malformation', *American Journal of Medical Genetics*, 29: 311–21.

Wimmer, H. and Perner, J. (1983) 'Beliefs about beliefs: representation and constraining function of wrong beliefs in young children's understanding of deception', *Cognition*, 13: 103–28.

Wing, L. and Gould, J. (1979) 'Severe impairments of social interaction and associated abnormalities in children: epidemiology and classification', *Journal of Autism and Developmental Disorders*, 9: 11–29.

Winkelman, M. (1989) 'Shamans and other "magico-religious" healers: a cross-cultural study of their origins, nature, and social transformations', *Ethos*, X: 308–52.

Winkelman, M. (2000) *Shamanism: the neural ecology of consciousness and healing*, Westport, CT: Bergin and Garvey.

Wise, S.M. (2001) 'A great shout: legal rights for great apes', in B.B. Beck, T.S. Stoinski, M. Hutchins, T.L. Maple, B. Norton, A. Rowan, E.F. Stevens and A. Arluke (eds) *Great Apes and Humans: the ethics of coexistence*, Washington, DC: Smithsonian Institution Press, pp. 274–94.

Wölwer, W., Streit, M., Polzer, U. and Gaebel, W. (1996) 'Facial affect recognition in the course of schizophrenia', *European Archives of Psychiatry and Clinical Neuroscience*, 246: 165–70.

Woodruff, P.W., Wright, I.C., Shuriquie, N., Russouw, H., Rushe, T., Howard, R.J., Graves, M., Bullmore, E.T. and Murray, R.M. (1997) 'Structural brain abnormalities in male schizophrenics reflect fronto-temporal dissociation', *Psychological Medicine*, 27: 1257–66.

World Health Organization (1973) *Report of the International Pilot Study of Schizophrenia*, vol.1. Geneva: WHO.

Wright, I.C., Sharma, T., Ellison, Z.R., McGuire, P.K., Friston, K.J., Brammer, M.J., Murray, R.M. and Bullmore, E.T. (1999) 'Supra-regional brain systems and the neuropathology of schizophrenia', *Cerebral Cortex*, 9: 366–78.

Wright, P.A. (1989) 'The nature of the shamanic state of consciousness: a review', *Journal of Psychoactive Drugs*, 21 (1): 25–33.

Wright, P.A. (1995) 'The interconnectivity of mind, brain and behaviour in altered states of consciousness: focus on shamanism', *Alternative Therapies*, 1 (3): 50–56.

Wylie, A. (1989) 'Archaeological cables and tacking: the implications of practice for Bernstein's "Options beyond objectivism and relativism"', *Philosophy of Science*, 19: 1–18.

Wynn, T. (1988) 'Tools and the evolution of human intelligence', in R.W. Byrne and A. Whiten (eds) *Machiavellian Intelligence: social expertise and the evolution of intellect in monkeys, apes, and humans*, Oxford: Clarendon Press, pp. 271–84.

Wynne-Edwards, V.C. (1962) *Animal Dispersion in Relation to Social Behaviour*, Edinburgh: Oliver and Boyd.

Young, A.W., Aggleton, J.P., Hellawell, D.J., Johnson, M., Broks, P. and Hanley, J.R. (1995) 'Face processing impairments after amygdalotomy', *Brain*, 118: 15–24.

Young, A.W., Hellawell, D.J., Van DeWal, W.C. and Johnson, M. (1996) 'Facial expression processing after amygdalotomy', *Neuropsychologia*, 34: 31–39.

Young, L.J. (2002) 'The neurobiology of social recognition, approach, and avoidance', *Biological Psychiatry*, 51: 18–26.

Young, M.P., Scannell, J.W., Burns, G.A. and Blakemore, C. (1994) 'Analysis of connectivity: neural systems in the cerebral cortex', *Review of Neuroscience*, 5: 227–50.

Yovel, G., Sirota, P., Mazeh, D., Shakar, G., Rosenne, E. and Ben-Eliyahu, S. (2000) 'Higher natural killer cell activity in schizophrenic patients: the impact of serum factors, medication, and smoking', *Brain Behaviour and Immunology*, 14: 153–69.

Yucel, M., Pantelis, C., Stuart, G.W., Wood, S.J., Maruff, P., Velakoulis, D., Pipingas, A., Crowe, S.F., Tochon-Danguy, H.J. and Egan, G.F. (2002) 'Anterior cingulate activation during Stroop task performance: a PET to MRI coregistration study of individual patients with schizophrenia', *American Journal of Psychiatry*, 159: 251–54.

Yurgelun-Todd, D.A., Renshaw, P.F., Gruber, S.A., Ed, M., Waternaux, C. and Cohen, B.M. (1996a) 'Proton magnetic resonance spectroscopy of the temporal lobes in schizophrenics and normal controls', *Schizophrenia Research*, 19: 55–59.

Yurgelun-Todd, D.A., Waternaux, C.M., Cohen, B.M., Gruber, S.A., English, C.D. and Renshaw, P.F. (1996b) 'Functional magnetic resonance imaging of schizophrenic patients and comparison subjects during word production', *American Journal of Psychiatry*, 153: 200–5.

Zahavi, D. (2001) 'Schizophrenia and self-awareness', *Philosophy, Psychiatry and Psychology*, 8 (4): 339–41.

Ziegler, B.P. (2002) 'The brain-machine disanalogy revisited', *Biosystems*, 64 (1–3): 127–40.

Zubin, J. (1985) 'Negative symptoms: are they indigenous to schizophrenia?' *Schizophrenia Bulletin*, 11: 461–69.

Zweig, A. (1908) 'Dementia praecox jenseits des 30. Lebensjahres', *Archiv für Psychiatrie*, 44: 1015–35.

INDEX

Note: page numbers in **bold** refer to diagrams and information contained in tables.

MACARONI AND VEGETABLE STEW

4 oz (100 g) wholewheat macaroni
2 oz (50 g) polyunsaturated margarine
1 large leek
1 parsnip
1 onion
1 potato
1 carrot
½ pt (275 ml) vegetable stock
Soy sauce
1-2 teaspoonsful mixed herbs
Seasoning to taste
Watercress to garnish

1. Peel and cube the parsnip, potato and carrot; slice the onion and leek.

2. Melt the margarine and gently *sauté* the vegetables for a few minutes; add the stock; season with soy sauce, herbs, sea salt and freshly ground black pepper.

3. Simmer until the vegetables are cooked but still hold their shape.

4. Meanwhile, cook the macaroni in boiling water.

5. Combine the drained macaroni with the vegetables and stock, and heat for 2 minutes; serve garnished with watercress.

PARSLEY EGG MACARONI

8 oz (225g) wholewheat macaroni
1 oz (25g) plain wholemeal flour
1 tablespoonful vegetable oil
¾ pt (425 ml) milk
Juice and grated rind of 1 lemon
3 hard-boiled eggs
3 tablespoonsful fresh chopped parsley
Seasoning to taste

1. Cook the macaroni in boiling salted water until just tender.

2. Meanwhile, heat the oil in a saucepan and *sauté* the flour for a few minutes; stir in the milk and bring to the boil, then simmer to make a sauce.

3. Remove the pan from the heat and add the lemon and rind, parsley, chopped eggs and seasoning; mix well.

4. Combine with the macaroni and re-heat gently for just a few minutes before serving.

Note: Some wholemeal breadcrumbs and/or a little grated cheese can be sprinkled on top, and the macaroni dish put under the grill for a few minutes if you prefer.

CHINESE-STYLE SPAGHETTI

8 oz (225 g) buckwheat spaghetti
4 oz (100 g) tofu (bean curd)
4 oz (100 g) mushrooms
1 medium green pepper
2 medium carrots
1 bunch watercress
2 tablespoonsful vegetable oil
Soy sauce
Seasoning to taste

1. Cook the spaghetti in boiling water for 10 minutes.

2. Heat the oil in a frying pan and add the cubed tofu; cook, stirring, until the tofu is lightly browned.

3. Peel the carrots, then slice lengthwise into thin strips; slice the mushrooms and pepper; wash and cut tough stems off the watercress.

4. Add the vegetables to the frying pan and cook over a moderate heat until tender but still crisp; sprinkle with soy sauce and season to taste.

5. Drain the spaghetti and arrange on a serving dish or individual plates; top with the tofu vegetable mixture and serve with more soy sauce if required.

PEANUTS AND PASTA

8 oz (225 g) wholewheat spaghetti
4 tablespoonsful smooth peanut butter
Approx. ¼ pt (140 ml) milk
Good pinch of chilli powder
Parsley to garnish
2 oz (50 g) roasted peanuts
Seasoning to taste

1. Cook the pasta and keep it warm.

2. In a pan, heat together the peanut butter, milk, chilli
    powder and seasoning; stir constantly until all the ingredients
    are well blended and heated through.

3. Adjust the milk, if necessary, to give the sauce a pouring
    consistency.

4. Drain the spaghetti. Arrange on serving dish, and pour the
    sauce over it.

5. Coarsely chop the parsley and peanuts and scatter on top.

SPAGHETTI 'BOLOGNESE'

8 oz (225g) wholewheat spaghetti
6 oz (175g) brown or green lentils, soaked overnight
1 oz (25g) polyunsaturated margarine
1 tablespoonful vegetable oil
1 clove garlic, crushed
1 large onion
1 large green pepper
4 large ripe tomatoes or 3 tablespoonsful tomato *purée*
4 oz (100g) mushrooms
1-2 teaspoonsful oregano
Seasoning to taste

1. Cook the lentils in boiling water until almost tender.

2. Heat the margarine and oil together in a large saucepan; fry the crushed garlic, sliced onion and pepper for several minutes over a low heat.

3. Add the chopped mushrooms and cook for a minute or two longer.

4. Stir in the lentils, chopped tomatoes or *purée*, oregano and seasoning.

5. Cover the pan and simmer gently for 15 minutes, or until cooked. (If using fresh tomatoes, the sauce may seem dry, in which case, add a little of the water in which the lentils were cooked, or tap water.)

6. Whilst the sauce is cooking, prepare the spaghetti in the usual way.

7. Drain the spaghetti, arrange on a serving dish or individual plates, and cover with the 'bolognese' sauce.

PASTA PILAF

10 oz (275 g) wholewheat spaghetti or spaghetti rings
2 oz (25 g) polyunsaturated margarine
1 large onion
2 oz (50 g) currants
2 oz (50 g) cooked peas
4 oz (100 g) pine nuts or cashew pieces
3 large tomatoes
½-1 teaspoonful ground coriander
½-1 teaspoonful ground cardamom
½-1 teaspoonful turmeric
Seasoning to taste

1. Cook the pasta in boiling water until just tender, then drain. (If using spaghetti, break it into small pieces first.)

2. Melt the margarine in a pan and gently *sauté* the chopped onion together with the spices for a few minutes.

3. Mix in the drained pasta, currants, peas, nuts and coarsely chopped tomatoes; stir so that all the ingredients are well combined; heat through for a few minutes only.

4. Season to taste, and serve hot.

CLIVE BIRCH

SPAGHETTI WITH GARLIC YOGURT

8 oz (225 g) wholewheat spaghetti
2 medium courgettes
1 oz (25 g) polyunsaturated margarine
2 cloves garlic, crushed
½ pt (275 ml) plain yogurt
Seasoning to taste

1. Cook the spaghetti in the usual way.

2. Meanwhile, top and tail the courgettes, then cut into fine slivers.

3. Melt the margarine in a pan; add the courgettes and *sauté* gently, stirring continually, until just turning brown.

4. Remove the courgettes and set aside in a warm spot.

5. Add the garlic to the pan and cook a minute or so longer.

6. Mix the contents of pan with the yogurt; add seasoning.

7. Stir the courgette slivers into the cooked, drained spaghetti; top with the garlic yogurt sauce.

PASTA OMELETTE

6 oz (175g) wholewheat noodles
2 oz (50g) polyunsaturated margarine
1 medium onion
4 eggs
2 oz (50g) bean sprouts
Seasoning to taste
Watercress to garnish

1. Cook the noodles in boiling water, until just tender; drain well.

2. Melt the margarine in another pan; *sauté* the chopped onion for 5 minutes.

3. Add the bean sprouts and drained noodles; cook for a few minutes more.

4. Beat the eggs; season well; pour into the pan evenly.

5. Continue cooking until almost set, then carefully turn the omelette; cook until browned on both sides and completely set. (This can also be done by putting the omelette under the grill.)

6. Serve cut into slices, and garnished with watercress.

BUCKWHEAT NOODLES WITH MISO-TAHINI SAUCE

8 oz (225 g) buckwheat noodles
1 large onion
1 tablespoonful vegetable oil
1 teaspoonful miso
2 tablespoonsful tahini sesame paste
Approx. ¹/₃ pt (190 ml) water
1 oz (25 g) plain wholemeal flour

1. Cook the noodles in the usual way.

2. Meanwhile, heat the oil and gently *sauté* the sliced onion until just tender.

3. Sprinkle in the flour and cook briefly.

4. Remove the pan from the heat and add the water, then bring to boil, stirring continually.

5. As the sauce begins to thicken add the miso and tahini, and continue cooking until they have dissolved and blended completely.

6. If the sauce is too thick, add a little more water.

7. Serve the miso-tahini sauce over the drained noodles.

NOODLES WITH WALNUT SAUCE

8 oz (225 g) wholewheat noodles
2 oz (50 g) walnuts
1 oz (25 g) fine wholemeal breadcrumbs
2 oz (50 g) polyunsaturated margarine
2 tablespoonsful vegetable oil
2 tablespoonsful creamy milk
Parsley to garnish
Seasoning to taste

1. Remove the skins from the walnuts if preferred.

2. Pound or grind the nuts to make a paste; add the finely chopped parsley and seasoning and mix well.

3. Use a wooden spoon to mix in the margarine, oil and crumbs; continue blending until you have a thick, creamy sauce.

4. Stir in the milk and adjust the seasoning. (If the sauce is too thick, add oil or cream to adjust the consistency.)

5. Cook the noodles in boiling water until tender; drain and serve with the walnut sauce, and a garnish of parsley.

SESAME NOODLES WITH CABBAGE

10 oz (275 g) wholewheat noodles
1 small white cabbage
2 medium onions
4 oz (100 g) polyunsaturated margarine
2 oz (50 g) sesame seeds
2 tablespoonsful tahini sesame paste
Seasoning to taste

1. Cook the noodles in plenty of water, then set aside.

2. Meanwhile, *sauté* the peeled, sliced onions in the melted margarine until transparent.

3. Finely shred the cabbage and add to the pan, cooking gently until tender.

4. Stir in the drained noodles and combine thoroughly.

5. Add the tahini and seeds; season to taste; serve hot.

SOYA SPAGHETTI

8 oz (225 g) wholewheat spaghetti
4 oz (100 g) soya grits
½ pt (275 ml) vegetable stock
1-2 teaspoonsful yeast extract
½-1 clove garlic, crushed
1 onion
1 tablespoonful vegetable oil
1-2 teaspoonsful oregano
4 tablespoonsful tomato *purée*
1 oz (25 g) polyunsaturated margarine
Seasoning to taste
Parsley to garnish

1: Soak the grits for a few hours or overnight in the vegetable stock, then bring to the boil for 10 minutes and simmer until the grits are soft.

2. Cook the spaghetti in the usual way.

3. Heat the oil and gently *sauté* the sliced onion with the garlic until soft but not browned.

4. Add the grits with whatever stock is left; stir in the *purée*, yeast extract, herbs and seasoning; simmer for 5-10 minutes.

5. Add a little more liquid to the grits if necessary to make a sauce; stir in the margarine until melted.

6. Arrange the spaghetti on a serving dish and pour on the sauce; garnish with fresh parsley.

SPINACH NOODLE RING

For Ring
8 oz (225 g) wholewheat noodles
¼ pt (140 ml) milk
3 oz (75 g) Cheddar cheese
2 eggs, separated
Seasoning to taste

For Filling
1 lb (450 g) spinach
2 oz (50 g) polyunsaturated margarine
Pinch of raw cane sugar
Pinch of grated nutmeg

1. Cook the noodles in boiling water; drain and chop coarsely.

2. Mix the noodles with the egg yolks and milk; add the grated cheese and season.

3. Add the whisked egg whites and pour mixture into a greased ring mould.

4. Bake in the oven at 325°F/170°C (Gas Mark 3) for 50 minutes to an hour, or until set.

5. Wash the spinach and shred; steam until cooked, then drain and chop finely.

6. Add the margarine, sugar and nutmeg to the spinach and mix thoroughly.

7. Turn the noodle ring onto a serving plate and fill the centre with the spinach mixture; serve at once.

Note: Any vegetable mixture can be used in the centre of this ring. Try a ratatouille made with aubergine, tomatoes, onions and courgettes; or cabbage with walnuts; brussels sprouts with chestnuts also go well. Serve alone, or with a tomato or cheese sauce.

HUMMUS WITH PASTA

8 oz (225g) wholewheat noodles
2 tablespoonsful vegetable oil
1 onion
4 tomatoes
1-2 teaspoonsful oregano
4-6 tablespoonsful hummus*
Seasoning to taste
2 tablespoonsful cooked chick peas – optional

1. Cook the noodles in boiling salted water until just tender.

2. Heat the oil and *sauté* the sliced onion for a few minutes,
    then add the coarsely chopped tomatoes and cook for a few
    minutes more.

3. Season the mixture, add the herbs and enough water to just
    cover; simmer for 15 minutes.

4. Stir the hummus into the tomato sauce until it has blended
    in completely, making the sauce creamy and golden; adjust
    the seasoning.

5. Serve the pasta with the sauce poured over it; garnish with
    coarsely chopped chick peas and parsley.

*To make hummus, grind some cooked chick peas to a paste
and stir in tahini to taste; add a squeeze of lemon juice, garlic salt
and/or seasoning, a trickle of vegetable oil, and enough of the
water in which the chick peas were cooked to make the
consistency you require. Hummus can also be served as a dip
with salad vegetables, a sauce for hot vegetables, a spread in
sandwiches, or as an accompaniment to deep-fried falafels – just
adjust the consistency and seasoning to suit.

PEAS, PASTA AND CURRY CREAM SAUCE

6 oz (175 g) wholewheat noodles
6 oz (175 g) peas
1 oz (25 g) polyunsaturated margarine
1 oz (25 g) wholemeal flour
½ pt (275 ml) creamy milk or milk with 2 tablespoonsful
  skimmed milk powder added
1 teaspoonful turmeric
1 teaspoonful ground cumin
½ teaspoonful ground cardamom
2 oz (50 g) peanuts
Seasoning to taste
Pinch of paprika
Parsley to garnish

1. Cook the peas in boiling water; drain and set aside.

2. Melt the margarine in a saucepan and add the flour and spices; *sauté* for a few minutes until the flour begins to brown; pour in the milk and bring to the boil, then simmer.

3. Continue cooking and stirring until the sauce thickens.

4. Meanwhile, cook the pasta in boiling salted water until just tender.

5. Add the peas to the curry cream sauce, season, and heat through for a few minutes before stirring into the drained noodles; add the cashews.

6. Serve garnished with paprika and parsley.

Note: This is a delicate tasting sauce, and although the quantities of the spices can be increased slightly, too much will change its character completely. If you like a stronger curry flavour, use a standard sauce made the way you like, add the peas and nuts, and serve with the noodles.

ORIENTAL NOODLES

6 oz (175g) wholewheat noodles
2 tablespoonsful vegetable oil
½ clove garlic, crushed
2 oz (50g) hydrated soya 'meat' slices
¾ pt (425 ml) hot vegetable stock
½ small white cabbage
2 oz (50g) bean sprouts
Good pinch of ginger
Soy sauce
Seasoning to taste

1. In a large saucepan heat the oil and gently *sauté* the crushed garlic for a minute.

2. Cut the soya 'meat' into strips and add to the pan; *sauté* for 5 minutes, turning frequently.

3. Add the stock to the pan together with the shredded cabbage, ginger, soy sauce, seasoning, and the noodles.

4. Bring to the boil, then cook over a medium heat until the cabbage and noodles are tender, and much of the liquid has been absorbed.

5. Stir in the bean sprouts and serve at once.

Note: If there is still a good deal of liquid left, you can either drain some of it off, or mix a tablespoonful of arrowroot with cold water and add this slowly to the saucepan, then cook until the sauce thickens. Adjust the seasoning. An omelette cut into strips can be arranged over the noodles for an even more filling dish.

TAGLIATELLE WITH TOFU TOMATO SAUCE

10 oz (275 g) wholewheat tagliatelle
1 lb (450g) tomatoes
1 large onion
2 sticks celery
½-1 clove garlic
2 tablespoonsful vegetable oil
Approx. ¼ pt (140ml) vegetable stock or water
12 oz (350g) tofu
Seasoning to taste
Chives to garnish

1. Cook the pasta in plenty of boiling water and keep warm.

2. Heat the oil in a saucepan and *sauté* the finely chopped onion and celery sticks for a few minutes; add the garlic and the skinned, chopped tomatoes and cook a little longer.

3. Drain any excess liquid from the tofu then mash it into the ingredients in the pan – the more you break it up, the smoother your sauce will be.

4. Add a very small amount of stock, cover the pan, and simmer the sauce until it is thick; add more water if necessary during cooking process.

5. Season the tofu tomato sauce to taste and serve poured over the drained tagliatelle; sprinkle with chives.

KASHA AND PASTA

8 oz (225 g) wholewheat pasta shells
4 oz (100 g) kasha (roasted buckwheat)
½ pt (275 ml) water
1 red pepper
1 large onion
10 black olives
Capers
2 oz (50 g) polyunsaturated margarine
1 small carton soured cream
Seasoning to taste

1. Add the kasha to the water, bring to the boil, then simmer until just tender; keep warm.

2. At the same time, cook the pasta in a large pan of boiling water.

3. Melt the margarine and gently cook the sliced onion, pepper, halved olives and capers for about 10 minutes, stirring frequently.

4. Stir the soured cream into the vegetables and heat through briefly; season.

5. Combine the drained kasha and pasta and serve topped with the sauce.

WINTER VEGETABLES PASTA

8 oz (225g) wholewheat macaroni
8 oz (225g) parsnips
8 oz (225g) carrots
8 oz (225g) turnips
2 tablespoonsful vegetable oil
Approx. ½pt (275 ml) vegetable stock
4 oz (100g) peas
1 teaspoonful basil
4 oz (100g) Lancashire cheese
Seasoning to taste

1. Peel and cube the root vegetables; heat the oil and *sauté* them briefly, turning frequently.

2. Pour in the stock, add the herbs, bring to the boil then cover and simmer for 20-30 minutes, or until tender.

3. Meanwhile, cook the pasta in boiling water; drain well.

4. Mix together the vegetables and pasta and transfer to a shallow heat-proof dish – most of the liquid will probably have been absorbed, but if not, drain off the excess first.

5. Season to taste; sprinkle with the grated cheese, and pop under the grill for a minute or two. Serve as the main dish, or make smaller portions and serve as a vegetable with such savouries as fritters, nut loaves, etc.

BAKED DISHES

BLUE CHEESE LASAGNE

6 oz (175 g) wholewheat lasagne
4 oz (100 g) Danish blue cheese ⎞
4 oz (100 g) Cheddar cheese ⎭ grated and mixed
1½ pts (825 ml) milk
2 oz (50 g) polyunsaturated margarine
2 oz (50 g) plain wholemeal flour
½ small carton soured cream
Seasoning to taste

1. Cook the lasagne in boiling water until just tender; rinse in cold water and set aside.

2. Melt the margarine in a pan; stir in the flour and cook gently until beginning to brown; add the milk and continue stirring until the sauce thickens.

3. Remove from the heat and blend in most of the grated cheese with the soured cream; season to taste, (you will need little, if any, sea salt).

4. Layer the prepared lasagne with the sauce in a shallow ovenproof dish, finishing with sauce. (If necessary, add a little more milk to make the sauce easier to pour.)

5. Sprinkle with the remaining cheese.

6. Bake at 400°F/200°C (Gas Mark 6) for 30 minutes.

LASAGNE WITH RED PEPPERS

6 oz (175g) wholewheat lasagne
2 medium onions
2 medium red peppers
3 medium tomatoes
10 black olives
2 tablespoonsful vegetable oil
1 teaspoonful basil
2 oz (50g) walnut pieces
¾ pt (425 ml) plain yogurt
2 eggs
2 oz (50g) Cheddar cheese
Seasoning to taste

1. Cook the lasagne; drain, then rinse thoroughly in cold water.

2. Heat the vegetable oil and gently *sauté* the sliced onions and peppers until they start to soften.

3. Add the walnuts and cook for a few minutes more.

4. Chop the tomatoes and add to the pan with the basil and seasoning; simmer for 5 minutes, stirring often.

5. Stone and halve the olives; stir into the vegetables.

6. Layer half the lasagne in a greased heatproof dish; top with the vegetable nut mixture; cover with the rest of the lasagne.

7. Beat the eggs lightly; add to the yogurt; season well.

8. Pour the sauce over the lasagne, tipping the dish so that it runs down between the ingredients.

9. Sprinkle with the grated cheese.

10. Bake at 400°F/200°C (Gas Mark 6) for 30-40 minutes, or until set.

VEGETABLE LASAGNE WITH TAHINI

4 oz (100g) wholewheat lasagne
2 tablespoonsful vegetable oil
2 medium onions
2 sticks celery
2 medium carrots
½ small cauliflower, broken into florets
4 oz (100g) cooked green peas
2 oz (50g) plain wholemeal flour
2 tablespoonsful tahini, or to taste
Seasoning to taste
Parsley to garnish

1. Cook the lasagne in boiling water; when just tender, remove
    at once from the heat and rinse through with cold water. Set
    aside.

2. Heat the oil in a large pan; gently *sauté* the peeled and
    chopped onions and carrots with the sliced celery, stirring
    occasionally.

3. When the vegetables are beginning to colour, add the flour
    and cook for a few minutes, then stir in the cauliflower
    florets, and enough water to cover.

4. Simmer until all the ingredients are cooked but still firm;
    add the drained peas carefully, and tahini to flavour the
    sauce.

5. In a shallow ovenproof dish layer the lasagne with the
    vegetables, finishing with lasagne and then a few spoonsful
    of sauce (or use a little more tahini with water).

6. Bake at 400°F/200°C (Gas Mark 6) for 20-30 minutes. Serve
    garnished with plenty of fresh parsley.

GREEK-STYLE LASAGNE

6 oz (175g) wholewheat lasagne
8 oz (225g) soya 'minced meat'
1 medium onion
4 medium tomatoes
2 medium aubergines
2 tablespoonsful vegetable oil
1 clove garlic, crushed
Parsley
1-2 teaspoonsful oregano
1 small carton soured cream or plain yogurt
2 oz (50g) grated Parmesan cheese
Seasoning to taste

1. Cook the lasagne in the usual way; after rinsing in cold water, set aside.

2. Cut the aubergine into ½ in. slices – arrange on a plate; sprinkle with sea salt and leave to drain for 30 minutes.

3. Hydrate the soya 'meat' according to instructions.

4. Heat the oil in a pan; add the sliced onion and garlic and cook gently for 5 minutes.

5. Rinse and dry the aubergine, chop into cubes and add to the pan; cook for 5 minutes more, stirring frequently.

6. Add the chopped tomatoes, herbs and seasoning.

7. Spoon in the soya 'meat' with just a little of the liquid in which it was cooked; cover the pan and simmer all the ingredients for about 10 minutes.

8. Layer a third of the lasagne in the base of a greased, heatproof dish; top with half the 'meat' mixture; add a few spoonsful of soured cream.

9. Repeat this pattern once more.

10. Top with the rest of the lasagne, then the soured cream; sprinkle with the grated cheese; season.

11. Bake, uncovered, at 375°F/190°C (Gas Mark 5) for 30 minutes, or until the top is golden.

ADUKI BEAN AND VEGETABLE LASAGNE

4 oz (100g) wholewheat lasagne
4 oz (100g) cooked aduki beans
2 medium onions
2 medium leeks
2 medium carrots
1 tablespoonful vegetable oil
1 oz (25g) polyunsaturated margarine
1 oz (25g) plain wholemeal flour
½ pt (275 ml) milk
3 oz (75g) Cheddar cheese
1-2 teaspoonsful sage
Seasoning to taste

1. Cook the lasagne for 15 minutes in boiling water; drain, then rinse in cold water. Set aside.

2. Heat the oil in a pan and gently *sauté* the sliced onions, leeks and carrots for 10 minutes.

3. Add a sprinkling of water, the sage and seasoning; cover the pan and simmer until the vegetables are tender.

4. Meanwhile, melt the margarine in another pan; sprinkle in the flour and *sauté* briefly.

5. Add the milk; bring to boil, then cook over a low heat, stirring continually, until the sauce thickens.

6. Grease a shallow heatproof dish and cover the bottom with half the lasagne.

7. Mix together the vegetables and drained beans, and distribute evenly in the dish.

8. Pour on half the white sauce (if too thick, add a little extra milk or water); cover with the remaining lasagne.

9. Add the rest of the sauce, spreading it to make an even topping; sprinkle with grated Cheddar cheese.

10. Bake at 400°F/200°C (Gas Mark 6) for 30 minutes.

BOSTON BAKED BEANS LASAGNE

4 oz (100g) wholewheat lasagne

For Beans
8 oz (225g) haricot beans, soaked overnight
1 oz (25g) polyunsaturated margarine
2 onions
8 oz (225g) cooking tomatoes
3 tablespoonsful tomato *purée*
2 teaspoonsful muscovado raw cane sugar
2 teaspoonsful molasses
1 teaspoonful dry mustard
Good pinch of ground cinnamon and cloves
Seasoning to taste
3 oz (75g) Cheddar cheese – optional

1. Drain the beans; add fresh water; bring to the boil for 10 minutes then simmer for an hour.

2. Heat the margarine and *sauté* the skinned and chopped tomatoes and onions until just softening; add the tomato *purée*, sugar, molasses, mustard, spices and seasoning.

3. Drain the beans and add about ½ pt (275 ml) of the liquid to the sauce; bring to the boil, stirring, then tip the beans back into the saucepan and blend well.

4. Transfer the mixture to an ovenproof dish, cover, and bake at 300°F/150°C (Gas Mark 2) for about 4 hours, or until the beans are tender. (Stir the mixture occasionally and add more liquid if necessary.)

5. Meanwhile, cook the pasta in boiling water for 10-15 minutes; drain, and rinse with cold water.

6. Place a layer of lasagne in the bottom of a shallow ovenproof dish, cover with some of the beans and sauce; repeat this until all the ingredients have been used; top with grated cheese (or finish with a generous layer of sauce).

7.   Bake at 400°F/200°C (Gas Mark 6) for 20-30 minutes.

Note: In an emergency, you can use tinned baked beans in this dish – they will taste more authentic if you simmer them briefly with some onion and molasses before making up the lasagne.

CANNELLONI WITH 'MINCED MEAT'

8 oz (225 g) basic pasta dough
6 oz (175 g) cooked spinach
3 oz (75 g) soya 'minced meat' (dry weight)
1 clove garlic, crushed
1 medium onion
4 tablespoonsful vegetable oil
4 oz (100 g) grated Parmesan cheese
1 oz (25 g) plain wholemeal flour
½ pt (275 ml) milk
1 oz (25 g) polyunsaturated margarine
Seasoning to taste

1. Roll out the pasta dough as thinly as possible; cut into 8 rectangles approximately 5 in. x 4 in. in size.

2. Cook the pasta in boiling salted water, stirring occasionally, for 5-10 minutes, or until tender but still firm.

3. Remove from the pan with a perforated spoon; drain and pat dry; spread on a plate and leave covered.

4. Hydrate the soya 'minced meat' according to the instructions on the packet.

5. Heat 2 tablespoonsful of the oil in a pan; add the sliced onion and garlic; fry gently until soft.

6. Add the drained 'meat' and simmer until cooked, (you may need to sprinkle with some water or stock).

7. Stir in the finely chopped spinach, seasoning, and 2 oz (50 g) of the grated cheese; mix thoroughly.

8. Divide the filling between the rectangles of dough; roll up carefully; place neatly in a greased heatproof dish, with the joint side down.

9. Make the white sauce; heat the rest of the oil in a pan, *sauté* the flour, then pour in the milk and bring to a boil before simmering to thicken the sauce.

10. Pour the sauce over the cannelloni; top with the rest of the grated cheese; dot with the margarine.

11. Bake at 400°F/200°C (Gas Mark 6) for 20 minutes.

WALNUT CANNELLONI

8 oz (225 g) basic pasta dough
1 large onion
2 large courgettes
2 tablespoonsful vegetable oil
4 oz (100 g) wholemeal breadcrumbs, soaked in water
1 large egg
2 oz (50 g) chopped walnuts
Parsley
1 small carton plain yogurt
2 oz (50 g) grated Parmesan cheese
Seasoning to taste

1. Roll out the pasta dough as thinly as possible; cut into 8 rectangles approximately 5 in. x 4 in. in size.

2. Cook the pasta in boiling salted water, stirring occasionally, for 5-10 minutes, until tender but still firm.

3. Remove from the pan with a perforated spoon; drain and pat dry; spread on a plate and leave covered.

4. Heat the oil in another pan and lightly *sauté* the finely chopped onion and courgettes for 5 minutes.

5. Drain, then squeeze the breadcrumbs and add them to the pan with the parsley, chopped nuts and seasoning; cook until golden.

6. Cool slightly, then add the egg to the mixture, blending thoroughly.

7. Divide the filling between the rectangles of dough; roll them up and place close together, joint side down, in a greased heatproof dish.

8. Cover with the plain yogurt, sprinkle with cheese; bake at 400°F/200°C (Gas Mark 6) for about 30 minutes.

CABBAGE AND SOUR CREAM CANNELLONI

8 oz (225g) basic pasta dough
1 large onion
½ small white cabbage
2 oz (50g) pumpkin or sunflower seeds
2 oz (50g) polyunsaturated margarine
1 small carton soured cream
2 oz (50g) grated Parmesan cheese
Seasoning to taste

1. Roll out the pasta dough and, when it is as thin as you can make it, cut into 8 rectangles approximately 5 in. x 4 in. in size.

2. Add carefully to the boiling salted water and cook, stirring occasionally, for 5-10 minutes, until tender but still firm.

3. Remove from the pan with a perforated spoon; drain and pat dry; spread on a plate and leave covered.

4. Heat the margarine in a pan and gently cook the finely sliced onion for 5 minutes; add the grated cabbage and continue cooking over a low heat, stirring occasionally, until soft.

5. Mix in the seeds, season, then divide the filling between the pasta rectangles.

6. Roll them carefully and place, with the join on the bottom, side by side in a greased ovenproof dish.

7. Stir together the soured cream and grated cheese, season to taste, then pour over the pasta rolls.

8. Bake at 400°F/200°C (Gas Mark 6) for 20 minutes.

Note: If desired, you can also mix a little soured cream and/or cheese with the cabbage before filling the cannelloni.

LENTIL CANNELLONI

8 oz (225 g) basic pasta dough
8 oz (225 g) small red lentils
3 tablespoonsful vegetable oil
2 onions
½-1 clove garlic, crushed
1 bay leaf
1 teaspoonful chopped parsley
1 teaspoonful thyme
4 tablespoonsful bean sprouts – optional
Approx. ¾ pt (425 ml) vegetable stock
4-6 tablespoonsful tomato *purée* or home-made tomato
   sauce
Seasoning to taste

1. Roll out the pasta to a thin sheet; cut into 8 rectangles
   approximately 5 in. x 4 in. in size.

2. Add the pasta to boiling salted water and cook for 5-10
   minutes, or until just tender.

3. Remove carefully with a perforated spoon, then pat dry; lay
   on a plate and leave covered.

4. Heat the oil in a pan; add the crushed garlic and finely sliced
   onions; cook gently until softening.

5. Add the lentils and cook for just a few minutes before
   pouring in the stock; sprinkle with the herbs and seasoning,
   and bring to the boil for 10 minutes.

6. Lower the heat, cover the pan, and simmer until all the
   liquid has been absorbed, which should take 30-40 minutes.
   (Add a tiny amount of liquid if necessary.)

7. Remove the bay leaf, then use a wooden spoon to mash the
   lentils to a thick *purée*; leave to cool slightly.

8. Mix in the bean sprouts, if using them.

9. Divide the mixture between the rectangles of dough, and roll each one carefully.

10. Place them neatly, side by side, in a shallow greased ovenproof dish, preferably with the joint facing downwards.

11. Cover generously with tomato *purée* or sauce, season, and bake at 400°F/200°C (Gas Mark 6) for 20-30 minutes.

'SAUSAGE ROLLS'

8 oz (225 g) basic pasta dough or wholewheat lasagne
5 oz (150 g) nut and cereal mix or soya 'sausage' mix (from
   a health food shop)
2 tablespoonsful vegetable oil
1 onion
1 green pepper
1 lb (450 g) cooking tomatoes
2 tablespoonsful tomato *purée*
1-2 teaspoonsful oregano
Seasoning to taste
2 oz (50 g) cottage cheese mixed with 1 oz (25 g) grated
Parmesan cheese – optional

1. Roll out the pasta dough as thinly as you can; cut into strips
    about 2 in.-3 in. x 5 in. in size; cook the pasta in plenty of
    boiling salted water for about 10 minutes, or until just
    cooked.

2. Drain the pasta, rinse in cold water and set aside.

3. Make up the filling according to the packet instructions.

4. If using lasagne strips, cut into half so that you have small
    rectangles similar in size to those described above, (exact
    size is not that important).

5. Fill each rectangle with some of the mixture and roll up into
    a sausage shape; place them neatly side by side in a greased
    ovenproof dish.

6. Make the sauce: heat the oil and gently *sauté* the sliced onion
    and pepper for 5 minutes, then add the chopped tomatoes,
    purée and seasoning with about ½ pt (275 ml) water.

7. Bring to the boil, then simmer the sauce until thick.

8. Pour this mixture over the 'sausage' rolls; spread with cheese if liked, and bake at 400°F/200°C (Gas Mark 6) for 20-30 minutes.

Note: You can also make this dish with ready-cooked soya 'meat' sausages, bought tinned from most health food shops. And try it with a bechamel or cheese sauce instead of tomato sauce for a change.

CANNELLONI WITH EGG FILLING

8 oz (225 g) basic pasta dough
4 hard-boiled eggs
4 medium carrots
1 oz (25 g) polyunsaturated margarine
1 oz (25 g) plain wholemeal flour
¾ pt (425 ml) milk
4 oz (100 g) Cheddar cheese
3 tablespoonsful wholemeal breadcrumbs
Seasoning to taste

1. Roll out the pasta as thinly as possible; cut into 8 rectangles approximately 5 in. x 4 in. in size.

2. Bring a large pan of salted water to the boil; add the pasta and cook for 5-10 minutes, or until just tender.

3. Use a perforated spoon to remove the pasta from the pan; drain and pat dry, then arrange on a plate and leave covered.

4. Chop the peeled carrots into small pieces and steam until cooked but still crisp; drain, and mix with the finely chopped eggs.

5. Make a white sauce by melting the margarine in a pan, gently *sautéeing* the flour for a few minutes, then pouring in most of the milk and stirring until the mixture thickens.

6. Season the sauce, then add about half of it to the egg and carrot, blending well.

7. Adjust the seasoning, then use this mixture to fill the rectangles of pasta; roll them up and lay close together, join facing downwards, in a greased ovenproof dish.

8. Add the rest of the milk to the sauce, if necessary, to make a pouring consistency, then spread it over the cannelloni.

9. Sprinkle the dish with the grated cheese and breadcrumbs, and bake at 400°F/200°C (Gas Mark 6) for 20-30 minutes.

PASTA SOUFFLÉ

4 oz (100 g) wholewheat spaghetti rings
1 oz (25 g) polyunsaturated margarine
½ oz (15 g) plain wholemeal flour
¼ pt (140 ml) milk
3 oz (75 g) Cheddar cheese
3 eggs, separated
Pinch of cayenne pepper
Seasoning to taste

1. Cook the spaghetti rings in the usual way; drain well and set aside.

2. Melt the margarine in a saucepan, add the flour, and cook for a few minutes.

3. Remove from the heat and stir in the milk; then continue cooking until sauce boils, stirring continually.

4. Simmer briefly, then set aside to cool slightly.

5. Stir in the grated cheese; add the pasta; season and blend well.

6. Add the egg yolks, one at a time.

7. Whisk the egg whites until stiff and carefully fold them into the pasta sauce.

8. Grease a medium-sized *soufflé* or casserole dish, and pour in the mixture.

9. Bake at 375°F/190°C (Gas Mark 5) for 25-30 minutes, or until well risen and set. Serve at once.

BEAN AND BRUSSELS HOT-POT

4 oz (100g) wholewheat spaghetti rings
3 oz (75 g) well cooked butter beans
2 tablespoonsful vegetable oil
2 onions
1-2 garlic cloves, crushed
10 oz (275 g) small brussels sprouts
4 tomatoes
Approx. ½ pt (275 ml) vegetable stock
1 teaspoonful yeast extract, or to taste
Seasoning to taste

1. Heat the oil in a pan and *sauté* the sliced onions and garlic until lightly browned.

2. Add the cleaned brussels sprouts with the stock, yeast extract, seasoning, coarsely chopped tomatoes and drained beans.

3. Turn the mixture into a casserole and cook, covered, in the oven, at 350°F/180°C (Gas Mark 4) for 10 minutes.

4. Stir in the pasta, adjust the liquid if necessary (remember the pasta will absorb quite a bit).

5. Return to the oven at the same temperature and continue cooking for 15-20 minutes, or until the pasta is just tender.

SPAGHETTI BAKE

8 oz (225g) wholewheat spaghetti
1 lb (450g) fresh spinach
8 oz (225g) curd or cream cheese
A little milk
1 oz (25g) polyunsaturated margarine
3 oz (75g) wholemeal breadcrumbs
Seasoning to taste

1. Cook the spaghetti in boiling salted water until barely
    tender; drain and set aside.

2. Steam the washed spinach; when cooked, drain and chop
    finely.

3. Soften the curd cheese and combine with the spinach; add a
    little milk if the mixture is very firm; season generously.

4. Toss the spaghetti with the creamed spinach until thoroughly
    combined; pile the mixture into an ovenproof dish; spread
    as evenly as possible.

5. In a saucepan, melt the margarine over a low heat; add the
    breadcrumbs and fry them briefly; sprinkle them over the
    spaghetti.

6. Bake at 350°F/180°C (Gas Mark 4) for 20 minutes, or until
    the top is crisp and golden.

BAKED AUBERGINE WITH PASTA

2 medium aubergines
2 onions
3 tomatoes
½-1 clove garlic, crushed
1 tablespoonful vegetable oil
1 oz (25 g) polyunsaturated margarine
3 oz (75 g) wholewheat pasta shells
2 oz (50 g) grated Cheddar cheese
2 oz (50 g) walnuts
Seasoning to taste

1. Cook the pasta in boiling salted water until just tender; drain and set aside.

2. Wash the aubergines and boil them for a few minutes; cool slightly; cut carefully in half lengthways and scoop out the flesh. (Keep the skins.)

3. Heat the oil and margarine together in a pan, and *sauté* the sliced onions with the garlic until just beginning to colour.

4. Add the coarsely chopped aubergine flesh and tomatoes, and continue cooking gently, stirring occasionally, for 10 more minutes.

5. Remove the pan from the heat and mix the pasta with the vegetables; season to taste; divide the mixture between the four shell-halves.

6. Arrange them on a lightly greased baking sheet; sprinkle with grated cheese and chopped walnut pieces.

7. Bake at 350°F/180°C (Gas Mark 4) for 20 minutes, or until cooked.

BAKED MACARONI WITH CAULIFLOWER

6 oz (175 g) wholewheat macaroni
1 medium cauliflower
1 tablespoonful vegetable oil
1 oz (25 g) plain wholemeal flour
½ pt (275 ml) milk or stock from cauliflower with 2
    tablespoonsful skimmed milk powder
4 oz (100 g) Edam cheese
2 tablespoonsful soya 'bacon' or wholemeal breadcrumbs
Good pinch of nutmeg
Seasoning to taste

1. Cook the macaroni in the usual way, then drain well.

2. Break the cauliflower into florets and steam, or cook in the minimum amount of water, until just tender.

3. Heat the oil in another pan, add the flour and cook for a few minutes.

4. Remove from the heat and stir in the milk, then bring to the boil and simmer until the sauce thickens.

5. Add the grated cheese and the seasoning; combine with the cauliflower and macaroni.

6. Pour into a casserole, smooth the top, and sprinkle with the soya 'bacon' or breadcrumbs; add the nutmeg.

7. Bake at 350°F/180°C (Gas Mark 4) for 15 minutes, or until heated through.

BRAZIL NUT BAKE

4 oz (100g) wholewheat macaroni
4 oz (100g) Brazil nuts, ground finely
4 oz (100g) Cheddar cheese
1 large egg
1 medium courgette
1-2 teaspoonsful mixed herbs
Seasoning to taste

1. Cook the macaroni until just tender, then drain well and chop coarsely.

2. Grate the cheese and the washed courgette (leave the skin on).

3. In a bowl, mix together the macaroni, ground Brazil nuts, grated cheese and courgette, herbs and seasoning.

4. Lightly beat the egg and add to the other ingredients.

5. Grease a shallow dish, pour in the mixture, and bake at 325°F/170°C (Gas Mark 3) for 30-40 minutes, or until set.

SESAME-TOPPED MACARONI

8 oz (225 g) wholewheat macaroni
1 onion
2 green peppers
2 tablespoonsful vegetable oil
1-2 teaspoonsful mixed herbs
Approx. ¼ pt (140 ml) plain yogurt or soured cream
4 oz (100 g) sesame seeds, ground to a powder
1 oz (25 g) polyunsaturated margarine
Seasoning to taste

1. Cook the macaroni in boiling salted water; when just tender, remove from the cooker and drain.

2. In a saucepan, heat the oil and *sauté* the sliced onion and peppers until softened; add the herbs and seasoning.

3. Stir together the pasta, vegetable mixture and enough yogurt to make a creamy sauce.

4. Turn the mixture into an ovenproof dish.

5. Melt the margarine and mix with the powdered seeds; spread this over the top of the pasta and vegetables.

6. Bake at 350°F/180°C (Gas Mark 4) for about 15 minutes.

CREAMY NOODLES BAKE

8 oz (225g) wholewheat noodles
8 oz (225g) cottage cheese
2 oz (50g) polyunsaturated margarine
1 medium onion
1 medium red pepper
2 large eggs
Chives to garnish
Seasoning to taste

1. Cook the noodles in the usual way; drain well.

2. Sieve, blend or mash the cottage cheese to make a smooth sauce.

3. Mix the cheese sauce and noodles; stir in the margarine until it melts.

4. Finely chop the peeled onion and the pepper, and add to the mixture with the beaten eggs and seasoning.

5. Lightly grease a flan dish, pour in the noodle mixture, and bake at 350°F/180°C (Gas Mark 4) for 30 minutes, or until set.

6. Sprinkle with chives before serving.

PASTA-STUFFED PEPPERS

4 large peppers
4 oz (100g) wholewheat noodles
1 medium onion
2 medium sticks celery
4 oz (100g) ground nuts
2 oz (50g) Edam cheese
1 large egg
1-2 teaspoonful mixed herbs
Soy sauce
1 tablespoonful vegetable oil
Seasoning to taste

1. Break the noodles into pieces and cook in boiling water until just tender; drain, then set aside.

2. Peel and chop the onion as finely as possible; slice the celery sticks finely; grate the cheese.

3. In a bowl, combine the noodles, chopped onion and celery, nuts and cheese.

4. Beat the egg lightly, then add to the other ingredients with the herbs, seasoning, and a sprinkling of soy sauce.

5. Wash the peppers and slice off the tops; remove the core and pips.

6. Stand the peppers close together in a small greased heat-proof dish; spoon in the pasta stuffing.

7. Replace the pepper tops and brush lightly with a little vegetable oil; bake at 400°F/200°C (Gas Mark 6) for 30-40 minutes, or until the peppers and stuffing are cooked.

GOLDEN VEGETABLE NOODLES

10 oz (275 g) wholewheat noodles
1 large parsnip
1 large carrot
1 large potato
4 oz (100 g) cooked sweet corn
Approx. ¾ pt (425 ml) milk
1 teaspoonful dill
1 oz (25 g) polyunsaturated margarine
Seasoning to taste
2 oz (50 g) grated Cheddar cheese
2 tomatoes

1. Cook the noodles in boiling salted water until just tender;
    drain and set aside.

2. Peel and finely chop the parsnip, carrot and potato.

3. Heat the margarine in a saucepan; when melted, add the
    prepared vegetables and cook gently for 10 minutes, stirring
    frequently.

4. Pour in the milk, add the herbs and seasoning; cover the pan
    and simmer for 20 minutes.

5. Cool the vegetables slightly, then put them into a blender to
    make a thick, golden *purée*; adjust the liquid if necessary.

6. Layer half the noodles in a shallow ovenproof dish; cover
    with half the vegetable *purée*; sprinkle with half the cooked,
    drained sweet corn. Repeat this to use up all the ingredients.

7. Cover the top of the dish with grated cheese; decorate with
    slices of tomato.

8. Bake at 350°F/180°C (Gas Mark 4) for 20 minutes.

EGG AND ONION LASAGNE

6 oz (175g) wholewheat lasagne
1½lb (675g) onions
2 oz (50g) polyunsaturated margarine
1 teaspoonful caraway seeds – optional
1 oz (25g) plain wholemeal flour
4 hard-boiled eggs
4 oz (100g) Parmesan cheese
Seasoning to taste

1. Cook the lasagne in boiling water and, when tender, rinse in cold water; drain and set aside.

2. Melt the margarine and *sauté* the crushed caraway seeds for a minute, then add the thickly sliced onions and cook gently for 5-10 minutes, stirring frequently.

3. Cover the pan and leave to cook over a low heat for 10 minutes more – if the pan seems dry add a spoonful of water.

4. Stir in the flour, cook briefly, add the milk and continue cooking and stirring until the onions are coated in a white sauce; add extra milk if it is too thick, and season well.

5. Layer the ingredients in an ovenproof dish in the following order: lasagne, sliced eggs, onions in sauce, then repeat.

6. Finish with the grated cheese, and bake at 400°F/200°C (Gas Mark 6) for 20-30 minutes.

PASTA DISHES

AUBERGINE YOGURT LAYER

8 oz (225 g) wholewheat macaroni
2 aubergines
3 tablespoonsful vegetable oil
2 oz (50 g) plain wholemeal flour
1 clove garlic, crushed
1 large onion
8 oz (225 g) tomatoes
2 oz (50 g) polyunsaturated margarine
2 oz (50 g) plain wholemeal flour
¾ pt (415 ml) milk
½ pt (275 ml) yogurt
3 oz (75 g) wholemeal breadcrumbs
Parsley
Seasoning to taste

1. Slice the aubergines; arrange them on a plate and sprinkle with salt; leave for 30 minutes.

2. Rinse and dry the aubergine slices and dip into the seasoned flour; fry gently in 2 tablespoonsful of the oil until tender on the inside, crisp and brown on the outside; drain on paper towels.

3. Heat the rest of the oil and *sauté* the garlic and finely chopped onion; add the peeled, crushed tomatoes and cook to make a thick *purée*.

4. In another pan, melt the margarine and sprinkle in the flour; *sauté* briefly; add the milk and stir whilst cooking until the sauce thickens; remove from the heat, season, and add the yogurt.

5. Cook the macaroni in boiling water then drain well.

6. Arrange half the macaroni in the base of an ovenproof dish; spread with half the tomato *purée*; cover with half of the aubergine slices; top with half the yogurt sauce.

7. Repeat this to use up the rest of the ingredients, and top with a mixture of the crumbs, chopped parsley and seasoning.

8. Bake this dish at 350°F/180°C (Gas Mark 4) for about 30 minutes.

Note: You can speed up the time spent preparing this dish by using ready-made tomato *purée* or sauce, or simply use slices of fresh tomatoes; and the yogurt sauce can be replaced by plain yogurt.

PASTA HOT-POT

4 oz (100g) wholewheat macaroni
4 oz (100g) hydrated soya 'meat' chunks
8 oz (225g) carrots
2 onions
8 oz (225g) peas
4 oz (100g) mushrooms
4 tomatoes
1-2 teaspoonsful mixed herbs
Approx. 1 pt (550ml) vegetable stock
Seasoning to taste

1. In a large saucepan, combine the drained 'meat' chunks, sliced carrots, onions and peas; pour the stock over them and bring to the boil.

2. Transfer the ingredients to a casserole, cover, and cook in the oven at 325°F/170°C (Gas Mark 3) for about 30 minutes.

3. Add the seasoning and herbs, sliced mushrooms and quartered tomatoes; stir in the macaroni having first cooked it for 10 minutes in boiling water.

4. Leave the casserole uncovered and continue cooking for 15-30 minutes more, or until all the ingredients are cooked.

PASTA DESSERTS

VERMICELLI PEACH CONDÉ

3 oz (75 g) wholewheat vermicelli
1 pt (550 ml) milk
2 oz (50 g) light muscovado raw cane sugar
Pure vanilla essence to taste
2 large fresh peaches
$1/3$ pt (190 ml) pure orange juice
Barely 1 oz (25 g) arrowroot
2 oz (50 g) desiccated or flaked coconut to garnish

1. Simmer the vermicelli in the milk for 10-20 minutes, or until the pasta is tender and most of the milk has been absorbed.

2. Add the sugar and essence; spoon the slightly cooled mixture into 4 dessert dishes or glasses.

3. Mix a little of the fruit juice with the arrowroot, then add to the rest and heat gently in a pan, stirring continually, to make a sauce.

4. Halve and stone the peaches; place one half cut-side down on the top of each dish.

5. Pour the fruit sauce over the fruit and pasta carefully and leave to set in the cool; serve sprinkled with coconut.

DRIED FRUIT BAKE

4 oz (100g) wholewheat macaroni
1 pt (550ml) milk
2 oz (50g) dried apricots, soaked overnight
2 oz (50g) dried prunes, soaked overnight
2 oz (50g) raisins
½ teaspoonful mixed spice, or to taste
1-2 teaspoonsful grated orange or lemon peel
Cream to serve – optional

1. Cook the macaroni in the milk for 15-20 minutes, or until tender.

2. Wash the dried fruit, pat dry, and chop the apricots and prunes into smaller pieces.

3. Combine all the ingredients and transfer to an ovenproof dish.

4. Bake at 350°F/180°C (Gas Mark 4) for 20 minutes.

5. Serve hot or cold, with cream if liked.

Note: With so much dried fruit, this dish should be sweet enough without additional sugar. If, however, you have an especially sweet tooth, you could mix the spice with a little raw cane sugar and sprinkle it over the top before baking.

PASTA CARAMEL

4oz (100g) wholewheat macaroni
1pt (550ml) milk
2oz (50g) light muscovado raw cane sugar
2 tablespoonsful water
Knob of polyunsaturated margarine

1. Put the sugar into a saucepan with the water; heat gently, stirring continually, until the sugar dissolves; cook a little longer to form a brown caramel mixture.

2. Add the milk and heat gently.

3. Add the macaroni and the margarine; continue cooking until the pasta is tender and most of the liquid has been absorbed.

4. If you prefer, this mixture can be transferred to an ovenproof dish and baked at 300°F/150°C (Gas Mark 2) for 30 minutes.

NOODLES WITH FRUIT SAUCE

3 oz (75 g) wholewheat noodles
3 cooking apples
8 oz (225 g) blackcurrants
2 tablespoonsful pure honey or raw sugar blackcurrant jam
Good squeeze of lemon juice
Plain yogurt to serve

1. Cook the noodles in boiling water for 5-10 minutes or until tender.

2. Peel, core and slice the apples; wash the blackcurrants; cook the fruit together in a heavy pan with enough water to cover.

3. When soft, mash or sieve the fruit to make a *purée*; sweeten with honey or jam; add the lemon juice.

4. Serve the pasta with the hot fruit sauce poured over it and well mixed in. A few whole blackcurrants could be reserved and sprinkled on top. Serve the yogurt separately.

Note: This can be eaten as you would eat a savoury noodle dish, with a spoon and fork, or break the pasta into small pieces before cooking so that it can be easily picked up in a spoon.

PEAR, DATE AND PASTA COMPOTE

4 dessert pears
4 oz (100 g) whole dates
4 oz (100 g) wholewheat spaghetti rings
1 lemon
3 oz (75 g) light muscovado raw cane sugar
¾ pt (425 ml) water
Vanilla raw sugar ice cream to serve

1. In a saucepan, combine the water, sugar, lemon juice and some of the grated rind; bring to the boil and continue boiling for about 15 minutes.

2. Peel, core and halve the pears.

3. Simmer the pears in the syrup until just tender; add the washed dates and cook for a few minutes longer.

4. Meanwhile, cook the pasta rings in boiling water for 10 minutes; drain and add to the fruit and syrup; mix well.

5. Serve hot; or leave to get cold, during which time the pasta will absorb some of the syrup flavour. Ice cream goes well with this compote.

MACARONI AND GOOSEBERRY CRUNCH

3 oz (75 g) wholewheat macaroni
1 pt (550 ml) milk
3 oz (75 g) light muscovado raw cane sugar
1 egg
8 oz (225 g) gooseberries
4 oz (100 g) muesli
1 oz (25 g) polyunsaturated margarine

1. Cook the cleaned gooseberries with 2 oz (50 g) of sugar and a little water.

2. Simmer the macaroni in the milk for 20-30 minutes or until soft. Sweeten with the rest of the sugar.

3. Remove from the heat, cool slightly; add the beaten egg, and continue cooking over a low heat, stirring continually, for 5 minutes more or until thick and creamy.

4. Spoon the macaroni into a shallow ovenproof dish, smooth the top.

5. Cover with the softened gooseberries (strain first if very liquid).

6. Melt the margarine in a pan and toss in the muesli; cook gently for just a minute; sprinkle this mixture over the prepared dish.

7. Put under the grill briefly to make the topping crisp; serve hot.

STUFFED APPLES

4 large apples
4 oz (100g) raw sugar mincemeat
2 oz (50g) wholewheat spaghetti rings
2 oz (50g) chopped roasted hazelnuts
½ oz (15g) polyunsaturated margarine
1 tablespoonful pure honey
Squeeze of lemon juice
1 small carton plain yogurt – optional
¼ pt (140ml) single cream – optional

1. Cook the pasta in boiling water until tender; drain, then set aside.

2. Wash, dry, and remove the centre cores from the apples; make a slit around the skins so that the apples do not burst in the oven.

3. In a bowl, mix together the pasta, mincemeat, nuts and margarine. Stuff the apples with this mixture.

4. Arrange the apples side-by-side in an ovenproof dish; mix the honey with the lemon juice and trickle over the top of the apples.

5. Bake at 350°F/180°C (Gas Mark 4) for about 40 minutes, or until the apples are cooked.

6. Serve hot or cold.

Note: Yogurt and single cream whipped lightly together, then chilled, make a fresh contrast to the sweetness of this dish.

INDIAN-STYLE VERMICELLI

4 oz (100g) wholewheat vermicelli
2 oz (50g) polyunsaturated margarine
½ teaspoonful cardamom powder, or to taste
1 pt (550 ml) milk
3 oz (75g) demerara raw cane sugar
1 oz (25g) raisins
1-2 oz (25-50g) pistachio nuts

1. Heat half the margarine and gently fry the raisins and coarsely chopped nuts for 5 minutes, stirring continually.

2. Transfer them to another bowl; add the rest of the margarine, and when melted, add the spice and cook briefly.

3. Add the vermicelli, broken into pieces, to the pan and fry gently, stirring frequently, until it begins to change colour.

4. Pour in the milk, add the sugar and bring to boil; simmer until the pasta is soft and the mixture thick and creamy.

5. Spoon into individual glasses or dessert dishes and sprinkle generously with the nuts and raisins.

6. Serve hot or cold.

NOODLE PUDDING

8 oz (225g) wholewheat noodles
2 eggs, separated
2 apples
2 oz (50g) chopped dried apricots
2 oz (50g) walnuts
1 teaspoonful mixed spice
2 tablespoonsful pure honey
Pinch of sea salt

1. Cook the noodles in boiling water until just tender; drain well.

2. Core, and chop the apples coarsely.

3. Beat the egg yolks lightly; add the apple, apricot pieces, chopped nuts, spice, honey and salt.

4. Stir in the drained pasta, making sure all the ingredients are well mixed together.

5. Whisk the egg whites until just stiff enough to hold a shape; fold into the noodles.

6. Lightly grease an ovenproof dish and turn the mixture into it; bake at 350°F/180°C (Gas Mark 4) for 30 minutes, or until firm. Serve piping hot.

MELON WITH PASTA SHELLS

1 large melon
10 black grapes
10 white grapes
10 cherries or strawberries
2 bananas
2 oz (50g) wholewheat pasta shells
3 tablespoonsful raw sugar apricot jam
Squeeze of lemon juice
Whipped cream – optional

1. Cook the pasta shells in boiling water until tender; drain and rinse immediately with cold water.

2. Cut the top off the melon; remove the seeds and most of the flesh.

3. Make a sauce by heating the sieved jam, lemon juice, and some water in a saucepan, stirring frequently.

4. Wash and dry the grapes and cherries; peel and chop the bananas; chop the melon flesh that was removed earlier.

5. Mix all the fruit and the drained pasta into the sauce, making sure all the ingredients are coated; if necessary, make up some extra sauce.

6. Pile back carefully into the melon shell; pour on any extra sauce.

7. Serve, if liked, with whipping cream.

Note: Any fruit can be used in this dessert, including dried varieties. Nuts can be added, and the sauce can be made of pure honey and lemon juice instead of jam. Alternatively, try mixing the fruit with a honey and yogurt sauce, and sprinkling with coconut.

EGG CUSTARD SURPRISES

4 oz (100g) wholewheat spaghetti rings
1 pt (550ml) milk
2 or 3 eggs
1 oz (25g) raw cane sugar
2 oz (50g) candied peel
2 oz (50g) raisins
Grated nutmeg

1. Cook the spaghetti rings in water (or milk) until just tender;
   drain well and divide between 4 small *soufflé* or ovenproof
   dishes.

2. Sprinkle each one with some of the raisins and chopped
   peel.

3. In a bowl, whisk together the eggs and warmed milk; add the
   sugar; pour over the pasta and fruit, preferably through a
   strainer; sprinkle with nutmeg

4. Stand the dishes in a tin of hot water and bake at 325°F/170°C
   (Gas Mark 3) for 1 hour, or until set.

APRICOT FLAN

For Pastry
5 oz (150g) plain wholemeal flour
3 oz (75g) polyunsaturated margarine
1 egg

For Filling
6 apricots
3 oz (75g) almonds, preferably roasted
1 teaspoonful pure vanilla essence
½pt (275ml) plain yogurt
6 oz (175g) cream cheese
1 tablespoonful honey

3 oz (75g) wholewheat spaghetti rings

1. Put the flour into a bowl; rub in the fat with the finger-tips; use the beaten egg to bind to make a firm dough.

2. Knead the dough lightly then roll it out to line an 8in. flan dish; bake blind at 400°F/200°C (Gas Mark 6) for about 30 minutes, or until cooked.

3. In a bowl, blend together the cream cheese, yogurt, honey and vanilla essence.

4. Cook the pasta in water until tender; drain well.

5. Distribute the pasta across the base of the cooled flan; halve and stone the apricots and arrange them attractively on top, cut-side down.

6. Spoon over the yogurt mixture and smooth the top; sprinkle with the chopped nuts; put the flan in a cool spot until the filling sets.

SWEET APPLE LASAGNE

6 oz (175 g) wholewheat lasagne
2 lb (900 g) cooking apples
4 oz (100 g) raw cane sugar, or to taste
2 teaspoonsful ground cinnamon, or to taste
1-2 tablespoonsful lemon or orange juice
2 oz (50 g) walnuts, coarsely chopped
2 oz (50 g) wholemeal breadcrumbs
½ oz (15 g) polyunsaturated margarine

1. Cook the lasagne in boiling water, then rinse in cold water and set aside.

2. Core and slice the apples and put into a pan with the spice, lemon juice, sugar, and enough water to cover; simmer until soft.

3. Place a layer of the lasagne in an ovenproof dish; cover with half the apple *purée*; use the rest of the lasagne and apples in the same way, sprinkling the walnuts in with the other ingredients.

4. Top the final layer of lasagne with the breadcrumbs, and dot with the margarine (if liked add some more cinnamon and a few chopped nuts to the crumbs).

5. Bake at 350°F/180°C (Gas Mark 4) for about 20 minutes, or until cooked and golden. Serve hot.

INDEX